Holt McDougal
Algebra 1

Chapter Resources
Volume 1

HOLT McDOUGAL

 HOUGHTON MIFFLIN HARCOURT

ISBN 978-0-547-71053-2

1 2 3 4 5 6 7 8 9 10 0928 20 19 18 17 16 15 14 13 12 11

4500303652 ^ B C D E F G

Contents

Holt McDougal Algebra 1

Description of Contents

Family Letter

A two-page letter is provided for each chapter in both English and Spanish. The letter describes some of the math concepts covered in the chapter. A list of key vocabulary words from the chapter is included, and some worked-out examples are provided.

Practice A, B, and C

There are three practice worksheets for every lesson. All of these reinforce the content of the lesson. Practice B is shown with answers in the Teacher's Edition and is appropriate for the on-level student. It is also available as a workbook (Practice Workbook).

Practice A is easier than Practice B but still practices the content of the lesson. Practice C is more challenging than Practice B.

Review for Mastery

The Review for Mastery worksheet (one per lesson) provides an alternate way to teach or review the main concepts of the lesson. This worksheet is two pages long and the first page with answers is shown in the Teacher's Edition.

Challenge

The Challenge worksheet (one per lesson) enhances critical thinking skills and extends the lesson. This worksheet is shown with answers in the Teacher's Edition.

Problem Solving

The Problem Solving worksheet (one per lesson) provides practice in problem solving and opportunities for real-world applications and for interdisciplinary connections. There are both multiple choice and short response problems. This worksheet is shown in the Teacher's Edition.

Reading Strategies

The Reading Strategies worksheet (one per lesson) provides tools to help the student master math vocabulary or symbols. This worksheet is shown with answers in the Teacher's Edition.

Date _____

Dear Family,
Your child will write and evaluate algebraic expressions and solve a variety of equations in one variable, including equations that result from proportion and percent problems. They will also compare measurements and choose which is the more precise.

An **equation** is a mathematical statement showing two expressions are equal. A **solution** to an equation is a value of the variable that makes the equation true.

Equation:	$x + 8 = 12$
Solution:	4 is a solution because $4 + 8 = 12$.

Equations are solved by **isolating the variable** using **inverse operations**. You must perform the same inverse operations on *both sides* of the equation.

$x - 6 = 3$	*x has had 6 subtracted from it.*
$+ 6 \quad + 6$	*Undo that by adding 6.*
$x \quad\quad = 9$	*9 is the solution.*

Many equations require multiple steps to isolate the variable. The variable might appear several times, or on both sides of the equation.

$5(1 - 2x) + 4x = 17$	
$5 - 10x + 4x = 17$	*Distribute 5.*
$5 \quad -6x \quad = 17$	*Combine $-10x$ and $4x$ to get $-6x$.*
$-5 \quad\quad\quad -5$	*Subtract 5 from each side.*
$-6x \quad = 12$	
$\dfrac{-6x}{-6} \quad = \dfrac{12}{-6}$	*Divide both sides by -6.*
$x \quad = -2$	*-2 is the solution.*

A **formula** is an equation that states a relationship between several quantities. Solving a formula for a given variable is similar to solving a multi-step equation.

For example, $d = rt$ can be written as $\dfrac{d}{t} = r$ by dividing both sides by t.

A **ratio** is a comparison of two quantities. A ratio such as 2 boys to 5 girls can be written as 2:5 or $\frac{2}{5}$. A **proportion** is an equation that relates two equivalent ratios. For example, $\frac{1}{3} = \frac{4}{12}$ is a proportion.

Holt McDougal Algebra 1

When part of a proportion is unknown, you can use a variable for the unknown quantity and solve by using **cross products**.

$$\frac{1}{16} \diagdown \frac{x}{20}$$

$1(20) = 16(x)$ *Use cross products.*

$\dfrac{20}{16} = \dfrac{16x}{16}$ *Divide both sides by 16.*

$1.25 = x$

Ratios and proportions have many useful applications, including rates, scale drawings, similarity, and indirect measurement.

Precision is the level of detail in a measurement and is determined by the smallest unit or fraction of a unit that you can reasonably measure.

Different Units	Equivalent Measures	Same Unit
8.2 kg 8231 g	4 ft 48 in.	8.3 cm 8.32 cm
8.2 kg is measured in tenths; 8231 is measured in whole grams.	Since 1 ft = 12 in., 4 ft = 48 in.	8.3 cm is measured in tenths; 8.32 cm is measured in hundredths.
Since a gram is smaller than a tenth of a kilogram, 8231 g is more precise.	Since an inch is smaller than an inch, 48 in. is more precise.	Since a hundredth of a centimeter is smaller than a tenth of a centimeter, 8.32 cm is more precise.

     Holt McDougal Algebra 1

LESSON 1-1

Practice A
Variables and Expressions

Give one way to write each algebraic expression in words.

1. $a + 3$

2. $2x$

_____

3. $5 - y$

4. $\dfrac{n}{4}$

_____

5. $10 + t$

6. $3s$

_____

7. Clint runs c miles each week. Brenda runs 2 miles more each week than Clint. Write an expression for the number of miles Brenda runs each week.   _____

8. Tom pays 5 cents per minute to use his cell phone. Write an expression for the cost in cents of using his cell phone for m minutes.   _____

Evaluate each expression for $a = 2$ and $b = 6$.

9. $a + b$

10. $b - a$

11. ab

_____

Evaluate each expression for $c = 12$ and $d = 4$.

12. $c \div d$

13. $c + d$

14. $c - d$

_____

15. Tina is 4 years younger than her brother Jeff.

  a. Write an expression for Tina's age when Jeff is j years old.

  _____

  b. Find Tina's age when Jeff is 15, 20, and 58 years old.

  _____

Holt McDougal Algebra 1

LESSON 1-1

Practice B
Variables and Expressions

Give two ways to write each algebraic expression in words.

1. $15 - b$

2. $\dfrac{x}{16}$

_____

_____

_____

_____

3. $x + 9$

4. $(2)(t)$

_____

_____

_____

_____

5. $z - 7$

6. $4y$

_____

_____

_____

_____

7. Sophie's math class has 6 fewer boys than girls, and there are g girls. Write an expression for the number of boys. _____

8. A computer printer can print 10 pages per minute. Write an expression for the number of pages the printer can print in m minutes. _____

Evaluate each expression for $r = 8$, $s = 2$, and $t = 5$.

9. st

10. $r \div s$

11. $s + t$

_____ _____ _____

12. $r - t$

13. $r \cdot s$

14. $t - s$

_____ _____ _____

15. Paula always withdraws 20 dollars more than she needs from the bank.

   a. Write an expression for the amount of money Paula withdraws if she needs d dollars. _____

   b. Find the amount of money Paula withdraws if she needs 20, 60, and 75 dollars. _____

LESSON 1-1

Practice C
Variables and Expressions

Give two ways to write each algebraic expression in words.

1. $k + 2.5$

_____

_____

2. $-5n$

_____

_____

3. $b \div 25$

_____

_____

4. $100 - x$

_____

_____

5. Corey's motorcycle gets 35 miles per gallon of gasoline. Write an expression for how many miles the motorcycle can travel with g gallons of gasoline.

6. Paulette buys a bag of candy for a party. The bag contains 150 pieces of candy. Write an expression for the number of pieces each person gets if there are p people at the party. _____

Evaluate each expression for $x = 28$, $y = 14$, and $z = 4$.

7. $x - y$

_____

8. yz

_____

9. $\dfrac{z}{x}$

_____

10. At the video arcade, Jorge buys 25 tokens. He uses 2 tokens for each game that he plays.

    a. Write an expression for the number of tokens Jorge has left after playing g games.

    _____

    b. Find the number of tokens he has left after playing 1, 4, 10, and 12 games.

Write an algebraic expression for each verbal expression. Then write a real-world situation that could be modeled by the expression.

11. 8 less than n

_____

_____

12. the product of x and 4

_____

_____

Review for Mastery

LESSON 1-1

Variables and Expressions

To translate words into algebraic expressions, find words like these that tell you the operation.

+	−	•	÷
add	subtract	multiply	divide
sum	difference	product	quotient
more	less	times	split
increased	decreased	per	ratio

Kenny owns v video games. Stan owns 7 more video games than Kenny. Write an expression for the number of video games Stan owns.

v represents the number of video games Kenny owns.

$v + 7$ *Think: The word "more" indicates addition.*

Order does not matter for addition. The expression $7 + v$ is also correct.

Jenny is 12 years younger than Candy. Write an expression for Jenny's age if Candy is c years old.

c represents Candy's age.

The word "younger" means "less," which indicates subtraction.

$c - 12$ *Think: Candy is older, so subtract 12 from her age.*

Order does matter for subtraction. The expression $12 - c$ is incorrect.

---

1. Jared can type 35 words per minute. Write an expression for the number of words he can type in m minutes.

   _____

2. Mr. O'Brien's commute to work is 0.5 hour less than Miss Santos's commute. Write an expression for the length of Mr. O'Brien's commute if Miss Santos's commute is h hours.

   _____

3. Mrs. Knighten bought a box of c cookies and split them evenly between the 25 students in her classroom. Write an expression for the number of cookies each student received.

   _____

4. Enrique collected 152 recyclable bottles, and Latasha collected b recyclable bottles. Write an expression for the number of bottles they collected altogether.

   _____

5. Tammy's current rent is r dollars. Next month it will be reduced by $50. Write an expression for next month's rent in dollars.

   _____

Holt McDougal Algebra 1

LESSON 1-1

Review for Mastery

Variables and Expressions continued

The value of $\boxed{} - 9$ depends on what number is placed in the box.

Evaluate $\boxed{} - 9$ when 20 is placed in the box.

$$\boxed{} - 9$$

$$\boxed{20} - 9$$

$$11$$

In algebra, variables are used instead of boxes.

Evaluate $x \div 7$ for $x = 28$.

$$x \div 7$$

$$28 \div 7$$

$$4$$

Sometimes, the expression has more than one variable.

Evaluate $x + y$ for $x = 6$ and $y = 2$.

$$x + y$$

$$6 + 2$$

$$8$$

Evaluate $5 + \boxed{}$ when each number is placed in the box.

6. 3

7. 5

8. 24

_____   _____   _____

Evaluate each expression for $x = 4$, $y = 6$, and $z = 3$.

9. $x + 15$

10. $3y$

11. $15 - z$

_____   _____   _____

Evaluate each expression for $x = 2$, $y = 18$, and $z = 9$.

12. $x \cdot z$

13. $y - x$

14. $y \div z$

_____   _____   _____

15. $\dfrac{y}{x}$

16. xy

17. $z - x$

_____   _____   _____

Holt McDougal Algebra 1

Name _____ Date _____ Class_____

 LESSON 1-1

Challenge
Comparing Phone Plans

A cell phone company is offering two different monthly plans. Each plan charges a monthly fee and then an additional cost per minute.

Plan A	$40 fee	45 cents per minute
Plan B	$70 fee	35 cents per minute

The mathematical expression for Plan A that represents the charges for the monthly fee plus the charge per minute *m* for one month is:

$$40 + 0.45(m)$$

1. Write the expression which represents the charges for the monthly fee plus the charge per minute *m* for Plan B for one month. _____

Use the expressions above to complete the chart.

Number of Minutes	Expression for Plan A	Cost of Plan A	Expression for Plan B	Cost for Plan B
100	40 + 0.45(100)	$85		
200				
300				
400				
500				

2. Which plan is less expensive for 200 minutes or less each month? _____

3. Which plan is less expensive for 400 minutes or more each month? _____

4. Suppose a friend asks you which of the two plans is less expensive. How would you respond?

_____

_____

_____

_____

Holt McDougal Algebra 1

Problem Solving

LESSON 1-1

Variables and Expressions

Write the correct answer.

1. For her book club, Sharon reads for 45 minutes each day. Write an expression for the number of hours she reads in d days.

2. The minimum wage in 2003 was $5.15. This was w more than the minimum wage in 1996. Write an expression for the minimum wage in 1996.

3. According to the 2000 census, the number of people per square mile in Florida was about 216 more than the number of people per square mile in Texas. Write an expression for the number of people per square mile in Florida if there were t people per square mile in Texas.

4. The cost of a party is $550. The price per person depends on how many people attend the party. Write an expression for the price per person if p people attend the party. Then find the price per person if 25, 50, and 55 people attend the party.

Use the table below to answer questions 5–6, which shows the years five states entered the Union. Select the best answer.

5. North Carolina entered the Union x years after Pennsylvania. Which expression shows the year North Carolina entered the Union?

   A $1845 + x$ C $1787 + x$

   B $1845 - x$ D $1787 - x$

6. The expression $f - 26$ represents the year Alabama entered the Union, where f is the year Florida entered. In which year did Alabama enter the Union?

   F 1819   H 1837

   G 1826   J 1871

State	Year Entered into Union
Florida	1845
Indiana	1816
Pennsylvania	1787
Texas	1845
West Virginia	1863

7. The number of states that entered the Union in 1889 was half the number of states s that entered in 1788. Which expression shows the number of states that entered the Union in 1889?

   A $2s$ C $s + 2$

   B $s \div 2$ D $2 - s$

Name _____ Date _____ Class _____

Reading Strategies
Connecting Words and Symbols

To translate between phrases and algebraic expressions, you must connect words with symbols. Look at the examples in the table below.

Operations	Words	Symbols
Addition	"sum of 3 and *n*" "*n* more than 3" "3 plus *n*"	$3 + n$
Subtraction	"difference of 3 and *n*" "*n* less than 3" "3 minus *n*"	$3 - n$
Multiplication	"product of 3 and *n*" "3 times *n*" "3 groups of *n*"	$3n$ $3 \cdot n$ $3 \times n$ $3(n)$
Division	"quotient of 3 and *n*" "3 divided by *n*" "3 separated into *n* groups"	$3 \div n$ $\dfrac{3}{n}$

Solve each problem.

1. Write "10 times the value of *y*" in symbols in three different ways.

   _____

2. Write "*k* ÷ 6" in words in two different ways.

   _____

3. Write "4 less than *b*" in symbols. _____

4. Write "*b* less than 4" in symbols. _____

Translate each word phrase into an algebraic expression.

5. Craig types 20 words per minute. Write an expression
   for the number of words Craig types in *m* minutes. _____

6. Jeana is 58 inches tall. Her sister Janelle is *t* inches
   taller. Write an expression for Janelle's height. _____

Holt McDougal Algebra 1

LESSON 1-2 **Practice A**
Solving Equations by Adding or Subtracting

Solve each equation by using addition. Check your answers.

1. $m - 2 = 5$

2. $t - 9 = 14$

3. $p - 6 = -2$

_____

_____

_____

4. $a - 4.5 = 3.5$

5. $-3 = c - 8$

6. $y - \dfrac{1}{5} = \dfrac{2}{5}$

_____

_____

_____

Solve each equation by using subtraction. Check your answers.

7. $b + 4 = 4$

8. $-8 + w = 1$

9. $p + 6 = 10$

_____

_____

_____

10. $25 = x + 21$

11. $x + 17 = 15$

12. $-9.3 + r = 5.1$

13. James took two math tests. He scored 86 points on the second test. This was 18 points higher than his score on the first test. Write and solve an equation to find the score James received on the first test. Show that your answer is reasonable.

_____

_____

14. The noontime temperature was 29°F. This was 4°F lower than predicted. Write and solve an equation to determine the predicted noontime temperature. Show that your answer is reasonable.

_____

_____

15. For two weeks, Gabrielle raised money by selling magazines. She raised $72 during the second week, which brought her total to $122. Write and solve an equation to find how much Gabrielle raised during the first week. Show that your answer is reasonable.

_____

_____

Holt McDougal Algebra 1

LESSON	**Practice B**
1-2	*Solving Equations by Adding or Subtracting*

Solve each equation. Check your answers.

1. $g - 7 = 15$

2. $t + 4 = 6$

3. $13 = m - 7$

_____   _____   _____

4. $x + 3.4 = 9.1$

5. $n - \dfrac{3}{8} = \dfrac{1}{8}$

6. $p - \dfrac{1}{3} = \dfrac{2}{3}$

_____   _____   _____

7. $-6 + k = 32$

8. $7 = w + 9.3$

9. $8 = r + 12$

_____   _____   _____

10. $y - 57 = -40$

11. $-5.1 + b = -7.1$

12. $a + 15 = 15$

_____   _____   _____

13. Marietta was given a raise of $0.75 an hour, which brought her hourly wage to $12.25. Write and solve an equation to determine Marietta's hourly wage before her raise. Show that your answer is reasonable.

_____

_____

14. Brad grew $4\dfrac{1}{4}$ inches this year and is now $56\dfrac{7}{8}$ inches tall. Write and solve an equation to find Brad's height at the start of the year. Show that your answer is reasonable.

_____

_____

15. Heather finished a race in 58.4 seconds, which was 2.6 seconds less than her practice time. Write and solve an equation to find Heather's practice time. Show that your answer is reasonable.

_____

_____

16. The radius of Earth is 6378.1 km, which is 2981.1 km longer than the radius of Mars. Write and solve an equation to determine the radius of Mars. Show that your answer is reasonable.

_____

_____

LESSON 1-2 **Practice C**

Solving Equations by Adding or Subtracting

Solve each equation. Check your answers.

1. $d - 17 = 4$

2. $f + 9.3 = 8$

3. $\dfrac{5}{6} = n - \dfrac{1}{6}$

_____

_____

_____

4. $-5 + x = 8$

5. $h + \dfrac{5}{8} = \dfrac{1}{8}$

6. $-6 + y = -23$

_____

_____

_____

Write an equation for each relationship. Then solve the equation.

7. A number increased by 12 is equal to 27.

8. Seven less than a number is 3.

_____

_____

9. The difference of a number and 6 is –2.

10. The sum of a number and 4.7 is 8.1.

_____

_____

11. Terrell's plant grew $2\dfrac{5}{8}$ inches in one month, and it is now $7\dfrac{1}{4}$ inches tall. Write and solve an equation to find the height of the plant at the start of the month. Show that your answer is reasonable.

_____

_____

12. After installing new software, the available memory on Joy's computer dropped by 36.8 MB, leaving her with 475.2 MB of memory. Write and solve an equation to determine the amount of available memory on Joy's computer before installing the new software. Show that your answer is reasonable.

_____

_____

_____

13. For all sanctioned USA swim meets in Indiana in 2004, the fastest time for the 50-meter freestyle in the girls' age group 11–12 was 28.3 seconds. This time was 0.43 seconds faster than the fastest time in 2002. Write and solve an equation to determine the fastest time for this swim event in Indiana in 2002. Show that your answer is reasonable.

_____

_____

_____

Holt McDougal Algebra 1

LESSON 1-2

Review for Mastery

Solving Equations by Adding or Subtracting

Use counters to model solving equations.

Solve $x + 2 = 5$.

Using counters	Using numbers
$x + $ 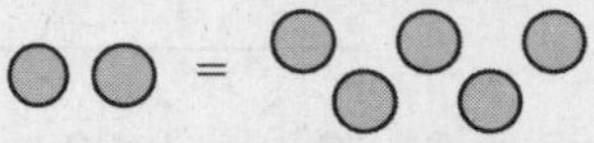 ⊙ ⊙ $=$ ⊙ ⊙ ⊙ ⊙ ⊙	$x + 2 = 5$
$x + $ 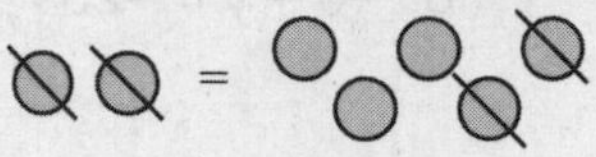 ⊘ ⊘ $=$ ⊙ ⊙ ⊙ ⊘ ⊘	$x + 2 = 5$ $\underline{\quad -2 \quad -2}$
$x + 0 \;=\;$ 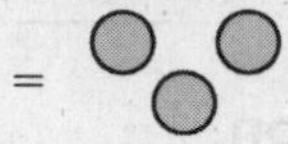 ⊙ ⊙ ⊙	$x + 0 = 3$
$x =$ 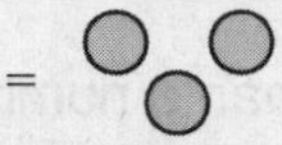 ⊙ ⊙ ⊙	$x = 3$
Check: 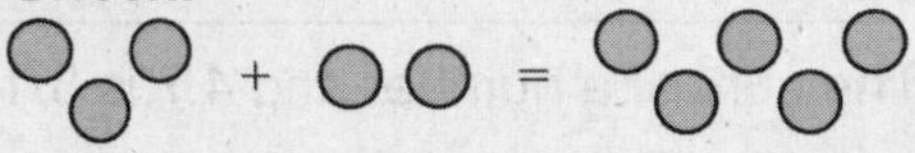 ⊙ ⊙ ⊙ $+$ ⊙ ⊙ $=$ ⊙ ⊙ ⊙ ⊙ ⊙	*Check:* $x + 2 = 5$ $3 + 2 \overset{?}{=} 5$ $5 \overset{?}{=} 5 \checkmark$

Solve the following by drawing counters. Check your answers.

1. $x + 1 = 5$ 2. $7 = x + 2$

Solve each equation. Check your answers.

3. $x + 4 = 12$ 4. $21 = x + 2$ 5. $x + 3 = 8$

Holt McDougal Algebra 1

LESSON 1-2

Review for Mastery

Solving Equations by Adding or Subtracting *continued*

Any addition equation can be solved by adding the opposite. If the equation involves subtraction, it helps to first rewrite the subtraction as addition.

Solve $x + 4 = 10$.

Find the opposite of this number.

$$x + 4 = 10$$
$$\underline{-4 \quad -4}$$
$$x = 6$$

The opposite of 4 is –4.
Add –4 to each side.

Check:
$$x + 4 = 10$$
$$6 + 4 \overset{?}{=} 10$$
$$10 \overset{?}{=} 10 ✓$$

Solve $-5 = x - 8$.

Find the opposite of this number.

$$-5 = x + -8$$

$$\underline{+8 \qquad +8}$$
$$3 = x$$

Rewrite subtraction as addition.
The opposite of –8 is 8.
Add 8 to each side.

Check:
$$-5 = x - 8$$
$$-5 \overset{?}{=} 3 - 8$$
$$-5 \overset{?}{=} -5 ✓$$

Solve $x - (-6) = 2$.

Find the opposite of this number.

$$x + 6 = 2$$

$$\underline{-6 \quad -6}$$
$$x = -4$$

Rewrite subtraction as addition.
The opposite of 6 is –6.
Add –6 to each side.

Check:
$$x - (-6) = 2$$
$$4 - (-6) \overset{?}{=} 2$$
$$2 \overset{?}{=} 2 ✓$$

Rewrite each equation with addition. Then state the number that should be added to each side.

6. $x - 7 = 12$

_____

_____

7. $x - (-1) = -5$

_____

_____

8. $-4 = x - 2$

_____

_____

Solve each equation. Check your answers.

9. $x + 10 = -6$

_____

10. $-8 = x - 2$

_____

11. $x - (-5) = -2$

_____

Holt McDougal Algebra 1

Challenge

Rate Problems

The function of an odometer is to measure the distance that a vehicle has traveled, either in miles or in kilometers. When you use an odometer for this purpose, you can answer the question, "How far have I traveled?" The reasoning that you used to answer the question can be applied to stating and solving new related problems.

Answer the following questions.

1. You are on a trip traveling from town A to town B. When you start the trip, your odometer reading is 37,538 miles. When you get to town B, your odometer reading is 37,781.

   a. Write an equation relating your initial reading, distance traveled, and final reading. _____

   b. Find the distance traveled from town A to town B. _____

2. Let *s* represent the initial reading, *d* represent the distance traveled, and *e* represent the final reading. Write an addition equation relating *s*, *d*, and *e*.

   _____

3. Using your equation from Exercise 2, solve for the specified variable.

   a. $s =$ _____   b. $d =$ _____   c. $e =$ _____

4. Use one of the equations that you wrote in Exercise 3 and the given values to find the value of the third variable.

   a. $s = 27,281$ and $e = 28,978$ b. $e = 17,349$ and $d = 197$

   _____   _____

   c. $s = 62,979$ and $d = 798$ d. $s = 69,876$ and $e = 70,987$

   _____   _____

The water level in a storage tank is currently $10\frac{1}{2}$ feet.

5. Water is drained from the tank, and the level drops $2\frac{5}{6}$ feet. Find the new water level.

   _____

6. Let *o* represent the original water level, *d* represent the change in water level, and *f* represent the final water level. Write three equations relating *o*, *d*, and *f*.

   _____

7. The water level rises $1\frac{3}{4}$ feet from $7\frac{2}{3}$ feet. Choose an equation from Exercise 6 and find the new water level.

   _____

Holt McDougal Algebra 1

LESSON 1-2

Problem Solving
Solving Equations by Adding or Subtracting

Write the correct answer.

1. Michelle withdrew $120 from her bank account. She now has $3345 in her account. Write and solve an equation to find how much money *m* was in her account before she made the withdrawal.

_____

2. Max lost 23 pounds while on a diet. He now weighs 184 pounds. Write and solve an equation to find his initial weight *w*.

_____

_____

3. Earth takes 365 days to orbit the Sun. Mars takes 687 days. Write and solve an equation to find how many more days *d* Mars takes than Earth to orbit the Sun.

_____

4. In 1990, 53.4% of commuters took public transportation in New York City, which was 19.9% greater than the percentage in San Francisco. Write and solve an equation to find what percentage of commuters *p* took public transportation in San Francisco.

_____

_____

Use the circle graph below to answer questions 5–7. Select the best answer. The circle graph shows the colors for SUVs as percents of the total number of SUVs manufactured in 2000 in North America.

5. The percent of silver SUVs increased by 7.9% between 1998 and 2000. If *x*% of SUVs were silver in 1998, which equation represents this relationship?

   A $x + 7.9 = 14.1$ C $7.9x = 14.1$

   B $x - 7.9 = 14.1$ D $7.9 - x = 14.1$

6. Solve the equation from problem 5. What is the value of *x*?

   F 1.8   H 7.1

   G 6.2   J 22

7. The sum of the percents of dark red SUVs and white SUVs was 26.3%. What was the percent of dark red SUVs?

   A 2.3%   C 12.2%

   B 3.2%   D 18%

Percent of SUVs by Color

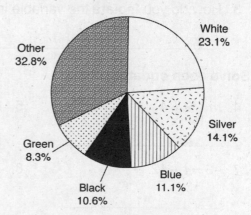

Other 32.8%
White 23.1%
Silver 14.1%
Blue 11.1%
Black 10.6%
Green 8.3%

LESSON 1-2

Reading Strategies
Vocabulary Development

To solve equations, you must know many mathematical words and phrases. Look at the diagram below to help you better understand this vocabulary.

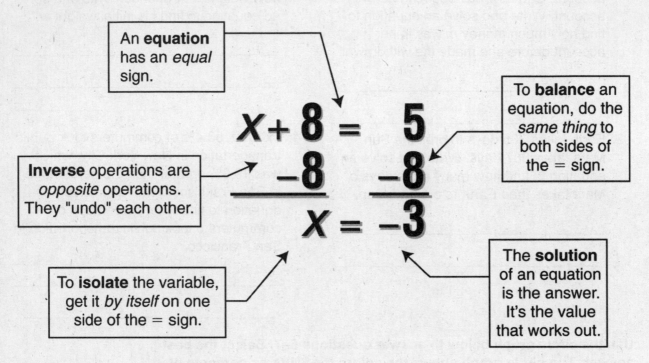

An **equation** has an *equal* sign.

To **balance** an equation, do the *same thing* to both sides of the = sign.

Inverse operations are *opposite* operations. They "undo" each other.

To **isolate** the variable, get it *by itself* on one side of the = sign.

The **solution** of an equation is the answer. It's the value that works out.

Answer each of the following.

1. What is the **inverse** operation of subtraction? _____

2. If you add 5 to the right side of an equation, how do you keep the equation **balanced?**

   _____

3. How do you **isolate** the variable in the equation $p - 4 = 12$?

   _____

Solve each equation.

4. $m - 9 = 4$

5. $13 = g + 8$

6. $k + 5.8 = 2.8$

_____   _____   _____

7. $-3 = t + 12$

8. $-30 = y - 32$

9. $-2 + h = 9$

_____   _____   _____

LESSON 1-3

Practice A
Solving Equations by Multiplying or Dividing

Solve each equation by using multiplication. Check your answers.

1. $\dfrac{d}{2} = 9$

_____

2. $-3 = \dfrac{n}{7}$

_____

3. $\dfrac{t}{-3} = 5$

_____

4. $\dfrac{2}{5} r = 8$

_____

5. $2.5 = \dfrac{b}{7}$

_____

6. $\dfrac{v}{-4} = -9$

_____

Solve each equation by using division. Check your answers.

7. $-50 = 10y$

_____

8. $2p = 20$

_____

9. $3m = 3$

_____

10. $-12 = -6x$

_____

11. $14y = -2$

_____

12. $6 = 0.5k$

_____

Answer each of the following.

13. The students at a school assembly were divided into 4 equal groups. There were 63 students in each group. Write and solve an equation to determine the number of students that were at the assembly.

14. Anna shipped a small package from North Carolina to Virginia for $1.15. Her package weighed 5 ounces. Write and solve an equation to determine the shipping cost per ounce.

15. The perimeter of a square is 64 mm. Write and solve an equation to determine the length of each side of the square.

_____

_____

_____

Holt McDougal Algebra 1

Practice B
Solving Equations by Multiplying or Dividing

Solve each equation. Check your answers.

1. $\dfrac{d}{8} = 6$

2. $-5 = \dfrac{n}{2}$

3. $2p = 54$

_____   _____   _____

4. $\dfrac{-t}{2} = 12$

5. $-40 = -4x$

6. $\dfrac{2r}{3} = 16$

_____   _____   _____

7. $-49 = 7y$

8. $-15 = -\dfrac{3n}{5}$

9. $9m = 6$

_____   _____   _____

10. $\dfrac{v}{-3} = -6$

11. $2.8 = \dfrac{b}{4}$

12. $\dfrac{3r}{4} = \dfrac{1}{8}$

_____   _____   _____

Answer each of the following.

13. The perimeter of a regular pentagon
    is 41.5 cm. Write and solve an equation
    to determine the length of each side
    of the pentagon.

14. In June 2005, Peter mailed a package
    from his local post office in Fayetteville,
    North Carolina to a friend in Radford,
    Virginia for $2.07. The first-class rate at
    the time was $0.23 per ounce. Write and
    solve an equation to determine the weight
    of the package.

15. Lola spends one-third of her allowance
    on movies. She spends $8 per week
    at the movies. Write and solve an equation
    to determine Lola's weekly allowance.

_____

_____

_____

Holt McDougal Algebra 1

LESSON 1-3

Practice C
Solving Equations by Multiplying or Dividing

Solve each equation. Check your answers.

1. $\dfrac{e}{5} = 15$

2. $-14 = \dfrac{g}{-4}$

3. $8d = 56$

_____   _____   _____

4. $-\dfrac{n}{3} = 3$

5. $-65 = -5t$

6. $\dfrac{4r}{5} = 32$

_____   _____   _____

7. $-2.7 = 0.3y$

8. $-\dfrac{4}{7} = -\dfrac{2f}{3}$

9. $12m = -8$

_____   _____   _____

Write and solve an equation to represent each relationship.

10. The product of 9 and a number is −72.   _____

11. A number divided by −3 is equal to −2.8.   _____

12. Two thirds of a number is equal to 14.   _____

Answer each of the following.

13. The perimeter of a regular octagon
    is 55.2 mm. Write and solve an equation
    to determine the length of each side
    of the octagon.

    _____

14. In April 2005, Roland mailed a package
    from his local post office in Albemarle,
    North Carolina to a friend in Fishers,
    Indiana for $2.76. The first-class domestic
    rate at the time was $0.23 per ounce.
    Write and solve an equation to determine
    the weight of the package.

    _____

15. Jasmine earned a mean score of
    34,250 points on the video game that
    she played 6 times. Write and solve an
    equation to determine the total number
    of points Jasmine earned in the 6 games.

    _____

Holt McDougal Algebra 1

LESSON 1-3

Review for Mastery

Solving Equations by Multiplying or Dividing

Solve equations involving multiplication and division by performing the inverse operation.

Solve $\dfrac{x}{5} = 4$.   **Check:** $\dfrac{x}{5} = 4$

$\dfrac{x}{5} = 4$ *x* is <u>divided</u> by 5. $\dfrac{20}{5} \overset{?}{=} 4$

$5 \cdot \dfrac{x}{5} = 4 \cdot 5$ *Multiply* both sides by 5. $4 \overset{?}{=} 4 \checkmark$

$\dfrac{5x}{5} = 20$ *Simplify.*

$x = 20$

Solve $-3x = 27$.   **Check:** $-3x = 27$

$-3x = 27$ *x* is <u>multiplied</u> by -3. $-3(-9) \overset{?}{=} 27$

$\dfrac{-3x}{-3} = \dfrac{27}{-3}$ <u>Divide</u> both sides by -3. $27 \overset{?}{=} 27 \checkmark$

$x = -9$ *Simplify.*

Circle the correct word in each sentence. Then solve the equation.

1. $\dfrac{x}{-2} = 7$ 2. $5m = -40$

    x is <u>multiplied/divided</u> by -2.   *m* is <u>multiplied/divided</u> by 5.

    To solve, <u>multiply/divide</u> both sides by -2.   To solve, <u>multiply/divide</u> both sides by 5.

    $x = $ _____ $m = $ _____

Solve each equation. Check your answers.

3. $-2x = -20$ 4. $\dfrac{w}{5} = -7$ 5. $6z = -42$

_____   _____   _____

LESSON 1-3

Review for Mastery

Solving Equations by Multiplying or Dividing continued

Equations with fractions can be solved by multiplying by the reciprocal.

Solve $\dfrac{2}{3}x = 8$.

$\dfrac{2}{3}x = 8$	*x* is multiplied by $\dfrac{2}{3}$.
$\dfrac{3}{2} \cdot \dfrac{2}{3}x = 8 \cdot \dfrac{3}{2}$	Multiply both sides by $\dfrac{3}{2}$.
$\dfrac{6}{6}x = \dfrac{24}{2}$	Simplify.
$x = 12$	

Check: $\dfrac{2}{3}x = 8$

$\dfrac{2}{3}(12) \stackrel{?}{=} 8$

$\dfrac{24}{3} \stackrel{?}{=} 8$

$8 \stackrel{?}{=} 8 \checkmark$

Solve $-\dfrac{3}{4}x = \dfrac{2}{5}$.

$-\dfrac{3}{4}x = \dfrac{2}{5}$	*x* is multiplied by $-\dfrac{3}{4}$.
$-\dfrac{4}{3} \cdot -\dfrac{3}{4}x = \dfrac{2}{5} \cdot -\dfrac{4}{3}$	*x* is multiplied by $-\dfrac{4}{3}$.
$\dfrac{12}{12}x = -\dfrac{8}{15}$	Simplify.
$x = -\dfrac{8}{15}$	

Check: $-\dfrac{3}{4}x = \dfrac{2}{5}$

$-\dfrac{3}{4}\left(-\dfrac{8}{15}\right) \stackrel{?}{=} \dfrac{2}{5}$

$\dfrac{24}{60} \stackrel{?}{=} \dfrac{2}{5}$

$\dfrac{2}{5} \stackrel{?}{=} \dfrac{2}{5} \checkmark$

Find the reciprocal.

6. $\dfrac{2}{5}$

7. $-\dfrac{5}{7}$

8. 7

_____

_____

_____

Solve each equation. Check your answers.

9. $\dfrac{5}{6}x = 10$

10. $6 = -\dfrac{3}{5}x$

11. $\dfrac{2}{3}x = -\dfrac{3}{5}$

_____

_____

_____

Holt McDougal Algebra 1

LESSON 1-3 Challenge

Deriving the Division Property of Equality

The Multiplication Property of Equality states that if *a*, *b*, and *c* are numbers and *a* = *b*, then *ac* = *bc*. That is, when you multiply each side of an equation by a fixed number, the resulting products are equal.

By itself, you can use the Multiplication Property of Equality to solve equations of the form *ax* = *b* as well as equations of the form $\frac{x}{a} = b$.

You can see this fact at work in the solution below.

$$3x = 6$$

$$\frac{1}{3}(3x) = \frac{1}{3}(6)$$

$$\left[\frac{1}{3}(3)\right]x = \frac{1}{3}(6)$$

$$1x = \frac{1}{3}(6)$$

$$x = 2$$

Notice that you multiply by a fraction whose numerator is 1, that is, by the reciprocal of *a*.

Solve each equation by using only the Multiplication Property of Equality. Show your work.

1. 4*x* = 12 _____

2. −3*x* = 15 _____

3. −7*x* = −21 _____

4. 10*t* = 12 _____

5. 18*w* = 9 _____

6. −3*d* = −90 _____

7. Suppose that *a* ≠ 0. Using the process that you followed in Exercises 1–6, solve *ax* = *b* for *x*.

_____

8. Use the Division Property of Equality to solve *ax* = *b* for *x*.

_____

9. Compare the method of solving an equation of the form *ax* = *b* by using the Multiplication Property of Equality with that of solving the same type of equation by using the Division Property of Equality.

_____

_____

LESSON 1-3

Problem Solving
Solving Equations by Multiplying or Dividing

Write the correct answer.

1. John threw a surprise birthday party for his friend. Food, drinks, and a DJ cost $480 for a group of 32 people. Write and solve an equation to find the cost c per person.

   _____

2. One serving of soybeans contains 10 grams of protein, which is 4 times the amount in one serving of kale. Write and solve an equation to find the amount of protein x in one serving of kale.

   _____

3. Maria earned $10.50 per hour working at an ice cream shop. She earned $147 each week before taxes. Write and solve an equation to find the number of hours h she worked each week.

   _____

4. Ben is saving $\frac{1}{5}$ of his weekly pay to buy a car. Write and solve an equation to find what weekly pay w results in savings of $61.50.

   _____

Use the table below to answer questions 5–7. Select the best answer.
The table shows the maximum speed in miles per hour for various animals.

5. The speed of a snail is how many times that of a cat?

   A $\frac{1}{1000}$ C 100

   B $\frac{1}{100}$ D 1000

Animal	mi/h
Falcon	200
Zebra	40
Cat (domestic)	30
Black Mamba Snake	20
Snail	0.03

6. A cheetah's maximum speed of 70 mi/h is x times faster than a black mamba snake's maximum speed. Which equation shows this relationship?

   F $20 + x = 70$ H $70 = \frac{20}{x}$

   G $20 = 70x$ J $70 = 20x$

7. Use your equation in problem 6 to find how many times faster a cheetah is than a black mamba snake if they are both traveling at their maximum speed.

   A 0.3 times   C 10 times

   B 3.5 times   D 50 times

    Holt McDougal Algebra 1

LESSON 1-3

Reading Strategies

Make Predictions

When solving multiplication and division equations, people often make mistakes that can easily be avoided by making a prediction first. Look at the examples below to see how you can make predictions.

EX. $\frac{n}{8} = 2$ 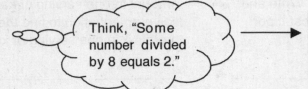 Think, "Some number divided by 8 equals 2."

> When dividing with whole numbers, the dividend is the greatest value.

Prediction: *n* is greater than both 8 and 2.

If your solution is *n* = 4, you know it's incorrect. Here, *n* = 16.

EX. $8 = 2n$ 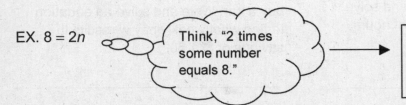 Think, "2 times some number equals 8."

> When multiplying with whole numbers, the factors are less than the product.

Prediction: *n* is less than 8.

If your answer is *n* = 16, you know it's incorrect. Here, *n* = 4.

EX. $\frac{1}{2}n = 8$ 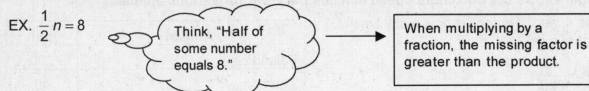 Think, "Half of some number equals 8."

> When multiplying by a fraction, the missing factor is greater than the product.

Prediction: *n* is greater than 8.

If your solution is *n* = 4, you know it's incorrect. Here, *n* = 16.

Make predictions by filling in each blank with "less" or "greater".

1. For $6t = 12$, *t* must be _____ than 12.

2. For $\frac{1}{4}f = 16$, *f* must be _____ than 16.

3. For $5 = \frac{y}{10}$, *y* must be _____ than 5.

Make a mental prediction about each solution. Then solve.

4. $3b = 12$ 5. $\frac{1}{3}c = 6$ 6. $10 = \frac{k}{2}$

_____   _____   _____

LESSON 1-4

Practice A

Solving Two-Step and Multi-Step Equations

Fill in the blanks to solve each equation.

1. $8 = 5n - 2$

    $\underline{+2} \quad +\underline{}$

    $\underline{} = 5n$

    $\underline{} = n$

2. $2d + 3 = 11$

    $-\underline{} \ -3$

    $2d \ = \underline{}$

    $d = \underline{}$

3. $3(b + 7) = 30$

    $3b + \underline{} = 30$

    $-21 \quad -21$

    $3b = \underline{}$

    $b = \underline{}$

Solve each equation. Check your answers.

4. $4t + 13 = 5$

    _____

5. $6.3 = 2x - 4.5$

    _____

6. $12 = -r - 11$

    _____

7. $-5y + 6 = -9$

    _____

8. $-1 = \dfrac{b}{4} - 7$

    _____

9. $\dfrac{5}{8} = 2m + \dfrac{3}{8}$

    _____

10. $x + -4 + 2x = 14$

    _____

11. $4(y + 1) = -8$

    _____

12. $-2(d + 6) = -10$

    _____

13. If $7x + 5 = -2$, find the value of $8x$.

The sum of the measures of the angles shown is 90°.   _____

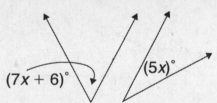

14. Write an equation to determine the value of x.   _____

15. Find the value of x.   _____

Holt McDougal Algebra 1

Practice B

Solving Two-Step and Multi-Step Equations

Solve each equation. Check your answers.

1. $-4x + 7 = 11$

2. $17 = 5y - 3$

3. $-4 = 2p + 10$

_____

_____

_____

4. $3m + 4 = 1$

5. $12.5 = 2g - 3.5$

6. $-13 = -h - 7$

_____

_____

_____

7. $-6 = \dfrac{y}{5} + 4$

8. $\dfrac{7}{9} = 2n + \dfrac{1}{9}$

9. $-\dfrac{4}{5}t + \dfrac{2}{5} = \dfrac{2}{3}$

_____

_____

_____

10. $-(x - 10) = 7$

11. $-2(b + 5) = -6$

12. $8 = 4(q - 2) + 4$

_____

_____

_____

13. If $3x - 8 = -2$, find the value of $x - 6$.

_____

14. If $-2(3y + 5) = -4$, find the value of $5y$.

_____

Answer each of the following.

15. The two angles shown
form a right angle.
Write and solve an
equation to find the
value of *x*.

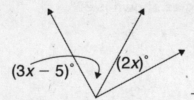

$(3x - 5)°$ $(2x)°$

_____

16. For her cellular phone service, Vera pays $32 a
month, plus $0.75 for each minute over the
allowed minutes in her plan. Vera received a bill
for $47 last month. For how many minutes did
she use her phone beyond the allowed minutes? _____

LESSON 1-4

Practice C
Solving Two-Step and Multi-Step Equations

Solve each equation. Check your answers.

1. $5r + 2 = 17$

2. $25 = -2w - 3$

3. $-7 = 4y + 9$

4. $-3f + 19 = 4$

5. $-22 = -p - 12$

6. $6.5 = 2.5r - 11$

7. $\dfrac{y}{3} - 8 = 1$

8. $\dfrac{2h}{3} - \dfrac{1}{4} = \dfrac{1}{3}$

9. $-\dfrac{2}{5} = -\dfrac{1}{3}m + \dfrac{3}{5}$

10. $-5v = 6v + 5 - v$

11. $-3(b + 9) = -6$

12. $6\dfrac{1}{2} = -4(n - 1)$

13. If $9x - 13 = -31$, find the value of $x - 8$. _____

14. If $4\left(y + \dfrac{3}{2}\right) = -18$, find the value of $2y$. _____

Answer each of the following.

15. Angle *A* is three
    times the size of
    angle *B*. The sum
    of the angle measures
    is 128°. Find the value of *x*.

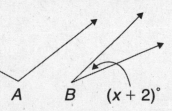

$A \qquad B \qquad (x + 2)°$

_____

16. Tina sold cookies at her club's bake sale. She
    spent $18.50 on supplies. She sold her cookies
    for $0.75 each and made a profit of $24.25.
    Write and solve an equation to find how
    many cookies Tina sold.

_____

Holt McDougal Algebra 1

LESSON 1-4

Review for Mastery

Solving Two-Step and Multi-Step Equations

When solving multi-step equations, first combine like terms on each side if possible. Then use inverse operations.

	Operations	Solve using Inverse Operations
$4x - 3 = 15$	• x is multiplied by 4. • Then 3 is subtracted.	• Add 3 to both sides. • Then divide both sides by 4.
$\dfrac{x}{3} + 2 = 9$	• x is divided by 3. • Then 2 is added.	• Add -2 to both sides. • Then multiply both sides by 3.

The order of the inverse operations is the order of operations in reverse.

Solve $2x - 7 + 3x = 13$.

		Check:
$2x + 3x - 7 = 13$	*Group like terms together.*	$2x - 7 + 3x = 13$
$5x - 7 = 13$	*Add like terms.*	$2(4) - 7 + 3(4) \overset{?}{=} 13$
$5x - 7 = 13$	*x is multiplied by 5. Then 7 is subtracted.*	
$\underline{+7 \ +7}$	*Add 7 to both sides.*	$8 - 7 + 12 \overset{?}{=} 13$
$5x = 20$		$13 \overset{?}{=} 13 \checkmark$
$\dfrac{5x}{5} = \dfrac{20}{5}$	*Divide both sides by 5.*	
$x = 4$		

Solve each equation. Check your answers.

1. $3x - 8 = 4$

2. $\dfrac{b}{2} - 4 = 26$

3. $5y + 4 - 2y = 9$

4. $14 = 3(x - 2) + 5$

Holt McDougal Algebra 1

LESSON 1-4

Review for Mastery

Solving Two-Step and Multi-Step Equations *continued*

A two-step equation with fractions can be simplified by multiplying each side by the LCD. This will clear the fractions.

Solve $\frac{x}{4} + \frac{2}{3} = 2$.

$$\frac{x}{4} + \frac{2}{3} = 2$$

$$12\left(\frac{x}{4} + \frac{2}{3}\right) = (12)2 \qquad \text{Multiply both sides by the LCD 12.}$$

$$12\left(\frac{x}{4}\right) + 12\left(\frac{2}{3}\right) = 12(2)$$

$$3x + 8 = 24 \qquad x \text{ is multiplied by 3. 8 is added.}$$

$$\underline{ -8 \quad -8} \qquad \text{Add } -8 \text{ to both sides.}$$

$$3x = 16$$

$$\frac{3x}{3} = \frac{16}{3} \qquad \text{Divide both sides by 3.}$$

$$x = \frac{16}{3}$$

Check:

$$\frac{x}{4} + \frac{2}{3} = 2$$

$$\frac{1}{4}x + \frac{2}{3} = 2$$

$$\frac{1}{4}\left(\frac{16}{3}\right) + \frac{2}{3} \overset{?}{=} 2$$

$$\frac{16}{12} + \frac{2}{3} \overset{?}{=} 2$$

$$\frac{4}{3} + \frac{2}{3} \overset{?}{=} 2$$

$$\frac{6}{3} \overset{?}{=} 2$$

$$2 \overset{?}{=} 2 \checkmark$$

Solve each equation. Check your answers.

5. $\frac{x}{2} + \frac{3}{8} = 1$

6. $\frac{w}{3} + \frac{2}{5} = \frac{1}{15}$

7. $3 = \frac{a}{5} + \frac{1}{2}$

Holt McDougal Algebra 1

Name _____ Date _____ Class_____

Challenge

Using Two-Step Equations to Solve Geometry Problems

Many concepts of algebra can be applied to a wide range of geometry problems.

Suppose that you want to design a box. The base of the box will be a square that is 10 inches on each side, and the box will be h inches tall. The surface area of the box (that is, the area of cardboard needed to make the box, assuming no overlap) is given by $4 \cdot 10 \cdot h + 2 \cdot 10 \cdot 10$, or $40h + 200$. For a surface area of 360 square inches, you would solve $40h + 200 = 360$ in order to find the height of the box.

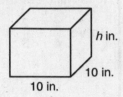

The base of a rectangular box is to be a square that is 10 inches on each side. For each given surface area, find the corresponding height of the box.

1. 360 square inches _____

2. 520 square inches _____

3. 240 square inches _____

4. 560 square inches _____

5. 800 square inches _____

6. 480 square inches _____

Now suppose that you want to design a cylindrical box whose base is a circle with a radius of 5 inches. The surface area of the cylindrical box is given by $50\pi + 10\pi h$.

The base of a cylindrical box will be a circle with a radius of 5 inches. For each given surface area, find the corresponding height of the box.

7. 80π square inches _____

8. 120π square inches _____

9. 110π square inches _____

10. 160π square inches _____

11. 200π square inches _____

12. 90π square inches _____

Another geometric application of two-step equations relates to the interior angles of a polygon. If the polygon has n sides, the sum of the measures of its angles is $180n - 360$ degrees.

For example, in a triangle, $n = 3$, so the measures of the angles add up to 180°. For a trapezoid, $n = 4$, so the measures of the angles add up to 360°.

In the following exercises, the sum of the measures of the interior angles of a polygon is given. Find the number of sides of the polygon.

13. 540° _____

14. 1800° _____

15. 900° _____

16. 2880° _____

Holt McDougal Algebra 1

LESSON 1-4

Problem Solving

Solving Two-Step and Multi-Step Equations

Write the correct answer.

1. Stephen belongs to a movie club in which he pays an annual fee of $39.95 and then rents DVDs for $0.99 each. In one year, Stephen spent $55.79. Write and solve an equation to find how many DVDs *d* he rented.

   _____

   _____

2. In 2003, the population of Zimbabwe was about 12.6 million, which was 1 million more than 4 times the population in 1950. Write and solve an equation to find the population *p* of Zimbabwe in 1950.

   _____

   _____

3. Maggie's brother is three years younger than twice her age. The sum of their ages is 24. How old is Maggie?

   _____

4. Kate is saving to take an SAT prep course that costs $350. So far, she has saved $180, and she adds $17 to her savings each week. How many more weeks must she save to be able to afford the course?

   _____

Use the graph below to answer questions 5–7. Select the best answer. The graph shows the population density (number of people per square mile) of various states given in the 2000 census.

5. One seventeenth of Rhode Island's population density minus 17 equals the population density of Colorado. What is Rhode Island's population density?

   A 425   C 714

   B 697   D 1003

6. One more than sixteen times the population density of New Mexico equals the population density of Texas. To the nearest whole number, what is New Mexico's population density?

   F 5   H 13

   G 8   J 63

7. Three times the population density of Missouri minus 26 equals the population density of California. What is Missouri's population density?

   A 64   C 98

   B 81   D 729

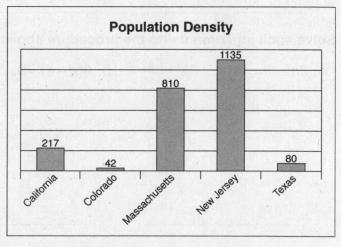

Population Density

California 217
Colorado 42
Massachusetts 810
New Jersey 1135
Texas 80

Holt McDougal Algebra 1

LESSON 1-4

Reading Strategies
Follow a Procedure

Use the example below to understand the procedure for solving multi-step equations. Not all problems will require all the steps.

Solve $-2(x - 5) + 4x = 17$.

$-2(x - 5) + 4x = 17$ ⟶ 1. Use the Distributive Property.

$-2x + 10 + 4x = 17$

$(-2x) + 10 + (4x) = 17$ ⟶ 2. Identify and combine like terms.

$2x + 10 = 17$

$2x + 10 = 17$

$\underline{-10 \quad -10}$ ⟶ 3. "Undo" addition (and subtraction).

$\dfrac{2x}{2} = \dfrac{7}{2}$ ⟶ 4. "Undo" division (and multiplication).

$x = 3.5$

Answer each question.

1. If an equation does not need the Distributive Property, what should you look for next?

   _____

2. To solve the equation $5x - 3 = 22$, would you "undo" subtraction or multiplication first?

   _____

3. Describe how you would solve $\dfrac{1}{5}x + 3 = 28$.

   _____

Solve each equation using the procedure shown. Show all your steps.

4. $3n - 1 = 14$ 5. $3(d - 4) = 9$ 6. $-4(j + 2) - 3j = 6$

_____   _____   _____

LESSON 1-5

Practice A

Solving Equations with Variables on Both Sides

Fill in the blanks to solve each equation.

1. $4a - 3 = 2a + 7$
    $-2a \quad - \underline{\quad}$
    $2a - 3 = 7$
    $+\underline{\quad} +3$
    $2a = \underline{\quad}$
    $a = \underline{\quad}$

2. $-3r + 9 = -4r + 5$
    $+\underline{\quad} +4r$
    $r + 9 = 5$
    $-9 \quad -\underline{\quad}$
    $r = \underline{\quad}$

3. $-2b = -5(b - 6)$
    $-2b = \underline{\quad} + \underline{\quad}$
    $+5b = +\underline{\quad}$
    $\underline{\quad} = 30$
    $b = \underline{\quad}$

Solve each equation.

4. $2(c + 3) = c - 13$

5. $5p - 8 = 1 + 5p - 9$

6. $3(2v - 1) = 6v - 4$

_____ _____ _____

Answer each of the following.

7. Gretchen lives in Florida, where the current temperature is 69°F and rising at a rate of 2°F per hour. She is talking on the phone to her friend in Indiana where the temperature is now 84°F and falling at a rate of 3°F per hour.

    a. If the temperatures continue changing at the same rates, how many hours would Gretchen and her friend have to talk before the temperatures become equal? _____

    b. What would that temperature be? _____

8. Marlo wants to rent and ride a bike at a state park. There are two parks in his area. One has an entrance fee of $8 and charges $2 per hour for bike rentals. The other park has an entrance fee of $2 and charges $5 per hour for bike rentals.

    a. After how many hours would the cost of renting and riding a bike be the same at both parks? _____

    b. What would that cost be? _____

Holt McDougal Algebra 1

LESSON 1-5

Practice B

Solving Equations with Variables on Both Sides

Solve each equation. Check your answers.

1. $3d + 8 = 2d - 17$

2. $2n - 7 = 5n - 10$

3. $p - 15 = 13 - 6p$

_____

_____

_____

4. $-t + 5 = t - 19$

5. $15x - 10 = -9x + 2$

6. $1.8r + 9 = -5.7r - 6$

_____

_____

_____

7. $2y + 3 = 3(y + 7)$

8. $4n + 6 - 2n = 2(n + 3)$

9. $6m - 8 = 2 + 9m - 1$

_____

_____

_____

10. $-v + 5 + 6v = 1 + 5v + 3$

11. $2(3b - 4) = 8b - 11$

12. $5(r - 1) = 2(r - 4) - 6$

_____

_____

_____

Answer each of the following.

13. Janine has job offers at two companies. One company offers a starting salary of $28,000 with a raise of $3000 each year. The other company offers a starting salary of $36,000 with a raise of $2000 each year.

    a. After how many years would Janine's salary be the same with both companies?

                                                 _____

    b. What would that salary be?

                                                 _____

14. Xian and his cousin both collect stamps. Xian has 56 stamps, and his cousin has 80 stamps. Both have recently joined different stamp-collecting clubs. Xian's club will send him 12 new stamps per month, and his cousin's club will send him 8 new stamps per month.

    a. After how many months will Xian and his cousin have the same number of stamps?

                                                 _____

    b. How many stamps will that be?

                                                 _____

Holt McDougal Algebra 1

LESSON 1-5

Practice C

Solving Equations with Variables on Both Sides

Solve each equation. Check your answers.

1. $9x - 2 = 2x + 12$

2. $2a - 11 = -8a + 19$

3. $2c + 6 = 1 - 3c$

_____

_____

_____

4. $-y - 22 = y - 16$

5. $5d - 8 = 3 + 7d$

6. $9 + 2.7t = -4.8t - 6$

_____

_____

_____

7. $-5m + 2 + 8m = 2m + 11$

8. $-y - 8 + 6y = -9 + 5y + 1$

_____

_____

9. $4(2x - 3) = 3 + 8x - 11$

10. $2\left(n + \dfrac{1}{3}\right) = \dfrac{3}{2}n + 1 + \dfrac{1}{2}n - \dfrac{1}{3}$

_____

_____

Answer each of the following.

11. The table at right shows the costs of ordering
T-shirts from two different companies. With
how many T-shirts would the cost of the order
be the same with both companies? What
would that cost be?

Company	Price Per Shirt	Shipping
Crazy Shirts	$8.00	$13.00
T's for All	$7.50	$16.00

_____

12. Brenn has $60 in his savings account. His brother Chris
has $135 in his. Brenn decides to save $5 of his allowance
each week, while Chris decides to spend his whole allowance
along with $10 of his savings each week. After how many weeks
will Brenn and Chris have the same amount of money in their
savings accounts? How much money will that be?

_____

Holt McDougal Algebra 1

LESSON
1-5

Review for Mastery
Solving Equations with Variables on Both Sides

Variables must be collected on the same side of the equation before the equation can be solved.

Solve $10x = 2x - 16$.

$10x = 2x - 16$		
$\underline{-2x \quad -2x}$	*Add $-2x$ to both sides.*	
$8x = -16$		
$\dfrac{8x}{8} = \dfrac{-16}{8}$	*Divide both sides by 8.*	
$x = -2$		

Check:

$10x = 2x - 16$

$10(-2) \overset{?}{=} 2(-2) - 16$

$-20 \overset{?}{=} -4 - 16$

$-20 \overset{?}{=} -20$ ✓

Solve $3x = 5(x + 2)$.

$3x = 5x + 10$	*Distribute.*
$\underline{-5x \quad -5x}$	*Add $-5x$ to both sides.*
$-2x = 10$	
$\dfrac{-2x}{-2} = \dfrac{10}{-2}$	*Divide both sides by -2.*
$x = -5$	

Check:

$3x = 5(x + 2)$

$3(-5) \overset{?}{=} 5(-5 + 2)$

$-15 \overset{?}{=} 5(-3)$

$-15 \overset{?}{=} -15$ ✓

Write the first step you would take to solve each equation.

1. $3x + 2 = 7x$ _____

2. $-4x - 6 = -10x$ _____

3. $15x + 7 = -3x$ _____

Solve each equation. Check your answers.

4. $4x + 2 = 5(x + 10)$ 5. $-10 + y + 3 = 4y - 13$ 6. $3(t + 7) + 2 = 6t - 2 + 2t$

_____   _____   _____

LESSON 1-5

Review for Mastery

Solving Equations with Variables on Both Sides *continued*

Some equations have infinitely many solutions. These equations are true for all values of the variable. Some equations have no solutions. There is no value of the variable that will make the equation true.

Solve $-3x + 9 = 4x + 9 - 7x$.

$-3x + 9 = -3x + 9$	Combine like terms.
$\underline{-3x \qquad +3x}$	Add 3x to each side.
$9 = 9$ ✓	True statement.

The solution is the set of all real numbers.

Check any value of x:
Try $x = 4$.
$-3x + 9 = 4x + 9 - 7x$
$-3(4) + 9 \overset{?}{=} 4(4) + 9 - 7(4)$
$-12 + 9 \overset{?}{=} 16 + 9 - 28$
$-3 \overset{?}{=} -3$ ✓

Solve $2x + 6 + 3x = 5x - 10$.

$2x + 6 + 3x = 5x - 10$	
$5x + 6 = 5x - 10$	Combine like terms.
$\underline{-5x \qquad -5x}$	Add −5x to each side.
$6 = -10$ ✗	False statement.

There is no solution.

Check any value of x:
Try $x = 1$.
$2x + 6 + 3x = 5x - 10$
$2(1) + 6 + 3(1) \overset{?}{=} 5(1) - 10$
$2 + 6 + 3 \overset{?}{=} 5 - 10$
$11 \overset{?}{=} -5$ ✗

Solve each equation.

7. $x + 2 = x + 4$

8. $-2x + 8 = 2x + 4$

9. $5 + 3g = 3g + 5$

10. $5x - 1 - 4x = x + 7$

11. $2(f + 3) + 4f = 6 + 6f$

12. $3x + 7 - 2x = 4x + 10$

Holt McDougal Algebra 1

LESSON 1-5

Challenge

Finding a Formula to Solve Linear Equations

A linear equation in one variable can take on many different appearances. Each of the equations below is an equation in one variable.

$$2x - 5 = 12 \qquad\qquad 2(x + 1) = 5 \qquad\qquad 3x - 4 = -2x + 1$$

Although these equations look different, you can transform each of them into the standard form for a linear equation in one variable.

In Exercises 1–4, each equation has the form $ax + b = 0$. Solve each equation.

1. $3x + 7 = 0$ _____

2. $-2x - 8 = 0$ _____

3. $\dfrac{2}{3}x - 5 = 0$ _____

4. $-4.1x - 8.2 = 0$ _____

You can always transform a given linear equation in one variable into the form $ax + b = 0$.

In Exercises 5–8, write each equation in the form $ax + b = 0$. Do not solve the resulting equation.

5. $3(x + 5) = x + 21$

6. $-2(-4 - 6x) = -10 + 3x$

_____

_____

7. $-7(-3 - x) = -2(3 - x)$

8. $8 - 2(x - 5) = x - 3$

_____

_____

9.   a. Solve $ax + b = 0$ for x. _____

     b. Explain how to write your answer to part **a** as a formula that you can use to solve a linear equation in x. _____

_____

Solve the specified equation by using your formula from Exercise 9.

10. Exercise 5 _____

11. Exercise 6 _____

12. Exercise 7 _____

13. Exercise 8 _____

14.   a. Let $ax + b = 0$, where $a = 0$ and $b = 0$. How many solutions does the equation have? _____

     b. Let $ax + b = 0$, where $a = 0$ and $b \neq 0$. How many solutions does the equation have? _____

Holt McDougal Algebra 1

LESSON 1-5

Problem Solving

Solving Equations with Variables on Both Sides

Write the correct answer.

1. Claire purchased just enough fencing to border either a rectangular or triangular garden, as shown, whose perimeters are the same.

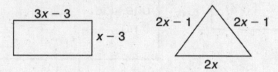

How many feet of fencing did she buy?

2. Celia and Ryan are starting a nutrition program. Celia currently consumes 1200 calories a day and will increase that number by 100 calories each day. Ryan currently consumes 3230 calories a day and will decrease that number by 190 each day. They will continue this pattern until they are both consuming the same number of calories per day. In how many days will that be?

_____

3. A moving company charges $800 plus $16 per hour. Another moving company charges $720 plus $21 per hour. How long is a job that costs the same no matter which company is used?

4. Aaron needs to take out a loan to purchase a motorcycle. At one bank, he would pay $2500 initially and $150 each month for the loan. At another bank, he would pay $3000 initially and $125 each month. After how many months will the two loan payments be the same?

_____

Use the table below to answer questions 5–7. Select the best answer.
The table shows the membership fees of three different gyms.

5. After how many months will the fees for Workout Now and Community Gym be the same?

  A 2.5   C 25

  B 15   D 30

6. Sal joined Workout Now for the number of months found in problem 5. How much did he pay?

  F $695   H $1325

  G $875   J $1550

7. After how many months will the fees for Workout Now and Ultra Sports Club be the same?

  A 7   C 12

  B 10   D 15

Gym	Fees
Workout Now	$200 plus $45 per month
Community Gym	$50 plus $55 per month
Ultra Sports Club	$20 plus $60 per month

Holt McDougal Algebra 1

LESSON 1-5

Reading Strategies
Use a Sequence Chain

Use the sequence chain below to guide you in solving equations.

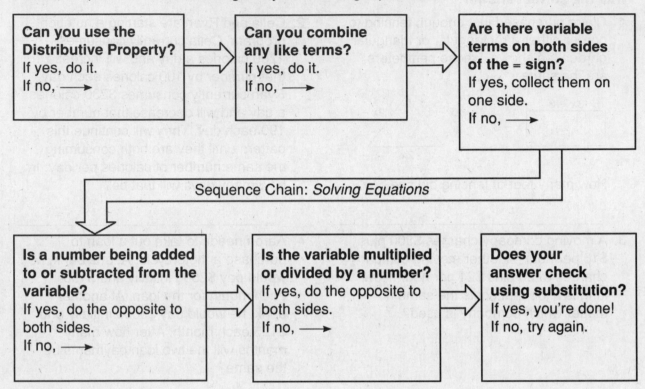

Sequence Chain: *Solving Equations*

Answer each question.

1. What is the first thing to look for when solving an equation?

_____

2. What should you do before collecting the variables on one side of the equal sign?

_____

3. Describe the first step in solving the equation $3x - 4 = 2x + 19$.

_____

Solve each equation using the sequence chain.

4. $7p - 2 = 9p + 10$ 5. $8 + 4x = 3(x - 1) + 12$ 6. $-2(t + 2) + 5t = 6t + 2$

_____   _____   _____

LESSON
1-6

Practice A
Solving for a Variable

Answer each of the following.

1. The formula $K = C + 273$ is used to convert temperatures from degrees Celsius to Kelvin. Solve this formula for C.

   _____

2. The formula $T = \dfrac{1}{f}$ relates the period of a sound wave T to its frequency f. Solve this formula for f.

   _____

Solve for the indicated variable.

3. $x = 5y$ for y

   _____

4. $s + 4t = r$ for s

   _____

5. $3m - 7n = p$ for m

   _____

6. $6 = hj + k$ for j

   _____

7. $\dfrac{v}{w} = 9$ for w

   _____

8. $\dfrac{a + 3}{b} = c$ for a

   _____

Answer each of the following.

9. The formula $d = rt$ relates the distance an object travels d, to its average rate of speed r, and amount of time t that it travels.

   a. Solve the formula $d = rt$ for t.

   _____

   b. How many hours would it take for a car to travel 150 miles at an average rate of 50 miles per hour?

   _____

10. The formula $F - E + V = 2$ relates the number of faces F, edges E, and vertices V, in any convex polyhedron.

   a. Solve the formula $F - E + V = 2$ for F.

   _____

   b. How many faces does a polyhedron with 20 vertices and 30 edges have?

   _____

Holt McDougal Algebra 1

LESSON 1-6 Practice B
Solving for a Variable

Answer each of the following.

1. The formula $C = 2\pi r$ relates the radius r of a circle to its circumference C. Solve the formula for r.

   _____

2. The formula $y = mx + b$ is called the slope-intercept form of a line. Solve this formula for m.

   _____

Solve for the indicated variable.

3. $4c = d$ for c

4. $n - 6m = 8$ for n

5. $2p + 5r = q$ for p

   _____ _____ _____

6. $-10 = xy + z$ for x

7. $\dfrac{a}{b} = c$ for b

8. $\dfrac{h-4}{j} = k$ for j

   _____ _____ _____

Answer each of the following.

9. The formula $c = 5p + 215$ relates c, the total cost in dollars of hosting a birthday party at a skating rink, to p, the number of people attending.

   a. Solve the formula $c = 5p + 215$ for p. _____

   b. If Allie's parents are willing to spend $300 for a party, how many people can attend? _____

10. The formula for the area of a triangle is $A = \dfrac{1}{2}bh$, where b represents the length of the base and h represents the height.

   a. Solve the formula $A = \dfrac{1}{2}bh$ for b. _____

   b. If a triangle has an area of 192 mm^2, and the height measures 12 mm, what is the measure of the base? _____

Holt McDougal Algebra 1

LESSON 1-6 Practice C

Solving for a Variable

Answer each of the following.

1. The formula $P = 2l + 2w$ relates the perimeter P of a rectangle to its length l and width w. Solve this formula for w.

_____

2. The formula $a = \dfrac{v_f - v_i}{t}$ is used to find an object's acceleration given initial velocity v_i, final velocity v_f, and time t. Solve this formula for v_f.

_____

Solve each literal equation for the indicated variable.

3. $-3f = g$ for f

4. $12 = a + 5b$ for a

5. $3x - 7y = z$ for x

_____ _____ _____

6. $5h - g = jk$ for h

7. $\dfrac{r}{s} = t - 9$ for r

8. $\dfrac{m+3}{n} = p$ for n

_____ _____ _____

Answer each of the following.

9. The formula $F = ma$ relates the force F exerted on an object, to the object's mass m, and acceleration a.

   a. Solve the formula $F = ma$ for a.   _____

   b. Suppose a shot-putter exerts a force of 123.5 kg • m/s^2 on a shot that has a mass of 6.5 kg. What is the rate of acceleration of the shot? (The answer will be in m/s^2.)   _____

10. The formula $I = Prt$ can be used to determine the interest I that is earned on a principal amount of money P, when the money is invested at an annual percentage rate r for t years.

   a. Solve the formula $I = Prt$ for t.   _____

   b. If a couple invests $5000 in an account that earns a 3% interest rate, how long will they need to invest it to earn $1200 in interest? (*Hint*: Convert the interest rate to a decimal.)   _____

Holt McDougal Algebra 1

LESSON 1-6

Review for Mastery
Solving for a Variable

Solving for a variable in a formula can make it easier to use that formula. The process is similar to that of solving multi-step equations. Find the operations being performed on the variable you are solving for, and then use inverse operations.

	Operations	Solve using Inverse Operations
$A = lw$ Solve for w.	• w is multiplied by l.	• Divide both sides by l.
$P = 2l + 2w$ Solve for w.	• w is multiplied by 2. • Then $2l$ is added.	• Add $-2l$ to both sides. • Then divide both sides by 2.

The formula $A = \dfrac{1}{2}bh$ relates the area A of a triangle to its base b and height h. Solve the formula for b.

> The order of the inverse operations is the order of operations in reverse.

$A = \dfrac{1}{2}bh$ *b is multiplied by $\dfrac{1}{2}$.*

$\left(\dfrac{2}{1}\right) \cdot A = \left(\dfrac{2}{1}\right)\dfrac{1}{2}bh$ *Multiply both sides by $\dfrac{2}{1}$.*

$2A = bh$ *b is multiplied by h.*

$\dfrac{2A}{h} = \dfrac{bh}{h}$ *Divide both sides by h.*

$\dfrac{2A}{h} = b$ *Simplify.*

Solve for the indicated variable.

1. $P = 4s$ for s

2. $a + b + c = 180$ for b

3. $P = \dfrac{KT}{V}$ for K

_____   _____

The formula $V = \dfrac{1}{3}lwh$ relates the volume of a square pyramid to its base length l, base width w, and height h.

4. Solve the formula for w.   _____

5. A square pyramid has a volume of 560 in³, a base length of 10 in., and a height of 14 in. What is its base width? _____

LESSON 1-6

Review for Mastery

Solving for a Variable continued

Any equation with two or more variables can be solved for any given variable.

Solve $x = \dfrac{y - z}{10}$ **for y.**

$x = \dfrac{y - z}{10}$ *y − z is divided by 10.*

$10(x) = 10\left(\dfrac{y - z}{10}\right)$ *Multiply both sides by 10.*

$10x = y - z$ *z is subtracted from y. Add z to both sides.*

$\underline{ +z \quad\quad +z}$

$10x + z = y$

Solve $a = b + \dfrac{c}{d}$ **for c.**

$a = b + \dfrac{c}{d}$

$\underline{-b \quad\quad -b}$ *Add −b to each side.*

$a - b = \dfrac{c}{d}$

$d(a - b) = \left(\dfrac{c}{d}\right)d$ *Multiply both sides by d.*

$d(a - b) = c$ *Simplify.*

State the first inverse operation to perform when solving for the indicated variable.

6. $y = x + z$; for z _____

7. $\dfrac{f + g}{2} = h$; for g _____

8. $t = -3r + \dfrac{s}{5}$; for s _____

Solve for the indicated variable.

9. $3ab = c$; for a 10. $y = x + \dfrac{z}{3}$; for z 11. $\dfrac{m + 3}{n} = p$; for m

_____   _____   _____

Name _____ Date _____ Class_____

Challenge
A Formula of Interest

When you put your money in a savings account, the bank may pay you *simple interest*. Let *P* represent the dollar amount of your deposit (the principal), let *r* represent the interest rate, and let *t* represent the number of years. The amount of interest you earn, *I*, is given by the *simple interest formula*: $I = Prt$.

Note that banks typically use percents to describe their interest rates. Percent means "per hundred," so an interest rate of 5% means that you should use $r = \dfrac{5}{100}$, or 0.05.

Use the simple interest formula to solve the following problems:

1. If $P = 2500$, $r = 0.03$, and $t = 5$, what is *I*? _____

2. If $r = 0.025$, $t = 3$, and $I = 150$, what is *P*? _____

3. If $P = 500$, $r = 0.06$, and $I = 150$, what is *t*? _____

4. If $P = 3000$, $t = 4$, and $I = 384$, what is *r*? _____

5. Kevin is making a deposit of $1800 at his local bank. The bank pays 6.5% simple interest ($r = 0.065$). If Kevin leaves his deposit at the bank for 3 years, how much interest will he earn? _____

6. Cecelia made a deposit of $600 at a bank paying 4% simple interest ($r = 0.04$). How long should she leave her deposit at the bank in order to earn $72 in interest? _____

7. Darryl opened an account at a bank which paid 5.5% simple interest ($r = 0.055$). After 6 years, he had earned $726 in interest. What was the amount of his original deposit? _____

8. Sophia deposited $150 at a savings and loan association paying simple interest. If she earned $27 in interest after 6 years, what was the interest rate? _____

9. Nathan made a deposit of $650 at a bank paying 3.8% simple interest ($r = 0.038$). If he leaves his deposit at the bank for 10 years, how much interest will he earn? _____

10. Susie made a deposit of $980 at a credit union paying 7% simple interest ($r = 0.07$). How long should she leave her deposit at the credit union in order to earn $343 in interest? _____

11. Guillermo deposited $1350 at a bank paying simple interest. If he earned $109.35 in 3 years, what was the interest rate? _____

Holt McDougal Algebra 1

LESSON 1-6

Problem Solving

Solving for a Variable

Use the table below, which shows some track and field gold medal winners, to answer questions 1–4. Round all answers to the nearest tenth.

1. Solve the formula $d = rt$ for r.

   _____

2. Find Johnson's average speed in meters per second.

   _____

3. Find Garcia's average speed in meters per second.

   _____

4. The world record of 19.32 seconds in the 200-meter race was set by Michael Johnson in 1996. Find the difference between Johnson's average speed and Kenteris' average speed.

2000 Summer Olympics		
Gold Medal Winner	**Race**	**Time (s)**
M. Greene, USA	100 m	9.87
K. Kenteris, Greece	200 m	20.09
M. Johnson, USA	400 m	43.84
A. Garcia, Cuba	110 m hurdles	13.00

   _____

Select the best answer.

5. The cost to mail a letter in the United States in 2008 was $0.41 for the first ounce and $0.26 for each additional ounce. Solve
   $C = 0.41 + 0.26(z - 1)$ for z.

   A $z = \dfrac{C - 0.41}{0.26}$

   B $z = \dfrac{C - 0.41}{0.26} + 1$

   C $z = \dfrac{C + 0.15}{0.26}$

   D $z = C - 0.67$

6. The formula $V = \dfrac{Bh}{3}$ shows how to find the volume of a pyramid. Solve for B.

   F $B = \dfrac{3V}{h}$ H $B = 3Vh$

   G $B = 3V - h$ J $B = 3V + h$

7. Degrees Celsius and degrees Fahrenheit are related by the equation
   $C = \dfrac{5}{9}(F - 32)$. Solve for F.

   A $F = 9C + 27$ C $F = \dfrac{5}{9}C + 32$

   B $F = \dfrac{9}{5}C$ D $F = \dfrac{9}{5}C + 32$

8. The cost of operating an electrical device is given by the formula $C = \dfrac{Wtc}{1000}$ where W is the power in watts, t is the time in hours, and c is the cost in cents per kilowatt-hour. Solve for W.

   F $W = 1000C - tc$

   G $W = \dfrac{Ctc}{1000}$

   H $W = 1000C + tc$

   J $W = \dfrac{1000C}{tc}$

Holt McDougal Algebra 1

LESSON 1-6

Reading Strategies
Use a Concept Map

Use the concept map below to help you understand literal equations.

Definition

Literal equations are equations with two or more variables.

Facts

Formulas are literal equations.

Literal equations are solved the same way as equations, by using inverse operations.

Literal Equations

Examples

$d = rt$

$A = \frac{1}{2}bh$

$m + n = 3p$

Non-Examples

$-4x = 20$

$10 = \frac{1}{3}(y - 6)$

$n + 5 = 2n - 14$

Answer each question.

1. Give your own example of a literal equation.

   _____

2. Why is $n + 5 = 2n - 14$ given as a non-example?

   _____

3. Is an equation with four different variables a literal equation? Why?

   _____

4. Describe how to solve $d = rt$ for t.

   _____

5. Solve the literal equation $3t + 8 = b$ for t.

   _____

6. The formula for the volume of a rectangular prism is $V = lwh$.

   a. Solve this formula for h.   _____

   b. Find the height of a rectangular prism with a volume of 189 cm^2, a length of 9 cm, and a width of 7 cm.   _____

LESSON 1-7

Practice A
Solving Absolute-Value Equations

Fill in the blanks to solve each equation.

1. $|x| + 3 = 5$

   ___ −3

   $|x| =$ ___

Case 1	Case 2
$x =$ ___	$x =$ ___

2. $|x + 4| = 7$

Case 1	Case 2
$x + 4 =$ ___	$x + 4 =$ ___
− ___ − ___	− ___ − ___
$x =$ ___	$x =$ ___

3. $5|x − 1| = 30$

   $|x − 1| =$ ___

Case 1	Case 2
$x − 1 =$ ___	$x − 1 =$ ___
$x =$ ___	$x =$ ___

Solve each equation.

4. $|x| = 8$

   _____

5. $|x| = 14$

   _____

6. $|x| − 6 = 3$

   _____

7. $|x| − 7 = 10$

   _____

8. $|x + 2| = 9$

   _____

9. $|x − 5| = 6$

   _____

10. $3|x| = 15$

    _____

11. $4|x + 2| = 20$

    _____

12. $|x + 1| − 2 = 8$

    _____

Troy's car can go 24 miles on one gallon of gasoline. However, his gas mileage can vary from this value by 2 miles per gallon depending on where he drives.

13. Write an absolute-value equation that you can use to find the minimum and maximum gas mileage.

    _____

14. Solve the equation to find the minimum and maximum gas mileage.

    _____

Holt McDougal Algebra 1

LESSON 1-7

Practice B

Solving Absolute-Value Equations

Solve each equation.

1. $|x| = 12$

2. $|x| = \dfrac{1}{2}$

3. $|x| - 6 = 4$

_____ _____ _____

4. $5 + |x| = 14$

5. $3|x| = 24$

6. $|x + 3| = 10$

_____ _____ _____

7. $|x - 1| = 2$

8. $4|x - 5| = 12$

9. $|x + 2| - 3 = 9$

_____ _____ _____

10. $|6x| = 18$

11. $|x - 1| = 0$

12. $|x - 3| + 2 = 2$

_____ _____ _____

13. How many solutions does the equation $|x + 7| = 1$ have?   _____

14. How many solutions does the equation $|x + 7| = 0$ have?   _____

15. How many solutions does the equation $|x + 7| = -1$ have?   _____

Leticia sets the thermostat in her apartment to 68 degrees. The actual temperature in her apartment can vary from this by as much as 3.5 degrees.

16. Write an absolute-value equation that you can
    use to find the minimum and maximum temperature.   _____

17. Solve the equation to find the minimum and
    maximum temperature.   _____

Holt McDougal Algebra 1

LESSON 1-7

Practice C
Solving Absolute-Value Equations

Solve each equation.

1. $|x| = \dfrac{3}{5}$

2. $2|x| = 0$

3. $|x| - 2.5 = 8$

_____

4. $|x| + 6 = -4$

5. $-9|x| = -63$

6. $|x + 11| = 0$

_____

7. $\left|x - \dfrac{1}{2}\right| = 2$

8. $3|x - 1| = -15$

9. $|x - 1| - 1.4 = 6.2$

_____

10. $|2x + 5| = 11$

11. $|4x - 7| + 3 = 0$

12. $15 = 7 - |2x|$

_____

Answer each question.

13. A carpenter cuts boards for a construction project. Each board must be 3 meters long, but the length is allowed to differ from this value by at most 0.5 cm. Write and solve an absolute-value equation to find the minimum and maximum acceptable lengths for a board.

_____

14. The owner of a butcher shop keeps the shop's freezer at –5°C. It is acceptable for the temperature to differ from this value by 1.5°. Write and solve an absolute-value equation to find the minimum and maximum acceptable temperatures.

_____

Holt McDougal Algebra 1

LESSON 1-7 Review for Mastery

Solving Absolute-Value Equations

There are three steps in solving an absolute-value equation. First use inverse operations to isolate the absolute-value expression. Then rewrite the equation as two cases that do not involve absolute values. Finally, solve these new equations.

Solve $|x - 3| + 4 = 8$.

Step 1: Isolate the absolute-value expression.

$|x - 3| + 4 = 8$

$$\underline{\quad\quad -4 \quad -4\quad}$$ *Subtract 4 from both sides.*

$|x - 3| = 4$

Step 2: Rewrite the equation as two cases.

$$|x - 3| = 4$$

	Case 1	**Case 2**	
Step 3:	$x - 3 = -4$	$x - 3 = 4$	
Solve.	$\underline{\quad +3 \quad +3\quad}$	$\underline{\quad +3 \quad +3\quad}$	*Add 3 to both sides.*
	$x = -1$	$x = 7$	

The solutions are -1 and 7.

Solve each equation.

1. $|x - 2| - 3 = 5$

2. $|x + 7| + 2 = 10$

3. $4|x - 5| = 20$

4. $|2x| + 1 = 7$

Holt McDougal Algebra 1

LESSON
1-7
Review for Mastery
Solving Absolute-Value Equations continued

Some absolute-value equations have two solutions. Others have one solution or no solution. To decide how many solutions there are, first isolate the absolute-value expression.

Original Equation	Simplified Equation	Solutions
$|x| + 5 = 7$	$|x| + 5 = 7$ $\underline{\quad -5 \quad -5}$ $|x| = 2$	$|x| = 2$ has two solutions, $x = -2$ and $x = 2$. The solutions are -2 and 2.
$|x - 5| + 2 = 2$	$|x - 5| + 2 = 2$ $\underline{\quad -2 \quad -2}$ $|x - 5| = 0$	$|x - 5| = 0$ means $x - 5 = 0$, so there is one solution $x = 5$. The solution is 5.
$|x + 7| + 4 = 1$	$|x + 7| + 4 = 1$ $\underline{\quad -4 \quad -4}$ $|x + 7| = -3$	$|x + 7| = -3$ has no solutions because an absolute-value expression is never negative. There is no solution.

Solve $|2x + 1| - 3 = -7$.

$$|2x + 1| - 3 = -7$$

$\underline{\quad +3 \quad +3}$ *Add 3 to both sides.*

$$|2x + 1| = -4$$ *Absolute value cannot be negative.*

The equation has no solution.

Solve each equation.

5. $8 + |x - 2| = 8$

6. $|x + 1| + 5 = 2$

_____

_____

7. $4|x - 3| = -16$

8. $3|x + 10| = 0$

_____

_____

Name _____ Date _____ Class_____

Challenge

Writing an Absolute-Value Equation Given the Solutions

It is sometimes useful to construct an equation from given solutions. For example, consider the solutions −3 and 7. To write an absolute-value equation with these solutions, first plot the points on a number line.

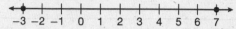

Find the value that is midway between −3 and 7. One way to do this is to find the mean:

$$\frac{-3 + 7}{2} = \frac{4}{2} = 2$$

Now find the distance of −3 and 7 from this midpoint. The distance is 5 units.

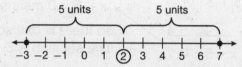

The required absolute-value equation will be in the form $|x - m| = d$, where m is the midpoint and d is the distance of each solution from the midpoint. Therefore, the absolute-value equation with the solutions −3 and 7 is $|x - 2| = 5$.

1. Show how to check that −3 and 7 are solutions of $|x - 2| = 5$.

   _____

2. Are there other absolute-value equations with the same solutions? If so, give an example of such an equation. (*Hint:* Consider performing the same operation on each side of the equation $|x - 2| = 5$.)

   _____

Write an absolute-value equation with the given solutions.

3. 1, 9   4. −4, 8   5. −5, 11   6. −9, −1

_____   _____   _____   _____

7. $-\dfrac{1}{3}, \dfrac{1}{3}$ 8. 5, 6   9. −4.5, 9.5   10. $-\dfrac{1}{2}, \dfrac{5}{2}$

_____   _____   _____   _____

LESSON 1-7 Problem Solving

Solving Absolute-Value Equations

Write the correct answer.

1. A machine manufactures wheels with a diameter of 70 cm. It is acceptable for the diameter of a wheel to be within 0.02 cm of this value. Write and solve an absolute-value equation to find the minimum and maximum acceptable diameters.

_____

_____

2. A pedestrian bridge is 53 meters long. Due to changes in temperature, the bridge may expand or contract by as much as 21 millimeters. Write and solve an absolute-value equation to find the minimum and maximum lengths of the bridge.

_____

_____

3. Two numbers on a number line are represented by the absolute-value equation $|n - 5| = 6$. What are the two numbers?

_____

_____

4. A jewelry maker cuts pieces of wire to shape into earrings. The equation $|x - 12.2| = 0.3$ gives the minimum and maximum acceptable lengths of the wires in centimeters. What is the minimum acceptable length of a wire?

_____

_____

The table shows the recommended daily intake of several minerals for adult women. Use the table for questions 5–7. Select the best answer.

5. Which absolute-value equation gives the minimum and maximum recommended intakes for zinc?

   A $|x - 8| = 32$ C $|x - 16| = 24$

   B $|x - 24| = 16$ D $|x - 40| = 32$

6. For which mineral are the minimum and maximum recommended intakes given by the absolute-value equation $|x - 31.5| = 13.5$?

   F Fluoride   H Zinc

   G Iron   J None of these

7. Jason writes an equation for the minimum and maximum intakes of fluoride. He writes it in the form $|x - b| = c$. What is the value of b?

   A 3   C 6.5

   B 3.5   D 7

Mineral	Daily Minimum (mg)	Daily Maximum (mg)
Fluoride	3	10
Iron	18	45
Zinc	8	40

Source:
http://www.supplementquality.com/news/multi_mineral_chart.html

Holt McDougal Algebra 1

LESSON 1-7 Reading Strategies
Make Predictions

An absolute-value equation may have two solutions, one solution, or no solution. The following examples show how you can think about an absolute-value equation and make a prediction about the number of solutions.

$|x - 2| = 5$

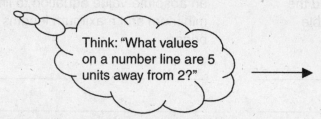

There are *two* values that are 5 units away from 2 on the number line.

Prediction: The equation has two solutions.

$7 + |x - 3| = 7$

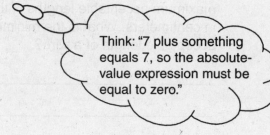

$|x - 3| = 0$ means $x - 3 = 0$. This has only *one* solution, $x = 3$.

Prediction: The equation has one solution.

$|x + 2| = -3$

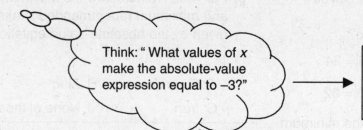

An absolute-value expression is *never* negative.

Prediction: The equation has no solutions.

Predict the number of solutions of each absolute-value equation.

1. $6 + |x + 2| = 6$

2. $|x - 10| = 1$

3. $5 + |x - 1| = 0$

_____

4. $2\left|x + \dfrac{1}{2}\right| = 0$

5. $6|x + 1| = -12$

6. $2 + |x - 4| = 3$

_____

Holt McDougal Algebra 1

LESSON 1-8

Practice A

Rates, Ratios, and Proportions

1. The ratio of boys to girls in an art class is 3:5. There are 12 boys in the class. How many girls are in the class?

_____

Find each unit rate.

2. An ostrich can run 174 feet in 3 seconds.

3. It costs $6.30 to mail a 6-pound package.

_____   _____

4. Eric read 150 pages in one hour. What is Eric's reading rate in pages per minute?

_____

Solve each proportion.

5. $\dfrac{y}{8} = \dfrac{2}{4}$

6. $\dfrac{1}{3} = \dfrac{6}{x}$

7. $\dfrac{10}{m} = \dfrac{25}{5}$

_____   _____   _____

8. $\dfrac{3}{4} = \dfrac{t}{100}$

9. $\dfrac{2}{100} = \dfrac{b}{-200}$

10. $\dfrac{x+1}{6} = \dfrac{1}{3}$

_____   _____   _____

11. Ron has a model car. The scale of the model to the actual car is 1:10. The length of the model car is 15 inches. How long is the actual car?

_____

12. On a map, the distance between Jacksonville, FL and Tallahassee, FL is about 8 inches. According to the scale, 1 inch represents 20 miles. About how far apart are the two cities?

_____

LESSON
1-8

Practice B

Rates, Ratios, and Proportions

1. The ratio of freshman to sophomores in a drama club is 5:6. There are 18 sophomores in the drama club. How many freshmen are there?

_____

Find each unit rate.

2. Four pounds of apples cost $1.96.

3. Sal washed 5 cars in 50 minutes.

_____   _____

4. A giraffe can run 32 miles per hour. What is this speed in feet per second? Round your answer to the nearest tenth.

_____

Solve each proportion.

5. $\dfrac{y}{4} = \dfrac{10}{8}$

6. $\dfrac{2}{x} = \dfrac{30}{-6}$

7. $\dfrac{3}{12} = \dfrac{-24}{m}$

_____   _____   _____

8. $\dfrac{3t}{10} = \dfrac{1}{2}$

9. $\dfrac{32}{4} = \dfrac{b+4}{3}$

10. $\dfrac{7}{x} = \dfrac{1}{0.5}$

_____   _____   _____

11. Sam is building a model of an antique car. The scale of his model to the actual car is 1:10. His model is $18\dfrac{1}{2}$ inches long. How long is the actual car?

_____

12. The scale on a map of Virginia shows that 1 centimeter represents 30 miles. The actual distance from Richmond, VA to Washington, DC is 110 miles. On the map, how many centimeters are between the two cities? Round your answer to the nearest tenth.

_____

Holt McDougal Algebra 1

LESSON 1-8

Practice C
Rates, Ratios, and Proportions

1. A cell phone company found that 15 of their phones sold in June were defective. The company sold 250 phones in June. How many of the 300 phones sold in July should they expect to be defective?

_____

Find each unit rate.

2. Thirty textbooks weigh 144 pounds.

3. Doug makes $43.45 in 5.5 hours.

_____   _____

4. A peregrine falcon flew $16\frac{2}{3}$ miles in 5 minutes.

   What is this speed in feet per second? Round your answer to the nearest tenth.

_____

Solve each proportion.

5. $\dfrac{-2.25}{x} = \dfrac{9}{6}$

6. $\dfrac{1}{b} = \dfrac{-3}{b+2}$

7. $\dfrac{-4}{0.8} = \dfrac{2}{s-1}$

_____   _____   _____

8. $\dfrac{4}{y+2} = \dfrac{10}{5y}$

9. $\dfrac{x-4}{6} = \dfrac{x+2}{12}$

10. $\dfrac{y+2}{y+7} = \dfrac{11}{31}$

_____   _____   _____

11. A model of a building was built to a scale of 1:65.5. One side of the model is 23 inches long. How long, in feet, is this side of the actual building? Round your answer to the nearest tenth.

_____

12. A map of Indiana is being made to a scale of $\frac{1}{2}$ in:20 mi.

   Indianapolis is 128 miles from Fort Wayne. How far apart from each other will they appear on this map?

_____

Holt McDougal Algebra 1

LESSON 1-8

Review for Mastery

Rates, Ratios, and Proportions

Multiplying by 1 does not change the value of a number: $33 \cdot 1 = 33$.

So, multiplying by a fraction equal to 1 does not change the value either: $33 \cdot \frac{5}{5} = 33$.

Multiplying by 1 is the idea behind converting rates.

Convert 33 feet per second to miles per hour.

Start by converting feet to miles.

$$\frac{33 \text{ ft}}{1 \text{ s}} \qquad \textit{Write the rate as a fraction.}$$

$$\frac{33 \text{ ft}}{1 \text{ s}} \cdot \mathbf{1} = \frac{33 \text{ ft}}{1 \text{ s}} \cdot \frac{1 \text{ mi}}{5280 \text{ ft}} = \frac{33 \text{ mi}}{5280 \text{ s}}$$

> Write the ratio so that feet is in the denominator.

> 1 mile is equal to 5280 feet, so $\frac{1 \text{ mile}}{5280 \text{ ft}} = 1$.

Now convert seconds to hours.

$$\frac{33 \text{ mi}}{5280 \text{ s}} \cdot \mathbf{1} \cdot \mathbf{1} = \frac{33 \text{ mi}}{5280 \text{ s}} \cdot \frac{60 \text{ s}}{1 \text{ min}} \cdot \frac{60 \text{ min}}{1 \text{ h}} = \frac{118,800 \text{ mi}}{5280 \text{ h}} \quad 22.5 \text{ mi/h}$$

> Multiply by 1 twice to convert seconds to minutes and minutes to hours.

Write a fraction equal to 1 for the relationship between these units.

1. feet and yards

$$\frac{\text{ft}}{\text{yd}} = \mathbf{1}$$

2. meters and centimeters

$$\frac{\text{m}}{\text{cm}} = \mathbf{1}$$

3. fluid ounces and cups

$$\frac{\text{fl oz}}{\text{c}} = \mathbf{1}$$

4. The 2004 Tour de France was 3391.1 kilometers. Lance Armstrong won the race in a little over 83.5 hours. Fill in the blanks to find his average speed in meters per hour.

$$\frac{3391.1 \text{ km}}{83.5 \text{ h}} \cdot \mathbf{1} = \frac{3391.1 \text{ km}}{83.5 \text{ h}} \cdot \underline{\hspace{2cm}} = \frac{\hphantom{m}}{\text{h}} \approx \underline{\hspace{2cm}} \text{m/h}$$

5. A soft-serve ice cream machine makes 1200 gallons per hour. Convert this rate to cups per minute.
(*Hint:* 1 gallon is equal to 16 cups.) _____

LESSON 1-8

Review for Mastery

Rates, Ratios, and Proportions continued

Use cross products to solve proportions.

Solve $\dfrac{x}{10} = \dfrac{4}{25}$.

$\dfrac{x}{10} \diagdown \dfrac{4}{25}$

Multiply x by 25. Write the product on the left.
Multiply 10 by 4. Write the product on the right.

$25x = 40$

$\dfrac{25x}{25} = \dfrac{40}{25}$ *Divide both sides by 25.*

$x = 1.6$

Sometimes it is necessary to use the Distributive Property.

Solve $\dfrac{4}{x+2} = \dfrac{2}{5}$.

$\dfrac{4}{x+2} \diagdown \dfrac{2}{5}$ *Multiply 4 by 5 and x + 2 by 2.*

$20 = 2(x+2)$

$20 = 2x + 4$ *Distribute 2.*

$\underline{-4 -4}$ *Subtract 4 from both sides.*

$\dfrac{16}{2} = \dfrac{2x}{2}$ *Divide both sides by 2.*

$8 = x$

Solve each proportion.

6. $\dfrac{x}{20} = \dfrac{1}{8}$

7. $\dfrac{5}{12} = \dfrac{1.25}{k}$

8. $\dfrac{3}{4} = \dfrac{a+5}{21}$

9. $\dfrac{3}{y-3} = \dfrac{1}{9}$

LESSON 1-8 Challenge

Using Cross Products to Derive New Proportions

In Lesson 1-8, you learned that in a true proportion, the cross products are equal. $\dfrac{a}{b} = \dfrac{c}{d}$

If $\dfrac{a}{b} = \dfrac{c}{d}$, then $ad = bc$. $bd\left(\dfrac{a}{b}\right) = bd\left(\dfrac{c}{d}\right)$ Multiplication Property of Equality

The proof to the statement above is shown at right. $da = bc$ Inverse Property of Multiplication

$ad = bc$ Commutative Property of Multiplication

Using $\dfrac{a}{b} = \dfrac{c}{d}$, you can write and prove that other proportions involving

a, b, c, and d are true.

In each proportion, assume that the denominator is not equal to 0.

1. Let $\dfrac{a}{b} = \dfrac{c}{d}$, where $a = 5$, $b = 7$, $c = 15$, and $d = 21$. Verify that

   the cross products are equal. _____

2. a. Let $\dfrac{a}{b} = \dfrac{c}{d}$. What can be done to each side of $\dfrac{a}{b} = \dfrac{c}{d}$, in order to get $\dfrac{d}{c} = \dfrac{b}{a}$?

   _____

   b. Justify each step in the reasoning below in order to show that $\dfrac{d}{c} = \dfrac{b}{a}$.

   $\dfrac{a}{b} = \dfrac{c}{d}$

   $ad = bc$ _____

   $\left(\dfrac{1}{ac}\right)ad = \left(\dfrac{1}{ac}\right)bc$ _____

   $\dfrac{d}{c} = \dfrac{b}{a}$ _____

3. Let $\dfrac{a}{b} = \dfrac{c}{d}$. Show that $\dfrac{d}{b} = \dfrac{c}{a}$. Write your reasons to the right of your steps.

   _____

   _____

   _____

Holt McDougal Algebra 1

LESSON 1-8 Problem Solving
Rates, Ratios, and Proportions

Write the correct answer.

1. A donut shop bakes 4 dozen donuts every 18 minutes. Find the unit rate to the nearest hundredth.

2. At one time, the ratio of in-state to out-of-state tuition at Texas A & M University in College Station, Texas was about 3:11. About how much was the out-of-state tuition if the in-state tuition at that time was about $2400?

3. The birth rate in Namibia is 35 babies to every 1000 people. In 2001, the country had a population of about 1,800,000 people. How many babies were there?

4. A boat travels 160 miles in 5 hours. What is its speed in miles per minute?

Use the table below to answer questions 5–8. Select the best answer. The table shows the ratio of female to male students at various institutions in 2002.

5. If there are 209 women at the US Naval Academy, how many men are there?

   A 11   C 3971

   B 190   D 4180

Institution	female:male
Massachusetts Institute of Technology	41:59
Tulane University	53:47
US Naval Academy	1:19
Georgia Institute of Technology	29:71
University of Massachusetts at Amherst	51:49
Baylor University	29:21

6. If there are 7282 male students at the Georgia Institute of Technology, how many females are there?

   F 2427   H 8282

   G 2974   J 17,828

7. If there are 4959 male students at Baylor University, which proportion can be used to find the number of female students?

   A $\dfrac{21}{4959} = \dfrac{x}{21}$ C $\dfrac{21}{29} = \dfrac{x}{4959}$

   B $\dfrac{21}{4959} = \dfrac{x}{29}$ D $\dfrac{29}{21} = \dfrac{x}{4959}$

8. For which institution is the ratio of female to male students the greatest?

   F Baylor University

   G Tulane University

   H University of Massachusetts at Amherst

   J US Naval Academy

              Holt McDougal Algebra 1

Reading Strategies
Focus on Vocabulary

The diagram below shows the connections between several related
vocabulary terms and gives an example of each.

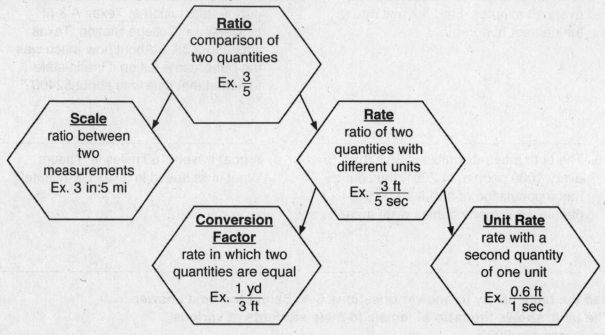

Ratio
comparison of
two quantities
Ex. $\frac{3}{5}$

Scale
ratio between
two
measurements
Ex. 3 in:5 mi

Rate
ratio of two
quantities with
different units
Ex. $\frac{3 \text{ ft}}{5 \text{ sec}}$

**Conversion
Factor**
rate in which two
quantities are equal
Ex. $\frac{1 \text{ yd}}{3 \text{ ft}}$

Unit Rate
rate with a
second quantity
of one unit
Ex. $\frac{0.6 \text{ ft}}{1 \text{ sec}}$

Answer each question.

1. There are 16 ounces in a pound. Write this as a conversion factor. _____

2. Is $\frac{1 \text{ ft}}{2 \text{ sec}}$ a unit rate? Explain. _____

3. Why is $\frac{12 \text{ inches}}{1 \text{ foot}}$ a conversion factor?

_____

4. Fill in the blanks with the most appropriate vocabulary terms:

   A rate is a type of _____.

   A unit rate is a type of _____.

   So, a unit rate is also a type of _____.

5. Write $\frac{84 \text{ pages}}{3 \text{ hours}}$ as a unit rate. _____

6. A *proportion* is an equation showing two equal ratios. Give an example.

_____

Holt McDougal Algebra 1

LESSON 1-9

Practice A
Applications of Proportions

Find the value of *x* in each diagram.

1. ΔACD ~ ΔDEF

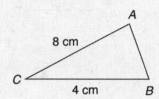

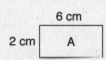

2. *RSTV ~ WXYZ*

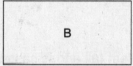

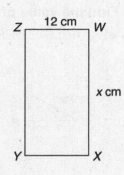

_____   _____

3. Sam is 5 feet tall and casts a shadow 4 feet long. At the same time, a nearby tree casts a shadow 12 feet long. Write and solve a proportion to find the height of the tree.   _____

Every dimension of rectangle A has been multiplied by 2 to form rectangle B.

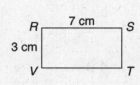

4. What are the new dimensions of rectangle B?   _____

5. What is the ratio of the corresponding sides?   _____

6. Complete the table.

	Rectangle A	Rectangle B
Perimeter		
Area		

7. What is the ratio of the perimeters?   _____

8. How is the ratio of perimeters related to the ratio in problem 5?

_____

9. What is the ratio of the areas?   _____

10. How is the ratio of the areas related to the ratio in problem 5?

_____

Holt McDougal Algebra 1

LESSON
1-9

Practice B
Applications of Proportions

Find the value of *x* in each diagram.

1. △ABC ~ △DEF

 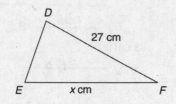

2. FGHJK ~ MNPQR

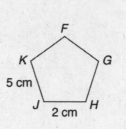 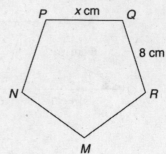

_____   _____

3. A utility worker is 5.5 feet tall and is casting a shadow
4 feet long. At the same time, a nearby utility pole casts
a shadow 20 feet long. Write and solve a proportion to
find the height of the utility pole.

_____

4. A cylinder has a radius of 3 cm and a length of 10 cm.
Every dimension of the cylinder is multiplied by 3 to form
a new cylinder. How is the ratio of the volumes related to
the ratio of corresponding dimensions?

_____

5. A rectangle has an area of 48 in². Every dimension of
the rectangle is multiplied by a scale factor, and the
new rectangle has an area of 12 in².
What was the scale factor?

_____

Holt McDougal Algebra 1

LESSON
1-9

Practice C
Applications of Proportions

Find the value of *x* in each diagram.

1. △*ACD* ~ △*ABE*

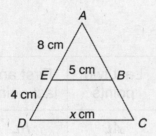

2. △*QRV* ~ △*TRS*

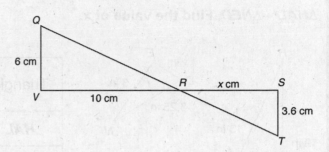

_____ _____

3. Keshawn is 5 ft 6 in. tall and casts a shadow
that is one-fourth his height. At the same time,
a nearby tree casts a shadow that is twice
Keshawn's height. Write and solve a proportion
to find the height of the tree.

4. A triangle has an area of 20 in². Every dimension
of the triangle is multiplied by a scale factor, and
the new triangle has an area of 180 in². What
was the scale factor?

_____

5. A rectangular prism has a volume of 112 cm³.
Every dimension of the rectangular prism is
multiplied by a scale factor and the new volume
is 1.75 cm³. What was the scale factor?

_____

Holt McDougal Algebra 1

LESSON 1-9

Review for Mastery

Applications of Proportions

To find missing lengths in similar polygons, you must know which sides correspond (match). Making a table can help.

ΔHAL ~ ΔNED. Find the value of x.

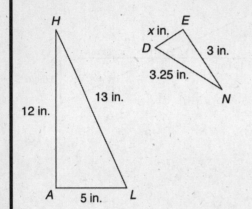

Triangle	First two points	Last two points	First and last points
HAL	**HA**	**AL**	**HL**
	12 in.	**5 in.**	**13 in.**
NED	**NE**	**ED**	**ND**
	3 in.	**x in.**	**3.25 in.**

$\dfrac{HA}{NE} = \dfrac{AL}{ED}$ *Choose any two columns from the table to set up a proportion.*

$\dfrac{12}{3} = \dfrac{5}{x}$ *Substitute.*

$12x = 15$ *Use cross products.*

$x = 1.25$ *Divide both sides by 12.*

Find the value of x in each diagram.

1. ΔABC ~ ΔDEF

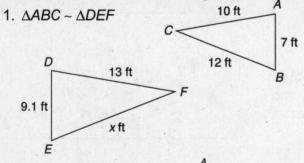

x = _____

2. LADY ~ GENT

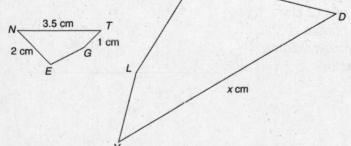

x = _____

LESSON 1-9

Review for Mastery
Applications of Proportions continued

When you multiply every dimension of a figure by a scale factor k, you create similar figures. You can determine the ratios of perimeters, areas, and volumes between those figures by thinking about the units that are used to measure perimeter, area, and volume.

Measurement	Measurement Units	Ratio Between
Perimeter	*single* units (in., ft, cm, m)	*single* ratio (k)
Area	*square* units (in^2, ft^2, cm^2, m^2)	*square* ratio (k^2)
Volume	*cubic* units (in^3, ft^3, cm^3, m^3)	*cubic* ratio (k^3)

The dimensions of a rectangular cake measure 12 in. by 18 in. by 4 in. Every dimension is multiplied by $\frac{1}{2}$ to create a smaller, similar cake. How is the ratio of the volumes related to the ratio of corresponding dimensions? What is the ratio of the volumes?

Think: Volume is measured in *cubic* units. So the ratio of the volumes is the cube of the ratio of the corresponding dimensions: $\left(\frac{1}{2}\right)^3 = \frac{1}{8}$.

Complete the table by filling in the missing ratios.

	Scale Factor	Ratio of Perimeters	Ratio of Areas	Ratio of Volumes
3.	5		$(5)^2 =$	
4.	$\frac{2}{3}$			$\left(\frac{2}{3}\right)^3 =$
5.			$\left(\quad\right)^2 = \frac{100}{49}$	

6. A stop sign has the shape of an octagon with each side measuring 0.5 ft. To make a scale model of the sign, every dimension is multiplied by $\frac{1}{20}$. How is the ratio of the areas related to the ratio of the corresponding dimensions? What is the ratio of the areas?

7. A circular plate has radius 15 cm. Every dimension is multiplied by 4 to create a larger, similar plate. How is the ratio of the circumferences related to the ratio of the corresponding dimensions? What is the ratio of the circumferences? (*Hint*: Think of circumference as perimeter of a circle.)

Holt McDougal Algebra 1

LESSON
1-9

Challenge
Trigonometric Ratios

Trigonometry is the study of angle and side relationships in triangles. Right triangles are especially important in trigonometry. In a right triangle, the side opposite the right angle is always called the **hypotenuse**, and the remaining sides are called the **legs**. Each leg can be described as **opposite** or **adjacent** to a given acute angle.

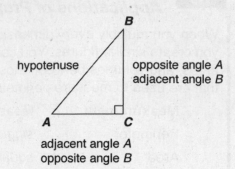

hypotenuse — opposite angle *A*
adjacent angle *B*

adjacent angle *A*
opposite angle *B*

Use these similar right triangles to fill in the table.

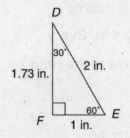 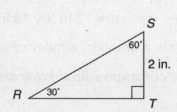 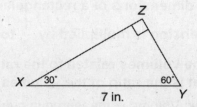

	ΔDEF	ΔRST	ΔXYZ
1. Name the side opposite the 30° angle in each triangle.	$\overline{EF}$		
2. What is the length of the side opposite the 30° angle?			
3. Name the hypotenuse.		$\overline{RS}$	
4. What is the length of the hypotenuse?			7 in.
5. Calculate $\dfrac{\text{length of side opposite } 30°}{\text{length of hypotenuse}}$.	$\dfrac{1}{2} = 0.5$		

6. The ratio in problem 5 is called the **sine** of the angle. Based on your results, what is the sine of a 30° angle in any right triangle? _____

7. Use the triangles above to determine the sine of a 60° angle. _____

8. The ratio $\dfrac{\text{length of adjacent side}}{\text{length of hypotenuse}}$ is called the **cosine** of the angle.

   a. Use the triangles above to determine the cosine of a 30° angle. _____

   b. Use the triangles above to determine the cosine of a 60° angle. _____

9. Explain how the sines of 30° and 60° are related to the cosines of 30° and 60°.

_____

_____

Problem Solving

LESSON 1-9

Applications of Proportions

Write the correct answer.

1. A 4 by 5 inch photo is enlarged by multiplying every dimension by 2 to form a similar 8 by 10 inch photo. What is the ratio of the perimeter of the smaller rectangle to that of the larger? What is the ratio of the two areas?

_____

_____

2. Pamela wants to buy a suitcase whose dimensions are $1\frac{1}{2}$ times those of her $28 \times 16 \times 8$ inch suitcase. How is the ratio of the volumes related to the ratio of corresponding dimensions? What is the ratio of the volumes?

_____

_____

_____

_____

3. The Taylors plan to expand their 80 square foot garage by tripling the dimensions. What will be the area of the new garage?

_____

4. A tent has a volume of 26.25 in^3. Every dimension is multiplied by a scale factor so that the new tent has a volume of 1680 in^3. What was the scale factor?

_____

Complete the table below and use it to answer questions 5–8. Select the best answer. Assume the shadow lengths were measured at the same time of day.

5. The flagpole casts an 8 foot shadow, as shown in the table. At the same time, the oak tree casts a 12 foot shadow. How tall is the oak tree?

Object	Length of Shadow (ft)	Height (ft)
Flagpole	8	20
Oak tree	12	
Goal post	18	
Telephone pole		17.5
Fence		6.5

  A 4.8 ft   C 30 ft

  B 24 ft   D 32 ft

6. How tall is the goal post?

  F 7.2 ft   H 38 ft

  G 30 ft   J 45 ft

7. What is the length of the telephone pole's shadow?

  A 5.5 ft   C 25.5 ft

  B 7 ft   D 43.8 ft

8. What is the length of the fence's shadow?

  F 1.5 ft   H 16.25 ft

  G 2.6 ft   J 21.5 ft

Holt McDougal Algebra 1

Reading Strategies
Understanding Symbols

Use the table below to help you understand the symbols commonly used
in geometry.

Symbols	Words
$\overline{XY}$	segment XY
$\angle X$	angle X
$\triangle XYZ$	triangle XYZ
XY	the length of segment XY
$m\angle X$	the measure of angle X
$\sim$	is similar to

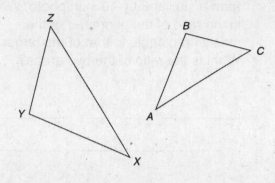

Answer each question.

1. Write "triangle ABC" in symbols. _____

2. Write $m\angle B = 93°$ in words. _____

_____

3. Write $\triangle XYZ \sim \triangle ABC$ in words. _____

_____

_____

4. Use the information given in symbols below to label the diagram shown above.

   $m\angle X = 38°$ $m\angle B = 93°$ $m\angle C = 49°$

   $XY = 18$ cm $YZ = 15$ cm $BC = 10$ cm

Corresponding angles of similar triangles have the same measure.

5. What is $m\angle Z$? _____   6. What is $m\angle A$? _____

7. Write a proportion relating AB, BC, XY, and YZ. _____

8. Substitute the known values into the proportion from problem 7, and then solve it find AB.

_____

_____

Holt McDougal Algebra 1

Name ________________________ Date ______________ Class ______________

LESSON 1-10

Practice A

Precision and Accuracy

Choose the more precise measurement in each pair.

1. 3.21 kg; 3215 g
2. 4 ft; 48 in.
3. 3.8 cm; 3.82 cm

____

4. 5 lb; 81 oz
5. 3 L; 3002 mL
6. 4.2 m; 421 cm

____

7. 4 qt; 1 gal
8. 2.9 ft; 3 yd
9. 3 c; 25 oz

____

Write the possible range of each measurement to the nearest tenth.

10. 20 lb ± 2%
11. 30 cm ± 4%
12. 100 ft ± 5.2%

____

13. 60 m ± 4.5%
14. 80°F ± 6%
15. 18L ± 5%

____

Use the following information for 16 and 17.

Jordan is testing the scales in a butcher shop. He uses a standard weight of 16 ounces. The results are shown below.

Scale	Measurement (oz)
A	16.1 oz
B	15.9 oz
C	16.05 oz

16. Which scale is the most precise?

____

17. Which scale is the most accurate?

____

LESSON	**Practice B**
1-10	*Precision and Accuracy*

Choose the more precise measurement in each pair.

1. 2.78 L; 2782 mL

2. 6 ft; 72.3 in.

3. 2 c; 15 oz

_____   _____   _____

4. 52 mm; 5.24 cm

5. 3 lb; 47 oz

6. 5.2 km; 5233 m

_____   _____   _____

Write the possible range of each measurement. Round to the nearest hundredth if necessary.

7. 50 m ± 4%

8. 90 °F ± 15%

9. 15 L ± 2%

_____   _____   _____

10. 16 ft ± 1.5%

11. 9 in. ± 10%

12. 66 g ± 3%

_____   _____   _____

Use the following information for 13 and 14.

Marcel is measuring the volume of a liquid for chemistry class. He uses a beaker, a measuring cup, and a test tube. The teacher measures the liquid with a graduated cylinder, which gives the most accurate reading of 26.279 milliliters (mL). Marcel's measurements are shown below.

Measuring Device	Measurement (mL)
Beaker	26.3
Measuring Cup	25
Test Tube	26.21

13. Which device used by Marcel recorded the most precise measurement?

_____

14. Which device used by Marcel recorded the most accurate measurement?

_____

LESSON
1-10

Practice C
Precision and Accuracy

Choose the more precise measurement in each pair. If they are equally precise, write "neither."

1. 5.26 kg; 5260.0 g

2. 48 mg; 0.048 g

3. 4.2 cm; 420.0 mm

_____

_____

_____

4. 5.1 lb; 82.1 oz

5. 4.1 L; 4102 mL

6. 128 min; 2.1 hr

_____

_____

_____

Write the possible range of each measurement to the nearest hundredth.

7. 70 m ± 6.5%

8. 62.5°F ± 8.2%

9. 22.5 mg ± 5%

_____

_____

_____

Rewrite each specified tolerance as a percent.

10. 120 lb ± 4.8 lb

11. 300 cm ± 22.5 cm

12. 210 ft ± 19.11 ft

_____

_____

_____

13. A professional baseball's circumference and weight must fall within given tolerance levels of regulation measurements. The table shows these tolerance levels as well as measurements taken on three different baseballs. Which baseball meets both of the specified tolerances?

	Circumference (cm)	Weight (oz)
Tolerance	**23.1775 ± 0.3175**	**5.125 ± 0.125**
Baseball #1	24.005	5.249
Baseball #2	23.382	5.181
Baseball #3	23.997	4.998

_____

Holt McDougal Algebra 1

LESSON 1-10 Review for Mastery

Precision and Accuracy

The *precision* of a measurement is determined by the smallest unit or fraction of a unit used.

Choose the more precise measurement in each pair.

a. 16.7 kg; 16.66 kg

    Compare the two measurements: 16.7 kg is to the nearest tenth.

                                       16.66 kg is to the nearest hundredth.

    Because a hundredth of a kilogram is smaller than a tenth of a kilogram, 16.66 kg is more precise.

b. 8.5 km; 8532 m

    Note that the units are different, but they can easily be converted:

    8532 m = 8.532 km   [1000 m = 1 km]

    Compare the two measurements: 8.5 km is to the nearest tenth.

                                         8.532 km is to the nearest thousandth.

    Because a thousandth of a meter is smaller than a tenth of a meter, 8532 m is more precise.

Choose the more precise measurement in each pair.

1. 73.71 cm; 736.2 cm

    73.71 cm is to the nearest _____ of a centimeter.

    736.2 cm is to the nearest _____ of a centimeter.

    _____ cm is more precise.

2. 4732 mL; 4.73 L

    4732 mL = _____ L, which is to the nearest _____ of a liter.

    4.73 L is to the nearest _____ of a liter.

    _____ is more precise.

3. An object is weighed on three different scales. The results are shown in the table. Which scale is the most precise?

Scale	Measurement (lb)
1	44.9
2	45.105
3	45.01

    Scale 1 measures to the nearest _____ of a pound.

    Scale 2 measures to the nearest _____ of a pound.

    Scale 3 measures to the nearest _____ of a pound.

    Scale _____ is the most precise.

Holt McDougal Algebra 1

LESSON 1-10 Review for Mastery

Precision and Accuracy continued

Tolerance describes how much a measurement may vary from a specified value.

A bolt can be 50 mm ± 1.5 mm. Write the possible range of the measurement.

$50 - 1.5 = 48.5$ The bolt cannot be smaller than 48.5 mm.

$50 + 1.5 = 51.5$ The bolt cannot be larger than 51.5 mm.

Written as a range, the bolt can be 48.5 mm–51.5 mm.

Tolerance can also be expressed as a percent.

A bolt can be 50 mm ± 5%. Write the possible range of the measurement.

5% of 50 is $0.05 \bullet 50 = 2.5$.

$50 - 2.5 = 47.5$ The bolt cannot be smaller than 47.5 mm.

$50 + 2.5 = 52.5$ The bolt cannot be larger than 52.5 mm.

Written as a range, the bolt can be 47.5 mm–52.5 mm.

Write the possible range of each measurement.

4. 42 g ± 5 g

$42 - 5 =$ _____

$42 + 5 =$ _____

The range is _____ g – _____ g.

5. 3.2 mi ± 0.01 mi

$3.2 - 0.01 =$ _____

$3.2 + 0.01 =$ _____

The range is _____ mi – _____ mi.

6. 25 L ± 5%

5% of 25 is _____ • 25 = _____

$25 -$ _____ = _____

$25 +$ _____ = _____

The range is _____ L– _____ L.

7. 40 m ± 2%

2% of 40 is _____ • 40 = _____

$40 -$ _____ = _____

$40 +$ _____ = _____

The range is _____ m– _____ m.

Holt McDougal Algebra 1

Challenge
Precision and Accuracy

When aiming a projectile, such as an arrow, at a target, very small changes in aim can make a large difference in where the arrow lands. For example, the distance between the center and the edge of an archery target is about 2 ft. But if you aim your arrow at the center of the target and then move it two feet to one side, you will miss the target by a large distance!

The distance from an arrow's starting point to its landing point can be represented by the radius of a circle, with the starting point at the center of the circle and the landing point on the circle. In the diagram below, *A* represents the target and *B* represents where the arrow lands. The distance by which the arrow misses the target is the distance from *A* to *B*.

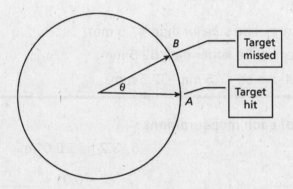

The circumference of a circle is 2π times the radius. Therefore, the distance from *A* to *B* is $AB = \dfrac{\theta}{360} 2\pi r$.

1. William is 90 m from an archery target. His arrow lands 0.3 m left of the target. By how many degrees should he adjust his aim to hit the target? Round to the nearest hundredth of a degree. (*Hint: AB* = 0.3 m; *r* = 90 m)

2. Sharon and Tony have built a catapult for the Medieval Festival. They enter a contest to hit a 20-ft target that is 250 ft away. How wide is the angle, in degrees, that the catapult can be aimed and hit the target?

3. An engineer is launching a rocket to the moon. He accidentally enters the angle of the rocket's trajectory as 45.5°, instead of 45.05°. How far off target will the rocket be when it crosses the moon's orbit? Round to the nearest hundred kilometers. (*Hint:* The moon is about 384,000 km from Earth.)

Holt McDougal Algebra 1

LESSON
1-10

Problem Solving
Precision and Accuracy

Write the correct answer.

1. Rolondo is measuring the length of his lawn. Using a board that is 10 feet long, he measures his lawn to be 70 feet long. He then uses his foot, which is 12 inches long, to measure his lawn to be 864 inches. Which is the more precise measurement? Which is the more precise tool?

_____

2. A bolt used to assemble a car must have a length of 37.5 mm ± 4%. Does a bolt that is 39.3 mm long fall within the specified tolerance? Why or why not?

_____

3. According to the Billiard Congress of America, BCA Equipment Specification, the diameter of a billiard ball is 2.25 inches with a tolerance of 0.005 inch. Which billiard ball(s) in the table below meet(s) this standard?

Ball	1	2	3	4	5
Diameter (in.)	2.255	2.249	2.251	2.250	2.2
Ball	6	7	8	9	10
Diameter (in.)	2.251	2.244	2.239	2.249	2.251
Ball	11	12	13	14	15
Diameter (in.)	2.250	2.219	2.247	2.257	2.288

Select the best answer.

4. Ann is measuring the capacity of a 16-oz water bottle. She first uses a measuring cup and finds that the water bottle holds 16.2 oz of water. She then uses a graduated cylinder and finds that the water bottle holds 16.18 oz of water. Which is the more precise measurement? Which is the more precise tool?

A 16.2 oz; measuring cup

B 16.2 oz; graduated cylinder

C 16.18 oz; measuring cup

D 16.18 oz; graduated cylinder

5. Ina added 32.155 milliliters (mL) of HCL to 64 mL of H_2O. How much solution does Ina have to the nearest milliliter?

F 95 mL   H 97 mL

G 96 mL   J 98 mL

6. Jesse mixed 8.24 oz of paprika with 12.23 oz of pepper. How much of the spice combination does Jesse have to the nearest tenth of an ounce?

A 20.0 oz   C 20.5 oz

B 20.4 oz   D 21.0 oz

7. An aquarium must be heated to 30°C ± 1.5%. What is the acceptable temperature range for this aquarium?

F 25.5 °C–34.5 °C

G 28.5 °C–31.5 °C

H 29.55 °C–30.45 °C

J 29.85 °C–30.15 °C

Holt McDougal Algebra 1

LESSON 1-10

Reading Strategies
Precision and Accuracy

Precision and accuracy refer to two different characteristics of a measurement. Precision describes the level of detail in a measurement, whereas accuracy describes how close the measurement is to the true value.

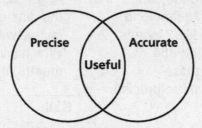

Tolerance refers to the amount a measurement is allowed to vary from a specified value. For example, a specified value of 8 with a tolerance of ± 2 can be written 8 ± 2. Measurements within this tolerance are in the range 6–10. This range can be shown on a number line.

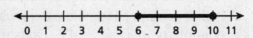

Write the range shown on each number line to the nearest tenth.

1. 8.0 ± 1.0

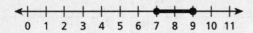

_____

2. 3.2 ± 0.8

_____

For 3 and 4, *C* represents the specified value. What is the tolerance?

3.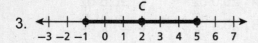

_____

4.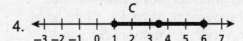

_____

For 5 and 6, a specified value is given. Which point is most accurate?

5. Specified value: 3.19

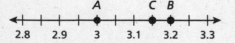

_____

6. Specified value: 6.05

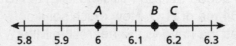

_____

　　　　　　　　　　　　　Holt McDougal Algebra 1

Date _____

Dear Family,

Your child will learn to solve inequalities in one variable.

An **inequality** is a statement that two quantities or expressions are *not* equal. An inequality looks very much like an equation, but it contains a sign other than the equal sign (=).

A **solution** is a value that makes the inequality true. Inequalities frequently have too many solutions to name individually, so all of the possibilities are shown by graphing them on a number line.

Inequality Signs	
>	greater than
<	less than
≥	greater than or equal
≤	less than or equal
≠	not equal

Inequality: $x - 2 > 5$

Solution: Any value of x greater than 7 makes the inequality true, or $x > 7$.

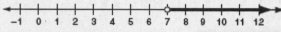

Graph:

Graphing Inequalities on a Number Line	
For a boundary point that **is a solution**...	...use a **solid** circle.
For a boundary point that **is not a solution**...	...use an **open** circle.
For a continuous series of points **greater than**...	...use an arrow to the **right**.
For a continuous series of points **less than**...	...use an arrow to the **left**.

You solve an inequality in much the same way that you solve an equation: you **isolate the variable** by using **inverse operations** in the reverse order. However, there is one major difference: when you multiply or divide both sides of the inequality by a *negative* number, you must reverse the inequality sign. You can see why this is true with a simple example:

True Inequality:	8	>	−2	
	8(−3)		−2(−3)	*Multiply both sides by −3.*
True Inequality:	−24	<	6	*> must change to <.*

With this one exception, solving one-step inequalities, multi-step inequalities, and inequalities with variables on both sides follows the same process as solving an equation.

Solve $5x - 4 \le 8x + 2$.

$$\underline{-8x \qquad\qquad -8x}$$ *Collect the variables on one side.*

$$-3x - 4 \le \qquad 2$$

$$\underline{\quad + 4 \qquad\qquad + 4}$$ *Collect the constants on the other side.*

$$\frac{-3x}{-3} \le \frac{6}{-3}$$ *Divide both sides by −3.*

$$x \ge -2$$ *Reverse the inequality when dividing by a negative.*

Holt McDougal Algebra 1

Also like equations, inequalities can result in identities and contradictions. An **identity** is an inequality that is *always* true. A **contradiction** is an inequality that is *never* true.

Identities:	$3 < 5$	$x \geq x$	$x + 2 > x + 1$
Contradictions:	$2 > 10$	$x < x$	$x + 5 \leq x$

A **compound inequality** is formed when two inequalities are combined using the words AND or OR. On a number-line graph, a compound inequality with AND represents the overlap, or **intersection**, of two inequalities. A compound inequality with OR represents the combined total, or **union**, of two inequalities.

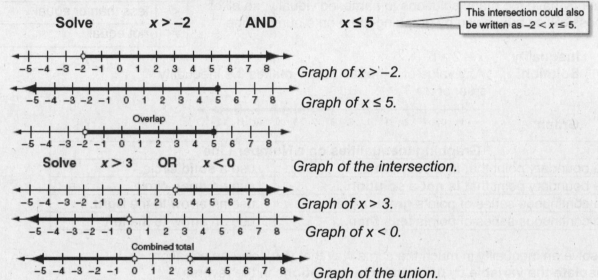

Solve $x > -2$ **AND** $x \leq 5$

> This intersection could also be written as $-2 < x \leq 5$.

Graph of $x > -2$.

Graph of $x \leq 5$.

Overlap

Graph of the intersection.

Solve $x > 3$ **OR** $x < 0$

Graph of $x > 3$.

Graph of $x < 0$.

Combined total

Graph of the union.

As with all topics in algebra, inequalities can be applied to model and solve real-world problems. Here's an example:

Karyn has a coupon for 15% off at an online bookstore. If the total of her purchases *after* any discounts is at least $25, she will get free shipping. How much do her purchases need to total *before* the coupon in order to get free shipping?

Let x represent the total of Karyn's purchases *before* the coupon. Then $x - 0.15x$ represents her purchases *after* the coupon.

"At least" means the purchases must equal or be greater than $25.

Inequality: $x - 0.15x \geq 25$

Holt McDougal Algebra 1

**LESSON
2-1**

Practice A

Graphing and Writing Inequalities

Match each inequality with its description.

1. $a + 2 \leq 6$ _____

2. $3n < 3$ _____

3. $f - 2 > 0$ _____

4. $8 \leq \dfrac{1}{2} y$ _____

a. all real numbers less than 1

b. all real numbers greater than 2

c. all real numbers less than or equal to 4

d. all real numbers greater than or equal to 16

Graph each inequality.

5. $t \geq 15$

6. $h > -12$

7. $b < 3 - 10$

8. $3^2 \geq w$

Match each inequality with its graph by writing the letter on the line.

9. $x \geq -4$ _____

10. $x \leq -4$ _____

11. $x > -4$ _____

12. $x < -4$ _____

a.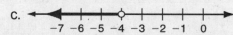

b.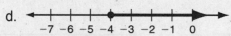

c.

d.

For each situation: Define a variable. Write an inequality. Graph the solutions.

13. To enter the play area, children must be more than 4 feet tall.

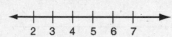

_____

14. As of July 1988, the speed limit on rural interstates in Virginia is 65 mph.

_____

Holt McDougal Algebra 1

LESSON 2-1

Practice B

Graphing and Writing Inequalities

Describe the solutions of each inequality in words.

1. $2m \geq 6$ _____

2. $t + 3 < 8$ _____

3. $1 < x - 5$ _____

4. $-10 \geq \dfrac{1}{2}c$ _____

Graph each inequality.

5. $x > -7$

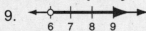

6. $p \geq 2^3$

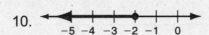

7. $4.5 \geq r$

8. $y < -\sqrt{14 - 5}$

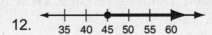

Write the inequality shown by each graph.

9.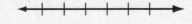

_____

10.

_____

11.

_____

12.

_____

Define a variable and write an inequality for each situation. Graph the solutions.

13. Josephine sleeps more than 7 hours each night.

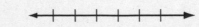

_____

14. In 1955, the minimum wage in the U.S. was $0.75 per hour.

_____

Holt McDougal Algebra 1

LESSON
2-1

Practice C
Graphing and Writing Inequalities

Describe the solutions of each inequality in words.

1. $t - 1 \geq 7$ _____

2. $-6 > 2d$ _____

3. $-4 < r + 5$ _____

4. $\frac{1}{2}x \leq 9$ _____

Graph each inequality.

5. $k > -12$

6. $-6\frac{1}{2} \leq w$

graph:

graph:

7. $b \leq 2^3 - 10$

8. $n < -\sqrt{2(5)+6}$

graph:

graph:

Write the inequality shown by each graph.

9.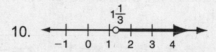

_____

10.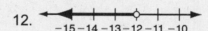

_____

11.

_____

12.

_____

Define a variable and write an inequality for each situation.

13. To qualify for the job, applicants must have more than 3 years of experience in the field.

_____

14. As of Aug. 1996, the speed limit on rural interstates in North Carolina is 70 mph.

_____

15. In 2005, the minimum wage in the U.S. was $5.15 per hour.

_____

Holt McDougal Algebra 1

LESSON 2-1

Review for Mastery

Graphing and Writing Inequalities

Describe the solutions of $x + 2 < 6$.

Choose different values for x. Be sure to choose positive and negative values as well as zero.

	$x = 0$	$x = 2$	$x = -4$	$x = 5$	$x = 4$	$x = 3$	$x = 3.5$
$x + 2 < 6$	$\overset{?}{0+2<6}$ $\overset{?}{2<6}$ True	$\overset{?}{2+2<6}$ $\overset{?}{4<6}$ True	$\overset{?}{-4+2<6}$ $\overset{?}{-2<6}$ True	$\overset{?}{5+2<6}$ $\overset{?}{7<6}$ False	$\overset{?}{4+2<6}$ $\overset{?}{6<6}$ False	$\overset{?}{3+2<6}$ $\overset{?}{5<6}$ True	$\overset{?}{3.5+2<6}$ $\overset{?}{5.5<6}$ True

Plot the points on a number line. Use T to label points that make the inequality true.

Use F to label points that make the inequality false.

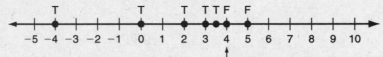

Look for the point at which the True statements turn to False statements. Numbers less than 4 make the statement true. The solutions are all real numbers less than 4.

Test the inequalities for the values given. Then describe the solutions of the inequality.

	$x = 0$	$x = 1$	$x = -3$	$x = -4$	$x = 2$	$x = 3$	$x = 1.5$
1. $5x \le 10$							

	$x = 0$	$x = 3$	$x = -4$	$x = -3$	$x = -2$	$x = -2.5$	$x = -5$
2. $m + 1 < -2$							

Describe the solutions of each inequality in words.

3. $\dfrac{x}{3} > 4$ _____

4. $g - 4 \le -3$ _____

Holt McDougal Algebra 1

LESSON 2-1

Review for Mastery
Graphing and Writing Inequalities continued

Graph $x \le 3$.

Step 1: Draw a circle on the number.

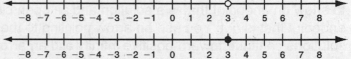

Step 2: Decide whether to fill in the circle.

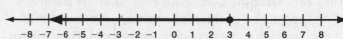

    If > or <, *leave empty.*

    If ≥ or ≤, *fill in.*

Step 3: Draw an arrow.

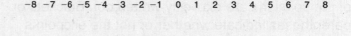

    If < or ≤, *draw arrow to left.*

    If > or ≥, *draw arrow to the right.*

Write the inequality shown by the graph.

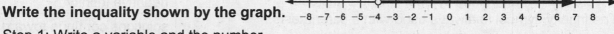

Step 1: Write a variable and the number
indicated by the circle.

                     $x \; ? \; -4$

Step 2: Look at the direction of the arrow.

    If arrow points left, use < or ≤. $x >$ or ≥ -4

    If arrow points right, use > or ≥.

Step 3: Look at the circle.

    If circle is empty, use > or <.

    If circle is filled in use, ≥ or ≤. $x > -4$

Graph each inequality.

5. $m \ge 8 - 3$

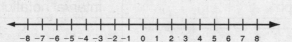

6. $p < 3.5$

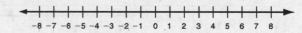

Write the inequality shown by the graph.

7.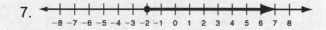

_____

8.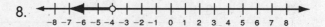

_____

LESSON 2-1 Challenge

Interval Notation

When you graph the solutions of an inequality, you use a solid circle to show an endpoint that is a solution and an open circle to show an endpoint that is not. You use an arrow pointing to the right to show when solutions continue toward positive infinity and an arrow pointing to the left to show when solutions continue toward negative infinity.

Interval notation is another way to show solutions of an inequality. In interval notation, the endpoints of the solutions are explicitly written out. Brackets or parentheses indicate whether or not the endpoints themselves are solutions. If the solutions continue toward infinity, an infinity symbol is written instead. The infinity symbol is always used with a parenthesis.

Interval Notation	
[or]	endpoint is a solution
(or)	endpoint is not a solution
$(-\infty$	solutions continue toward negative infinity
$\infty)$	solutions continue toward positive infinity

Here are the graph and interval notation for $x \geq 1$.

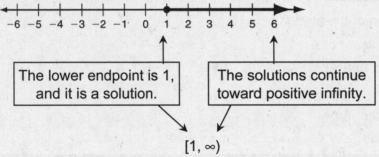

The lower endpoint is 1, and it is a solution.

The solutions continue toward positive infinity.

$[1, \infty)$

Complete the table. Problems 7–10 preview compound inequalities, which you'll learn more about in Lesson 3–6.

	inequality	graph	interval notation
1.	$x > 4$		
2.			$(-\infty, -2]$
3.	$x < 3$		
4.			
5.			$(0, \infty)$
6.	$x \leq -1$		
7.	$-3 \leq x \leq 2$		
8.			$(0, 3]$
9.			$[-4, 5)$
10.	$-1 < x < 1$		

LESSON
2-1
Problem Solving
Graphing and Writing Inequalities

Write the correct answer.

1. A citizen must be at least 35 years old in order to run for the Presidency of the United States. Define a variable and write an inequality for this situation.

   _____

   _____

2. A certain elevator can hold no more than 2500 pounds. Define a variable and write an inequality for this situation.

   _____

   _____

3. Approximately 30% of the land on Earth is forested, but this percent is decreasing due to construction. Write and graph an inequality for this situation.

   _____

   _____

4. Khalil weighed 125 pounds before he started to gain weight to play football. Write and graph an inequality for this situation.

   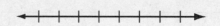

The Sanchez family is visiting an amusement park. When they enter the park, they receive a brochure which lists several requirements and restrictions. Select the best answer.

5. You must be at least 50 inches tall to ride The Wild Tornado roller coaster. Which of the following inequalities fits this situation?

   A $h \le 50$ C $h \ge 50$

   B $h < 50$ D $h > 50$

6. Children less than 12 years old must be accompanied by an adult inside The Haunted House. Which of the following inequalities shows the ages of children who require an adult inside the house?

   F $y \le 12$ H $y \ge 12$

   G $y < 12$ J $y > 12$

7. Totland is an area of the amusement park set aside for children who are 6 years old or younger. Which of the following inequalities represents the ages of children who are allowed in Totland?

   A $a \le 6$ C $a \ge 6$

   B $a < 6$ D $a > 6$

8. The Bumpy Cars will not be turned on if there are 5 or more empty cars. Which of the following inequalities shows the possible numbers of empty cars if the ride is going to start?

   F $c \le 5$ H $c \ge 5$

   G $c < 5$ J $c > 5$

Holt McDougal Algebra 1

Reading Strategies
Connecting Words and Symbols

To write and graph inequalities, you must connect words with symbols.
Look at the information in the table below.

Symbol	Words	Graph
<	"less than"	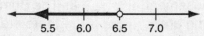
≤	"less than or equal to" "no more than" "at most"	
>	"greater than"	
≥	"greater than or equal to" "no less than" "at least"	

Answer each question.

1. What are three ways to say $x \geq 5$ in words?

   _____

   _____

   _____

2. Does the graph of $p > 8$ have an empty circle or a solid circle? Why?

   _____

   _____

3. Draw the graph of $m \leq -2$.

   _____

4. Write the inequality that represents the graph, once with symbols and
   once with words.

   5.5   6.0   6.5   7.0

   _____   _____

5. Mitchell's goal is to get a grade g of at least 85% on his next Algebra
   quiz. Translate these words into symbols. Then graph the inequality.

   _____   graph:

LESSON 2-2

Practice A
Solving Inequalities by Adding or Subtracting

Solve each inequality and graph the solutions.

1. $t - 3 > 5$

_____

2. $x + 7 \geq 0$

_____

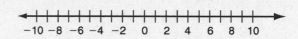

3. $4 \leq p - 1$

_____

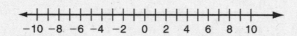

4. $m + 15 > 6$

_____

5. $-8 \geq w - 11$

_____

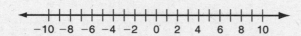

6. $-5 + g > -5$

_____

Answer each question.

7. Joy wants to save at least $40 for her trip to the amusement park. So far, she has $32. She plans to save *d* more dollars. Write, solve, and graph an inequality to show the values of *d* that will allow Joy to meet her goal.

_____

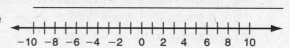

8. Penelope's MP3 player has 20 megabytes of memory. She has already downloaded 11 megabytes. She will continue to download *m* more megabytes. Write and solve an inequality that shows all the values of *m* that Penelope can download to her MP3 player.

_____

9. Roy works more than 30 hours each week. He has worked 17 hours already. Write and solve an inequality that shows the numbers of hours *h* that Roy has left to work.

_____

Holt McDougal Algebra 1

LESSON 2-2

Practice B

Solving Inequalities by Adding or Subtracting

Solve each inequality and graph the solutions.

1. $b + 8 > 15$

_____

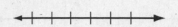

2. $t - 5 \geq -2$

_____

3. $-4 + x \geq 1$

_____

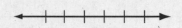

4. $g + 8 < 2$

_____

5. $-9 \geq m - 9$

_____

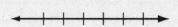

6. $15 > d + 19$

_____

Answer each question.

7. Jessica makes overtime pay when she works more than 40 hours in a week. So far this week she has worked 29 hours. She will continue to work *h* hours this week. Write, solve, and graph an inequality to show the values of *h* that will allow Jessica to earn overtime pay.

8. Henry's MP3 player has 512MB of memory. He has already downloaded 287MB and will continue to download *m* more megabytes. Write and solve an inequality that shows how many more megabytes he can download.

_____

9. Eleanor needs to read at least 97 pages of a book for homework. She has read 34 pages already. Write and solve an inequality that shows how many more pages *p* she must read.

_____

Holt McDougal Algebra 1

LESSON 2-2

Practice C
Solving Inequalities by Adding or Subtracting

Solve each inequality and graph the solutions.

1. $h + 5 > 12$

2. $1 \leq b - 4$

_____

graph:

_____

graph:

3. $-11 + y \geq 8$

4. $n + 8.2 < 2.2$

_____

graph:

_____

graph:

5. $r - \dfrac{1}{2} \leq -7\dfrac{1}{2}$

6. $-4 > t - 12$

_____

graph:

_____

graph:

Answer each question.

7. Leo has an outdoor painting project he wants to complete today. The directions on the paint can indicate that the minimum temperature for proper adherence and drying is 10ºC. Early in the morning the thermometer read –3ºC. The temperature will rise d degrees throughout the day. Write, solve, and graph an inequality to show the values of d that will allow Leo to paint.

_____

graph:

8. Kalista spent $29.75 at the gift shop of the science museum. She took $40 to the museum and still needs to buy lunch. Write and solve an inequality that shows how much money m Kalista can spend on her lunch.

9. Grace is at least 8 inches taller than her younger sister. Her sister is 4 feet tall. Write and solve an inequality that shows how tall g Grace can be.

_____

LESSON
2-2

Review for Mastery

Solving Inequalities by Adding or Subtracting

The method for solving one-step inequalities by adding is just like the method
for solving one-step equations by adding.

Solve x – 2 = 1 and graph the solution.

x – 2 = 1

  +2   +2   Add 2 to each side.
   x = 3

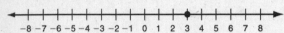

Solve x – 2 ≥ 1 and graph the solutions.

x – 2 ≥ 1

  +2 +2   Add 2 to each side.
   x ≥ 3

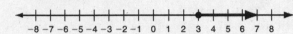

Solve –4 = a – 3 and graph the solution.

–4 = a – 3

+3   +3   Add 3 to each side.
–1 = a

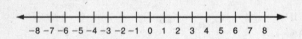

Solve –4 > a – 3 and graph the solutions.

–4 > a – 3

+3   +3   Add 3 to each side.
–1 > a

a < –1

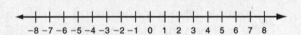

Solve each inequality and graph the solutions.

1. b – 4 < 3

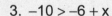

2. x – 5 < –2

3. –10 > –6 + x

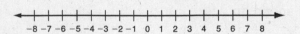

4. 1 ≤ f – 3

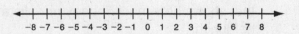

LESSON 2-2 **Review for Mastery**

Solving Inequalities by Adding or Subtracting *continued*

The method for solving one-step inequalities by subtracting is just like the method for solving one-step equations by subtracting.

Solve $x + 3 = 7$ and graph the solution.

$x + 3 = 7$

$\underline{\quad -3 \quad -3}$ *Subtract 3 from each side.*

$x = 4$

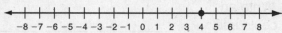

Solve $x + 3 < 7$ and graph the solutions.

$x + 3 < 7$

$\underline{\quad -3 \quad -3}$ *Subtract 3 from each side.*

$x < 4$

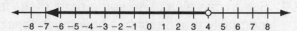

Solve $-4 = h + 2$ and graph the solution.

$-4 = h + 2$

$\underline{-2 \quad\quad -2}$ *Subtract 2 from each side.*

$-6 = h$

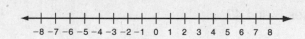

Solve $-4 \le h + 2$ and graph the solutions.

$-4 \le h + 2$

$\underline{-2 \quad\quad -2}$ *Subtract 2 from each side.*

$-6 \le h$

$h \ge -6$

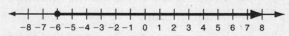

Solve each inequality and graph the solutions.

5. $c + 3 \le -2$

_____

6. $4 + x < 6$

_____

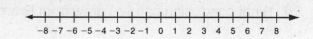

7. $4 < w + 7$

_____

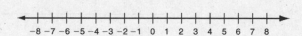

8. $9 \le 5 + n$

_____

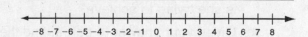

LESSON 2-2

Challenge

Solving One-Step Inequalities by Adding and Subtracting

Susan has 200 feet of fencing and wants to use it to enclose a rectangular garden. She knows that the formula for the perimeter of a rectangle is $P = 2(L + W)$. Susan also knows that the area A of a rectangle is found by using $A = LW$.

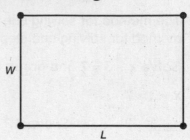

Answer the following questions in order to help Susan plan how to use the fencing.

1. Susan can either use some or all of the fencing. Write an inequality that describes how much fencing she could use. _____

2. Would a length of 70 feet and a width of 40 feet satisfy the inequality in Exercise 1? Explain.

   _____

3. a. If Susan decides to use all of the fencing and chooses a length of 20 feet, find the width. _____

   b. What would the length be if she chooses a width of 20 feet? _____

   c. Given these dimensions, find the area of the garden. _____

4. a. If Susan decides to use all of the fencing and chooses a length of 40 feet, find the width. _____

   b. What would the length be if she chooses a width of 40 feet? _____

   c. Given these dimensions, find the area of the garden. _____

5. What conclusion can you draw from Exercises 3 and 4?

   _____

6. a. If Susan would like the length and the width to be as close to one another as possible and to be whole numbers, what might the dimensions be? _____

   b. Given her intention in part **a**, what shape is she trying to achieve? _____

   c. Given your answer to part **a**, find the area of the garden. _____

7. Susan's friend, Jack, has 160 feet of fencing. He wants to use all his fencing to make a garden with the greatest possible area. Without using inequalities, what dimensions should he choose? _____

Holt McDougal Algebra 1

LESSON 2-2

Problem Solving

Solving Inequalities by Adding or Subtracting

Write the correct answer.

1. Sumiko is allowed to watch no more than 10 hours of television each week. She has watched 4 hours of television already. Write and solve an inequality to show how many more hours of television Sumiko can watch.

   _____

2. A satellite will be released into an orbit of more than 400 miles above the Earth. The rocket carrying it is currently 255 miles above Earth. Write and solve an inequality to show how much higher the rocket must climb before it releases the satellite.

   _____

3. Wayne's homework is to solve at least 20 questions from his textbook. So far, he has completed 9 of them. Write, solve, and graph an inequality to show how many more problems Wayne must complete.

   _____

   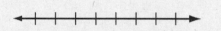

4. Felix wants to get at least one hour of exercise each day. Today, he has run for 40 minutes. Write, solve, and graph an inequality that shows how much longer Felix needs to exercise to reach his goal.

   _____

The high school has been raising money for charity and the class that raises the most will be awarded a party at the end of the year. The table below shows how much money each class has raised so far. Use this information to answer questions 5–7.

5. The school has a goal of raising at least $3000. Which inequality shows how much more money m they need to raise to reach their goal?

   A $m \geq 215$ C $m \leq 215$

   B $m < 215$ D $m > 2785$

Class	Amount Raised ($)
Seniors	870
Juniors	650
Sophomores	675
First-Years	590

6. The juniors would like to raise more money than the seniors. The seniors have completed their fundraising for the year. Which expression shows how much more money j the juniors must raise to overtake the seniors?

   F $j \leq 220$ H $j \geq 220$

   G $j < 220$ J $j > 220$

7. A local business has agreed to donate no more than half as much as the senior class raises. Which inequality shows how much money b the business will contribute?

   A $\frac{1}{2}(870) \leq b$ C $\frac{1}{2}(870) \geq b$

   B $870 \leq \frac{1}{2}b$ D $870 \geq \frac{1}{2}b$

LESSON 2-2

Reading Strategies
Follow a Procedure

There are two parts to checking solutions to inequalities: checking the endpoint and checking the direction of the inequality symbol.

Check that $x > -3$ represents the solutions to $x - 4 > -7$.

Step 1
$$x - 4 = -7$$
$$-3 - 4 = -7$$
$$-7 = -7 \checkmark$$
Write the related equation.
Substitute -3 for x in the related equation.
If the statement is true, the value is an endpoint.

Step 2
$$x - 4 > -7$$
$$10 - 4 > -7$$
$$6 > -7 \checkmark$$
Write the original inequality.
Substitute a value greater than -3 in the original inequality.
If the statement is true, the symbol is correct.

Both steps check, so $x > -3$ correctly represents the solutions.

Answer each question.

1. Which Step confirms that the endpoint is correct? _____

2. What is being checked in Step 2?

_____

3. Describe Step 1 when checking that $8 \leq m$ represents the solutions to $14 \leq m + 6$.

_____

4. Give a value that could be used in Step 2 when
   checking that $8 \leq m$ represents the solutions
   to $14 \leq m + 6$.   _____

For each problem, check that the given solutions represent the inequality by using the two-step procedure shown above.

5. $t + 5 < -9$ <u>Step 1</u>   <u>Step 2</u>   correct?
   $t > -14$

   _____   _____   _____

6. $b - 6 \geq 2$ <u>Step 1</u>   <u>Step 2</u>   correct?
   $b \geq 8$

   _____   _____   _____

Name _____ Date _____ Class _____

Practice A

Solving Inequalities by Multiplying or Dividing

Solve each inequality and graph the solutions.

1. $2x \geq 6$

2. $\dfrac{a}{5} < 1$

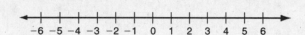

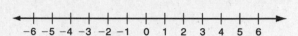

3. $\dfrac{3}{4}b > 3$

4. $15y \leq -30$

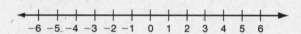

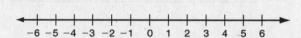

Solve each inequality and graph the solutions.
Remember to switch the inequality sign.

5. $-3x < 12$

6. $\dfrac{k}{-2} > 1.5$

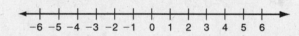

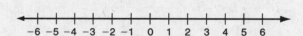

7. $-\dfrac{2}{3}n \geq -4$

8. $-7x \leq 0$

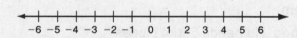

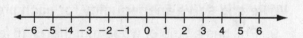

Write and solve an inequality for each problem.

9. Joe goes to the store with $15 to buy salad. Bags
   of pre-washed salad are on sale for $2 each. What
   are the possible numbers of bags Joe can buy?

   _____

10. By selling old CDs, Sarah has a store credit
    for $153. A new CD costs $18. What are the
    possible numbers of new CDs Sarah can buy?

    _____

Holt McDougal Algebra 1

LESSON 2-3

Practice B

Solving Inequalities by Multiplying or Dividing

Solve each inequality and graph the solutions.

1. $4a > 32$

2. $-7y < 21$

3. $1.5n \leq -18$

4. $-\dfrac{3}{8}c \geq 9$

5. $\dfrac{y}{5} > 4$

6. $2s \leq -3$

7. $-\dfrac{1}{3}b < -6$

8. $\dfrac{z}{-8} \geq -0.25$

Write and solve an inequality for each problem.

9. Phil has a strip of wood trim that is 16 feet long. He needs 5-foot pieces to trim some windows. What are the possible numbers of pieces he can cut?

_____

10. A teacher buys a 128-ounce bottle of juice and serves it in 5-ounce cups. What are the possible numbers of cups she can fill?

_____

11. At an online bookstore, Kendra bought 4 copies of the same book for the members of her book club. She got free shipping because her total was at least $50. What was the minimum price of each book?

_____

Holt McDougal Algebra 1

LESSON 2-3

Practice C

Solving Inequalities by Multiplying or Dividing

Solve each inequality.

1. $68 < 4a$

2. $-13b \geq 78$

3. $6c \leq -10$

_____

_____

_____

4. $7.3 \geq \dfrac{x}{-2}$

5. $-\dfrac{y}{3} \leq 2.5$

6. $1.8z > 9.36$

_____

_____

_____

7. $-6n > \dfrac{3}{4}$

8. $-\dfrac{3}{8}p < \dfrac{9}{10}$

9. $-16 \leq \dfrac{2}{5}k$

_____

_____

_____

Write an inequality for each statement.
Solve the inequality and graph the solutions.

10. The product of a number and −4 is at most 24.

inequality: _____   solution: _____

graph:

11. The quotient of a number and 15 is at least 3.

inequality: _____   solution: _____

graph:

12. The product of $\dfrac{2}{3}$ and x is no more than −16.

inequality: _____   solution: _____

graph:

Write and solve an inequality for the problem.

13. Ms. Malek is planning a breakfast meeting for 45 people. She wants
at least one donut per person, but donuts are only sold in boxes of a
dozen. What is the least number of boxes she should buy?

_____

LESSON 2-3

Review for Mastery

Solving Inequalities by Multiplying or Dividing

The inequality sign must be reversed when multiplying by a negative number.

Multiplying by a positive number:		Multiplying by a negative number:	
$2 < 5$	*True*	$2 < 5$	*True*
$3 \cdot 2 \overset{?}{<} 3 \cdot 5$	*Multiply both sides by a positive number.*	$(-3) \cdot 2 \overset{?}{<} (-3) \cdot 5$	*Multiply both sides by a negative number.*
$6 \overset{?}{<} 15$ ✓	*Statement is true.*	$-6 \overset{?}{<} -15$ ☐	*Statement is false.*
		$-6 > -15$ ✓	*Reverse inequality sign so statement is true.*

Solve $\dfrac{x}{3} > -2$ and graph the solution.   **Solve $\dfrac{x}{-4} \geq 1$ and graph the solutions.**

$\dfrac{x}{3} > -2$ 　　　　　　　　　　　　　 $\dfrac{x}{-4} \geq 1$

$3 \cdot \dfrac{x}{3} > 3 \cdot (-2)$ 　*Multiply both sides by 3.*　 $(-4) \cdot \dfrac{x}{-4} \geq (-4) \cdot 1$ 　*Multiply both sides by −4.*

$x > -6$

$x \leq -4$ 　　　 Reverse inequality sign.

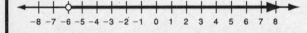

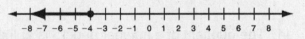

Solve each inequality and graph the solutions.

1. $\dfrac{x}{3} \geq -2$ 　　　　　　　　　　2. $-\dfrac{3}{4}g < -3$

_____ 　　　_____

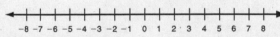 　　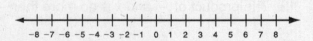

Solve each inequality.

3. $-1 < \dfrac{v}{-5}$ 　　　　　　　　4. $\dfrac{5}{6}m > 10$

_____ 　　　_____

Review for Mastery

Solving Inequalities by Multiplying or Dividing continued

The inequality sign must also be reversed when dividing by a negative number. Dividing by a negative number:

$8 > 6$ *True*

$\dfrac{8}{-2} > \dfrac{6}{-2}$ *Divide both sides by a negative number.*

$-4 \overset{?}{>} -3$ *Statement is false.*

$-4 < -3$ *Reverse inequality sign so statement is true.*

Solve 3x > −12 and graph the solution.   **Solve −2m ≤ 10 and graph the solutions.**

$3x > -12$ $-2m \le 10$

$\dfrac{3x}{3} > \dfrac{-12}{3}$ *Divide both sides by 3.* $\dfrac{-2m}{-2} \le \dfrac{10}{-2}$ *Divide both sides by −2.*

$x > -4$ Dividing by a positive. Do not reverse inequality sign. $m \ge -5$ Dividing by a negative. Reverse inequality sign

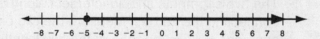

Solve each inequality and graph the solutions.

5. $-5q \ge -10$ 6. $4x < -16$

_____   _____

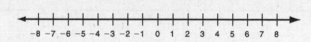

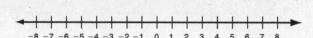

Solve each inequality.

7. $-x \le 5$ 8. $30 > -10d$

_____   _____

                 Holt McDougal Algebra 1

LESSON 2-3

Challenge
A Mathematical Lens

You will need a centimeter ruler for this activity.

1. Consider the inequality −1 < 3. Write the inequality you get when you multiply both sides by −2. _____

2. On the top number line, plot a point at −1. On the bottom number line, plot the value you get when you multiply by −2. Use your ruler to connect the two points with a straight segment.

3. Similarly, on the top, plot a point at 3. On the bottom, plot the value you get when you multiply by −2. Connect the two points with a segment.

4. Explain how the graph illustrates that you *reverse* an inequality when you multiply both sides by a negative number.

_____

_____

5. The two segments should intersect along the dashed segment connecting the zeroes. Measure the two pieces of the dashed segment. How is the ratio of the two lengths related to the factor −2?

_____

6. Try it again. Multiply both sides of the inequality 9 < 15 by $-\dfrac{1}{3}$.

   Plot points and connect them. Do you see the same patterns?

_____

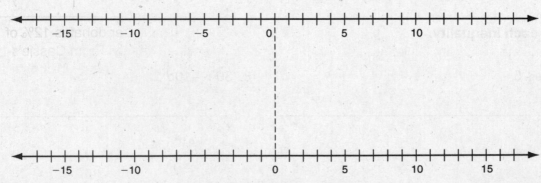

7. Where along the dashed line would the segments intersect if you multiplied both sides of any inequality by −1?

_____

LESSON 2-3	**Problem Solving**

Solving Inequalities by Multiplying or Dividing

Write and solve an inequality for each situation.

1. Karin has $3 to spend in the arcade. The game she likes costs 50¢ per play. What are the possible numbers of times that she can play?

_____

_____

2. Tyrone has $21 and wants to buy juice drinks for his soccer team. There are 15 players on his team. How much can each drink cost so that Tyrone can buy one drink for each person?

_____

3. A swimming pool is 7 feet deep and is being filled at the rate of 2.5 feet per hour. How long can the pool be left unattended without the water overflowing?

_____

_____

4. Megan is making quilts that require 11 feet of cloth each. She has 50 feet of cloth. What are the possible numbers of quilts that she can make?

_____

_____

Alyssa, Reggie, and Cassie are meeting some friends at the movies and have stopped at the refreshment stand. The table below shows some of the items for sale and their prices. Use this information to answer questions 5–7.

5. Alyssa has $7 and would like to buy fruit snacks for as many of her friends as possible. Which inequality below can be solved to find the number of fruit snacks f she can buy?

   A $2f \le 7$ C $7f \le 2$

   B $2f > 7$ D $7f < 2$

Menu Item	Price($)
Popcorn	3.50
Drink	3.00
Hot Dog	2.50
Nachos	2.50
Fruit Snack	2.00

6. Reggie brought $13 and is going to buy popcorn for the group. Which answer below shows the possible numbers of popcorns p Reggie can buy for his friends?

   F 0, 1, or 2   H 0, 1, 2, 3, or 4

   G 0, 1, 2, or 3   J 0, 1, 2, 3, 4, or 5

7. The movie theater donates 12% of its sales to charity. From Cassie's purchases, the theater will donate at least $2.15. Which inequality below shows the amount of money m that Cassie spent at the refreshment stand?

   A $m \ge 17.92$ C $m \ge 25.80$

   B $m \le 17.92$ D $m \le 25.80$

Holt McDougal Algebra 1

LESSON 2-3

Reading Strategies
Recognize Errors

The rules for solving inequalities are the same as for solving equations, with one exception. Analyze the problems below to avoid common errors.

$-4n > 28$ $\dfrac{-4n}{-4} > \dfrac{28}{-4}$ $n < -7$ **Correct:** When dividing by a negative number, you must reverse the inequality symbol.	$\dfrac{x}{-8} \le 2$ $(-8)\dfrac{x}{-8} \le 2(-8)$ $x \ge -16$ **Correct:** When multiplying by a negative number, you must reverse the inequality symbol.
$\dfrac{t}{-5} \ge 4$ $(-5)\dfrac{t}{-5} \ge 4(-5)$ $t < -20$ **Error:** Don't drop the "or equal to" part of the inequality symbol.	$3p < -4.5$ $\dfrac{3p}{3} < \dfrac{-4.5}{3}$ $p > -1.5$ **Error:** Do not reverse the inequality symbol just because there is a negative in the problem.

Answer each question.

1. Would you reverse the inequality symbol when solving $2x > -20$? Explain.

_____

2. What are the *correct* answers for the two errors shown above?

_____   _____

Tell whether the solution for each of the inequalities shown below is correct or incorrect. If incorrect, describe the error.

3. $-2a \ge -6$; $a \le 3$ 4. $\dfrac{m}{-2} \le 9$; $m > -18$ 5. $15 > -15t$; $t < -1$

_____   _____   _____

_____   _____   _____

_____   _____   _____

_____   _____   _____

Name _____ Date _____ Class_____

Practice A
Solving Two-Step and Multi-Step Inequalities

Fill in the blanks to solve each inequality.

1. $2x - 5 \le 7$

   $ + \underline{\quad} + \underline{\quad}$

   $2x \le \underline{\quad}$

   $\div 2 \quad \div 2$

   $x \le \underline{\quad}$

2. $-3(k - 1) < 15$

   $-3k + \underline{\quad} < 15$

   $- \underline{\quad} - \underline{\quad}$

   $-3k < \underline{\quad}$

   $\div(-3) \div (-3)$

   $k \underline{\quad} \underline{\quad}$

3. $\dfrac{1}{2}n + \dfrac{5}{6} > \dfrac{2}{3}$

   $\underline{\quad}\left(\dfrac{1}{2}n + \dfrac{5}{6}\right) > \underline{\quad}\left(\dfrac{2}{3}\right)$

   $3n + 5 > \underline{\quad}$

   $- \underline{\quad} - \underline{\quad}$

   $3n > \underline{\quad}$

   $\div \underline{\quad} \div \underline{\quad}$

   $\underline{\quad} \underline{\quad} \underline{\quad}$

Solve each inequality and graph the solutions.

4. $5x + 7 \ge 2$

   _____

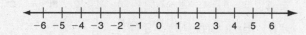

6. $6 - \dfrac{a}{3} < 2$

   _____

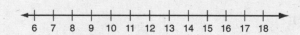

5. $5(z + 6) \le 40$

   _____

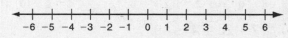

7. $-\dfrac{1}{3}x + 4 > 1$

   _____

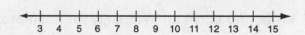

Write and solve an inequality for each problem.

8. Ted needs an average of at least 70 on his three history tests. He has already scored 85 and 60 on two tests. What is the minimum grade Ted needs on his third test?

   _____

9. A VHS tape holds at most 360 minutes. A tape already has a 120-minute movie on it. How many 30-minute sitcoms can be recorded on the remaining tape?

   _____

Holt McDougal Algebra 1

Name _____ Date _____ Class_____

Practice B
Solving Two-Step and Multi-Step Inequalities

Solve each inequality and graph the solutions.

1. $-3a + 10 < -11$

2. $4x - 12 \geq 20$

_____

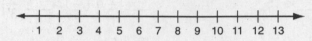

_____

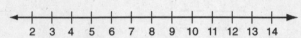

3. $\dfrac{2k - 3}{-5} > 7$

4. $-\dfrac{1}{5}z + \dfrac{2}{3} \leq 2$

_____

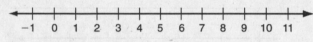

_____

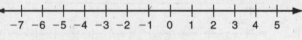

5. $6(n - 8) \geq -18$

6. $10 - 2(3x + 4) < 11$

_____

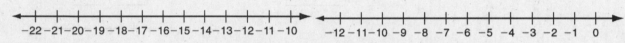

_____

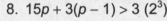

7. $7 + 2c - 4^2 \leq -9$

8. $15p + 3(p - 1) > 3(2^3)$

_____

_____

Write and solve an inequality for each problem.

9. A full-year membership to a gym costs $325 upfront with no monthly charge. A monthly membership costs $100 upfront and $30 per month. For what numbers of months is it less expensive to have a monthly membership?

_____

10. The sum of the lengths of any two sides of a triangle must be greater than the length of the third side. What are the possible values of x for this triangle?

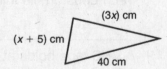

(3x) cm
(x + 5) cm
40 cm

_____

Holt McDougal Algebra 1

LESSON 2-4

Practice C

Solving Two-Step and Multi-Step Inequalities

Solve each inequality.

1. $4 \geq -3x + 5$

2. $-2.5(y - 6) \leq -4.5$

3. $5 > 12a - (3 - 4a)$

_____

4. $5 < \dfrac{7 - 3h}{-4}$

5. $\dfrac{x - 2}{3} \geq \dfrac{1}{2}$

6. $\dfrac{3}{8}n - 2 < \dfrac{1}{5}$

_____

7. $-2p - 3\dfrac{1}{4} \leq -1$

8. $2^2 - (3^2)x + 14x > \dfrac{4^3}{2}$

9. $\dfrac{3}{4}w - \dfrac{1}{2}(2w + 1) < \dfrac{2}{5}$

_____

Write, solve, and graph an inequality for each statement.

10. Two is greater than the sum of 3 and one-fourth of a number.

inequality: _____   solution: _____

graph:

11. The product of –2 and the sum of a number and 3 is at least 0.

inequality: _____   solution: _____

graph: _____

Write and solve an inequality for each problem.

12. Ann's grade is the average of four scores: three chapter tests and a final that counts as two chapter tests. She scored 72, 90, and 75 on the chapter tests. What score does she need on the final to have a grade of at least 80?

_____

13. Trey is limiting his diet to no more than 600 calories per meal. For lunch, he had a can of iced tea and two bowls of soup. The tea had 140 calories. What are the possible number of calories in each bowl of soup?

_____

LESSON 2-4

Review for Mastery
Solving Two-Step and Multi-Step Inequalities

When solving inequalities with more than one step, use inverse operations to isolate the variable. The order of the inverse operations is the order of the operations in reverse. You can check your solution by substituting the endpoint and another point in the solution back into the original inequality.

Solve $-5x + 3 < 23$ and graph the solutions.

$-5x + 3 < 23$

$\underline{\quad -3 \quad -3\quad}$

$-5x < 20$ *Add –3 to each side.*

$\dfrac{-5x}{-5} < \dfrac{20}{-5}$ *Divide both sides by –5.*

$x > -4$ *Reverse the inequality sign.*

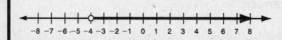

Check:

Try –4.	Try 6.
$-5x + 3 < 23$	$-5x + 3 < 23$
$-5(-4) + 3 \overset{?}{<} 23$	$-5(6) + 3 \overset{?}{<} 23$
$20 + 3 \overset{?}{<} 23$	$-30 + 3 \overset{?}{<} 23$
$23 \overset{?}{<} 23$ ✗	$-27 \overset{?}{<} 23$ ✓

The endpoint –4 is not a solution. The open circle on the graph is correct. The value 6 is a solution. The direction of the inequality symbol is correct.

Solve each inequality and graph the solutions.

1. $-3e - 10 \le -4$

_____

2. $\dfrac{c}{2} + 8 > 11$

_____

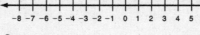

3. $15 \le 3 - 4s$

_____

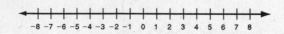

4. $\dfrac{3}{4}j + 1 > 4$

_____

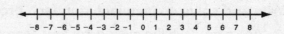

LESSON 2-4

Review for Mastery

Solving Two-Step and Multi-Step Inequalities continued

Solving inequalities may require using the Distributive Property, combining like terms, or clearing fractions. Remember that you can clear fractions by multiplying both sides of the inequality by the least common denominator (LCD).

Solve $\dfrac{3}{2}x + \dfrac{1}{6} \geq \dfrac{5}{3}$.

$$\frac{3}{2}x + \frac{1}{6} \geq \frac{5}{3}$$

$$6\left(\frac{3}{2}x + \frac{1}{6}\right) \geq 6\left(\frac{5}{3}\right)$$ *Multiply both sides by the LCD 6.*

$$6\left(\frac{3}{2}x\right) + 6\left(\frac{1}{6}\right) \geq 6\left(\frac{5}{3}\right)$$ *Distribute 6.*

$$9x + 1 \geq 10$$

$$\underline{\quad -1 \quad -1 \quad}$$ *Add −1 to both sides.*

$$9x \geq 9$$

$$\frac{9x}{9} \geq \frac{9}{9}$$ *Divide both sides by 9.*

$$x \geq 1$$

Check:

Try 1.

$$\frac{3}{2}x + \frac{1}{6} \geq \frac{5}{3}$$

$$\frac{3}{2}(1) + \frac{1}{6} \overset{?}{>} \frac{5}{3}$$

$$\frac{3}{2} + \frac{1}{6} \overset{?}{\geq} \frac{5}{3}$$

$$\frac{9}{6} + \frac{1}{6} \overset{?}{\geq} \frac{10}{6}$$

$$\frac{10}{6} \overset{?}{\geq} \frac{10}{6} \checkmark$$

Try 2.

$$\frac{3}{2}x + \frac{1}{6} \geq \frac{5}{3}$$

$$\frac{3}{2}(2) + \frac{1}{6} \overset{?}{\geq} \frac{5}{3}$$

$$3 + \frac{1}{6} \overset{?}{\geq} \frac{5}{3}$$

$$3\frac{1}{6} \overset{?}{\geq} 1\frac{2}{3} \checkmark$$

The endpoint 1 is a solution. The value 2 is a solution. The direction of the inequality symbol is correct.

Solve each inequality.

5. $-\dfrac{5}{6}x + 3 < \dfrac{1}{2}$

6. $2(b - 7) + -4b \geq 30 - 18$

7. $\dfrac{2}{3}(g + 4) - g > 1$

8. $-\dfrac{3}{5} + \dfrac{8}{5}k - (3k - 2) \leq 0$

LESSON 2-4

Challenge

Solving Multi-Step Inequalities

As you have already seen, when you solve a linear equation, you find a definite value. If the variable is equal to 3, then the number line is divided into three parts: the number 3, those numbers greater than 3, and those numbers less than 3. When you deal with multiple inequalities, you divide the number line into even more parts.

In Exercises 1–3, use the number line below.

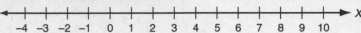

1. Draw a graph showing the solutions to $x \geq 3$ and $x < 7$.

2. What integers satisfy both of these inequalities? _____

3. What inequalities describe your response in Exercise 2?

_____

On a certain freeway, the minimum allowable speed is 40 miles per hour, and the maximum allowable speed is 55 miles per hour.

Use the information above to answer Exercises 4–6.

4. Write an inequality for each driving situation.

    a. A motorist is driving too fast. _____

    b. A motorist is driving too slow. _____

5. Is it technically correct to say that the speed limit is exactly 55 miles per hour?

_____

6. Write multiple inequalities for each situation.

    a. The driver's speed is within the speed limits. _____

    b. The driver's speed is outside of the speed limits. _____

People use multiple inequalities when they deal with real-estate situations.

7. John and Marsha would like to buy a house priced at $185,000, plus or minus $5,000.

    a. What are the maximum and minimum house price that they are willing to pay? _____

    b. Write a pair of inequalities describing their price range. _____

8. Use inequalities to describe the following sentence: "We sell houses priced at $80,000, plus or minus $5,000, to houses priced at $250,000, plus or minus $5,000." _____

Holt McDougal Algebra 1

Name _____ Date _____ Class _____

Problem Solving
Solving Two-Step and Multi-Step Inequalities

Write and solve an inequality for each situation.

1. Jillene is playing in a basketball tournament and scored 24 points in her first game. If she averages over 20 points for both games, she will receive a trophy. How many points can Jillene score in the second game and receive a trophy?

_____

2. Marcus has accepted a job selling cell phones. He will be paid $1500 plus 15% of his sales each month. He needs to earn at least $2430 to pay his bills. For what amount of sales will Marcus be able to pay his bills?

_____

3. A 15-foot-tall cedar tree is growing at a rate of 2 feet per year beneath power lines that are 58 feet above the ground. The power company will have to prune or remove the tree before it reaches the lines. How many years can the power company wait before taking action?

_____

4. Binh brought $23 with her to the county fair. She purchased a $5 T-shirt and now wants to buy some locally grown plants for $2.50 each. What are the numbers of plants that she can purchase with her remaining money?

_____

Benedict, Ricardo, and Charlie are considering opportunities for summer work. The table below shows the jobs open to them and the pay for each. Use this information to answer questions 5–7.

5. Benedict has saved $91 from last year and would like to baby-sit to earn enough to buy a mountain bike. A good quality bike costs at least $300. What numbers of hours h can Benedict baby-sit to reach his goal?

   A $h \geq 14$ C $h \geq 38$

   B $h \geq 23$ D $h \geq 71$

6. Ricardo has agreed to tutor for the school. He owes his older brother $59 and would like to end the summer with at least $400 in savings. How many sessions s can Ricardo tutor to meet his goal?

   F $s \geq 31$ H $s \geq 51$

   G $s \geq 38$ J $s \geq 83$

Job	Pay
Mowing Lawns	$15 per lawn
Baby-Sitting	$5.50 per hour
Tutoring	$9 per session

7. Charlie has agreed to mow his neighbor's lawn each week and will also baby-sit some hours. If he makes $100 or more each week, his parents will charge him rent. How many hours h should Charlie agree to baby-sit each week to avoid paying rent?

   A $h \leq 15$ C $h \leq 21$

   B $h \geq 15$ D $h \geq 21$

Holt McDougal Algebra 1

Reading Strategies

LESSON 2-4

Compare and Contrast

The chart below summarizes the similarities and differences between multi-step equations and multi-step inequalities when there is a variable on one side.

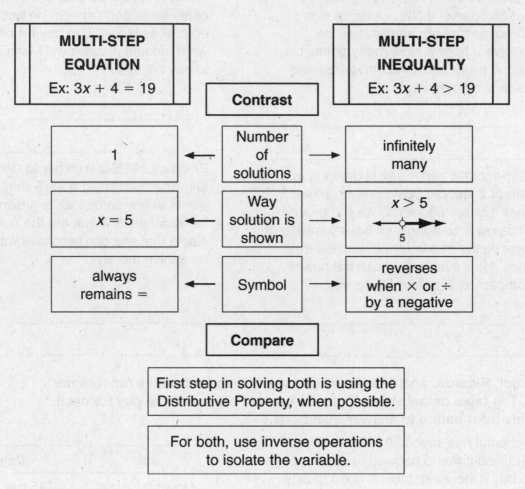

Answer each question.

1. Why are solutions to inequalities graphed on number lines?

   _____

2. Show what the solution $x = 5$ looks
   like when graphed on a number line.   _____

3. What one value is the solution to the equation $3(x + 4) = 9$?   _____

4. List five values that are solutions to the inequality
   $3(x + 4) < 9$.   _____

5. Do $-2x + 3 = 7$ and $-2x + 3 \geq 7$ have any solutions in common?   _____

   If so, what? _____

Holt McDougal Algebra 1

Name _____ Date _____ Class_____

LESSON 2-5

Practice A
Solving Inequalities with Variables on Both Sides

Fill in the blanks to solve each inequality.

1. $2x \le 3x + 8$

    $-$ _____   _____

      $-1x \le$ _____

    $\div (-1)$ $\div$ (-1)

    x _____ _____

2. $8y > -2(3y - 7)$

     $8y >$ _____ $+$ _____

      $+$ _____ $+$ _____

     $14y >$ _____

      $\div$ _____ $\div$ _____

       $y >$ _____

3. $3(5n + 6) < 10n - 4$

    _____ $+$ _____ $< 10n - 4$

     $-10n$ $-10n$

    _____ $+$ _____ < -4

      $-$ _____ $-$ _____

       $5n < -22$

      $\div$ _____ $\div$ _____

     _____ $\div$ _____ _____

Solve each inequality and graph the solutions.

4. $5x \ge 7x + 4$

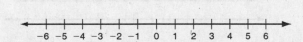

5. $3(b - 5) < -2b$

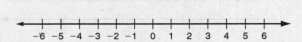

Identify each inequality as an identity (all real numbers are solutions) or contradiction (no solutions).

6. $10 < -2$ 7. $a - 7 \le a$ 8. $2(z + 3) > 2z$

_____   _____   _____

Write and solve an inequality for each problem.

9. Jay can buy a stereo either online or at a local store. If he buys online, he gets a 15% discount, but has to pay a $12 shipping fee. At the local store, the stereo is not on sale, but there is no shipping fee. For what regular prices is it cheaper for Jay to buy the stereo online?

_____

10. For what values of x is the area of the rectangle greater than the area of the triangle?

_____

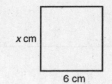

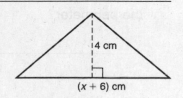

         Holt McDougal Algebra 1

LESSON 2-5

Practice B

Solving Inequalities with Variables on Both Sides

Solve each inequality and graph the solutions.

1. $2x + 30 \geq 7x$

2. $2k + 6 < 5k - 3$

_____

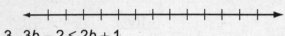

_____

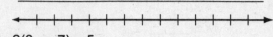

3. $3b - 2 \leq 2b + 1$

4. $2(3n + 7) > 5n$

_____

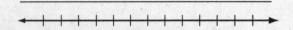

_____

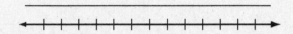

5. $5s - 9 < 2(s - 6)$

6. $-3(3x + 5) \geq -5(2x - 2)$

_____

_____

7. $1.4z + 2.2 > 2.6z - 0.2$

8. $\dfrac{7}{8}p - \dfrac{1}{4} \leq \dfrac{1}{2}p$

_____

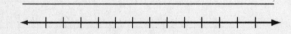

_____

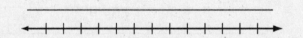

Solve each inequality.

9. $v + 1 > v - 6$

10. $3(x + 4) \leq 3x$

11. $-2(8 - 3x) \geq 6x + 2$

_____   _____   _____

Write and solve an inequality for each problem.

12. Ian wants to promote his band on the Internet. Site A offers website hosting for $4.95 per month with a $49.95 startup fee. Site B offers website hosting for $9.95 per month with no startup fee. For how many months would Ian need to keep the website for Site B to be less expensive than Site A?

_____

13. For what values of x is the area of the rectangle greater than the perimeter?

_____

Holt McDougal Algebra 1

LESSON 2-5

Practice C
Solving Inequalities with Variables on Both Sides

Solve each inequality.

1. $2x + 1 < 8x - 2$

2. $4(3p + 5) \geq -2p$

3. $-2s + 3 \geq -7s$

4. $\frac{1}{2}(5 - 2x) > -x + 1$

5. $5(n - 2) < 4(2n + 6) + 2$

6. $\frac{2}{3}y + 6 < \frac{2}{3}y - 6$

7. $\frac{3x}{8} + 4 \leq 0.2x + 5$

8. $-z + 20 > z + 20$

9. $2a + 10 \leq 2(-2a + 3) + 6a$

10. $5b + 20 > -2 + 3b$

11. $6(k - 5) > 3k - 26$

12. $0.42d < 152.5 + 0.17d$

For 13–17, use the table at right. The table gives the populations of Toledo, Ohio, and Lexington, Kentucky, during the last three U.S. Censuses.

	1980	1990	2000
Toledo, OH	350,000	330,000	310,000
Lexington, KY	200,000	230,000	260,000

13. About how much did the population of Toledo change each **year**? (Note: *Not* each decade!) _____

14. Write an expression for the population of Toledo any number of years after 1980. _____

15. About how much did the population of Lexington change each **year**? _____

16. Write an expression for the population of Lexington any number of years after 1980. _____

17. Assuming the patterns in the table continue, write and solve an inequality to find the years in which the population of Lexington will be greater than the population of Toledo. _____

LESSON 2-5

Review for Mastery

Solving Inequalities with Variables on Both Sides

Variables must be collected on the same side of an inequality before the inequality can be solved. If you collect the variables so that the variable term is positive, you will not have to multiply or divide by a negative number.

Solve $x > 8 (x - 7)$.

Collect the variables on the left.

$x > 8(x - 7)$	
$x > 8x - 56$	*Distribute.*
$\dfrac{-8x \quad -8x}{-7x > -56}$	*Add −8x to both sides.*
$\dfrac{-7x}{-7} > \dfrac{-56}{-7}$	*Divide both sides by −7.*
$x < 8$	*Reverse the sign.*

Notice that if you want to have the variable on the left to make graphing solutions easier, you may still need to switch the inequality sign, even if you did not multiply or divide by a negative number.

Solve $x > 8 (x - 7)$.

Collect the variables on the right.

$x > 8(x - 7)$	
$x > 8x - 56$	*Distribute.*
$\dfrac{-x \quad -x}{0 > 7x - 56}$	*Add −x to both sides.*
$\dfrac{+56 \qquad +56}{56 > 7x}$	
$\dfrac{56}{7} > \dfrac{7x}{7}$	*Divide both sides by 7.*
$8 > x$	
$x < 8$	

Write the first step you would take to solve each inequality if you wanted to keep the variable positive.

1. $6y < 10y + 1$ _____

2. $4p - 2 \geq 3p$ _____

3. $5 - 3r \leq 6r$ _____

Solve each inequality.

4. $8c + 4 > 4(c - 3)$ 　　　5. $5(x - 1) < 3x + 10 - 8x$ 　　　6. $-8 + 4a - 12 > 2a + 10$

_____ 　　　_____ 　　　_____

　　　Holt McDougal Algebra 1

LESSON 2-5
Review for Mastery
Solving Inequalities with Variables on Both Sides continued

An inequality with infinite solutions is called an identity.

Solve $-2x - 5 \leq 4x + 8 - 6x$.

			Check any value of x:
$-2x - 5 \leq 4x + 8 - 6x$			Try $x = 3$.
$-2x - 5 \leq -2x + 8$	Combine like terms.		$-2x - 5 \leq 4x + 8 - 6x$
$\underline{+2x \qquad +2x}$	Add 2x to each side.		$-2(3) - 5 \overset{?}{\leq} 4(3) + 8 - 6(3)$
$-5 \qquad \leq 8 \checkmark$	True statement. This is an identity.		$-6 - 5 \overset{?}{\leq} 12 + 8 - 18$
			$-11 \overset{?}{\leq} 2 \checkmark$

The solution is the set of all real numbers.

An inequality with no solutions is called a contradiction.

Solve $3(x - 4) > 7 + 3x$.

			Check any value of x:
$3(x - 4) > 7 + 3x$			Try $x = 2$.
$3x - 12 > 7 + 3x$	Distribute.		$3(x - 4) > 7 + 3x$
$\underline{-3x \qquad -3x}$	Add −3x to each side.		$3(2 - 4) \overset{?}{>} 7 + 3(2)$
$-12 > 7$ 8	False statement. This is a contradiction.		$3(-2) \overset{?}{>} 7 + 6$
			$-6 \overset{?}{>} 13$ 8

There are no solutions.

Solve each inequality.

7. $t + 5 < t + 5$

8. $x + 5 \leq x + 5$

_____   _____

9. $4y + 3(y - 2) < 7y$

10. $10n - 4 \leq 5(2n + 1)$

11. $9x + 3 - 5x \geq 2(2x + 5)$

_____   _____   _____

       Holt McDougal Algebra 1

LESSON 2-5

Challenge
Above and Below

The grid at right shows the graphs of two functions, $y_1 = x + 3$ and $y_2 = 2x - 1$. These functions can be graphed by creating a table of ordered pairs for each function and then plotting the ordered pairs. The ordered pairs of each function form straight lines as shown.

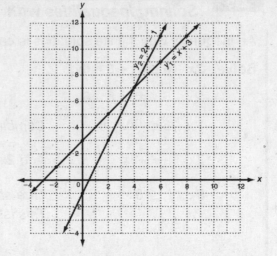

1. For what value of x is $y_1 = y_2$? What happens to the graphs at this x-value?

_____

2. For what values of x is $y_1 > y_2$? What happens to the graphs for these x-values?

_____

3. The equation $y_1 = x + 3$ tells you that y_1 is the same as the expression $x + 3$. Likewise, $y_2 = 2x - 1$ tells you that y_2 is the same as $2x - 1$. Use this information to rewrite $y_1 > y_2$ using the variable x.

y_1 > y_2

_____ _____ _____

4. Solve the inequality in problem 3. How do the solutions relate to your answer for problem 2?

_____

5. Explain how you could use the graph to solve this inequality: $2x - 1 \geq x + 3$.

_____

6. Generate ordered pairs for the functions below. For each, plot the points, connect them with straight lines, and label as in the example above.

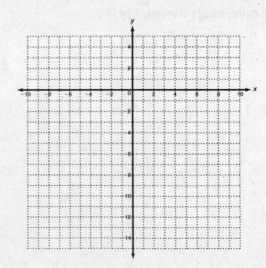

$y_1 = x - 3$	
x	**y**
−4	
−2	
0	
2	
4	

$y_2 = -3x - 11$	
x	**y**
−4	
−3	
−2	
−1	
0	

Use the graph to solve $x - 3 \leq -3x - 11$.

_____

           Holt McDougal Algebra 1

LESSON 2-5

Problem Solving
Solving Inequalities With Variables on Both Sides

Write and solve an inequality for each situation.

1. Rosa has decided to sell pet rocks at an art fair for $5 each. She has paid $50 to rent a table at the fair and it costs her $2 to package each rock with a set of instructions. For what numbers of sales will Rosa make a profit?

_____

_____

2. Jamie has a job paying $25,000 and expects to receive a $1000 raise each year. Wei has a job paying $19,000 a year and expects a $1500 raise each year. For what span of time is Jamie making more money than Wei?

_____

_____

3. Sophia types 75 words per minute and is just starting to write a term paper. Patton already has 510 words written and types at a speed of 60 words per minute. For what numbers of minutes will Sophia have more words typed than Patton?

_____

_____

4. Keith is racing his little sister Pattie and has given her a 15 foot head start. She runs 5 ft/sec and he is chasing at 8 ft/sec. For how long can Pattie stay ahead of Keith?

_____

_____

The table below shows the population of four cities in 2004 and the amount of population change from 2003. Use this table to answer questions 5–6.

5. If the trends in this table continue, after how many years y will the population of Manchester, NH, be more than the population of Vallejo, CA? Round your answer to the nearest tenth of a year.

   A $y > 0.2$ C $y > 34.6$

   B $y > 6.4$ D $y > 78.6$

6. If the trends in this table continue, for how long x will the population of Carrollton, TX be less than the population of Lakewood, CO? Round your answer to the nearest tenth of a year.

   F $x < 11.7$ H $x < 20.1$

   G $x < 14.6$ J $x < 28.3$

City	Population (2004)	Population Change (from 2003)
Lakewood, CO	141,301	−830
Vallejo, CA	118,349	−1155
Carrollton, TX	117,823	+1170
Manchester, NH	109,310	+261

LESSON 2-5

Reading Strategies
Analyze Choices

When solving an inequality with variables on both sides, you have a choice:
Collect the variables on the left, or collect the variables on the right.
There are advantages to each, depending on the inequality. Either way,
you should get the same answer.

<table>
<tr><td>

$x - 7 > 4x + 2$

$\underline{-4x \qquad -4x}$

$-3x - 7 > 2$

$\underline{\quad +7 \quad +7}$

$\dfrac{-3x}{-3} > \dfrac{9}{-3}$

$x < -3$

</td><td>

$x - 7 > 4x + 2$

$\underline{-x \quad -x}$

$-7 > 3x + 2$

$\underline{\quad -2 \qquad -2}$

$\dfrac{-9}{3} > \dfrac{3x}{3}$

$-3 > x$

$x < -3$

</td></tr>
</table>

| **Collect variables on the left.** | ⟺ $x - 7 > 4x + 2$ | **Collect variables on the right.** |

| Analysis | Analysis |
| With this choice, we divide by a negative. So we must remember to change the direction of the inequality symbol. | With this choice, the solution is "backwards". We must flip the solutions so that we can read it from left to right. |

Answer each question.

1. Kirby often forgets to switch the inequality symbol when dividing by a negative. When solving $3x - 10 \geq x$, should Kirby collect the variables on the left or the right? Why?

   _____

2. Rewrite the inequality $8 < t$ so that the variable is on the left. _____

3. Solve the inequality $-2(n + 3) > -4n + 8$
   by collecting variables on the left, then by
   collecting variables on the right.
   Which seems better in this case? Why?

   _____

LESSON 2-6

Practice A
Solving Compound Inequalities

Graph each inequality, and then graph the compound inequality.

1. $x > -3$

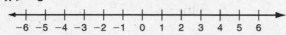

2. $z < 0$

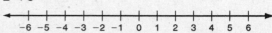

$x \le 4$

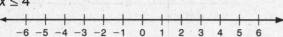

$z > 2$

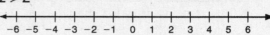

intersection: $x > -3$ AND $x \le 4$

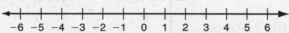

union: $z < 0$ OR $z > 2$

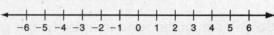

Write the compound inequality shown by each graph.

3.

_____

4.

_____

Fill in the blanks to solve each compound inequality. Graph the solutions.

5. $n + 5 < 2$ OR $n + 5 \ge 9$

  $-$____ $-$____ $-$____ $-$____

$n <$ ____   OR $n \ge$ ____

6. $-11 \le 2x - 1 \le 1$

$-11 \le 2x - 1$ AND $2x - 1 \le 1$

$+$____ $+$____ $+$____ $+$____

____ $\le 2x$ AND $2x \le$ ____

$\div$____ $\div$____ $\div$____ $\div$____

____ $\le x$ AND $x \le$ ____

Write a compound inequality for each problem. Graph the solutions.

7. To relieve arthritis, Dr. Stoll recommends taking between 400 and 600 mg of ibuprofen, inclusive.

_____

8. An advertisement for a part-time job says that the hourly rate is between $6.40 and $9.80 inclusive, depending on experience.

_____

Holt McDougal Algebra 1

LESSON
2-6

Practice B
Solving Compound Inequalities

Write the compound inequality shown by each graph.

1.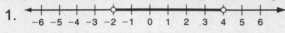

_____

2.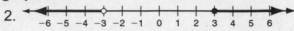

_____

3.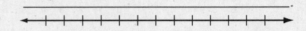

_____

4.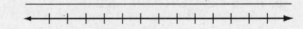

_____

Solve each compound inequality and graph the solutions.

5. $-15 < x - 8 < -4$

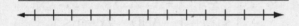

6. $12 \leq 4n < 28$

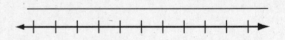

7. $-2 \leq 3b + 7 \leq 13$

8. $x - 3 < -3$ OR $x - 3 \geq 3$

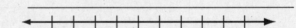

9. $5k \leq -20$ OR $2k \geq 8$

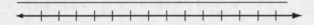

10. $2s + 3 \leq 7$ OR $3s + 5 > 26$

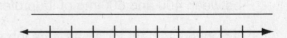

Write a compound inequality for each problem. Graph the solutions.

11. The human ear can distinguish sounds
    between 20 Hz and 20,000 Hz, inclusive.

_____

12. For a man to box as a welterweight, he must
    weigh more than 140 lbs, but at most 147 lbs.

_____

Holt McDougal Algebra 1

LESSON
2-6

Practice C
Solving Compound Inequalities

Solve each compound inequality and graph the solutions.

1. $-1 < 4x - 3 < 5$

_____

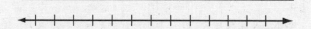

2. $3a - 5 \leq -2$ OR $3a - 5 \geq 13$

_____

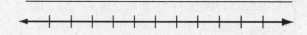

3. $-y - 2 < 6$ OR $4y + 8 \leq 20$

_____

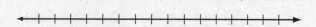

4. $3 \leq -2x + 1 \leq 9$

_____

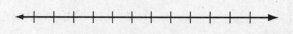

5. $-5k < -10$ OR $3k > -9$

_____

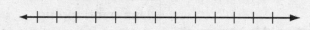

6. $\frac{1}{2}z + 3 < -4$ OR $\frac{2}{3}z - 1 \geq \frac{1}{5}$

_____

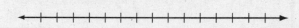

7. $-2 \leq \frac{n+2}{3} \leq 4$

_____

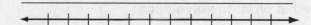

8. $p + 4 > 6$ AND $3p \leq -18$

_____

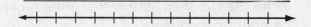

9. The United States Postal Service charges a "nonmachinable surcharge" for first-class mail if the length of the envelope (parallel to the address) divided by the height of the envelope is less than 1.3 or more than 2.5. Charlene has an envelope with a height of 3.5 inches. Write a compound inequality to show the lengths in inches for which Charlene will have to pay the surcharge.
Graph the solutions.

_____

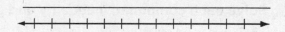

Holt McDougal Algebra 1

Name _____ Date _____ Class _____

Review for Mastery
Solving Compound Inequalities

Compound inequalities using AND require you to find solutions so that two inequalities will be satisfied at the same time.

Solve $2 < x + 3 \le 5$ and graph the solutions.

The two inequalities are: $2 < x + 3$ AND $x + 3 \le 5$.

Solve $2 < x + 3$.   Solve $x + 3 \le 5$.

$2 < x + 3$ $x + 3 \le 5$

$\underline{-3 \quad -3}$ *Add –3 to both sides.* $\underline{-3 \quad -3}$ *Add –3 to both sides.*

$-1 < x$ $x \le 2$

Graph $x > -1$.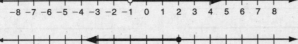

Graph $x \le 2$.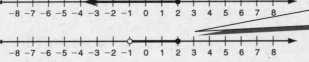

Graph $-1 < x \le 2$.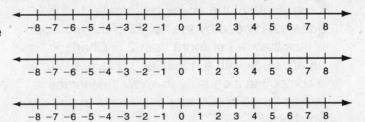

> Use **overlapping** regions for compound inequalities with **AND**.

Write the two inequalities that must be solved in order to solve each compound inequality.

1. $-3 < x - 4 \le 10$ _____ AND _____

2. $8 \le m + 4 \le 15$ _____ AND _____

3. Graph $-2 \le w < 6$ by graphing each inequality separately. Then graph the compound inequality.

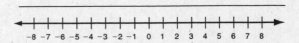

Solve each compound inequality and graph the solutions.

4. $-5 < k - 1 < 0$ 5. $-4 < 2x - 8 \le 6$

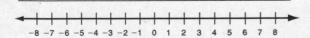

LESSON 2-6

Review for Mastery

Solving Compound Inequalities *continued*

Compound inequalities using OR require you to find solutions that satisfy either inequality.

Solve $4x > 12$ OR $3x \leq -15$ and graph the solutions.

The two inequalities are: $4x > 12$ OR $3x \leq -15$.

Solve $4x > 12$.

$$\frac{4x}{4} > \frac{12}{4} \quad \textit{Divide both sides by 4.}$$

$$x > 3.$$

Solve $3x \leq -15$.

$$\frac{3x}{3} \leq \frac{-15}{3} \quad \textit{Divide both sides by 3.}$$

$$x \leq -5$$

Graph $x > 3$.

Graph $x \leq -5$.

Graph $x > 3$ OR $x \leq -5$.

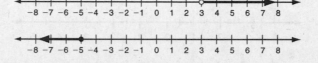

> Use **both** regions for compound inequalities with **OR**.

Write the compound inequality shown by each graph.

6. 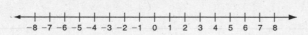 _____

7. _____

8. Graph $k \leq -1$ OR $k > 4$ by graphing each inequality separately. Then graph the compound inequality.

Solve each compound inequality and graph the solutions.

9. $x + 2 \geq 5$ OR $x + 6 < 2$

10. $6b \geq 42$ OR $3b \leq -3$

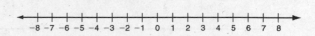

Holt McDougal Algebra 1

LESSON 2-6

Challenge

Solving Compound Inequalities

The inequality $a \le x \le b$, where $a < b$, is the set of all real numbers between a and b, including a and b. The corresponding set of points on the number line is called a *closed inverval*.

In Exercises 1–7, n is an integer and $n - \dfrac{1}{4} \le x \le n + \dfrac{1}{4}$. Graph the

solutions for the given values of n on the number line below.

1. $n = 0$ 2. $n = 0$ or $n = 1$

3. $n = 0$ or $n = -1$ 4. $n = -2, -1, 0, 1,$ or 2

5. $n = -3, -2, -1, 0, 1, 2,$ or 3 6. $n = -4, -3, -2, -1, 0, 1, 2, 3,$ or 4

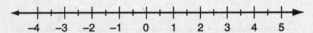

7. Suppose that the graphs for all values of n are shown on the number line. Describe the graph. _____

_____

Let n be an integer. For each set of intervals on the given number line, write a compound inequality involving n, x, and a conjunction to describe the entire graph.

8. _____

9. _____

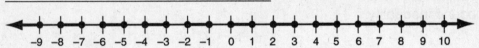

10. _____

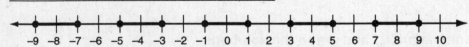

11. a. Let n be a nonzero integer. Describe the interval $1 - \dfrac{1}{n} \le x \le 1 + \dfrac{1}{n}$.

_____

   b. What can you say about the interval as n gets larger?

_____

LESSON
2-6

Problem Solving
Solving Compound Inequalities

Write and solve an inequality for each situation.

1. The Mexican Tetra is a tropical fish that requires a water temperature between 68 and 77 degrees Fahrenheit, inclusive. An aquarium is heated 8 degrees so that a Tetra can live in it. What temperatures could the water have been before the heating?

   _____

   _____

2. Nerissa's car can travel between 380 and 410 miles on a full tank of gas. She filled her gas tank and drove 45 miles. How many more miles can she drive without running out of gas?

   _____

   _____

3. A local company is hiring trainees with less than 1 year of experience and managers with 5 or more years of experience. Graph the solutions.

   _____

   _____

   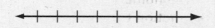

4. Marty's allowance is doubled and is now between $10 and $15, inclusive. What amounts could his allowance have been before the increase? Graph the solutions.

   _____

   _____

   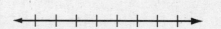

The elliptical orbits of planets bring them closer to and farther from the Sun at different times. The closest (perihelion) and furthest (aphelion) points are given for three planets below. Use this data to answer questions 5–7.

5. Which inequality represents the distances (in 10^6 km) d from the sun to Neptune?

   A $d \leq 4444.5$

   B $d \leq 4545.7$

   C $4444.5 \leq d \leq 4545.7$

   D $d = 4444.5$ OR $d \geq 4545.7$

Planet	Perihelion (in 10^6 km)	Aphelion (in 10^6 km)
Uranus	2741.3	3003.6
Neptune	4444.5	4545.7
Pluto	4435.0	7304.3

6. A NASA probe is traveling between Uranus and Neptune. It is currently between their orbits. Which inequality shows the possible distance p from the probe to the Sun?

   F $1542.1 < p < 1703.2$

   G $2741.3 < p < 4545.7$

   H $3003.6 < p < 4444.5$

   J $7185.8 < p < 7549.3$

7. At what distances o do the orbits of Neptune and Pluto overlap?

   A $4435.0 \leq o \leq 4444.5$

   B $4435.0 \leq o \leq 4545.7$

   C $4444.5 \leq o \leq 7304.3$

   D $4545.7 \leq o \leq 7304.3$

Holt McDougal Algebra 1

Name _____ Date _____ Class _____

Reading Strategies

Compare and Contrast

There are two types of compound inequalities: AND statements and OR statements. The chart below shows their similarities and differences.

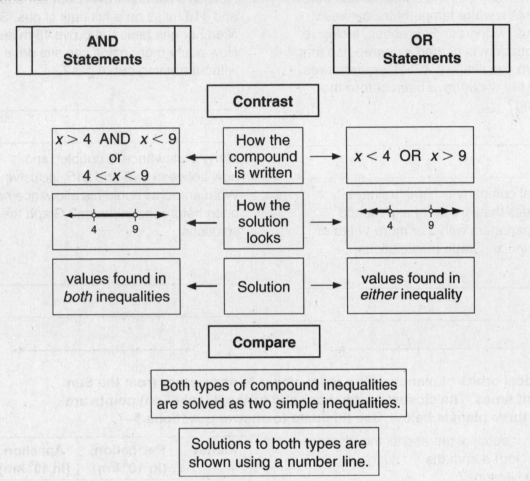

AND Statements		OR Statements
	Contrast	
$x > 4$ AND $x < 9$ or $4 < x < 9$	How the compound is written	$x < 4$ OR $x > 9$
(number line 4, 9)	How the solution looks	(number line 4, 9)
values found in *both* inequalities	Solution	values found in *either* inequality

Compare

Both types of compound inequalities are solved as two simple inequalities.

Solutions to both types are shown using a number line.

Answer each question using the examples given above.

1. Which has more *whole number* solutions: the AND or the OR statement? _____

2. List 3 *whole number* solutions to the AND statement. _____

3. List 3 *whole number* solutions to the OR statement. _____

4. Which is best described as having solutions *between* two values: the AND statement or the OR statement? _____

5. The shaded region in each Venn diagram represents the solutions to compound inequalities. Label them either *OR statement* or *AND statement*.

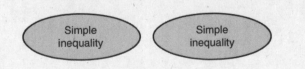

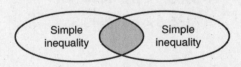

Holt McDougal Algebra 1

LESSON 2-7

Practice A
Solving Absolute-Value Inequalities

Fill in the blanks to solve each inequality.

1. $|x| + 7 \le 9$

    $-\underline{\quad} - \underline{\quad}$

    $\quad |x| \le \underline{\quad}$

    $x \ge \underline{\quad}$ AND $x \le \underline{\quad}$

2. $|x - 1| > 3$

    $x - 1 < \underline{\quad}$ OR $x - 1 > \underline{\quad}$

    $+ \underline{\quad} + \underline{\quad} \quad + \underline{\quad} + \underline{\quad}$

    $x < \underline{\quad}$ OR $\quad x > \underline{\quad}$

Solve each inequality and graph the solutions.

3. $|x| + 1 < 5$

    _____

    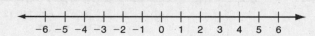

4. $|x + 2| \le 2$

    _____

    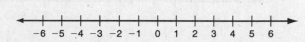

5. $5|x| \le 25$

    _____

    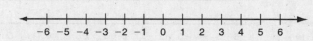

6. $|x| - 4 > -2$

    _____

    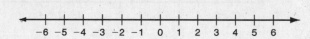

7. $|x - 1| \ge 3$

    _____

    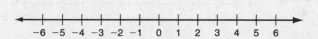

8. $|x + 3| - 3 > -1$

    _____

    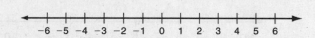

9. In Mr. Garcia's class, a student receives a B if the average of the student's test scores is 85 or if the average of the scores differs from this value by at most 4 points. Write and solve an absolute-value inequality to find the range of scores that results in a B.

    _____

    _____

Holt McDougal Algebra 1

Name _____ Date _____ Class_____

Practice B
Solving Absolute-Value Inequalities

Solve each inequality and graph the solutions.

1. $|x| - 2 \leq 3$

_____

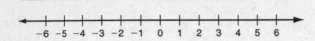

2. $|x + 1| + 5 < 7$

_____

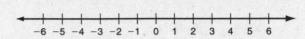

3. $3|x - 6| \leq 9$

_____

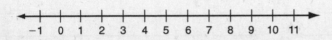

4. $|x + 3| - 1.5 < -2.5$

_____

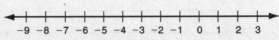

5. $|x| + 17 > 20$

_____

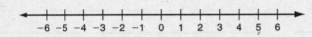

6. $|x - 6| - 7 > -3$

_____

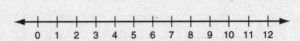

7. $\frac{1}{2}|x + 5| \geq 2$

_____

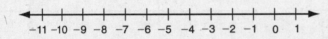

8. $2|x - 2| \geq 3$

_____

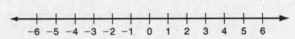

9. The organizers of a drama club wanted to sell 350 tickets to their show. The actual sales were no more than 35 tickets from this goal. Write and solve an absolute-value inequality to find the range of the number of tickets that may have been sold.

_____

10. The temperature at noon in Los Angeles on a summer day was 88 °F. During the day, the temperature varied from this by as much as 7.5 °F. Write and solve an absolute-value inequality to find the range of possible temperatures for that day.

_____

Holt McDougal Algebra 1

LESSON 2-7
Practice C
Solving Absolute-Value Inequalities

Solve each inequality and graph the solutions.

1. $|x| - 7 < -4$

2. $|x - 3| + 0.7 < 2.7$

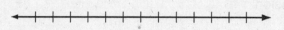

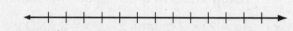

3. $\frac{1}{3}|x + 2| \leq 1$

4. $|x - 5| - 3 > 1$

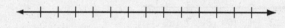

5. $|5x| \geq 15$

6. $\left|x + \frac{1}{2}\right| - 2 \geq 2$

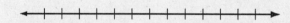

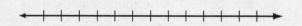

7. $|x - 2| + 7 \geq 3$

8. $4|x - 6| \geq -8$

9. The ideal temperature for a refrigerator is 36.5 °F. It is acceptable for the temperature to differ from this value by at most 1.5 °F. Write and solve an absolute-value inequality to find the range of acceptable temperatures.

_____

10. At a trout farm, most of the trout have a length of 23.5 cm. The length of some of the trout differs from this by as much as 2.1 cm. Write and solve an absolute-value inequality to find the range of lengths of the trout.

_____

Holt McDougal Algebra 1

LESSON 2-7

Review for Mastery

Solving Absolute-Value Inequalities

To solve an absolute-value inequality, first use inverse operations to isolate the absolute-value expression. Then write and solve a compound inequality.

Solve $|x - 2| + 8 < 10$.

Step 1: Isolate the absolute-value expression.

$|x - 2| + 8 < 10$

$\underline{ -8 \quad -8}$ *Subtract 8 from both sides.*

$|x - 2| \quad < \quad 2$

Step 2: Solve a compound inequality.

$|x - 2| < 2$ means $x - 2 > -2$ AND $x - 2 < 2$.

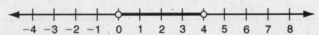   *Solve each inequality.*

$x \quad > \quad 0$ AND $x \quad < 4$

Graph the solution as shown.

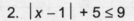

Solve each inequality and graph the solutions.

1. $|x| + 12 < 16$

_____

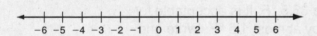

2. $|x - 1| + 5 \le 9$

_____

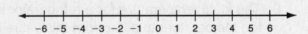

3. $7|x| \le 21$

_____

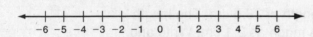

4. $|x + 4| - 3 < -2$

_____

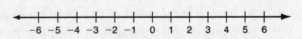

LESSON 2-7

Review for Mastery

Solving Absolute-Value Inequalities (continued)

You can use a similar method to solve absolute-value inequalities that involve a greater-than symbol (>). As always, the first step is to isolate the absolute-value expression. Then work with a compound inequality.

Solve $|x - 5| - 4 > -1$.

Step 1: Isolate the absolute-value expression.

$$|x - 5| - 4 > -1$$

$$\underline{\quad\quad +4 \quad +4} \qquad \text{Add 4 to both sides.}$$

$$|x - 5| \quad\quad > 3$$

Step 2: Solve a compound inequality.

$|x - 5| > 3$ means $x - 5 < -3$ OR $x - 5 > 3$.

$$\underline{+5 \quad +5} \qquad \underline{+5 \quad +5} \qquad \text{Solve each inequality.}$$

$$x \quad\quad < \quad 2 \text{ OR } x \quad\quad > 8$$

Graph the solution as shown.

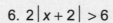

Solve each inequality and graph the solutions.

5. $4 + |x| \geq 5$

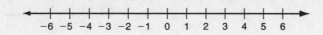

6. $2|x + 2| > 6$

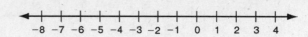

7. $|x| - 7 > -3$

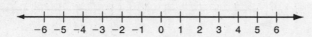

8. $|x - 4| + 5 \geq 8$

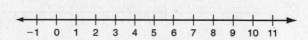

Holt McDougal Algebra 1

Name _____ Date _____ Class _____

Challenge
Solving More Complex Absolute-Value Inequalities

When you solve a multi-step inequality, you may need to simplify expressions, combine like terms, or use the Distributive Property. This also applies when you solve inequalities that involve absolute values.

For example, to solve $3(|x| + 4) < 18$, you can first use the Distributive Property on the left side of the equation to write $3|x| + 12 < 18$.

1. Show how to finish solving the above inequality. Graph the solutions.

_____

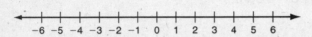

In some cases, you may need to combine like terms. For example, to solve $6|x| - 5 + 3|x| \geq 22$, first combine the absolute-value terms to write $9|x| - 5 \geq 22$.

2. Show how to finish solving the above inequality. Graph the solutions.

_____

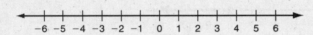

Solve each inequality and graph the solutions.

3. $5|x| + 1 - 3|x| \leq 3$

_____

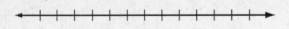

4. $2(5 + |x|) < 13$

_____

5. $7|x + 1| - 5|x + 1| > 4$

_____

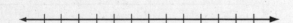

6. $3(|x - 2| + 1) \geq -1$

_____

Holt McDougal Algebra 1

LESSON 2-7

Problem Solving
Solving Absolute-Value Inequalities

Write the correct answer.

1. A carpenter cuts boards that are 2 meters long. It is acceptable for the length to differ from this value by at most 0.05 meters. Write and solve an absolute-value inequality to find the range of acceptable lengths.

   _____

   _____

2. During a workout, Vince tries to keep his heart rate at 134 beats per minute. His actual heart rate varies from this value by as much as 8 beats per minute. Write and solve an absolute-value inequality to find Vince's range of heart rates.

   _____

   _____

3. Mai thinks of a secret number. She says that her secret number is more than 11 units away from 50. Write an absolute-value inequality that gives the possible values of Mai's number.

   _____

   _____

4. Boxes of cereal are supposed to weigh 15.3 ounces each. A quality-control manager finds that the boxes are no more than 0.4 ounces away from this weight. Write an absolute-value inequality that gives the range of possible weights of the boxes.

   _____

   _____

The table gives the typical lifespan for several mammals. Use the table for questions 5-7. Select the best answer.

5. Which absolute-value inequality gives the number of years a goat may live?

   A $|x - 6| \leq 11$ C $|x - 24| \leq 6$

   B $|x - 15| \leq 9$ D $|x - 30| \leq 9$

7. The inequality $|x - 17| \leq c$ gives the number of years a panda may live. What is the value of c?

   A 3   C 14

   B 6   D 20

6. Which mammal has a lifespan that can be represented by the absolute-value inequality $|x - 12.5| \leq 2.5$?

   F Antelope   H Otter

   G Koala   J Wolf

Mammal	Lifespan (years)	Mammal	Lifespan (years)
Antelope	10 to 25	Otter	15 to 20
Goat	6 to 24	Panda	14 to 20
Koala	10 to 15	Wolf	13 to 15

Source:

http://www.sandiegozoo.org/animalbytes/a-mammal.html

LESSON 2-7

Reading Strategies
Use a Model

You can use a number line to help you solve absolute-value inequalities that have the form $|x - b| \leq c$ or $|x - b| < c$. The following steps show how to use this method to solve $|x - 1| \leq 3$.

Step 1: Plot the value of *b* on the number line.

In $|x - 1| \leq 3$, $b = 1$
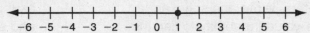

Step 2: Plot the two points that are *c* units away from *b*.

In this case, $c = 3$.
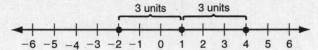

Step 3: Shade the points in between.

The solution is $-2 \leq x \leq 4$
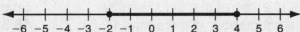

Answer each question.

1. When you use a number line to solve the inequality $|x - 5| < 4$, which point should you plot first?

   _____

2. Which points should you plot next?

   _____

3. Graph the solutions of $|x - 5| < 4$ on the number line.
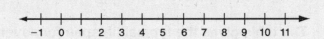

4. When you use a number line to solve the inequality $|x + 1| \leq 2$, which point should you plot first?
   (Hint: The inequality can be written as $|x - (-1)| \leq 2$)

   _____

5. Which points should you plot next?

   _____

6. Graph the solutions of $|x + 1| \leq 2$ on the number line.
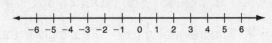

7. Use this method to graph the solutions of $|x + 2| < 1$.
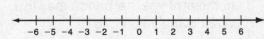

Holt McDougal Algebra 1

Date _____

Dear Family,

As you probably know from the news, media, or your own career, graphs are used to represent many different situations. Your child will make and interpret graphs that show how two variables are related. He or she will identify special relationships called *functions*, and use functions to model real-world data.

The graph at right shows how the speed of a horse changes with time during a race. Using words such as increasing, constant, or dropping, you could write a verbal description of how the speed changes. Likewise, you could use a verbal description to sketch a graph.

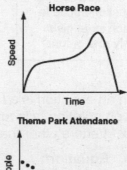

The horse race graph above is an example of a **continuous graph** because it is created by a connected line or curve. In contrast, **discrete graphs** show distinct points. The theme park graph at right is an example of a discrete graph, because years and people are counted with whole numbers.

Each point on a graph can be written as an ordered pair. So, a relationship can also be given as a set of ordered pairs. In mathematics, any set of ordered pairs is a **relation**. Here are four ways to represent the same relation:

List: {(5, 3), (4, 6), (3, 2), (1, 0)}

Table:

x	y
5	3
4	6
3	2
1	0

Mapping Diagram:

Graph:

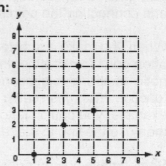

The **domain** of a relation is the set of *x*-coordinates. The **range** is the set of *y*-coordinates. When each value in the domain is paired with exactly one value in the range, you have a special type of relation called a **function**.

The relation shown above is a function.

Holt McDougal Algebra 1

Any equation with two variables represents a relation. If for each input (*x*-value) there is only one output (*y*-value), then the equation is a function.

Equation: $y = 3x + 2$

This equation is a function because each input gives only one output.

input	output
x	*y*
−2	−4
−1	−1
0	2
1	5

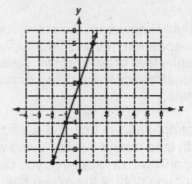

When an equation is a function, **function notation** can be used. In function notation, *y* is replaced with $f(x)$, read "function of *x*" or "*f* of *x*." Letters other than *f* can be used too: $g(x)$, $h(x)$, etc.

Equation: $y = 3x + 2$ **Function:** $f(x) = 3x + 2$

To evaluate a function, you input a value for *x*.

For $f(x) = 3x + 2$, find $f(x)$ when $x = 3$.
$$f(x) = 3x + 2$$
$$f(3) = 3(3) + 2$$
$$= 11$$

Input 3 for *x*.

The output is 11.

You graph a function by evaluating it for several *x*-values, plotting points, and connecting the points with a smooth line or curve.

When you make a **scatter plot** of real-world data, the points often don't form a smooth line or curve. However, you might notice a strong relationship that you can approximate with a function. With this scatter plot of snowboarding participants, for example, you could sketch a **trend line** that closely fits the data, then use the line to make predictions for the future.

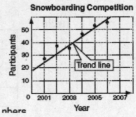

Snowboarding Competition

Sometimes you can notice a pattern in a list, or **sequence**, of numbers. If the pattern changes by a **common difference**, the sequence is called an **arithmetic sequence**.

In the sequence 5, 2, −1, −4, −7, ..., the common difference is −3 because $5 + (-3) = 2$, $2 + (-3) = -1$, and so on.
Using the formula, $a_n = a_1 + (n - 1)d$, students can find the value of any term in an arithmetic sequence as long as they know the first term a_1 and the common difference *d*.

LESSON 3-1

Practice A
Graphing Relationships

For each, write if the height is *rising*, *falling*, or *staying the same*.

1.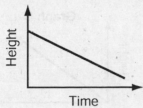

2.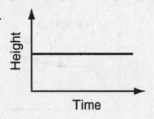

3.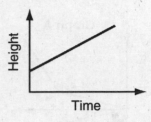

_____   _____   _____

Choose the graph that best represents each situation.

Graph A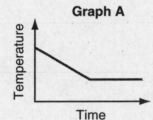

Graph B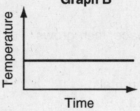

Graph C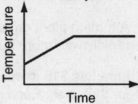

4. The temperature of the water in a glass remained constant.

_____

5. The temperature of the water in a glass rose steadily for several hours until it reached room temperature, then remained constant.

_____

6. The temperature of the water in a glass cooled down steadily with the addition of ice, then remained constant when all the ice had melted.

_____

7. Don's hair grows steadily longer between haircuts. Sketch a graph to show the length of Don's hair between two haircuts. Is the graph continuous or discrete?

_____

Write a possible situation for the graph.

8.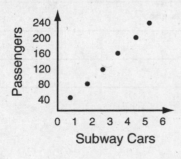

_____

_____

_____

LESSON 3-1

Practice B
Graphing Relationships

Choose the graph that best represents each situation.

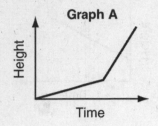

Graph A

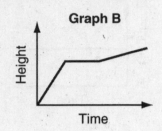

Graph B

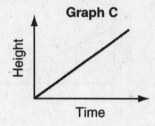

Graph C

1. A tomato plant grows taller at a steady pace. _____

2. A tomato plant grows quickly at first, remains a constant height during a dry spell, then grows at a steady pace. _____

3. A tomato plant grows at a slow pace, then grows rapidly with more sun and water. _____

4. Lora has $15 to spend on movie rentals for the week. Each rental costs $3. Sketch a graph to show how much money she might spend on movies in a week. Tell whether the graph is continuous or discrete.

_____

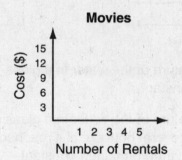

Movies

Write a possible situation for each graph.

5.

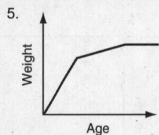

_____
_____
_____
_____

6.

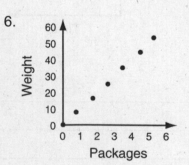

_____
_____
_____
_____

Holt McDougal Algebra 1

LESSON 3-1

Practice C

Graphing Relationships

Choose the graph that best represents each situation.

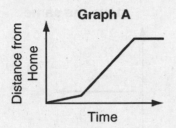

Graph A

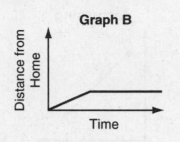

Graph B

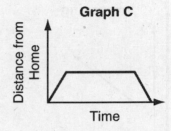

Graph C

1. A person leaves home, drives through town, then on the highway, and finally stops at a rest area.

   _____

2. A person leaves home, drives to the other end of town and buys groceries, then returns home.

   _____

3. A person walks to a friend's house where she stays overnight.

   _____

4. Franco's heart rate increases steadily as he does some warm-up exercises. He then maintains a steady heart rate for several minutes as he jogs. Finally, his heart rate slows down to normal with his cool-down walk. Sketch a graph to show Franco's heart rate over time as he exercises. Tell whether the graph is continuous or discrete.

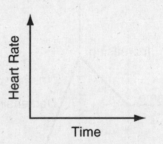

   _____

Write a possible situation for each graph.

5.

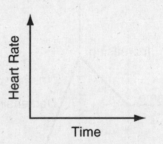

   _____

   _____

   _____

6.

   _____

   _____

   _____

Holt McDougal Algebra 1

Name _____ Date _____ Class _____

Review for Mastery
Graphing Relationships

Graphs are a way to turn words into pictures. Be sure to read the graphs from left to right.

increasing	**decreasing**	**stays the same**

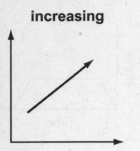 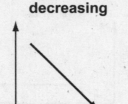 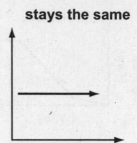

Other descriptions:	Other descriptions:	Other descriptions:
rose	fell	constant
gained	lessened	steady
grew	diminished	continuous

You can divide the graph into sections every time the graph changes directions. Then label each section.

Picture

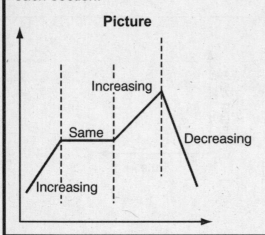

Words

This graph increases, then stays constant, increases again, and finally decreases sharply.

Divide each graph into sections where the graph changes directions.
Then label the sections as *increasing, decreasing,* or *same.*

1.
Graph A

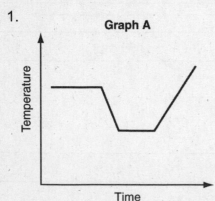

2.
Graph B

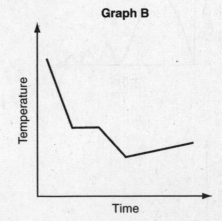

3. Which graph above shows that the air temperature
   fell steadily, leveled off, fell again, and then
   increased slightly?   _____

Review for Mastery

Graphing Relationships continued

A graph can be continuous or discrete. Continuous means the situation can include fractions or decimals. Discrete means the situation must have only specific amounts.

Continuous	**Discrete**
time	people
temperature	animals
distance	objects

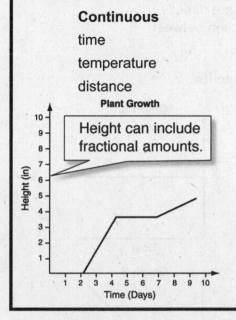

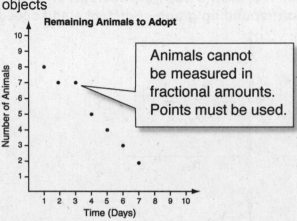

Sketch a graph of each situation. Tell whether the graph is continuous or discrete.

4. The heart rate of someone walking, then running, then resting.

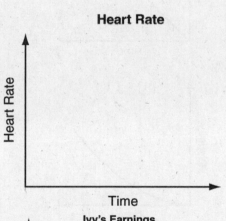

_____

5. Ivy is selling ice cream. Each ice cream costs $1.50. She has 6 ice creams to sell.

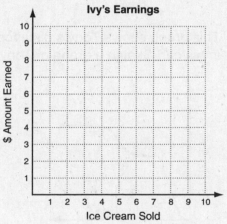

_____

Holt McDougal Algebra 1

LESSON 3-1

Challenge

Time, Distance, and Speed

You have already seen graphs that show an object's distance related to time or an object's speed related to time. However, for any one object, the distance it travels and how long it takes to travel that distance are directly related to its speed. See if you can make the graphical connection between distance and speed.

For 1–3, draw a line from each graph of distance and time to its corresponding graph of distance and speed.

1.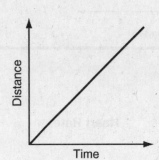

Graph A

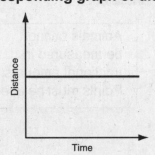

2.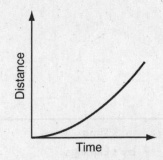

Graph B

Graph C

3.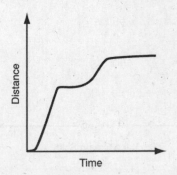

4. This graph shows Tony's distance from home as he drives away in his car. Sketch a graph of Tony's speed.

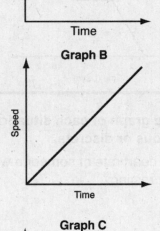

Holt McDougal Algebra 1

LESSON
3-1

Problem Solving
Graphing Relationships

Sketch a graph for the given situation. Tell whether the graph is discrete or continuous.

1. A giraffe is born 6 feet tall and continues to grow at a steady rate until it is fully grown.

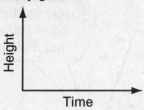

2. The price of a used car is discounted $200 each week.

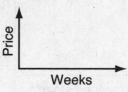

_____

3. A city planner buys more buses as the population of her city grows.

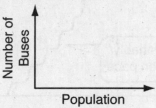

_____

4. Joseph is sky-diving. At first, he is free-falling rapidly and then he releases his parachute to slow his descent until he reaches the ground.

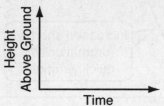

_____

Choose the graph that best represents the situation.

5. Rebekah turns on the oven and sets it to 300 °F. She bakes a tray of cookies and then turns the oven off.

   A Graph 1   C Graph 3

   B Graph 2   D Graph 4

6. Leon puts ice cubes in his soup to cool it down before eating it.

   F Graph 1   H Graph 3

   G Graph 2   J Graph 4

7. Barlee has the flu and her temperature rises slowly until it reaches 101 °F.

   A Graph 1   C Graph 3

   B Graph 2   D Graph 4

8. On a hot day, Karin walks into and out of an air-conditioned building.

   F Graph 1   H Graph 3

   G Graph 2   J Graph 4

Graph 1

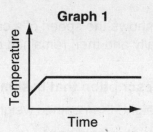

Graph 2

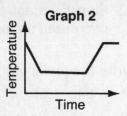

Graph 3

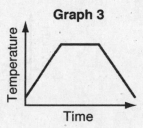

Graph 4

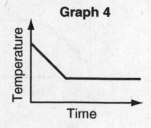

Holt McDougal Algebra 1

LESSON 3-1

Reading Strategies

Use a Model

A relationship between variables is often shown as a continuous graph.
Study the segments of the continuous graph below and the common
phrases that describe them.

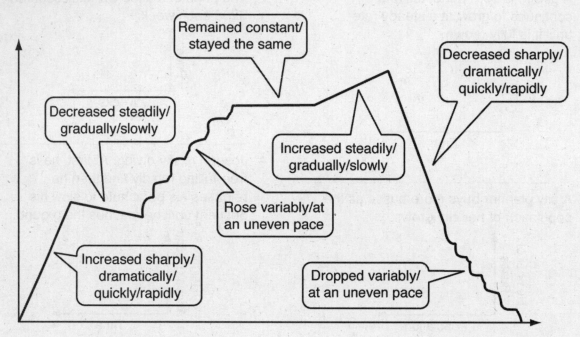

Answer the following.

1. Give two phrases that
   could describe this graph:

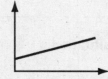

   _____

   _____

2. Sketch a graph that shows the speed of a car
   decreased dramatically and then remained constant.

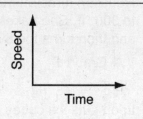

Write the letter of the description that best matches each graph.

A. A baby lost a little weight, then gained weight slowly.

B. A baby gained weight at a rapid pace.

C. A baby gained weight at an uneven pace, then maintained a constant weight.

3.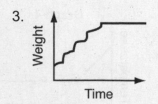

   _____

4.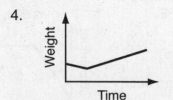

   _____

5.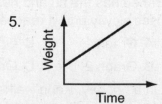

   _____

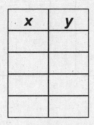

LESSON 3-2

Practice A
Relations and Functions

Express each relation as a table, as a graph, and as a mapping diagram.

1. {(–2, 5), (–1, 1), (3, 1), (–1, –2)}

x	y

2. {(5, 3), (4, 3), (3, 3), (2, 3), (1, 3)}

x	y

Give the domain and range of each relation. Tell whether the relation is a function. Explain.

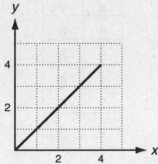

3.

D: _____

R: _____

Function? _____

Explain: _____

_____

_____

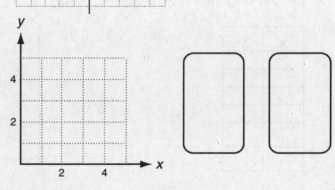

4.

D: _____

R: _____

Function? _____

Explain: _____

_____

_____

5.

x	y
1	4
2	5
0	6
1	7
2	8

D: _____

R: _____

Function? _____

Explain: _____

_____

_____

 Holt McDougal Algebra 1

LESSON 3-2

Practice B

Relations and Functions

Express each relation as a table, as a graph, and as a mapping diagram.

1. {(−5, 3), (−2, 1), (1, −1), (4, −3)}

x	y

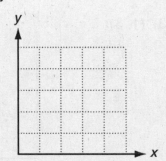

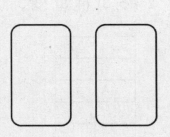

2. {(4, 0) (4, 1), (4, 2), (4, 3), (4, 4), (4, 5)}

x	y

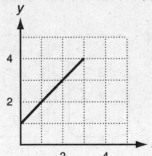

Give the domain and range of each relation. Tell whether the relation is a function. Explain.

3.

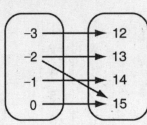

-3 → 12
-2 → 13
-1 → 14
0 → 15

4.

(graph)

5.

x	y
8	8
6	6
4	4
2	6
0	8

D: _____   D: _____   D: _____

R: _____   R: _____   R: _____

Function? _____   Function? _____   Function? _____

Explain: _____   Explain: _____   Explain: _____

_____   _____   _____

_____   _____   _____

_____   _____   _____

Practice C
Relations and Functions

Express each relation as a table, as a graph, and as a mapping diagram.

1. {(–3, 5), (–2, 4), (–1, 1), (–1, –3)}

x	y

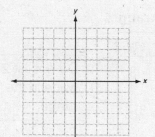

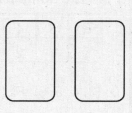

2. {(–2, 0), (–2, 1), (–2, 2), (–2, 3), (–2, 4), (–2, 5)}

x	y

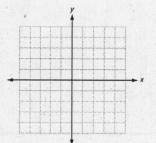

Give the domain and range of each relation. Tell whether the relation is a function. Explain.

3.

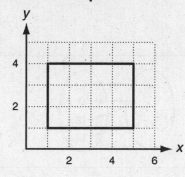

4.

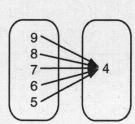

5.

x	y
1	1
2	2
3	3
4	4
5	5

D: _____   D: _____   D: _____

R: _____   R: _____   R: _____

Function? _____   Function? _____   Function? _____

Explain: _____   Explain: _____   Explain: _____

_____   _____   _____

_____   _____   _____

_____   _____   _____

Holt McDougal Algebra 1

Review for Mastery

Relations and Functions

A **relation** is a set of ordered pairs. The relation can be in the form of a table, graph, or mapping diagram. The **domain** is all the *x*-values. The **range** is all the *y*-values.

Find the domain and range.

x	3	4	5	6
y	1	2	2	3

Do not list 2 twice in the range.

D: {3, 4, 5, 6}; R: {1, 2, 3}

Find the domain and range.

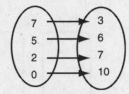

D: {7, 5, 2, 0}; R: {3, 6, 7, 10}

Find the domain and range.

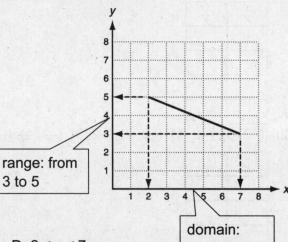

range: from 3 to 5

domain: from 2 to 7

D: 2 ≤ x ≤ 7
R: 3 ≤ y ≤ 5

Find the domain and range of each relation.

1.

x	−2	−1	0	1
y	4	1	0	4

_____

2. (4, 5) (−2, 6) (−5, 12)

_____

3.

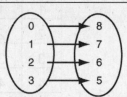

_____

4.

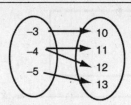

_____

5.

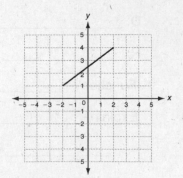

_____

6.

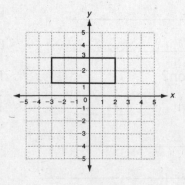

_____

Holt McDougal Algebra 1

LESSON
3-2

Review for Mastery

Relations and Functions continued

A **function** is a type of relation where each *x* value (domain) can be paired with only one *y* value (range).

Functions

x	2	3	4	5
y	3	4	4	6

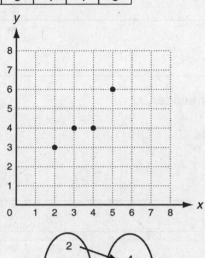

6 is paired with 2 and 3.

Not functions

x	5	6	6	7
y	1	2	3	4

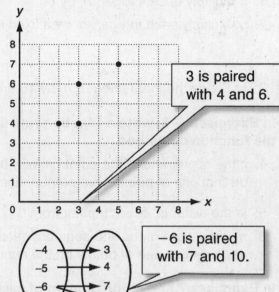

3 is paired with 4 and 6.

−6 is paired with 7 and 10.

Tell whether the relation is a function. Explain.

7.

x	−2	−3	−3	−4
y	1	2	3	4

8.

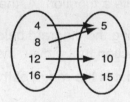

_____

_____

_____

_____

9.

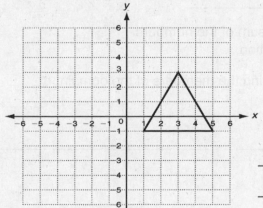

_____

_____

Holt McDougal Algebra 1

Name_____ Date _____ Class _____

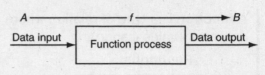

Challenge
Relations and Functions

A function is a correspondence, *f*, between two sets, *A* and *B*, such that each member of *A* is assigned exactly one member of *B*. The diagram shows a function as a dynamic process.

In Exercises 1–3, suppose that the input set, *A*, is the set of integers. Describe the range of each function.

1. *f*: Multiply each integer, *n*, by 5. _____

2. *g*: Multiply each integer, *n*, by a fixed integer, *k*.

   _____

3. *h*: Divide the input integer, *n*, by 10 and write the remainder, *r*. _____

In Exercises 4–6, write a function rule that represents the function described.

4. *j*: the coordinate of the point halfway between each distinct pair of points on a number line _____

5. *k*: the distance of each point from 0 _____

6. *m*: the length of the line segment determined by each distinct pair of points on the number line _____

In Exercises 7 and 8, the domain of each function is the set of all squares.

7. a. Write a function, *P*, that gives the perimeter of any square. _____

   b. Write a function, *A*, that gives the area of any square. _____

8. a. Using the diagram below, describe the function that moves the square from A to B. _____

   b. What is the range of the function in part **a**?

   _____

   _____

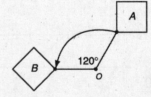

9. Suppose that you roll two number cubes. The sum of the numbers that are showing can be represented by a function.

   a. In the space at the right, make a table showing the members of the domain.

   b. What is the range of the function?

   _____

Holt McDougal Algebra 1

Name _____ Date _____ Class _____

Problem Solving
Relations and Functions

Give the domain and range of each relation and tell whether it is a function.

1. The mapping diagram shows the ages *x* and grade level *y* of four children.

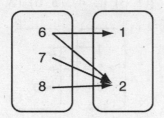

_____

_____

_____

2.

Age x	Shoe Size y
6	8
9	10
12	10
15	10.5
18	11

_____

_____

_____

3. The list represents the number of cars sold and the bonus received by the salespeople of a car dealership.

   {(1, 50), (2, 50), (3, 100), (4, 150)}

_____

_____

_____

4. A 2-inch-tall plant grows at a rate of 2.5 inches every week for 5 weeks. Let *x* represent the number of weeks and *y* represent the height of the plant.

_____

_____

_____

Use the graph below to answer questions 5–6. A conservation group has been working to increase the population of a herd of Asian elephants. The graph shows the results of their efforts. Select the correct answer.

5. Which relation represents the information in the graph?

   A {(1, 4.5), (2, 6), (3, 10), (4, 14.5)}

   B {(1, 5), (2, 6), (3, 10), (4, 15)}

   C {(4.5, 1), (6, 2), (10, 3), (14.5, 4)}

   D {(5, 1), (6, 2), (10, 3), (15, 4)}

6. What is the range of the relation shown in the graph?

   F {0, 1, 2, 3, 4, 5}

   G {1, 2, 3, 4}

   H {4.5, 6, 10, 14.5}

   J {5, 6, 10, 15}

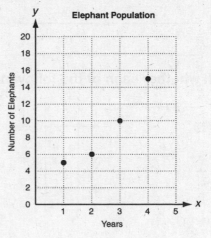

Holt McDougal Algebra 1

LESSON 3-2

Reading Strategies

Use Examples and Non-Examples

A **function** is defined as a relation that pairs each domain value with exactly one range value. No *x*-value can be repeated with a different *y*-value.

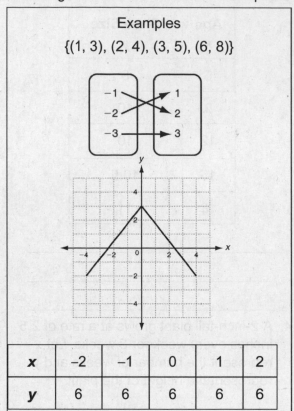

Examples

{(1, 3), (2, 4), (3, 5), (6, 8)}

x	−2	−1	0	1	2
y	6	6	6	6	6

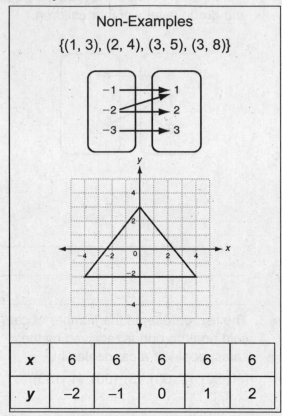

Non-Examples

{(1, 3), (2, 4), (3, 5), (3, 8)}

x	6	6	6	6	6
y	−2	−1	0	1	2

Answer the following.

1. Give your own example of a function in table form.

x				
y				

2. Give an example of a mapping diagram that is NOT a function.

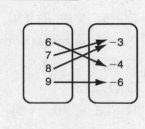

3. Explain why the relation in problem 2 is not a function.

_____

_____

Tell whether each of the following is a function by writing *yes* or *no*.

4. _____

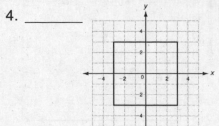

5. _____

x	y
−3	8
−2	5
−1	1
−1	4
−1	6

6. _____

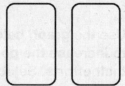

LESSON 3-3 Practice A
Writing Functions

Choose the equation from the box that describes each relationship.

1.

x	−3	−2	−1	0
y	−9	−6	−3	0

_____

$y = -3x$
$y = 3x$
$y = x - 3$

2. {(3, 0), (2, −1), (1, −2), (0, −3)} _____

3. {(0, 0), (1, −3), (2, −6), (3, −9)} _____

For each, write whether the given variable is *independent* or *dependent*.

4. Auto insurance costs increase with each accident and traffic violation.

• number of accidents/violations: _____

• cost of auto insurance: _____

5. Christian is buying several DVDs that cost $12 each.

• total cost of the DVDs: _____

• number of DVDs purchased: _____

Evaluate each function for the given input values.

6. For $f(x) = x + 7$, find $f(x)$ when $x = 3$ and when $x = -5$. _____ _____

7. For $g(x) = -2x$, find $g(x)$ when $x = 4$ and when $x = -1$. _____ _____

8. For $h(x) = 3x - 1$, find $h(x)$ when $x = -2$ and when $x = 7$. _____ _____

Complete the following.

9. Marlena is making her own beaded bracelets.   rule: _____
Each bracelet will have 10 beads. Write a function
rule to describe the number of beads she will use.   domain: _____
Find a reasonable domain and range for the function
if Marlena makes up to 7 bracelets.   range: _____

10. Giselle is going to rent a scooter for at least one   rule: _____
hour. The fee is $45 plus $5 for each hour it is
rented. Write a function rule to describe the total   domain: _____
cost of renting a scooter. Find a reasonable domain
and range for the function if Giselle has $65.   range: _____

Holt McDougal Algebra 1

LESSON
3-3

Practice B
Writing Functions

Determine a relationship between the *x*- and *y*-values. Write an equation.

1.

x	−4	−3	−2	−1
y	−1	0	1	2

_____

2. {(2, 3), (3, 5), (4, 7), (5, 9)}

_____

Identify the independent and dependent variables in each situation.

3. Ice cream sales increase when the temperature rises.

   I: _____

   D: _____

4. Food for the catered party costs $12.75 per person.

   I: _____

   D: _____

Identify the independent and dependent variables. Write a rule in function notation for each situation.

5. Carson charges $7 per hour for yard work.

   _____

   _____

   _____

6. Kay donates twice what Ed donates.

   _____

   _____

   _____

Evaluate each function for the given input values.

7. For $f(x) = 5x + 1$, find $f(x)$ when $x = 2$ and when $x = 3$. _____ _____

8. For $g(x) = -4x$, find $g(x)$ when $x = -6$ and when $x = 2$. _____ _____

9. For $h(x) = x - 3$, find $h(x)$ when $x = 3$ and when $x = 1$. _____ _____

Complete the following.

10. An aerobics class is being offered once a week for 6 weeks. The registration fee is $15 and the cost for each class attended is $10. Write a function rule to describe the total cost of the class. Find a reasonable domain and range for the function.

    _____

    _____

    _____

LESSON 3-3

Practice C

Writing Functions

Determine a relationship between the *x*- and *y*-values. Write an equation.

1.

x	−2	−1	0	1
y	4	1	0	1

_____

2. {(−1, −4), (0, −2), (2, 2), (5, 8)}

_____

Identify the independent and dependent variables in each situation.

3. More program money is given out to cities with a larger population.

I: _____

D: _____

4. Sales tax in the state of Maryland is 5% of the purchase price.

I: _____

D: _____

Identify the independent and dependent variables. Write a rule in function notation for each situation.

5. Meg earns a $5 flat fee plus $4.50 per student for a tutoring session.

_____

_____

_____

6. Jeb is allowed 2 hours less television time per week than his older brother.

_____

_____

_____

Evaluate each function for the given input values.

7. For $f(x) = 3x + 2$, find $f(x)$ when $x = 4$ and when $x = −1$. _____ _____

8. For $g(x) = −6x$, find $g(x)$ when $x = −5$ and when $x = 3$. _____ _____

9. For $h(x) = x^2 − 4$, find $h(x)$ when $x = 2$ and when $x = −7$. _____ _____

Complete the following.

10. A fitness class is being offered twice a week for four weeks. The registration fee is $8.50 and the cost for each class attended is $4.75. Write a function rule to describe the total cost of the class. Find a reasonable domain and range for the function.

_____

_____

_____

LESSON 3-3

Review for Mastery
Writing Functions

Functions have dependent and independent variables. The dependent variable will always depend on the independent variable.

Rewrite each situation using the word *depends*. Then identify the dependent and the independent variables.

An employee who works longer hours will receive a larger amount in her paycheck.

Rewrite sentence:

> The **amount of a paycheck** *depends* on the **number of hours worked**.

> Dependent: amount of paycheck   Independent: number of hours worked

A box with several books weighs more than a box with just a few books.

Rewrite sentence:

> The **weight of a box** *depends* on the **number of books in the box**.

> Dependent: weight of box   Independent: number of books in box

Rewrite each sentence using the word *depends*. Then identify the dependent and the independent variables.

1. A very large animal will eat many pounds of food.

   _____

   Dependent: _____

   Independent: _____

2. The fire was very large, so many firefighters were there.

   _____

   Dependent: _____

   Independent: _____

3. The temperature of the water on the heated stove rose each minute.

   _____

   Dependent: _____

   Independent: _____

4. The restaurant bill was low because only a few meals were ordered.

   _____

   Dependent: _____

   Independent: _____

LESSON 3-3

Review for Mastery

Writing Functions continued

After identifying the independent and dependent variables, you can write a rule in function notation. Remember that **f(x)** is the **dependent variable** and **x** is the **independent variable**.

Identify the dependent and independent variables. Write a function rule for each situation.

A zoo charges $6 for parking and $17.50 for each child.

1. *Identify the dependent and independent variables.*

The **cost of admission** *depends* on **the number of children**.

Dependent *f*(*x*): cost of admission   Independent *x*: number of children

2. *Write the equation in words.*

The cost of admission is $17.50 multiplied by the number of children plus $6 for parking.

3. *Write the function using cost of admission = f(x) and number of children = x.*

$$f(x) = \$17.50x + \$6.00$$

Evaluate the function above when x = 4 and x = 10.

x = 4	x = 10
$f(x) = \$17.50x + \$6.00$	$f(x) = \$17.50x + \$6.00$
$f(4) = \$17.50(4) + \$6.00$	$f(10) = \$17.50(10) + \$6.00$
$= \$70.00 + \$6.00$	$= \$175.00 + \$6.00$
$= \$76.00$	$= \$181.00$

Identify the dependent and the independent variables for each situation below. Write the function. Then evaluate the function for the given input values.

5. A limo service charges $90 for each hour.

Dependent *f*(*x*): _____

Independent *x*: _____

Function: _____

Evaluate for *x* = 2.

_____

Evaluate for *x* = 7.5.

_____

6. A computer support company charges $295 for the first hour plus $95 for each additional hour.

Dependent *f*(*x*): _____

Independent *x*: _____

Function: _____

Evaluate for *x* = 3.25.

_____

Evaluate for *x* = 8.

_____

LESSON 3-3

Challenge

Functioning in the Real World

A Celsius thermometer shows a reading of 40 °C. While you are looking at this thermometer, the local weather report on the radio gives a temperature of 104 °F. When you change to another local station, you hear a report of 112 °F.

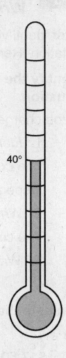

40°

1. Use the formula $F = \dfrac{9}{5}C + 32$ to find the Fahrenheit temperature

   corresponding to 40 °C. _____

2. Why do you suppose that you heard a different Fahrenheit temperature on one of the radio stations?

   _____

3. Explain why $F = \dfrac{9}{5}C + 32$ represents a function.

   _____

4. Complete the following ordered pairs for (C, F) by using the formula

   $F = \dfrac{9}{5}C + 32$:

   a. (25, _____)   b. (–10, _____)   c. (18, _____)   d. (_____, 86)

5. In part **d** of Exercise 4, you solved for C given F. Use the appropriate

   properties of equality to solve $F = \dfrac{9}{5}C + 32$ for C in terms of F. _____

6. Use the formula found in Exercise 5 to complete the following ordered pairs (C, F).

   a. (_____, 59)   b. (_____, 77)   c. (_____, –4)   d. (_____, 80)

7. Is this formula for C in terms of F also a function? Why or why not?

   _____

8. Functions that "undo" each other are called *inverse* functions. Start with 35 °C and use the first formula to find a value of F. Then use this value of F in the second formula to find a value of C. What happens?

   _____

9. Find the temperature at which the Celsius and the Fahrenheit temperatures are equivalent.

   _____

Holt McDougal Algebra 1

Name _____ Date _____ Class_____

LESSON 3-3

Problem Solving
Writing Functions

Identify the independent and dependent variables. Write a rule in function notation for each situation.

1. Each state receives electoral votes based on the number of representatives it has in the House of Representatives.

Representatives	2	4	6	8
Electoral Votes	4	6	8	10

_____

_____

_____

2. Terry has 30 pieces of gum and gives 2 pieces to each of his friends.

_____

_____

_____

3. Ronaldo is buying bacon that costs $4.29 per pound.

_____

_____

_____

4. A personal trainer charges $50 for the first session and $40 for every session thereafter.

_____

_____

_____

International travel and business require the conversion of American dollars into foreign currency. During part of 2005, one American dollar was worth 6 Croatian Kuna. Select the best answer.

5. An American bank wishes to convert d dollars into kuna. Which function rule describes the situation?

A $f(d) = \dfrac{d}{6}$ C $f(d) = \dfrac{6}{d}$

B $f(d) = 6d$ D $f(d) = d + 6$

6. A Croatian company already has $100,000 and is going to convert k kuna into dollars. Which function rule can be used to determine the total amount of American dollars this company will have?

F $f(x) = 100,000 + 6k$

G $f(x) = 100,000 + \dfrac{k}{6}$

H $f(x) = 100,000k + 6$

J $f(x) = 100,000 + \dfrac{6}{k}$

7. Macon has $100 and is thinking about converting some of it into kuna. What is a reasonable range for this situation?

A $0 \le y \le 6$ C $0 \le y \le 100$

B $0 \le y \le 16.7$ D $0 \le y \le 600$

8. Robin converts x dollars into y kuna. Which expression is the independent variable in this situation?

F x H $6x$

G y J $6y$

9. Jakov converts n kuna into c dollars. Which expression is the dependent variable in this situation?

A n C $\dfrac{n}{6}$

B c D $\dfrac{c}{6}$

Holt McDougal Algebra 1

LESSON 3-3 Reading Strategies
Understanding Vocabulary

To read and write functions, you must understand what is meant by an
independent variable and a *dependent variable*.

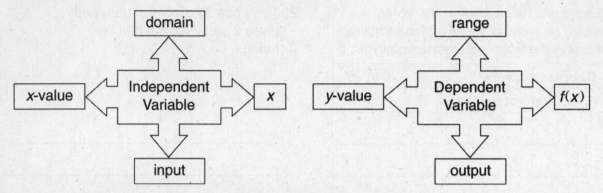

**Carmen attends a school with a dress code. She went
shopping and found acceptable shirts for $15 each.
Her mother has allowed her to buy up to 5 new shirts
for the school year.**

Independent variable: number of shirts
Dependent variable: total cost
The function that represents this relation is $f(x) = 15x$.
   Reasonable domain (*x*-values): {1, 2, 3, 4, 5}
   Reasonable range (*y*-values): {15, 30, 45, 60, 75}
When $x = 5$, $f(x) = 75$.
So, 5 shirts will cost $75.

Answer the following based on the situation below.

Molly is making greeting cards for 5 of her friends. Each card is to have 4 ribbons.

1. Identify each as either the independent or the dependent variable.

 "number of ribbons used"   _____

 "number of cards made"   _____

2. Write a function for the relation.   _____

3. What is the reasonable domain for this function? _____

4. What is the reasonable range for this function? _____

5. How many ribbons will Molly use if she makes 3 cards? _____

6. How many ribbons will Molly use if she makes 5 cards? _____

Name _____ Date _____ Class_____

LESSON 3-4

Practice A

Graphing Functions

Graph the function for the given domain.

1. $y = x + 2$; D: $\{-2, -1, 0, 1, 2\}$

x	$y = x + 2$	(x, y)

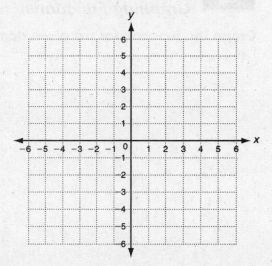

Graph the function. The domain is all real numbers.

2. $y = x^2 \div 2$

x	$y = x^2 \div 2$	(x, y)

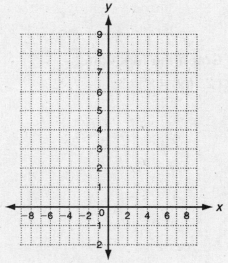

3. A Pacific salmon can swim at a maximum speed of 8 mi/h. The function $y = 8x$ describes how many miles *y* the fish swims in *x* hours. Graph the function. Use the graph to estimate the number of miles the fish swims in 3.5 hours.

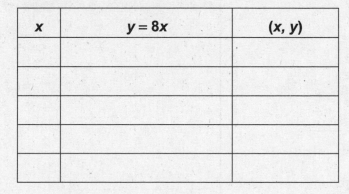

x	$y = 8x$	(x, y)

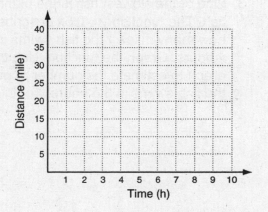

_____

Holt McDougal Algebra 1

LESSON
3-4

LESSON
3-4

Practice B

Graphing Functions

Graph the function for the given domain.

1. $y = |x| - 1$; D: $\{-1, 0, 1, 2, 3\}$

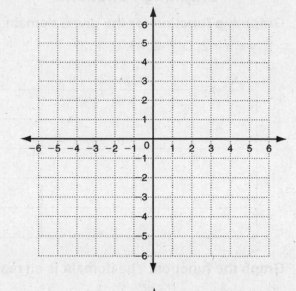

Graph the function.

2. $f(x) = x^2 - 3$

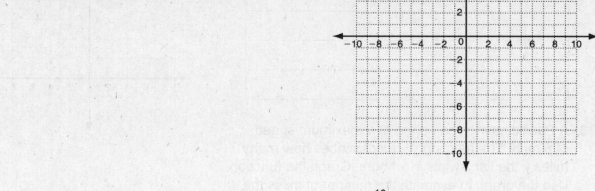

3. One of the slowest fish is the blenny fish. The function $y = 0.5x$ describes how many miles y the fish swims in x hours. Graph the function. Use the graph to estimate the number of miles the fish swims in 3.5 hours.

_____

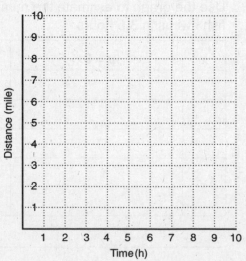

Holt McDougal Algebra 1

LESSON 3-4

Practice C
Graphing Functions

1. Graph $y = |x - 2| + 3$ for the following domain:
   $\{-2, 0, 2, 4, 6\}$

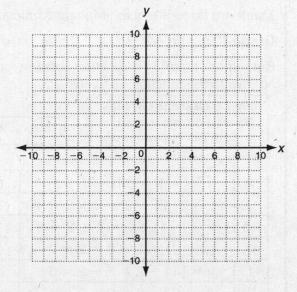

2. Graph $y = \left(\dfrac{x}{4}\right)^2 + 2$.

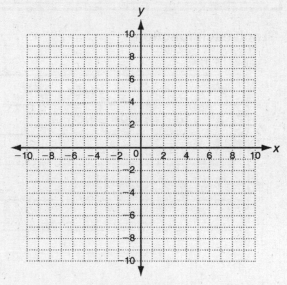

3. A human being can swim at a maximum rate of
   7.4 feet per second. The function $y = 7.4x$ describes
   how many feet y a person can swim in x seconds.
   Graph the function. Use the graph to estimate the
   maximum number of feet a person can swim in
   4.5 seconds.

   _____

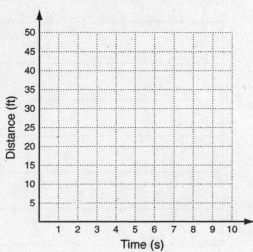

Holt McDougal Algebra 1

LESSON 3-4

Review for Mastery
Graphing Functions

There are three steps to graphing a function.

Graph $f(x) = |x| + 2$.

Remember that $f(x)$ is function notation for y, so rewrite the function as $y = |x| + 2$.

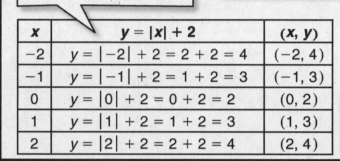

Step 1: Generate points.
Unless a domain is given, you can pick any values of x.

Step 2: Plot points.

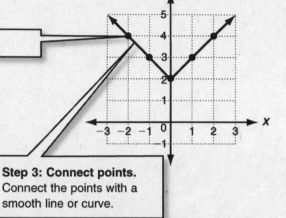

Step 3: Connect points.
Connect the points with a smooth line or curve.

x	$y = |x| + 2$	(x, y)
-2	$y = |-2| + 2 = 2 + 2 = 4$	$(-2, 4)$
-1	$y = |-1| + 2 = 1 + 2 = 3$	$(-1, 3)$
0	$y = |0| + 2 = 0 + 2 = 2$	$(0, 2)$
1	$y = |1| + 2 = 1 + 2 = 3$	$(1, 3)$
2	$y = |2| + 2 = 2 + 2 = 4$	$(2, 4)$

Graph each function.

1. $y = (x + 2)^2$

x	$y = (x + 2)^2$	(x, y)
-4	$y = (-4 + 2)^2 = (-2)^2 = $ _____	
-3	$y = (-3 + 2)^2 = (___)^2 = $ _____	
-2	$y = (___ + 2)^2 = (___)^2 = $ _____	
-1	$y = (____)^2 = (___)^2 = $ _____	
0	$y = $ _____	

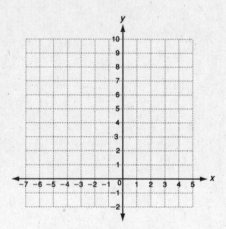

2. $f(x) = \dfrac{1}{2}x - 3$

x	$y = \dfrac{1}{2}x - 3$	(x, y)

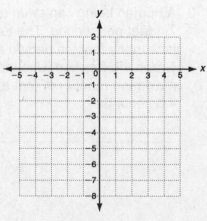

Holt McDougal Algebra 1

LESSON 3-4

Review for Mastery

Graphing Functions continued

You can use the graph of a function to find points that are generated by the function.

Use the graph of $f(x) = -x^2 + 4$ to find the value of $f(x)$ when $x = -3$.

Remember that $f(x)$ is function notation for y, so you need to find y when $x = -3$.

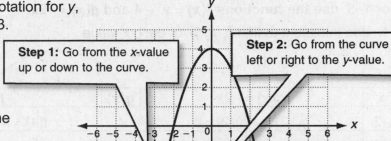

Step 1: Go from the x-value up or down to the curve.

Step 2: Go from the curve left or right to the y-value.

Because $(-3, -5)$ is a point on the graph of the function,

$f(x) = -5$ when $x = -3$.

Use this graph of $f(x) = 2x - 1$ to find these values.

3. $f(x) =$ _____ when $x = -1$

4. $f(x) =$ _____ when $x = 1$

5. $f(x) =$ _____ when $x = \frac{1}{2}$

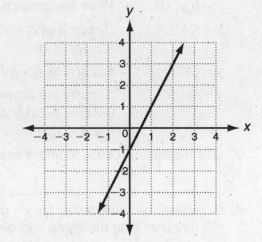

Use this graph of $f(x) = |5 - x|$ to find these values.

6. $f(x) =$ _____ when $x = 2$

7. $f(x) =$ _____ when $x = 6$

8. $x =$ _____ when $f(x) = 0$

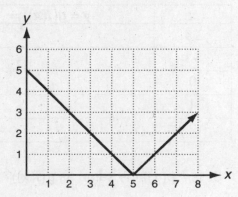

Holt McDougal Algebra 1

LESSON 3-4

Challenge
Composition of Functions

When the output of one function is used as the input of another, you have a **composition of functions.** The notation $f(g(x))$ means you input x into function g, and then use that output as the input for function f.

For 1–5, use the functions $f(x) = x^2 - 4$ and $g(x) = -2x$.

1. Use this table to find $f(g(x))$ for each x-value.

x	$g(x) = -2x$	$g(x)$	$f(x) = x^2 - 4$	$f(g(x))$
–2	$g(-2) = -2(-2) = 4$	4	$f(4) = 4^2 - 4 = 16 - 4 = 12$	12
–1				
0				
1				
2				

2. Use the first and last columns of the table to graph the function $y = f(g(x))$. Connect the points with a smooth curve.

Here is the algebra to find a "one-step" rule for $y = f(g(x))$.

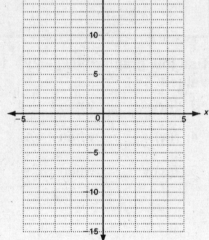

$y = f(g(x))$	*Write the composite function.*
$y = f(-2x)$	*Because $g(x) = -2x$, substitute $-2x$ for $g(x)$.*
$y = (-2x)^2 - 4$	*Substitute $-2x$ for x in $f(x) = x^2 - 4$.*
$y = 4x^2 - 4$	*Simplify the power:* $(-2x)^2 = (-2x)(-2x) = (-2)(-2)(x)(x) = 4x^2$.

3. Use a similar process to find a one-step rule for $y = g(f(x))$.

_____

4. Complete the table below for $y = g(f(x))$. Then graph the function. Use the same coordinate plane at right.

x	$y = g(f(x)) =$ _____	$(x, g(f(x)))$
–2		
–1		
0		
1		
2		

5. Is $f(g(x))$ the same as $g(f(x))$? _____

Holt McDougal Algebra 1

LESSON 3-4

Problem Solving

Graphing Functions

In 1998, Hurricane Bonnie approached the United States at a speed of 8 miles per hour. The function $y = 8x$ describes how many miles y Hurricane Bonnie traveled in x hours.

1. Complete the table by generating ordered pairs.

x	$y = 8x$	(x, y)
0		
1		
2		
3		
4		

2. Graph the function $y = 8x$.

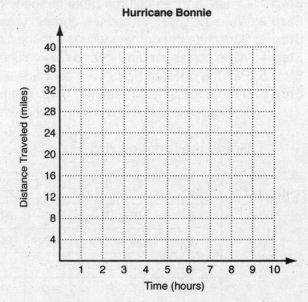

3. Use the graph to estimate how far Hurricane Bonnie traveled in 3.5 hours.

_____

Select the correct answer.

4. The graph below shows the relation between the cost of an item and the sales tax due. Which function is graphed below?

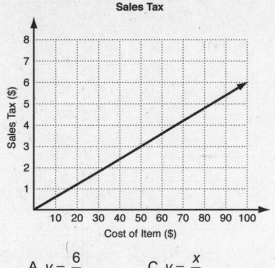

A $y = \dfrac{6}{x}$ C $y = \dfrac{x}{6}$

B $y = 0.06x$ D $y = 6x$

5. The graph below shows the relation between Jeremy's age and the number of times per year he refused to eat his brussel sprouts. Which function is graphed for the domain {1, 2, 3, 4, 5}?

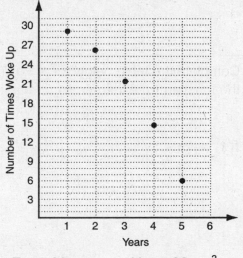

F $y = 30 - x$ H $y = 30 - x^2$

G $y = x + 28$ J $y = 29x$

Reading Strategies
Follow a Procedure

Whether graphing a function with a limited domain, or a domain of all real numbers, the procedure is almost the same. The steps of the procedure are listed below and shown in the following example.

Step 1: Create a three-column table headed "x", "$f(x)$", and "$(x, f(x))$".
Step 2: Write the given or chosen domain values in the "x" column.
Step 3: Substitute the domain values into the function and evaluate for $f(x)$.
Step 4: Write corresponding x- and $f(x)$-values as ordered pairs.
Step 5: Plot the ordered pairs on a coordinate grid.
Step 6: If the domain is all real numbers, connect the points with a smooth line/curve and put arrows on both ends.

Graph the function $f(x) = |x - 2|$.

Step1 →

x	$f(x)$	$(x, f(x))$
6	$|6 - 2| = |4| = 4$	$(6, 4)$
4	$|4 - 2| = |2| = 2$	$(4, 2)$
2	$|2 - 2| = |0| = 0$	$(2, 0)$
0	$|0 - 2| = |-2| = 2$	$(0, 2)$
-2	$|-2 - 2| = |-4| = 4$	$(-2, 4)$

Step5 →
Step6 →

Step2   Step3   Step4

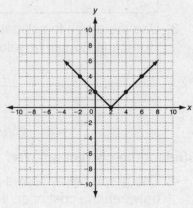

Graph each function using the procedure shown above.

1. $f(x) = x^2 - 8$; D: $\{-4, -2, 0, 2, 4\}$

2. $f(x) = -2x + 3$

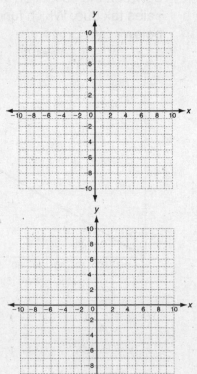

Holt McDougal Algebra 1

LESSON 3-5

Practice A

Scatter Plots and Trend Lines

1. The table shows the number of soft drinks sold at a small restaurant from 11:00 am to 1:00 pm. Graph a scatter plot using the given data.

Time of Day	11:00	11:30	12:00	12:30	1:00
Number of Drinks	20	29	34	49	44

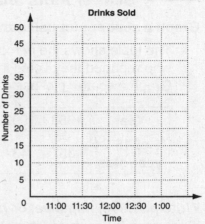

Write *positive, negative,* **or** *none* **to describe the correlation illustrated by each scatter plot.**

2.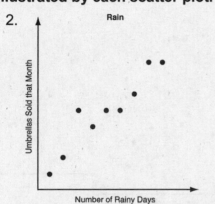

_____

3.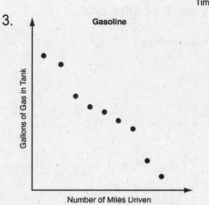

_____

Identify the correlation you would expect to see between each pair of data sets. Explain.

4. the temperature during the day and the number of people in the pool

_____

_____

5. the height of an algebra student and the number of phone calls they make in one week

_____

_____

6. The scatter plot at right shows a relationship between the number of batteries needed and the number of toys. Predict how many batteries will be needed for 11 toys.

_____

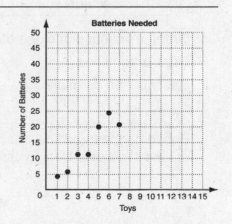

Holt McDougal Algebra 1

LESSON 3-5

Practice B

Scatter Plots and Trend Lines

Graph a scatter plot using the given data.

1. The table shows the percent of people ages 18–24 who reported they voted in the presidential elections. Graph a scatter plot using the given data.

Year	1988	1992	1996	2000	2004
% of 18-24 year olds	36	43	32	32	42

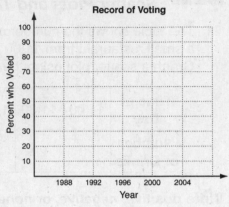

Write *positive*, *negative*, or *none* to describe the correlation illustrated by each scatter plot.

2.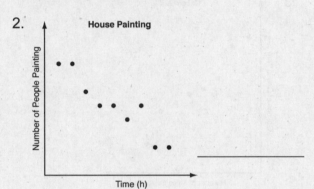

3.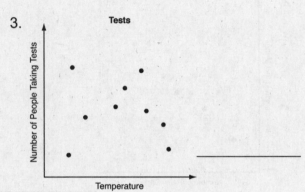

4. Identify the correlation you would expect to see between the number of pets a person has and the number of times they go to a pet store. Explain.

_____

_____

Neal kept track of the number of minutes it took him to assemble sandwiches at his restaurant. The information is in the table below.

Number of sandwiches	1	2	4	6	7
Minutes	3	4	5	6	7

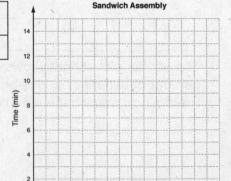

5. Graph a scatter plot of the data.

6. Draw a trend line.

7. Describe the correlation.

_____

8. Based on the trend line you drew, predict the amount of time it will take Neal to assemble 12 sandwiches.

_____

Holt McDougal Algebra 1

LESSON 3-5

Practice C
Scatter Plots and Trend Lines

Graph a scatter plot using the given data.

1. The table shows the average salary (rounded to the nearest hundred) for one type of worker, listed by decade. Graph a scatter plot using the given data.

Decade	1950	1960	1970	1980	1990
Avg. Salary	$2800	$4800	$8300	$15,400	$23,700

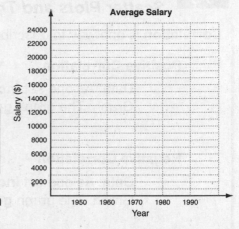

Average Salary

Identify the correlation you would expect to see between the pair of data sets. Explain.

2. The number of chicken pox vaccines given and the number of chicken pox cases reported.

_____

_____

3. The number of vacation days given to employees and their level of job satisfaction.

_____

_____

The average number of gallons of coffee per person consumed in the United States is shown in the table below.

Years	1998	1999	2000	2001	2002	2003
Avg. annual per capita consumption	23.9	25.1	26.3	24.2	23.6	24.3

4. Graph a scatter plot of the data.

5. Draw a trend line.

6. Describe the correlation.

_____

7. Based on the trend line you drew, predict the average amount of coffee consumed per person in 2007.

_____

8. How confident are you in your prediction? Explain.

_____

_____

_____

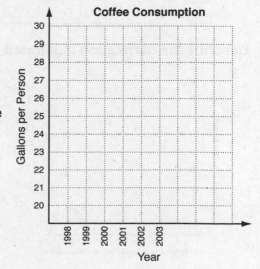

Coffee Consumption

Holt McDougal Algebra 1

Review for Mastery
Scatter Plots and Trend Lines

Correlation is one way to describe the relationship between two sets of data.

Positive Correlation

    Data: As one set **increases,** the other set **increases.**
    Graph: The graph **goes up** from left to right.

Negative Correlation

    Data: As one set **increases,** the other set **decreases.**
    Graph: The graph **goes down** from left to right.

No Correlation

    Data: There is **no relationship** between the sets.
    Graph: The graph has **no pattern.**

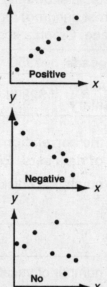

Identify the correlation you would expect to see between the number of grams of fat and the number of calories in different kinds of pizzas.

When you *increase* the amount of fat in a food, you also *increase* calories.
So you would expect to see a positive correlation.

Identify the correlation you would expect to see between each pair of data sets. Explain.

1. the number of knots tied in a rope and the length of the rope

_____

2. the height of a woman and her score on an algebra test

_____

Describe the correlation illustrated by each scatter plot.

3.

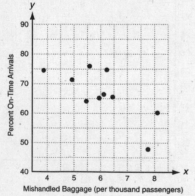

4.

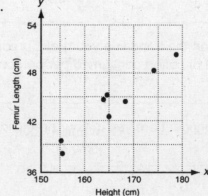

_____   _____

Holt McDougal Algebra 1

LESSON 3-5

Review for Mastery
Scatter Plots and Trend Lines continued

By drawing a **trend line** over a graph of data, you can make predictions.

The scatter plot shows a relationship between a man's height and the length of his femur (thigh bone). Based on this relationship, predict the length of a man's femur if his height is 160 cm.

Step 1: Draw a trend line through the points.

Step 2: Go from 160 cm on the *x*-axis up to the line.

Step 3: Go from the line left to the *y*-axis.

The point (160, 41) is on the line.

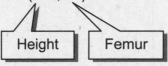

Height   Femur

A man that is 160 cm tall would have a femur about 41 cm long.

To find an *x*-value, go right from the *y*-value, and then down to the *x*-value. So, a man with a 42 cm femur would be about 162 cm tall.

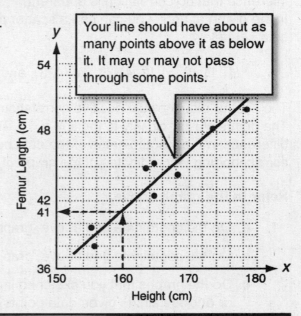

Your line should have about as many points above it as below it. It may or may not pass through some points.

The scatter plot shows a relationship between engine size and city fuel economy for ten automobiles.

5. Draw a trend line on the graph.

6. Based on the relationship, predict...

  a. the city fuel economy of an automobile with an engine size of 5 L.

  _____

  b. the city fuel economy of an automobile with an engine size of 2.8 L.

  _____

  c. the engine size of an automobile with a city fuel economy of 11 mi/gal.

  _____

  d. the engine size of an automobile with a city fuel economy of 28 mi/gal.

  _____

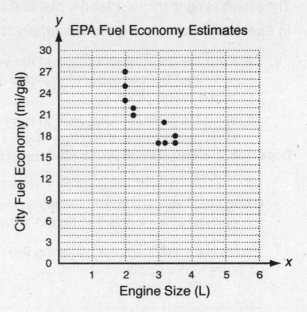

LESSON
3-5

Challenge
Bounding Data with Lines

A scatter plot that represents a data set has many advantages. When you visualize the data on the coordinate plane, you can draw an inference about whether there may be a correlation, positive or negative. You may also be able to draw the inference that no correlation is apparent.

In the graph at right, you can see a scatter plot for the data set below.

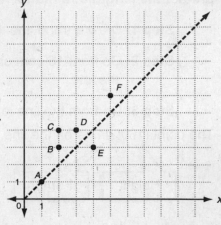

$$(1, 1), (2, 3), (2, 4), (3, 4), (4, 3), \text{ and } (5, 6)$$

The scatter plot shows a positive correlation between x and y. The points cluster closely to the line $y = x$. The greatest difference in the y-coordinates of the data points and the corresponding y-coordinates of the graph of $y = x$ is 2.

Refer to the graph above.

1. a. On the coordinate grid above, graph $y = x + 2$.

   b. On the coordinate grid above, graph $y = x - 1$.

   c. Do the graphs that you sketched in parts **a** and **b** bound or enclose all the given data points? Explain your response.

   _____

The graph at right shows a scatter plot and the line $y = x$.

In Exercises 2 and 3, refer to the graph at right.

2. a. Find the greatest difference in the y-coordinates of the data points above the graph of $y = x$ and the corresponding y-coordinates of the graph of $y = x$._____

   b. Find the greatest difference in the y-coordinates of the data points below the graph of $y = x$ and the corresponding y-coordinates of the graph of $y = x$._____

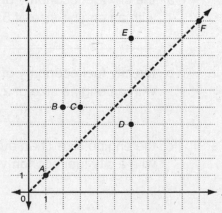

3. Using your answers from Exercise 2, sketch lines that are parallel to $y = x$ and that bound all the data points.

4. Explain how you can use bounding lines to analyze a data set with a positive correlation.

_____

_____

_____

Holt McDougal Algebra 1

LESSON 3-5

Problem Solving

Scatter Plots and Trend Lines

Fawn is trying to improve her reading skills by taking a speed-reading class. She is measuring how many words per minute (wpm) she can read after each week of the class.

1. Graph a scatter plot using the given data.

Weeks	1	2	3	4	5
wpm	220	230	260	260	280

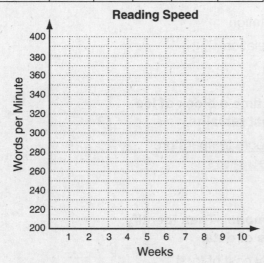

Reading Speed

2. Describe the correlation illustrated by the scatter plot.

_____

_____

3. Draw a trend line and use it to predict the number of words per minute that Fawn will read after 8 weeks of this class.

_____

4. Fawn is paying for this class each week out of her savings account. Identify the correlation between the number of classes and Fawn's account balance.

_____

Choose the scatter plot that best represents the described relationship.

5. the distance a person runs and how physically tired that person is

    A Graph 1   C Graph 3

    B Graph 2   D Graph 4

6. the price of a new car and the number of hours in a day

    F Graph 1   H Graph 3

    G Graph 2   J Graph 4

7. a person's age and the amount of broccoli the person eats

    A Graph 1   C Graph 3

    B Graph 2   D Graph 4

8. the number of cats in a barn and the number of mice in that barn

    F Graph 1   H Graph 3

    G Graph 2   J Graph 4

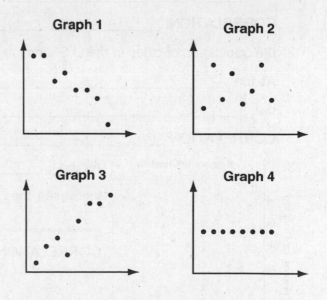

Graph 1   **Graph 2**

Graph 3   **Graph 4**

LESSON 3-5

Reading Strategies
Use a Model

The relationship between two variables can be described as having a *positive correlation*, a *negative correlation*, or *no correlation*. The sentence below can be used as a model to help you determine what type of relationship best fits each situation.

"As the (independent *x*-variable) increases, the (dependent *y*-variable) (increase/decrease/shows no pattern)."

If the dependent *y*-variable...

- increases ⟹ positive correlation
- decreases ⟹ negative correlation
- shows no pattern ⟹ no correlation

Determine the correlation between the amount of time a block of ice sits at room temperature and the amount of ice that remains.

MODEL: As the <u>amount of time a block of ice sits in room temperature</u> increases, the <u>amount of ice that remains</u> <u>decreases</u>.

CORRELATION: There is a negative correlation.

For each relationship, fill in the blanks using the model. Then identify the type of correlation found between the two sets of data.

1. the number of children in a family and the monthly cost of food

   As the _____ increases,

   the _____ _____.

   CORRELATION: _____

2. the population of cities in the U.S. and the average February temperature

   As the _____ increases,

   the _____ _____.

   CORRELATION: _____

3.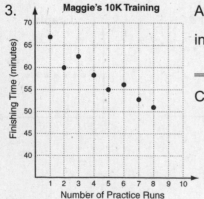

   As the _____

   increases, the _____

   _____.

   CORRELATION: _____

Holt McDougal Algebra 1

Practice A

Arithmetic Sequences

Determine if the sequence is arithmetic. Write *yes* or *no*.

1. 5, 9, 14, 20, …

2. 10, 22, 34, 46, …

_____   _____

Find the common difference for each arithmetic sequence.

3. 12, 15, 18, 21, …

4. 30, 24, 18, 12, …

_____   _____

Find the common difference for each arithmetic sequence. Then find the next three terms.

5. 20, 10, 0, −10, …

6. 100, 98, 96, 94, …

_____   _____

Find the indicated term of each arithmetic sequence.

7. 42nd term: $a_1 = 10$; $d = 6$

8. 27th term: 59, 56, 53, 50, …

_____   _____

A swim pass costs $30 for the first month. Each month after that, the cost is $20 per month. Riley wants to swim for 12 months.

9. The sequence for this situation is arithmetic. What is the first term of this sequence?

_____

10. What is the common difference?

_____

11. The 12th term will be the amount Riley spends for a one-year swim pass. Write the equation for finding the total cost of a one-year swim pass.

_____

12. What is the total amount of money Riley will spend for a one-year swim pass?

_____

Holt McDougal Algebra 1

LESSON 3-6 Practice B
Arithmetic Sequences

Determine whether each sequence is an arithmetic sequence. If so, find the common difference and the next three terms.

1. −10, −7, −4, −1, …

2. 0, 1.5, 3, 4.5, …

3. 5, 8, 12, 17, …

4. −20, −20.5, −21, −21.5, …

Find the indicated term of each arithmetic sequence.

5. 28th term: 0, −4, −8, −12, …

6. 15th term: 2, 3.5, 5, 6.5, …

7. 37th term: $a_1 = -3$; $d = 2.8$

8. 14th term: $a_1 = 4.2$; $d = -5$

9. 17th term; $a_1 = 2.3$; $d = -2.3$

10. 92nd term; $a_1 = 1$; $d = 0.8$

11. A movie rental club charges $4.95 for the first month's rentals. The club charges $18.95 for each additional month. How much is the total cost for one year? _____

12. A carnival game awards a prize if Kasey can shoot a basket. The charge is $5.00 for the first shot, then $2.00 for each additional shot. Kasey needed 11 shots to win a prize. What is the total amount Kasey spent to win a prize?

Holt McDougal Algebra 1

LESSON 3-6

Practice C

Arithmetic Sequences

Determine whether each sequence is an arithmetic sequence. If so, find the common difference and the next three terms.

1. 5, 4.25, 3.5, 2.75, …

2. $3, \dfrac{23}{8}, \dfrac{11}{4}, \dfrac{21}{8}, \ldots$

3. $\dfrac{1}{2}, \dfrac{1}{4}, \dfrac{1}{8}, \dfrac{1}{16}, \ldots$

4. $x, x+3, x+6, x+9, \ldots$

Find the indicated term of each arithmetic sequence.

5. 17th term: 0, −0.25, −0.5, −0.75, …

6. 99th term: $2, \dfrac{5}{2}, 3, \dfrac{7}{2}, \ldots$

7. 51st term: $a_1 = 7$; $d = -4.7$

8. 28th term: $a_1 = 5$; $d = \dfrac{1}{3}$

9. 46th term; $a_1 = 46$; $d = 46$

10. 92nd term; $a_1 = -63.7$; $d = 0.7$

11. A photographer charges a sitting fee of $69.95 for one person. Each additional person in the picture is $30. What is the total sitting fee charge if a group of 10 people wish to be photographed?

12. Grant is planting one large tree and several smaller trees. He has a budget of $1400. A large tree costs $200. Each smaller tree is $150. How many total trees can Grant purchase on his budget?

Holt McDougal Algebra 1

LESSON 3-6

Review for Mastery

Arithmetic Sequences

An **arithmetic sequence** is a list of numbers (or **terms**) with a **common difference** between each number. After you find the common difference, you can use it to continue the sequence.

Determine whether each sequence is an arithmetic sequence. If so, find the common difference and the next three terms.

1, 2, 4, 8, ...

+1   +2   +4

> Find how much you add or subtract to move from term to term.

The difference between terms is *not* constant.

This sequence is *not* an arithmetic sequence.

0, 6, 12, 18, ...

+6   +6   +6

> Find how much you add or subtract to move from term to term.

The difference between terms is constant.

This sequence is an arithmetic sequence with a common difference of 6.

0, 6, 12, 18, __24__, __30__, __36__

+6   +6   +6

> Use the difference of 6 to find three more terms.

Fill in the blanks with the differences between terms. State whether each sequence is an arithmetic sequence.

1. 14, 12, 10, 8, ...

____ ____ ____

Is this an arithmetic sequence? _____

2. 0.3, 0.6, 1.0, 1.5, ...

____ ____ ____

Is this an arithmetic sequence? _____

Use the common difference to find the next three terms in each arithmetic sequence.

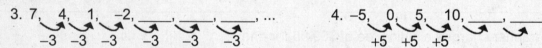

3. 7, 4, 1, −2, ____, ____, ____, ...

−3   −3   −3   −3   −3   −3

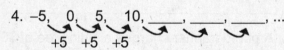

4. −5, 0, 5, 10, ____, ____, ____, ...

+5   +5   +5

Determine whether each sequence is an arithmetic sequence. If so, find the common difference and the next three terms.

5. −1, 2, −3, 4, ...

_____

6. 1.25, 3.75, 6.25, 8.75, ...

_____

Holt McDougal Algebra 1

LESSON 3-6

Review for Mastery

Arithmetic Sequences continued

You can use the first term and common difference of an arithmetic sequence to write a rule in this form: $a_n = a_1 + (n-1)d$

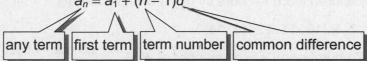

any term | first term | term number | common difference

After you write the rule, you can use it to find any term in the sequence.

Find the 50th term of this arithmetic sequence:

5, 3.8, 2.6, 1.4, ...

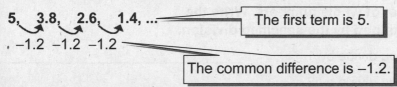

.−1.2 −1.2 −1.2

The first term is 5.

The common difference is −1.2.

First, write the rule.

$a_n = a_1 + (n-1)d$ *Write the general form for the rule.*

$a_n = 5 + (n-1)(-1.2)$ *Substitute the first term and common difference.*

Now, use the rule to find the 50th term.

$a_{50} = 5 + (50-1)(-1.2)$ *Substitute the term number.*

$a_{50} = 5 + (49)(-1.2)$ *Simplify.*

$a_{50} = 5 + (-58.8)$

$a_{50} = -53.8$

The 50th term is −53.8.

Use the first term and common difference to write the rule for each arithmetic sequence.

7. The arithmetic sequence with first term
   $a_1 = 10$ and common difference $d = 4$. _____

8. −5, 0, 5, 10, ...

   first term: $a_1 = $ _____

   common difference: $d = $ _____ _____

Find the indicated term of each arithmetic sequence.

9. $a_n = 16 + (n-1)(-0.5)$ 15th term:_____

10. $a_n = 6 + (n-1)(3)$ 32nd term: _____

11. −8, −6, −4, −2, ... 100th term: _____

LESSON 3-6

Challenge
Sequences

The sequence of numbers below is known as the sequence of whole numbers. At an early age, children learn to count by using whole numbers.

0, 1, 2, 3, 4, 5, 6, 7, 8, 9, 10, 11, 12, 13, 14, ...

When you divide each whole number by a fixed number of your choice, you can create a new sequence. The diagram at the right will help you recall the meaning of the terms related to division.

$$\text{divisor} \rightarrow 6\overline{)23} \quad \begin{array}{l} 3 \leftarrow \text{quotient} \\ \leftarrow \text{dividend} \\ 18 \end{array}$$

In Exercises 1–6, consider the set of whole numbers. Write the first 10 terms of the sequence defined by the specified division.

1. the remainder you get when you divide by 1   _____

2. the remainder you get when you divide by 2   _____

3. the remainder you get when you divide by 3   _____

4. the remainder you get when you divide by 4   _____

5. the remainder you get when you divide by 5   _____

6. the remainder you get when you divide by 6   _____

7. a. Suppose that you divide each of the whole numbers by 12. Without writing any division or remainders, write a conjecture about the sequence of remainders that you think you will get.

_____

   b. Write a brief justification of your conjecture from part **a.**

_____

_____

8. a. The following sequence of remainders is the result of dividing each whole number by an unknown number. By what number are the whole numbers being divided?

0, 1, 2, 3, 4, 5, 6, 7, 8, 9, 0, 1, 2, 3, 4, 5, 6, 7, 8, 9, 0, 1, 2, 3, 4, 5, 6, 7, 8, 9, ...

_____

   b. Write a brief justification of your conjecture from part **a.**

_____

9. It is noon. Use division and remainders to find what time will be 99 hours from now.

_____

Holt McDougal Algebra 1

LESSON 3-6

Problem Solving
Arithmetic Sequences

Find the indicated term of each arithmetic sequence.

1. Darnell has a job and is saving his paychecks each week.

Weeks	1	2	3	4
Savings	$130	$260	$390	$520

How much will Darnell have saved after 11 weeks?

_____

2. A tube containing 3 ounces of toothpaste is being used at a rate of 0.15 ounces per day. How much toothpaste will be in the tube after one week?

_____

3. A new car costs $13,000 and is depreciating by $900 each year. How much will the car be worth after 4 years?

_____

4. Jessie is playing an arcade game that costs 50¢ for the first game and 25¢ to continue if she loses. How much will she spend on the game if she continues 9 times?

_____

Use the graph below to answer questions 5–9. The graph shows the size of Ivor's ant colony over the first four weeks. Assume the ant population will continue to grow at the same rate. Select the best answer.

Ivor's Ant Farm

5. Which of the following shows how many ants Ivor will have in the next three weeks?

   A 315, 341, 367

   B 317, 343, 369

   C 318, 334, 350

   D 319, 345, 371

6. Which rule can be used to find how large the colony will be in *n* weeks?

   F $a_n = 215 + 26n$

   G $a_n = 215n + 26$

   H $a_n = 215(n - 1) + 26$

   J $a_n = 215 + 26(n - 1)$

7. How many ants will Ivor have in 27 weeks?

   A 891   C 5616

   B 917   D 5831

8. Ivor's ants weigh 1.5 grams each. How many grams do all of his ants weigh in 13 weeks?

   F 660.5   H 722

   G 683   J 790.5

9. When the colony reaches 1385 ants, Ivor's ant farm will not be big enough for all of them. In how many weeks will the ant population be too large?

   A 45   C 47

   B 46   D 48

Holt McDougal Algebra 1

**LESSON
3-6**

Reading Strategies
Use a Concept Map

Use the concept map below to help you understand arithmetic sequences.

Definition	**Formula**
An arithmetic sequence is a list of numbers whose terms all differ by the same non-zero number.	The *n*th term of an arithmetic sequence can be found using $$a_n = a_1 + (n-1)d$$ where a_1 is the first term and *d* is the common difference.

Arithmetic Sequence

Examples

−2, 1, 4, 7, 10, ...
+3 +3 +3 +3

9, 7.5, 6, 4.5, 3, ...
−1.5 −1.5 −1.5 −1.5

Non-Examples

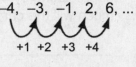
−4, −3, −1, 2, 6, ...
+1 +2 +3 +4

1, 2, 4, 8, 16, ...
×2 ×2 ×2 ×2

Answer each question.

1. Explain why −4, −3, −1, 2, 6, ... is given as a non-example of an arithmetic sequence.

   _____

2. Explain why 1, 2, 4, 8, 16, ... is given as a non-example of an arithmetic sequence.

   _____

3. Give an example of an arithmetic sequence whose common difference is 5.

   _____

4. Find the common difference and the next 3 terms of the sequence 8, $7\frac{1}{2}$, 7, $6\frac{1}{2}$, 6, ...

   _____   _____

Find the indicated term of each arithmetic sequence using the formula given above.

5. 25th term: −14, −8, −2, 4, 10, ...   6. 18th term: 122, 120, 118, 116, 114, ...

   _____   _____

Holt McDougal Algebra 1

Date _____

Dear Family,

Your child will learn to identify and graph **linear functions**.
A function is linear if its graph forms a non-vertical straight line. You can
also determine if a function is linear by looking at the differences in the
x- and *y*-values of a list of ordered pairs.

$\{(0, 3), (2, 6), (4, 9), (6, 12)\}$ — This function is linear because the *x*-values increase by a constant amount (2) while the *y*-values also increase by a constant amount (3).

Another way to determine if a function is linear is by determining whether its equation is linear.

> A linear equation can be written in the form $Ax + By = C$ where *A*, *B*, and *C* are real numbers and both *A* and *B* are not zero.

Students will also find the **slope** of a line, which tells how steep the line is.
The slope of a line is the ratio of *rise* to *run* for any two points on the line.

If you pick any two points on a line, the slope can be
found by first counting up or down, then left or right,
and then dividing.

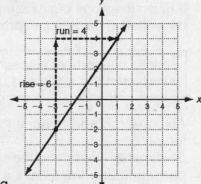

The slope of the line at right is $\frac{6}{4}$, which reduces

to $\frac{3}{2}$. From any point on the line, if you count up 3 units

and right 2 units, you will land on another point on the line.

Students will learn to graph linear functions other than by generating
ordered pairs. One way to graph a linear function is by using **intercepts**.
An intercept indicates where a line crosses an axis.

Graph $2x - 4y = 8$.

Step 1: Find the value of *x* when $y = 0$.
$$2x - 4y = 8$$
$$2x - 4(0) = 8$$
$$2x = 8$$
$$x = 4 \longrightarrow (4, 0)$$

Step 2: Find the value of *y* when $x = 0$.
$$2x - 4y = 8$$
$$2(0) - 4y = 8$$
$$-4y = 8$$
$$y = -2 \longrightarrow (0, -2)$$

Step 3: Plot $(4, 0)$ and $(0, -2)$.
Connect with a straight line.

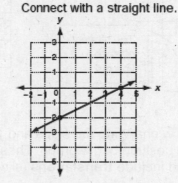

Holt McDougal Algebra 1

$Ax + By = C$ is called the **standard form of a line**, but a line can also be written in **slope-intercept** form or **point-slope form**.

> Slope-intercept form of a linear equation is $y = mx + b$,
> where m is the slope and b is the y-intercept.

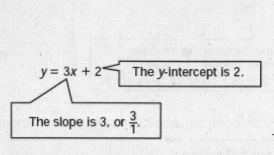

$y = 3x + 2$ — The y-intercept is 2.

The slope is 3, or $\frac{3}{1}$.

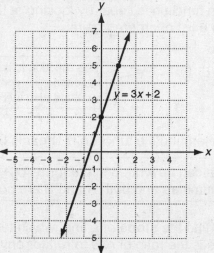

$y = 3x + 2$

To graph a line written in slope-intercept form, first plot the y-intercept, and then find another point on the line by using the slope.

If given the slope of a line and one point on the line, the equation of the line can be written in point-slope form.

> Point-slope form of a linear equation is $y - y_1 = m(x - x_1)$,
> where m is the slope and (x_1, y_1) is a point on the line.

An equation in point-slope form can be written in slope-intercept form by solving for y.
Students will learn that the slopes of **parallel lines** are equal, while the slopes of **perpendicular lines** have a product of -1.

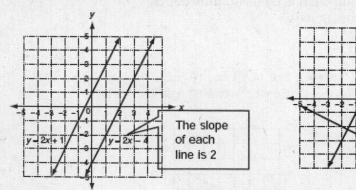

$y = 2x + 1$ $y = 2x - 4$

The slope of each line is 2

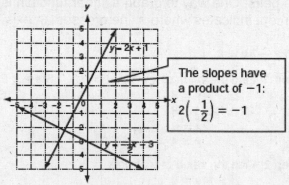

$y = 2x + 1$

$y = -\frac{1}{2}x - 3$

The slopes have a product of -1:
$2\left(-\frac{1}{2}\right) = -1$

Students will learn how changing the slope and y-intercept of a linear function changes the position of the graph. These changes are called **transformations**, and include **translations** (slides), **rotations** (turns), and **reflections** (flips).

Holt McDougal Algebra 1

LESSON 4-1

Practice A

Identifying Linear Functions

Use the graph for 1–3.

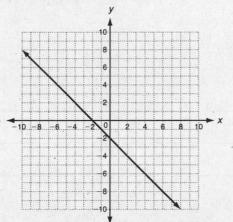

1. Is this graph a function? _____

2. Explain how you know it is a function.

   _____

   _____

3. If this graph is a function, is it also a linear function? _____

Use the set {(1, 8), (2, 6), (3, 4), (4, 2), (5, 0)} for 4–5.

4. Does the set of ordered pairs satisfy a linear function? _____

5. Explain how you decided. _____

   _____

6. Write the equation $y = x - 4$ in standard form $(Ax + By = C)$.

   _____

7. Is $y = x - 4$ a linear function?

   _____

8. Graph $y = x - 4$ to check.

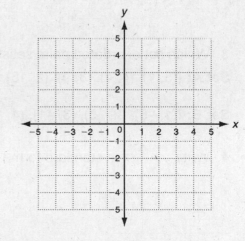

9. In 2005, a storm in Milwaukee, WI was dropping 2.5 inches of snow every hour. The total amount of snow is given by $f(x) = 2.5x$, where x is the number of hours. Graph this function and give its domain and range.

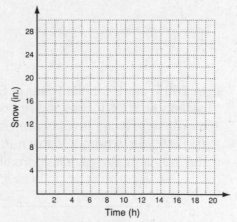

   _____

Holt McDougal Algebra 1

LESSON
4-1

Practice B
Identifying Linear Functions

Identify whether each graph represents a function. Explain. If the graph does represent a function, is the function linear?

1. 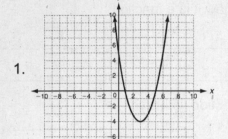 _____
   _____
   _____

2. 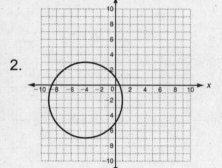 _____
   _____
   _____

3. Which set of ordered pairs satisfies a linear function? Explain.

Set A: $\{(5, 1), (4, 4), (3, 9), (2, 16), (1, 25)\}$ _____

Set B: $\{(1, -5), (2, -3), (3, -1), (4, 1), (5, 3)\}$ _____

4. Write $y = -2x$ in standard form. Then graph the function.

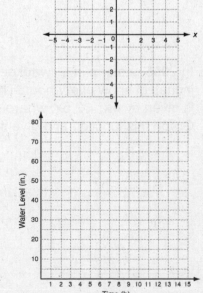

_____

5. In 2005, the Shabelle River in Somalia rose an estimated 5.25 inches every hour for 15 hours. The increase in water level is represented by the function $f(x) = 5.25x$, where x is the number of hours. Graph this function and give its domain and range.

_____

Holt McDougal Algebra 1

LESSON 4-1

Practice C

Identifying Linear Functions

Identify whether each graph represents a function. Explain. If the graph does represent a function, is the function linear?

1.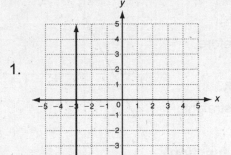

_____

_____

_____

2.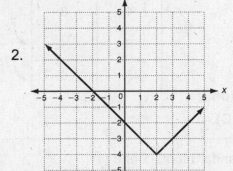

_____

_____

_____

3. Which of the sets of ordered pairs satisfies a linear function? Explain.

Set A: $\{(-10, 3), (-9.9, 4.5), (-9.8, 6), (-9.7, 7.5)\}$ _____

Set B: $\{(1, 5), (2, 10), (4, 15), (8, 20), (16, 25)\}$ _____

4. Write $y = -x + 3$ in standard form. Then graph the function.

_____

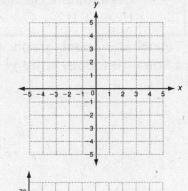

5. A campground charges $30 for 2 people plus $4 for each additional person. The total amount owed is given by $f(x) = 30 + 4x$ where x is the number of additional people. Graph this function and give its domain and range.

_____

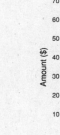

LESSON 4-1

Review for Mastery
Identifying Linear Functions

You can determine if a function is linear by its graph, ordered pairs, or equation.

Identify whether the graph represents a linear function.

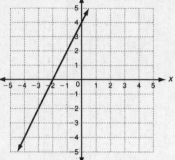

Step 1: Determine whether the graph is a function.

Every *x*-value is paired with exactly one *y*-value; therefore, the graph is a function. Continue to step 2.

Step 2: Determine whether the graph is a straight line.

Conclusion: Because this graph is a function and a straight line, this graph represents a linear function.

Identify whether {(4, 3), (6, 4), (8, 6)} represents a linear function.

Step 1: Write the ordered pairs in a table.

Step 2: Find the amount of change in each variable. Determine if the amounts are constant.

Conclusion: Although the *x*-values show a constant change, the *y*-values do not. Therefore, this set of ordered pairs does not represent a linear function.

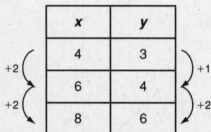

Identify whether the function $y = 5x - 2$ is a linear function.

Try to write the equation in standard form $(Ax + By = C)$.

$$y = 5x - 2$$
$$\underline{-5x \quad -5x}$$
$$-5x + y = -2$$

In standard form, *x* and *y*
- have exponents of 1
- are not multiplied together
- are not in denominators, exponents, or radical signs

Conclusion: Because the function can be written in standard form, $(A = -5, B = 1, C = -2)$, the function is a linear function.

Tell whether each graph, set of ordered pairs, or equation represents a linear function. Write *yes* or *no*.

1.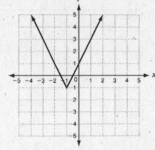

_____

2.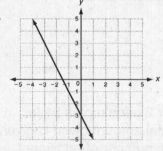

_____

3.

x	y
−9	5
−5	10
−1	15

_____

4. {(−3, 5), (−2, 8), (−1, 12)}

_____

5. $2y = -3x^2$

_____

6. $y = 4x - 7$

_____

LESSON 4-1

Review for Mastery

Identifying Linear Functions continued

In real-life problems, the domain and range are sometimes restricted.

Swimming at the park pool costs $2.75 for each person. The total cost is given by $f(x) = 2.75x$ where x is the number of people going swimming. Graph this function and give its domain and range.

Step 1: Graph.

x	$f(x) = 2.75x$
0	$f(0) = 2.75(0) = 0$
1	$f(1) = 2.75(1) = 2.75$
2	$f(2) = 2.75(2) = 5.50$
3	$f(3) = 2.75(3) = 8.25$

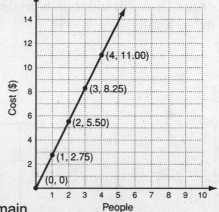

Step 2: Determine the domain and range.

Ask yourself the following questions to help determine the domain.

   Can the x-value be all fractions or decimals in between the whole numbers?

   Can the x-value be 0?

   Can the x-value be negative?

The domain is the number of people. So the domain is restricted to whole numbers. Because the range is determined by the domain, it is also restricted.

Domain: {0, 1, 2, 3, …}   Range: {$0, $2.75, $5.50, $8.25, …}

Give the domain and range for the graphs below.

7.
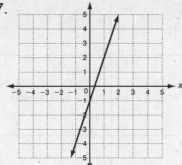

_____

8.
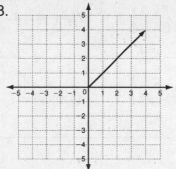

_____

9.
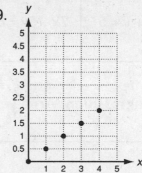

10. Tyler makes $10 per hour at his job. The function $f(x) = 10x$ gives the amount of money Tyler makes after x hours. Graph this function and give its domain and range.

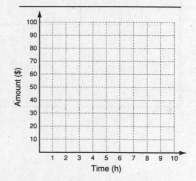

_____

Holt McDougal Algebra 1

LESSON 4-1 Challenge

Identifying Linear Functions

Linear functions are functions that can be written in the form $Ax + By = C$ where A, B, and C are real numbers and A and B are not both 0.

Follow a path from start to finish in the maze below. Each box you cross through must be a linear function. You may move horizontally or vertically.

Start

$3x + 2y = 7$	$y = 4x$	$y = -\dfrac{1}{2}x$	$\dfrac{5}{x} = y + 2$	$x^3 = 27$	$xy = 8$
$x(x + y) = 4$	$x^2 - 16 = 0$	$4x - y = 0$	$y = 3$	$\dfrac{x}{5} = y + 2$	$y = |x|$
$\dfrac{3}{x} + y = 0$	$x(3 + y) = 4$	$x + \dfrac{6}{y} = 3$	$y(x + 2y) = 9$	$-y = x$	$\dfrac{4}{y} + x = 16$
$|x| + y = 5$	$7x - 5y = 8$	$\dfrac{x}{8} = \dfrac{y}{3}$	$2(x + y) = 4$	$\dfrac{y}{4} = 3x$	$x(x + 2) = 5$
$xy + y = 10$	$-y = \dfrac{2}{5}$	$x^2 - y^2 = 1$	$x(4x + y) = 3$	$xy + x = 20$	$x^2 + 8 = -20$
$xy = 5$	$x = 3y$	$8(y + x) = 9$	$2x + 3y = x$	$12x = \dfrac{y}{6}$	$y = x^2$
$x^2 - 20 = 0$	$xy = 10$	$y = |x + 4|$	$x^3 = 10$	$5x - 4y = 8y$	$y(3x + y) = 4$

Finish

Name _____ Date _____ Class_____

Problem Solving

Identifying Linear Functions

Write the correct answer.

1. A daycare center charges a $75 enrollment fee plus $100 per week. The function $f(x) = 100x + 75$ gives the cost of daycare for x weeks. Graph this function and give its domain and range.

   _____

   _____

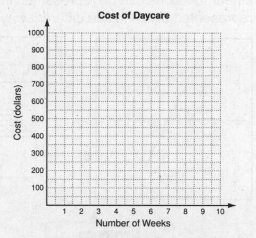

Cost of Daycare

2. A family swimming pool holds 60 m³ of water. The function $f(x) = 60 - 0.18x$ gives the cubic meters of water in the pool, taking into account water lost to evaporation over x days. Graph this function and give its domain and range.

   _____

   _____

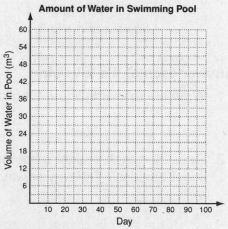

Amount of Water in Swimming Pool

Elijah is using a rowing machine. The table shows how many Calories he can burn for certain lengths of time. Select the best answer.

Time (min)	Calories
2	24
4	48
6	72
8	96
10	120

3. Which function could be used to describe the number of Calories burned after x minutes?

   F $y = 12 + x$　　　H $xy = 12$

   G $x + y = 12$　　　J $y = 12x$

4. What is the domain of the function?

   A {0, 1, 2, 3, ...}　　　C $x \geq 0$

   B {2, 4, 6, ...}　　　D $x \geq 2$

5. What is the range of the function?

   F {0, 12, 24, 36, ...}　H $y \geq 0$

   G {24, 48, 72, ...}　　J $y \geq 24$

6. Elijah graphed the function in problem 4. Which best describes the graph?

   A It is a line that increases from left to right.

   B It is a line that decreases from left to right.

   C It forms a U-shape.

   D It forms a V-shape.

　　　　　　Holt McDougal Algebra 1

LESSON
4-1

Reading Strategies
Use Multiple Representations

Linear functions can be represented in many forms. The same function is represented below in five different ways.

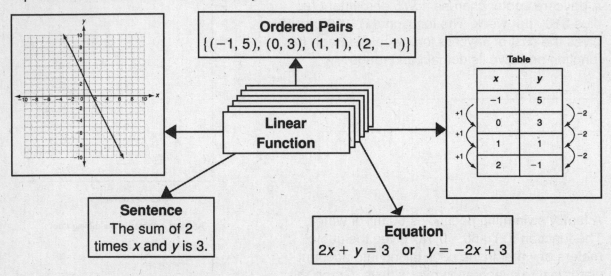

Ordered Pairs
$\{(-1, 5), (0, 3), (1, 1), (2, -1)\}$

Linear Function

Table

x	y
−1	5
0	3
1	1
2	−1

Sentence
The sum of 2 times x and y is 3.

Equation
$2x + y = 3$ or $y = -2x + 3$

Answer each of the following.

1. Write the following linear function as an equation: "The sum of x and $4y$ is 9."

   _____

2. Does the graph at right represent a linear function? Tell why or why not.

   _____

   _____

   _____

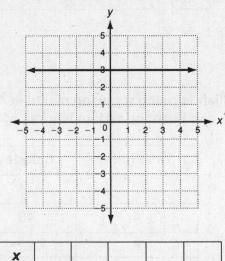

3. Represent the list of ordered pairs in table form: { (6, −3), (4, −1), (2, 0), (0, 2), (−2, 3) }. It this a linear function? Tell why or why not.

   _____

   _____

x				
y				

4. Write $y = -x + 4$ in standard form ($Ax + By = C$).

   _____

LESSON
4-2

Practice A
Using Intercepts

Find the *x*- and *y*-intercepts.

1.

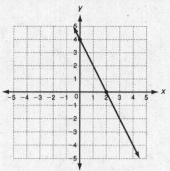

2.

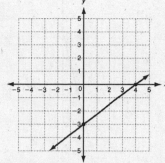

3.

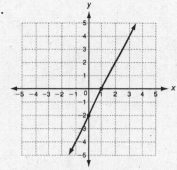

x-intercept: _____   *x*-intercept: _____   *x*-intercept: _____

y-intercept: _____   *y*-intercept: _____   *y*-intercept: _____

4. Find the intercepts of $2x + 3y = 6$ by following the steps below.

   a. Substitute $y = 0$ into the equation. Solve for *x*.

   _____

   b. The *x*-intercept is: _____

   c. Substitute $x = 0$ into the equation. Solve for *y*.

   _____

   d. The *y*-intercept is: _____

   e. Use the intercepts to graph the line described by the equation.

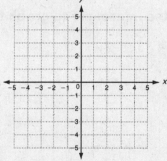

5. Jennifer started with $50 in her savings account. Each week
   she withdrew $10. The amount of money in her savings account
   after *x* weeks is represented by the function $f(x) = 50 - 10x$.

   a. Find the intercepts and graph the function.

   _____

   b. What does each intercept represent?

   _____

   _____

   _____

Holt McDougal Algebra 1

Practice B
Using Intercepts

Find the *x*- and *y*-intercepts.

1.
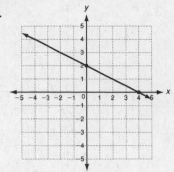

_____

_____

2.
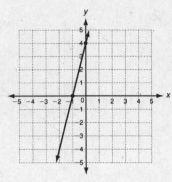

_____

_____

3.
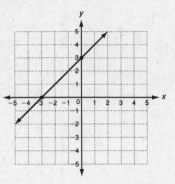

_____

_____

Use intercepts to graph the line described by each equation.

4. $3x + 2y = -6$

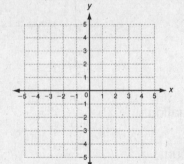

5. $x - 4y = 4$

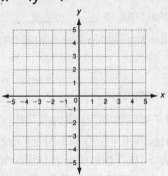

6. At a fair, hamburgers sell for $3.00 each and hot dogs sell for
$1.50 each. The equation $3x + 1.5y = 30$ describes the number
of hamburgers and hot dogs a family can buy with $30.

  a. Find the intercepts and graph the function.

  _____

  b. What does each intercept represent?

  _____

  _____

  _____

  _____

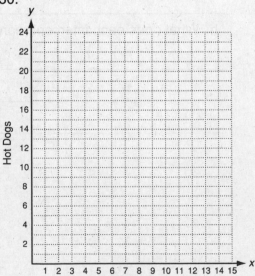

Practice C

Using Intercepts

Find the *x*- and *y*-intercepts.

1.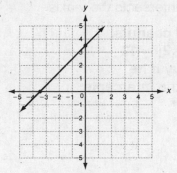

2.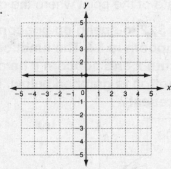

3.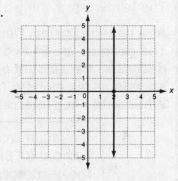

_____

_____

Use intercepts to graph the line described by each equation.

4. $y = 0.25x - 1$

5. $\frac{1}{3}x + y = 1$

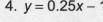

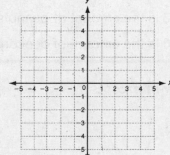

6. The change in water level of one portion of the Mississippi River is about −0.3 ft per day. If the water level starts at 17 feet and falls for *x* days, the level is represented by the function $f(x) = 17 - 0.3x$.

   a. Find the intercepts and graph the function.

   _____

   b. What does each intercept represent?

   _____

   _____

   _____

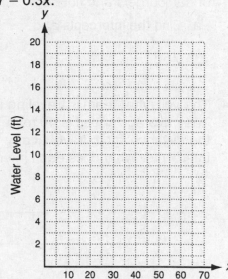

Holt McDougal Algebra 1

LESSON 4-2

Review for Mastery
Using Intercepts

The *x*-intercept is the *x*-coordinate of the point where the graph intersects the *x*-axis.
The *y*-intercept is the *y*-coordinate of the point where the graph intersects the *y*-axis.

At a baseball game, Doug has $12 to spend on popcorn and peanuts.
The peanuts are $4 and the popcorn is $2. The function $4x + 2y = 12$
describes the amount of peanuts *x* and popcorn *y* he can buy if he
spends all his money. The function is graphed below. Find the intercepts.
What does each intercept represent?

The graph crosses the
y-axis at (0, 6).
The *y*-intercept is 6.

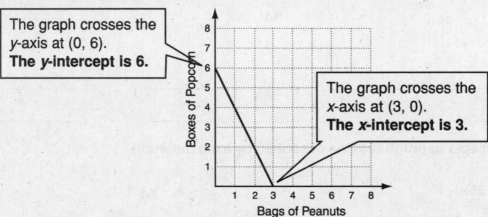

The graph crosses the
x-axis at (3, 0).
The *x*-intercept is 3.

The *x*-intercept 3 is the amount of peanuts Doug can buy if he buys no popcorn.

The *y*-intercept 6 is the amount of popcorn Doug can buy if he buys no peanuts.

Find the *x*- and *y*-intercepts.

1.

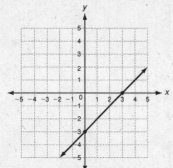

_____

2.

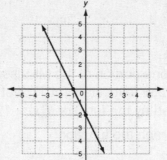

_____

3.

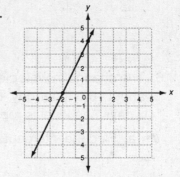

_____

4. The volleyball team is traveling to a game 120 miles away.
   Their average speed is 40 mi/h. The graphed line describes
   the distance left to travel at any time during the trip. Find the
   intercepts. What does each intercept represent?

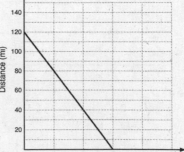

_____

_____

Holt McDougal Algebra 1

LESSON 4-2

Review for Mastery

Using Intercepts continued

You can find the *x*- and *y*-intercepts from an equation. Then you can use the intercepts to graph the equation.

Find the *x*- and *y*-intercepts of $4x + 2y = 8$.

To find the *x*-intercept, substitute 0 for *y*.

$$4x + 2x = 8$$
$$4x + 2(0) = 8$$
$$4x = 8$$
$$\frac{4x}{4} = \frac{8}{4}$$
$$x = 2$$

The *x*-intercept is 2.

To find the *y*-intercept, substitute 0 for *x*.

$$4x + 2y = 8$$
$$4(0) + 2y = 8$$
$$2y = 8$$
$$\frac{2y}{2} = \frac{8}{2}$$
$$y = 4$$

The *y*-intercept is 4.

Use the intercepts to graph the line described by $4x + 2y = 8$.

Because the *x*-intercept is 2, the point (2, 0) is on the graph.

Because the *y*-intercept is 4, the point (0, 4) is on the graph.

Plot (2, 0) and (0, 4).

Draw a line through both points.

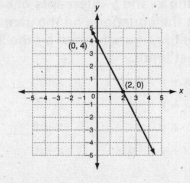

Use intercepts to graph the line described by each equation.

5. $3x + 9y = 9$

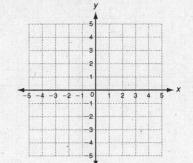

6. $4x + 6y = -12$

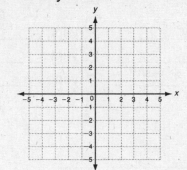

7. $2x - y = 4$

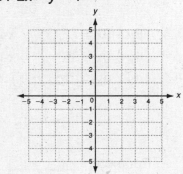

LESSON 4-2

Challenge

Intercepts and Perimeters

You can use the **distance formula** to find the distance between two ordered pairs.

$$d = \sqrt{(x_2 - x_1)^2 + (y_2 - y_1)^2}$$

where (x_1), (y_1) represents the first ordered pair and (x_2), (y_2) represents the second ordered pair.

Find the distance between the ordered pairs. Round your answer to the nearest tenth.

1. (3, 0) and (0, 5)

2. (−4, 0) and (0, 2)

_____   _____

Find the x- and y-intercepts of each equation. Use the intercepts to graph the equations on the same grid. Then find the perimeter of the geometric figure formed by the lines. Round all distances to the nearest tenth.

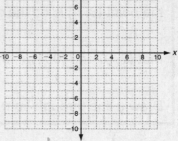

3. $-x + y = 4$ x-int: _____   y-int: _____

    $-x + y = -4$ x-int: _____   y-int: _____

    $x + y = 4$ x-int: _____   y-int: _____

    $x + y = -4$ x-int: _____   y-int: _____

Perimeter: _____

4. $8y + 9x = 72$ x-int: _____   y-int: _____

    $4y - 9x = 36$ x-int: _____   y-int: _____

    $16y - 9x = -72$ x-int: _____   y-int: _____

Perimeter: _____

LESSON 4-2

Problem Solving
Using Intercepts

Write the correct answer.

1. Naima has $40 to spend on refreshments for herself and her friends at the movie theater. The equation $5x + 2y = 40$ describes the number of large popcorns x and small drinks y she can buy. Graph this function and find its intercepts.

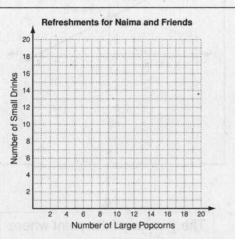

2. Turner is reading a 400-page book. He reads 4 pages every 5 minutes. The number of pages Turner has left to read after x minutes is represented by the function $f(x) = 400 - \frac{4}{5}x$. Graph this function and find its intercepts.

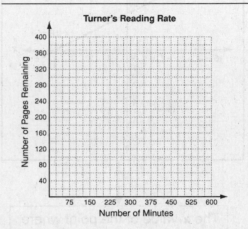

The graph shows the distance of an elevator at Chimney Rock, North Carolina, from its destination as a function of time. Use the graph to answer questions 3–6. Select the best answer.

3. What is the *x*-intercept of this function?

   A 0   C 258

   B 30   D 300

4. What does the *x*-intercept represent?

   F the total distance the elevator travels

   G the number of seconds that have passed for any given distance

   H the number of seconds it takes the elevator to reach its destination

   J the distance that the elevator has traveled at any given time

5. What is the *y*-intercept for this function?

   A 0   C 258

   B 30   D 300

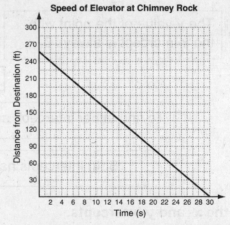

6. What does the *y*-intercept represent?

   F the total distance the elevator travels

   G the number of seconds that have passed for any given distance

   H the number of seconds it takes the elevator to reach its destination

   J the distance that the elevator has traveled at any given time

Holt McDougal Algebra 1

LESSON 4-2	# Reading Strategies

Compare and Contrast

Study the chart below to compare and contrast *x*- and *y*-intercepts.

	x-intercept	

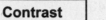

Contrast

	y-intercept	

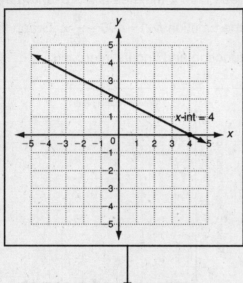
x-int = 4

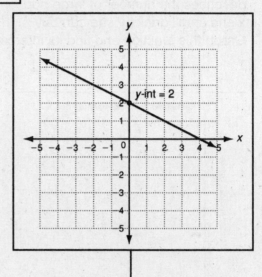
y-int = 2

The *x*-value of the point where a graph crosses the *x*-axis

The *y*-value of the point where a graph crosses the *y*-axis

The *y*-value of the point with the *x*-intercept is always 0.

The *x*-value of the point with the *y*-intercept is always 0.

Compare

To find either intercept, substitute 0 for the other variable and solve.

Both intercepts have meaning in real-world problems.

Find the *x*- and *y*-intercepts.

1. $3x - 2y = 6$

2.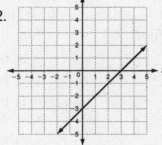

3. The graph intersects the two axes at $(-3, 0)$ and $(0, 5)$.

_____ _____ _____

Holt McDougal Algebra 1

LESSON
4-3

Practice A

Rate of Change and Slope

Fill in the blanks to define slope.

1. The _____ is the difference in the *y*-values of two points on a line.

2. The _____ is the difference in the *x*-values of two points on a line.

3. The slope of a line is the ratio of _____ to _____ for any two points on the line.

Find the rise and run between each set of points. Then, write the slope of the line.

4.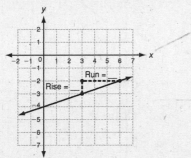

slope = _____

5.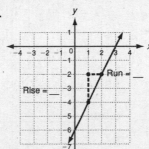

slope = _____

6.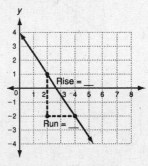

slope = _____

Tell whether the slope of each line is positive, negative, zero, or undefined.

7.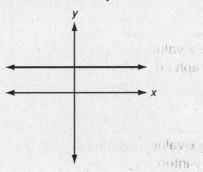

_____

8.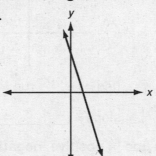

_____

9.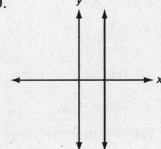

_____

10. The table shows a truck driver's distance from home during one day's deliveries. Find the rate of change for each time interval.

Time (h)	0	1	4	5	8	10
Distance (mi)	0	35	71	82	199	200

Hour 0 to Hour 1: _____   Hour 1 to Hour 4: _____   Hour 4 to Hour 5: _____

Hour 5 to Hour 8: _____   Hour 8 to Hour 10: _____

The rate of change represents the average speed. During which time interval was the driver's average speed the least? _____

Holt McDougal Algebra 1

LESSON 4-3

Practice B
Rate of Change and Slope

Find the rise and run between each set of points. Then, write the slope of the line.

1.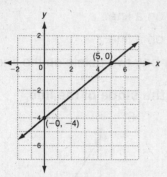

rise = _____ run = _____

slope = _____

2.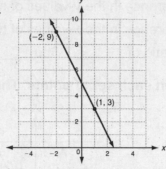

rise = _____ run = _____

slope = _____

3.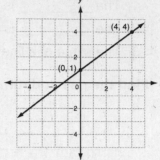

rise = _____ run = _____

slope = _____

4.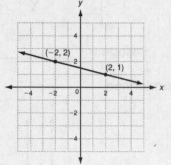

rise = _____ run = _____

slope = _____

5.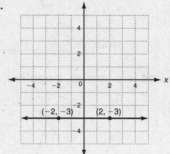

rise = _____ run = _____

slope = _____

6.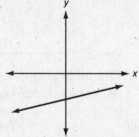

rise = _____ run = _____

slope = _____

Tell whether the slope of each line is positive, negative, zero, or undefined.

7.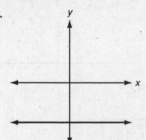

_____

8.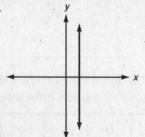

_____

9.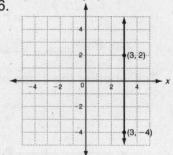

_____

10. The table shows the amount of water in a pitcher at different times. Graph the data and show the rates of change. Between which two hours is the rate of change the greatest? _____

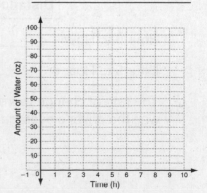

Time (h)	0	1	2	3	4	5	6	7
Amount (oz)	60	50	25	80	65	65	65	50

Holt McDougal Algebra 1

Name _____ Date _____ Class _____

Practice C
Rate of Change and Slope

Find the slope of each line.

1.
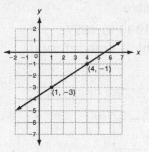
slope = _____

2.
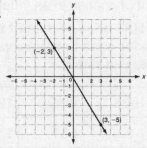
slope = _____

3.
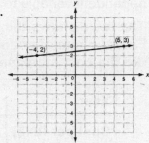
slope = _____

4.
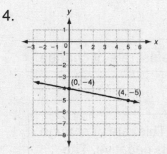
slope = _____

5.
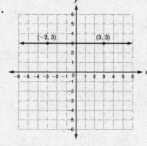
slope = _____

6.
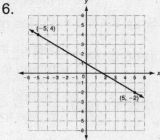
slope = _____

Tell whether the slope of each line is positive, negative, zero, or undefined.

7.
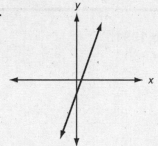

_____

8.
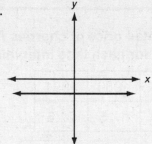

_____

9.
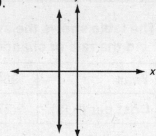

_____

10. The table shows the distance a car drove on one tank of gasoline.

Miles driven	0	60	150	170	230	260
Gas Used (gal)	0	2	5	6	9	11

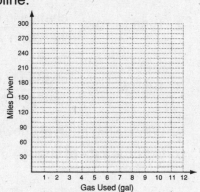

a. Graph the data and show the rates of change.

b. The rate of change represents the gas mileage in miles per gallon. Between which two measurements was the car's gas mileage least?

_____

Holt McDougal Algebra 1

**LESSON
4-3**

Review for Mastery

Rate of Change and Slope

A **rate of change** is a ratio that compares the amount of change in a dependent variable to the amount of change in an independent variable.

The table shows the average retail price of peanut butter from 1986 to 1997. Find the rate of change in cost for each time interval. During which time interval did the cost increase at the greatest rate?

Year	1986	1987	1989	1992	1997
Cost per lb ($)	1.60	1.80	1.81	1.94	1.78

Step 1: Identify independent and dependent variables.
    Year is independent. *Cost* is dependent.

Step 2: Find the rates of change.

1986 to 1987 $\dfrac{\text{change in cost}}{\text{change in years}} = \dfrac{1.80 - 1.60}{1987 - 1986} = \dfrac{0.20}{1} = 0.2$ → greatest rate of change

1987 to 1989 $\dfrac{\text{change in cost}}{\text{change in years}} = \dfrac{1.81 - 1.80}{1989 - 1987} = \dfrac{0.01}{2} = 0.005$

1989 to 1992 $\dfrac{\text{change in cost}}{\text{change in years}} = \dfrac{1.94 - 1.81}{1992 - 1989} = \dfrac{0.13}{3} \approx 0.043$

1992 to 1997 $\dfrac{\text{change in cost}}{\text{change in years}} = \dfrac{1.78 - 1.94}{1997 - 1992} = \dfrac{-0.16}{5} = -0.032$

This rate of change is negative. The price went down during this time period.

The cost increased at the greatest rate from 1986 to 1987.

The table shows the average retail price of cherries from 1986 to 1991. Find the rate of change in cost for each time interval.

Year	1986	1988	1989	1991
Cost per lb ($)	1.27	1.63	1.15	2.26

1. 1986 to 1988 $\dfrac{\text{change in cost}}{\text{change in years}} = \dfrac{\boxed{}}{\boxed{}} = \dfrac{\boxed{}}{\boxed{}} = \boxed{}$

2. 1988 to 1989 $\dfrac{\text{change in cost}}{\text{change in years}} = \dfrac{\boxed{}}{\boxed{}} = \dfrac{\boxed{}}{\boxed{}} = \boxed{}$

3. 1989 to 1991 $\dfrac{\text{change in cost}}{\text{change in years}} = \dfrac{\boxed{}}{\boxed{}} = \dfrac{\boxed{}}{\boxed{}} = \boxed{}$

4. Which time interval showed the greatest rate of change? _____

5. Was the rate of change ever negative? If so, when? _____

Holt McDougal Algebra 1

LESSON 4-3

Review for Mastery

Rate of Change and Slope continued

When graphing rates of change, if all the segments have the same rate of change (same steepness), they form a straight line. This rate of change is called the slope.

Find the slope of the line.

Step 1: First choose any two points on the line.

Step 2: Begin at one of the points.

Step 3: Count vertically until you are even with the second point.

This is the rise. If you go down the rise will be negative. If you go up the rise will be positive.

Step 4: Count over until you are at the second point.

This is the run. If you go left the run will be negative. If you go right the run will be positive.

Step 5: Divide to find the slope.

$$\text{slope} = \frac{\text{rise}}{\text{sun}} = -\frac{6}{2} = -3$$

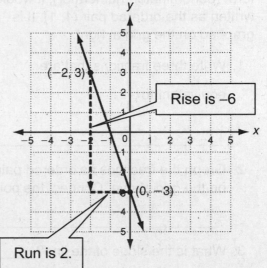

Rise is –6

Run is 2.

Find the slope of each line.

6.

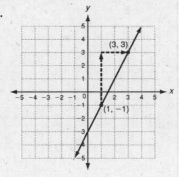

7.

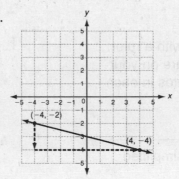

8.

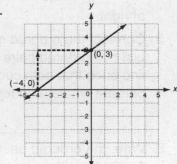

_____ _____ _____

9.

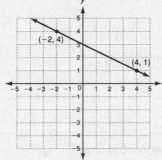

10.

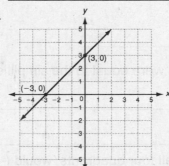

11.

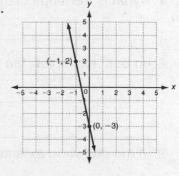

_____ _____ _____

Holt McDougal Algebra 1

LESSON 4-3

Challenge

Graphing Equivalent Fractions

If $\frac{1}{4}$ is written as an ordered pair in the

form (denominator, numerator), it would be
written as the ordered pair (4, 1). It is
graphed on the grid at right.

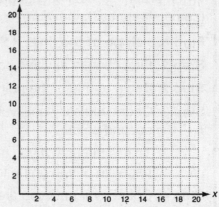

1. Write three fractions that are

   equivalent to $\frac{1}{4}$.

   _____

2. Graph the fractions as ordered pairs
   on the grid above. Connect the points. What do you notice?

   _____

3. What is the slope of the line? _____

4. Graph $\frac{1\frac{1}{2}}{2}$, $\frac{4\frac{1}{2}}{6}$, and $\frac{5\frac{1}{4}}{7}$ on the grid

   at right.

5. Connect the ordered pairs with a ruler.
   List two ordered pairs that are on your
   line such that both coordinates in each
   pair are whole numbers.

   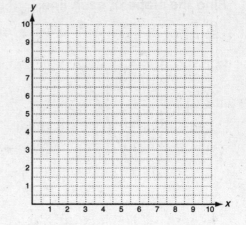

   _____

6. Write the ordered pairs as simplified
   fractions.

   _____

7. What is the slope of the line?

   _____

8. In both examples, the slopes were equal to the simplified fractions. Why?

   _____

   _____

9. If the grid were extended to all four quadrants, would (–4, –3) be on the line?

   Explain. _____

Holt McDougal Algebra 1

Name _____ Date _____ Class _____

Problem Solving

Rate of Change and Slope

Write the correct answer.

1. The table shows the cost per pound of Granny Smith apples.

Weight (lb)	1	2	3	4
Cost ($)	1.49	2.98	4.47	5.96

Describe the rate(s) of change shown by the data.

_____

_____

2. The table shows Gabe's height on his birthday for five years. Find the rate of change during each time interval.

Age	9	11	12	13	15
Height (in.)	58	59.5	61.5	65	69

_____

_____

When did the greatest rate of change occur? _____

When was the rate of change the least?

_____

During which two time periods were the rates of change the same?

_____

3. The table shows the distance of a courier from her destination.

Time (p.m.)	2:15	2:30	2:45	3:00
Distance (mi)	5.4	5.4	5.0	0.5

What is the rate of change from 2:15 p.m. to 2:30 p.m.? What does this rate of change mean?

_____

_____

The graph below tracks regular gasoline prices from July 2004 to December 2004. Use the graph to answer questions 5–7. Select the best answer.

4. What is the slope of the line from November to December?

   A −4   C −0.04

   B −1   D −0.01

5. During which time interval did the cost decrease at the greatest rate?

   F Jul to Aug   H Sep to Oct

   G Aug to Sep   J Oct to Nov

6. During which time interval was the slope positive?

   A Jul to Aug   C Sep to Oct

   B Aug to Sep   D Oct to Nov

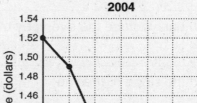

Regular Gasoline Prices 2004

7. What was the rate of change from October to December?

   F −0.05   H 0.025

   G −0.025   J 0.05

Reading Strategies
Focus on Vocabulary

Study the vocabulary web below to understand how rate of change and slope are related.

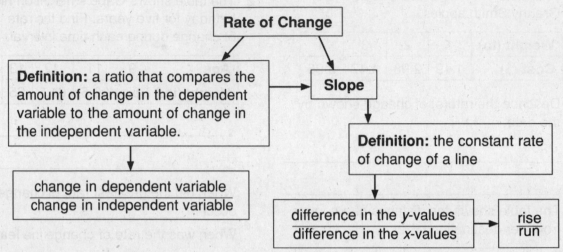

The table shows the temperatures (in °F) at one location at different times.

Time	8 am	11 am	1 pm	5 pm
Temperature	68	80	84	88

1. Which is the dependent variable? _____

2. Which is the independent variable? _____

3. Calculate the rate of change for each time interval.

   8 am to 11 am: _____ 11 am to 1 pm: _____ 1 pm to 5 pm: _____

4. In everyday life, *rise* means to move in an upward direction. How can this help you remember the math definition?

   _____

5. How can you use the everyday meaning of *run* to help you remember the math definition?

   _____

6. Find the slope of the line.

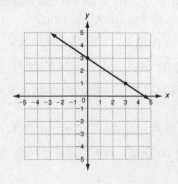

   _____

Holt McDougal Algebra 1

Name _____ Date _____ Class_____

LESSON 4-4

Practice A
The Slope Formula

Find the slope of the line that contains each pair of points.

1. (3, 1) and (9, 2)

$$m = \frac{y_2 - y_1}{x_2 - x_1}$$

$$= \frac{2-1}{\boxed{}-\boxed{}} = \frac{1}{\boxed{}}$$

2. (–2, 3) and (2, –1)

$$m = \frac{y_2 - y_1}{x_2 - x_1}$$

$$= \frac{-1-\boxed{}}{2-\boxed{}} = \frac{\boxed{}}{\boxed{}} = \boxed{}$$

3. (4, 6) and (0, –2)

$$m = \frac{y_2 - y_1}{x_2 - x_1}$$

$$= \frac{\boxed{}-\boxed{}}{\boxed{}-\boxed{}} = \frac{\boxed{}}{\boxed{}} = \boxed{}$$

Each graph or table shows a linear relationship. Find the slope.

4.

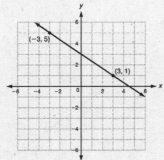

_____

5.

x	y
0	82
3	76
6	70
9	64
12	58

_____

6.

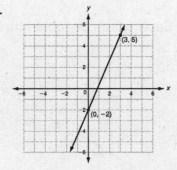

_____

Find the slope of each line. Then tell what the slope represents.

7.

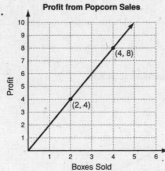

_____

_____

8.

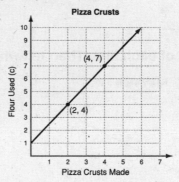

_____

_____

Complete the steps to find the slope of the line described by 2x + 5y = 10.

9. a. Find the *x*-intercept.

Let *y* = 0

2*x* + 5 (_____) = –10

_____ = –10

÷ _____ ÷ _____

x = _____

b. Find the *y*-intercept.

Let *x* = 0

2 (_____) + 5*y* = –10

_____ = –10

÷ _____ ÷ _____

y = _____

c. The line contains (___, 0) and (0, ____). Use the slope formula.

$$m = \frac{y_2 - y_1}{x_2 - x_1}$$

$$= \frac{\boxed{}-0}{0-\boxed{}} = \frac{\boxed{}}{\boxed{}}$$

Holt McDougal Algebra 1

LESSON 4-4

Practice B

The Slope Formula

Find the slope of the line that contains each pair of points.

1. (2, 8) and (1, −3)

$$m = \frac{y_2 - y_1}{x_2 - x_1}$$

$$= \frac{\boxed{} - \boxed{}}{\boxed{} - \boxed{}}$$

$$= \frac{\boxed{}}{\boxed{}} = \boxed{}$$

2. (−4, 0) and (−6, −2)

$$m = \frac{y_2 - y_1}{x_2 - x_1}$$

$$= \frac{\boxed{} - \boxed{}}{\boxed{} - \boxed{}}$$

$$= \frac{\boxed{}}{\boxed{}} = \boxed{}$$

3. (0, −2) and (4, −7)

$$m = \frac{y_2 - y_1}{x_2 - x_1}$$

$$= \frac{\boxed{} - \boxed{}}{\boxed{} - \boxed{}}$$

$$= \frac{\boxed{}}{\boxed{}}$$

Each graph or table shows a linear relationship. Find the slope.

4.

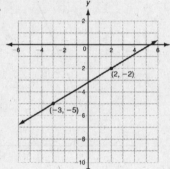

5.

x	y
1	3.75
2	5
3	6.25
4	7.50
5	8.75

6.

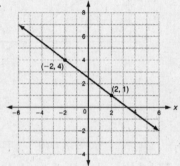

_____ _____ _____

Find the slope of each line. Then tell what the slope represents.

7.

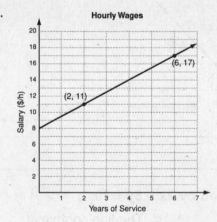

8.

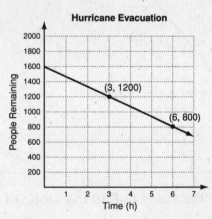

_____ _____

_____ _____

Find the slope of the line described by each equation.

9. $3x + 4y = 24$

10. $8x + 48 = 3y$

_____ _____

Holt McDougal Algebra 1

LESSON 4-4

Practice C
The Slope Formula

Find the slope of the line that contains each pair of points.

1. (2, –5) and (4, 3)

   m = _____

2. (0, –4) and (7, 1)

   m = _____

3. (6, 2) and (–9, –1)

   m = _____

4. (8, 8) and (2, –10)

   m = _____

5. (0, –1) and (–3, –1)

   m = _____

6. (6, 1) and (5, –2)

   m = _____

Each graph or table shows a linear relationship. Find the slope.

7.

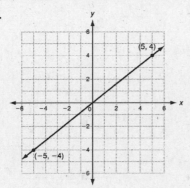

8.

x	y
10	–28
20	–24
30	–20
40	–16
50	–12

9.

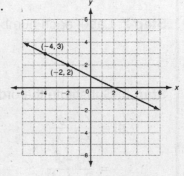

_____

_____

_____

Find the slope of each line. Then tell what the slope represents.

10.

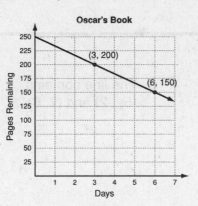

11.

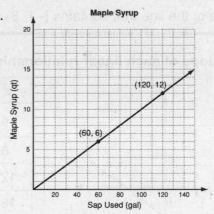

_____

_____

_____

_____

Find the slope of the line described by each equation.

12. $7x - 6y = 42$

13. $5x + 2y = 20$

14. $-2x + 8y = 24$

_____

_____

_____

15. $64 - 4y = -16x$

16. $8x = 4y - 1$

17. $y = 6x - 10$

_____

_____

_____

LESSON 4-4

Review for Mastery
The Slope Formula

You can find the slope of a line from any two ordered pairs. The ordered pairs can be given to you, or you might need to read them from a table or graph.

Find the slope of the line that contains (–1, 3) and (2, 0).

Step 1: Name the ordered pairs. (It does not matter which is first and which is second.)

first ordered pair ⟍ (–1, 3)　　　(2, 0) ⟋ second ordered pair

Step 2: Label each number in the ordered pairs.

$$(-1, 3) \qquad (2, 0)$$
$$(x_1, y_1) \qquad (x_2, y_2)$$

Step 3: Substitute the ordered pairs into the slope formula.

$$m = \frac{y_2 - y_1}{x_2 - x_1}$$

$$= \frac{0 - 3}{2 - (-1)}$$

$$= \frac{-3}{3}$$

$$= -1$$

The slope of the line that contains (–1, 3) and (2, 0) is –1.

Find the slope of each linear relationship.

1.

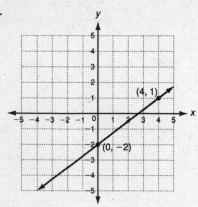

2.

x	y
4	–5
8	–3
12	–1
16	1

3. The line contains (5, –2) and (7, 6).

_____ _____ _____

Holt McDougal Algebra 1

LESSON 4-4

Review for Mastery

The Slope Formula continued

You can also find slope from an equation using the *x*- and *y*-intercepts.

Find the slope of the line described by $x - 3y = -9$.

Step 1: To find the *x*-intercept, substitute 0 for *y*.

$$x - 3y = -9$$
$$x - 3(0) = -9$$
$$x = -9$$

The *x*-intercept is –9.

Step 2: To find the *y*-intercept, substitute 0 for *x*.

$$x - 3y = -9$$
$$(0) - 3y = -9$$
$$-3y = -9$$
$$\frac{-3y}{-3} = \frac{-9}{-3}$$
$$y = 3$$

The *y*-intercept is 3.

Step 3: Use the slope formula with the points (–9, 0) and (0, 3).

$$m = \frac{y_2 - y_1}{x_2 - x_1}$$
$$= \frac{3 - 0}{0 - (-9)}$$
$$= \frac{3}{9}$$
$$= \frac{1}{3}$$

The slope of the line described by $x - 3y = -9$ is $\frac{1}{3}$.

Find the slope of the line described by each equation.

4. $-2x - 5y = 10$

5. $4x + 2y = 8$

6. $-6x + 2y = 12$

_____

_____

_____

7. $8y - 4x = 32$

8. $6y + 8x = 24$

9. $-\frac{1}{2}x + 2y = 3$

_____

_____

_____

Holt McDougal Algebra 1

Name _____ Date _____ Class_____

Challenge
Exploring the Meaning of a Difference Quotient

When two variables x and y are related and (x_1, y_1) and (x_2, y_2) satisfy the relationship, you can write the quotient as shown at right. The quotient is called a *difference quotient*.

$$\frac{y_2 - y_1}{x_2 - x_1}$$

The difference quotient can have different meanings in different situations.

In Exercises 1–5, use the grid at the right.

1. Graph and connect $A(-2, -3)$, $B(1, 3)$, and $C(3, 7)$.

2. Calculate the slope of $\overline{AB}$ and of $\overline{BC}$. _____

3. On the same grid, graph $D(2, 6)$. Connect A, B and D.

4. Calculate the slope of $\overline{AB}$ and of $\overline{BD}$. _____

5. Explain how to use a difference quotient to determine whether three points are collinear, that is, whether three points lie on the same line.

_____

Another application of the difference quotient is the measurement of the *grade*, or steepness, of a road. A grade of 3% means that the road surface rises 3 feet for every horizontal run of 100 feet. A roadway that slopes down has a negative grade.

6. If the vertical rise of a highway is 150 feet when the horizontal run is 5000 feet, what is the grade of the road?   _____

7. If the grade of a road is 5%, what is the vertical rise of the road when the horizontal run is 6000 feet?   _____

8. On a certain stretch of road, the point 420 feet east of point A is 24 feet lower than point A. Point B, 600 feet east of A, is 36 feet lower than point A.

   a. Find the grade of the road surface between points A and B. _____

   b. Would a motorist driving along a stretch of road from point B to point A report the same grade for the road as a motorist driving from A to B would report? Explain your response.

_____

In economics, the additional cost to produce one more unit of an item is called the *marginal cost* of the item. Marginal cost is found by computing the difference quotient, or difference in $\dfrac{\text{manufacturing cost}}{\text{difference in units made}}$.

9. The cost that a manufacturer pays for producing 5 pairs of shoes is $113. The cost to produce 12 pairs of shoes is $127. Use a difference quotient to find the marginal cost. _____

Holt McDougal Algebra 1

Name _____ Date _____ Class_____

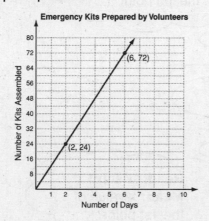

LESSON 4-4

Problem Solving
The Slope Formula

Write the correct answer.

1. The graph shows the number of emergency kits assembled by volunteers over a period of days. Find the slope of the line. Then tell what the slope represents.

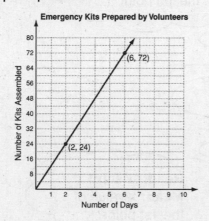

Emergency Kits Prepared by Volunteers

_____

_____

2. The graph shows how much flour is in a bag at different times. Find the slope of the line. Then tell what the slope represents.

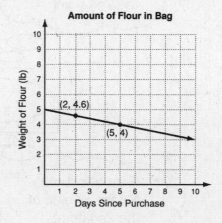

Amount of Flour in Bag

_____

_____

3. The function $20x - y = 250$ describes the profit y Bridget can make from selling x pairs of earrings. The graph of this function is a line. Find its slope.

_____

The graph below shows the cost of membership at Fabulously Fit.
Use the graph to answer questions 4–7. Select the best answer.

4. What is the slope of the line?

    A 24   C 50

    B 35   D 70

5. What does the slope represent?

    F the enrollment fee

    G the late payment fee

    H the total cost of membership

    J the monthly membership fee

6. A second line is graphed that shows the cost of membership at The Fitness Studio. The line contains (0, 35) and (5, 85). What is the slope of this line?

    A 10   C 45

    B 20   D 50

Membership at Fabulously Fit

7. How much greater is the monthly fee at Fabulously Fit than The Fitness Studio?

    F $15   H $35

    G $25   J $40

Holt McDougal Algebra 1

LESSON 4-4

Reading Strategies
Understanding Mathematical Notation

In the slope formula, *x*- and *y*-values of two different points are identified using subscripts, as described below.

> **Read:** "*y* sub 2"
> **Mean:** *y*-value of the 2nd point

> **Read:** "*y* sub 1"
> **Mean:** *y*-value of the 1st point

$$m = \frac{y_2 - y_1}{x_2 - x_1}$$

> **Read:** "*x* sub 2"
> **Mean:** *x*-value of the 2nd point

> **Read:** "*x* sub 1"
> **Mean:** *x*-value of the 1st point

Answer questions 1–3 using the table below.

x	−3	−2	−1	0	1
y	2	4	6	8	10

1. If you use −2 to represent x_1, what is the value of y_1? _____

2. Choose a different point to represent (x_2, y_2). _____

3. Calculate the slope of the line represented by the table. _____

Use the graph to complete questions 4 and 5.

4. Which two ordered pairs are plotted on the graph?

   _____

5. What is the slope of the line?

   _____

6. Find the slope of the line that contains

   (3, 6) and (−4, 6). _____

7. Describe the line in problem 6. _____

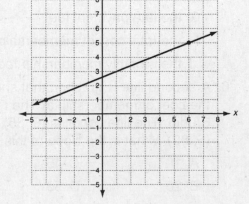

Holt McDougal Algebra 1

LESSON 4-5 Practice A
Direct Variation

Complete the table.

	Solve for y (if needed).	Is the equation in the form $y = kx$?	Is it a direct variation?	Constant of variation
1. $y = 7x$	$y = 7x$	yes	yes	
2. $y = 4x - 10$				
3. $5x - 2y = 0$				

Complete the table.

	Find the value of $\dfrac{y}{x}$ for each ordered pair.	Is the value of $\dfrac{y}{x}$ the same for each ordered pair?	Direct variation?
4. <table><tr><td>x</td><td>10</td><td>15</td><td>20</td></tr><tr><td>y</td><td>2</td><td>3</td><td>4</td></tr></table>			
5. <table><tr><td>x</td><td>4</td><td>8</td><td>12</td></tr><tr><td>y</td><td>16</td><td>20</td><td>24</td></tr></table>			

6. The value of y varies directly with x, and $y = -2$ when $x = -4$. Find y when $x = 8$.

   Find k: Use k to find y:

   $y = kx$ $y = kx$

   $-2 = k(-4)$ $y = (\underline{})(\underline{})$

   $\underline{} = k$ $y = \underline{}$

7. The value of y varies directly with x, and $y = 12$ when $x = 8$. Find y when $x = 15$.

   Find k: Use k to find y:

   $y = kx$ $y = kx$

   $12 = k(8)$ $y = (\underline{})(\underline{})$

   $\underline{} = k$ $y = \underline{}$

8. The number of hamburgers that can be made varies directly with the weight of ground beef used. Four hamburgers can be produced from every pound of ground beef. Write a direct variation equation for the number of hamburgers y that can be produced from x pounds of ground beef. Then graph the relationship.

   _____

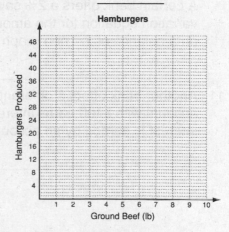

Hamburgers

Name _____ Date _____ Class _____

Practice B

Direct Variation

Tell whether each equation is a direct variation. If so, identify the constant of variation.

1. $y = 3x$ _____

2. $y = 2x - 9$ _____

3. $2x + 3y = 0$ _____

4. $3y = 9x$ _____

Find the value of $\frac{y}{x}$ for each ordered pair. Then, tell whether each relationship is a direct variation.

5.

x	6	15	21
y	2	5	7
$\frac{y}{x}$			

6.

x	6	10	25
y	24	40	100
$\frac{y}{x}$			

7.

x	10	15	20
y	3	5	9
$\frac{y}{x}$			

_____   _____   _____

8. The value of y varies directly with x, and $y = -18$ when $x = 6$.
   Find y when $x = -8$.

   Find k: Use k to find y:

   $y = kx$

   $y = (\underline{\quad})(\underline{\quad})$

   $\underline{\quad} = k$ $y = \underline{\quad\quad}$

9. The value of y varies directly with x, and $y = \frac{1}{2}$ when $x = 5$.
   Find y when $x = 30$.

   Find k: Use k to find y:

   $y = kx$

   $y = (\underline{\quad})(\underline{\quad})$

   $\underline{\quad} = k$ $y = \underline{\quad\quad}$

10. The amount of interest earned in a savings account varies directly with the amount of money in the account. A certain bank offers a 2% savings rate. Write a direct variation equation for the amount of interest y earned on a balance of x. Then graph.

_____

11. Another bank offers a different savings rate. If an account with $400 earns interest of $6, how much interest is earned by an account with $1800?

_____

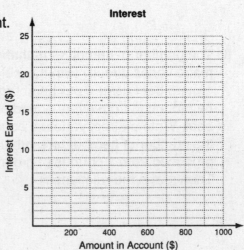

Holt McDougal Algebra 1

Name _____ Date _____ Class_____

Practice C
Direct Variation

Tell whether each equation is a direct variation. If so, identify the constant of variation.

1. $y = -2x$ _____

2. $8y = 3x + 1$ _____

3. $12y = 24x$ _____

4. $5x - 9y = 0$ _____

5. $6x + 3 = y$ _____

6. $y = 4x - 8$ _____

For 7–10, tell whether each relationship is a direct variation. Explain.

7.
x	−3	−6	−9
y	18	36	54

8.
x	8	0	−5
y	13	5	0

9.
x	−1	5	8.
y	−1.5	7.5	12

_____   _____   _____

_____   _____   _____

_____   _____   _____

10. The equation $F = \frac{9}{5}C + 32$ relates a temperature in degrees Fahrenheit F to the equivalent temperature in degrees Celsius C.

_____

11. The value of y varies directly with x, and $y = -14$ when $x = \frac{1}{2}$.

Find y when $x = -1$. _____

12. The value of y varies directly with x, and $y = 9$ when $x = 2$.

Find x when $y = 22.5$. _____

13. The area a painter can paint varies directly with the amount of time he works. One morning, he painted 204 ft^2 between 8 a.m. and 12:15 a.m. Write a direct variation equation to describe the area y covered in x hours.

_____

14. The number of people that can be seated in a lecture hall varies directly with the number of rows of seats. If 72 people can be seated in 4 rows, write a direct variation equation to describe the number of people y that can be seated in x rows. Then graph.

_____

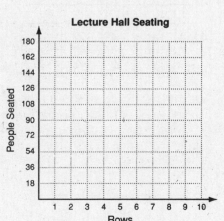

Lecture Hall Seating

People Seated: 18, 36, 54, 72, 90, 108, 126, 144, 162, 180

Rows: 1 2 3 4 5 6 7 8 9 10

Holt McDougal Algebra 1

LESSON 4-5 Review for Mastery

Direct Variation

A direct variation is a special type of linear relationship. It can be written in the form $y = kx$ where k is a nonzero constant called the constant of variation.

You can identify direct variations from equations or from ordered pairs.

Tell whether $2x + 4y = 0$ is a direct variation. If so, identify the constant of variation.

First, put the equation in the form $y = kx$.

$2x + 4y = 0$

$\underline{-2x \qquad -2x}$ *Add $-2x$ to each side.*

$4y = -2x$

$\dfrac{4y}{4} = -\dfrac{2x}{4}$ *Divide both sides by 4.*

$y = -\dfrac{1}{2}x$

Because the equation can be written in the form $y = kx$, it is a direct variation.

The constant of variation is $-\dfrac{1}{2}$.

Tell whether the relationship is a direct variation. If so, identify the constant of variation.

x	2	4	6
y	1	2	3

If we solve $y = kx$ for k, we get:

$y = kx \longrightarrow \dfrac{y}{x} = \dfrac{kx}{x} \longrightarrow \dfrac{y}{x} = k$

Find k for each ordered pair. This means find $\dfrac{y}{x}$ for each ordered pair. If they are the same, the relationship is a direct variation.

$\dfrac{1}{2} \qquad \dfrac{2}{4} = \dfrac{1}{2} \qquad \dfrac{3}{6} = \dfrac{1}{2}$

This is a direct variation.

Tell whether each equation or relationship is a direct variation. If so, identify the constant of variation.

1. $x + y = 7$

2. $4x - 3y = 0$

3. $-8y = 24x$

_____

4.

x	-4	2	10
y	2	-1	-5

5.

x	5	12	8
y	17.5	42	28

6.

x	6	8	10
y	8	10	12

_____   _____   _____

Holt McDougal Algebra 1

LESSON 4-5

Review for Mastery

Direct Variation continued

If you know one ordered pair that satisfies a direct variation, you can find and graph other ordered pairs that will also satisfy the direct variation.

The value of *y* varies directly with *x*, and *y* = 8 when *x* = 24. Find *y* when *x* = 27.

We have to find how the *y* varies with the change in *x*. Then we can find the value of *y* when *x* = 27.

$y = kx$	*Use the equation for direct variation.*
$8 = k(24)$	*Substitute 8 for y and 24 for x*
$\dfrac{8}{24} = \dfrac{k(24)}{24}$	*Solve for k.*
$\dfrac{1}{3} = k$	*Simplify.*
$y = \dfrac{1}{3}x$	*Write the direct variation equation.*
$y = \dfrac{1}{3}(27)$	*Substitute 27 for x.*
$y = 9$	

A garden snail can travel about 2.6 feet per minute. Write a direct variation equation for the distance *y* a snail will travel in *x* minutes. Then graph.

Step 1: Write an equation.

distance = 2.6 feet × minutes

$y = 2.6x$

Step 2: Generate ordered pairs.

x	$y = 2.6x$	(x, y)
0	$y = 2.6(0)$	$(0, 0)$
1	$y = 2.6(1)$	$(1, 2.6)$
2	$y = 2.6(2)$	$(2, 5.2)$

Step 3: Graph.

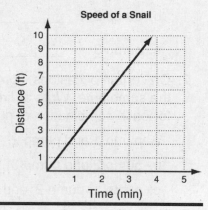

---

7. The value of *y* varies directly with *x*, and *y* = 8 when *x* = 2. Find *y* when *x* = 10.

   _____

8. The value of *y* varies directly with *x*, and *y* = 5 when *x* = –20. Find *y* when *x* = 35.

   _____

9. The cost of electricity to run a personal computer is about $2.13 per day. Write a direct variation equation for the electrical cost *y* of running a computer each day *x*. Then graph.

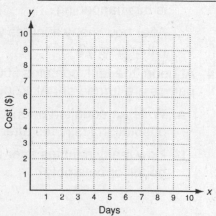

_____

Holt McDougal Algebra 1

LESSON 4-5

Challenge
Combining Direct-Variation Relationships

In Lesson 5.3, you learned that when y varies directly as x, there is a nonzero number, k, such that $y = kx$. There are many situations in which one variable varies directly with another variable.

A 700-gallon tank contains 500 gallons of a certain liquid. Three pumps feed three different ingredients into the tank at its top. A discharge pump at the base of the tank removes the mixed ingredients. The rates at which the pipes feed and remove liquid are shown at right.

Pump 1:	5 gallons per minute
Pump 2:	10 gallons per minute
Pump 3:	15 gallons per minute
Discharge pump:	35 gallons per minute

Let t represent the amount of time for which each pipe is operating.

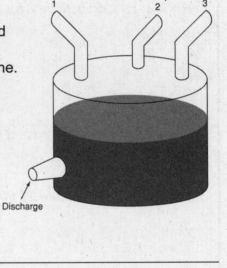

1. Write a direct-variation relationship for the gallons supplied by each pump. Then find the amount of time that it takes for each pump to fill the tank to capacity if each works alone.

   a. pump 1 _____

   b. pump 2 _____

   c. pump 3 _____

2. On certain occasions, some pumps are turned on at the same time. Write a direct-variation relationship for each combination of pumps operating simultaneously.

   a. pump 1 and pump 2 _____

   b. pump 2 and pump 3 _____

   c. pump 1, pump 2, and pump 3 _____

3. At noon, the tank contains 500 gallons of solution. At noon, all pumps, and the discharge pump, are turned on simultaneously.

   a. Write an equation for the quantity, Q, of solution t minutes after noon. _____

   b. Is the tank filling or emptying? At what rate is this happening? _____

   c. After how many minutes will the tank be full or empty? _____

4. At noon, the tank contains 500 gallons of solution and all feeder pumps are turned on. At 12:06 p.m., the discharge pump is turned on.

   a. Write an equation or equations for the quantity, Q, of solution t minutes after noon. _____

   b. How many minutes after noon will the tank either be full or be empty? _____

Holt McDougal Algebra 1

Name _____ Date _____ Class_____

Problem Solving
Direct Variation

Write the correct answer.

1. Wesley earns $6.50 per hour at the bookstore. The total amount of his paycheck varies directly with the number of hours he works. Write a direct variation equation for the amount of money y Wesley earns for working x hours.

   _____

2. The equation $-4x + y = 0$ relates the number of pages in a photo album y to the number of pictures in the album x. Tell whether the relationship is a direct variation. Explain your answer.

   _____

3. The formula $9x - 5y = -160$ relates the temperature in degrees Fahrenheit y to the temperature in degrees Celsius x. Tell whether the relationship is a direct variation. Explain your answer.

   _____

   _____

4. The number of miles driven varies directly with the number of gallons of gas used. Erin drove 297 miles on 9 gallons of gas. How far would she be able to drive on 14 gallons of gas?

   _____

Select the best answer.

5. The table shows the relationship between the number of lemons purchased and their cost.

Lemons x	1	2	3	4
Cost y	0.1	0.2	0.3	0.4

   Is the relationship a direct variation?

   A Yes; it can be written as $y = 0.1x$.

   B Yes; it can be written as $y = 10x$.

   C No; it cannot be written as $y = kx$.

   D No; the relationship is not a function.

6. The table shows the relationship between the hours since sunrise and the temperature in degrees Celsius.

Hour x	1	2	3	4
Temp. y	25	26	28	32

   Is the relationship a direct variation?

   F Yes; it can be written as $y = 25x$.

   G Yes; it can be written as $y = 8x$.

   H No; it cannot be written as $y = kx$.

   J No; the relationship is not a function.

7. The Diaz family is driving at a constant speed on the highway so their distance varies directly with their speed. They traveled 17.5 miles in 15 minutes. How far did they travel in 2 hours?

   A 50 miles   C 140 miles

   B 70 miles   D 262.5 miles
                           (17.5 times 15)

8. On July 26, 2005, it rained a record 37 inches in Mumbai, India, in a 24-hour period. Which equation of direct variation relates the number of inches of rain y to the number of hours x?

   F $y = \dfrac{24}{37}x$ H $y = 24x$

   G $y = \dfrac{37}{24}x$ J $y = 37x$

                                 Holt McDougal Algebra 1

LESSON 4-5

Reading Strategies

Applying a Formula

A *direct variation* is a special type of linear relationship. It can be expressed using the formula $y = kx$, where k is the *constant of variation*.

The equation $y = \frac{3}{4}x$ is a direct variation because it is in the form $y = kx$, where $k = \frac{3}{4}$

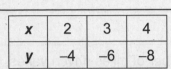

x	2	3	4
y	−4	−6	−8

The relationship shown in the table is a direct variation because

$k = \frac{y}{x} = -2$ for each ordered pair.

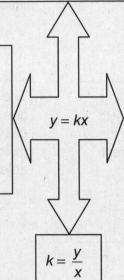

$y = kx$

$k = \frac{y}{x}$

The value of y varies directly with x and $y = 5$ when $x = 2$.

$$y = kx$$
$$5 = k2$$
$$\frac{5}{2} = k$$

Find y when $x = 8$.

$$y = \frac{5}{2}(8)$$
$$y = 20$$

Identify k, the constant of variation, for each direct variation.

1. $y = 8x$

2. $y = \frac{x}{3}$

3. $-2y = 5x$

_____   _____   _____

Solve each equation for y. Tell whether or not it is a direct variation.

4. $x + y = 12$

_____

5. $6x = 4y$

_____

6. Calculate $\frac{y}{x}$ for each ordered pair in the table.

x	−4	−2	4
y	−2	−1	2

_____

7. Is this a direct variation? _____

8. The value of y varies directly with x, and $y = 21$ when $x = 7$.
   Find y when $x = 4$. _____

Holt McDougal Algebra 1

LESSON 4-6

Practice A

Slope-Intercept Form

Write the equation that describes each line in slope-intercept form.

1. slope = $\frac{2}{3}$; *y*-intercept = 2

   $y = $ _____ $x +$ _____

2. slope = -1; *y*-intercept = -8

   $y = $ _____ $x -$ _____

3. slope = -2; (3, 5) is on the line.
   Find the *y*-intercept: $y = mx + b$

   $5 = (-2)(\_\_\_) + b$

   $5 = \_\_\_ + b$

   $+\_\_\_ + \_\_\_$

   $\_\_\_ = b$

   Write the equation: $y = $ _____ $x +$ _____

Write each equation in slope-intercept form. Then graph the line.

4. $y - 2x = -4$

5. $y - 3 = -\frac{1}{2}x$

6. $2x + 3y = 6$

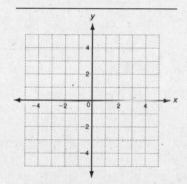

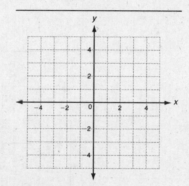

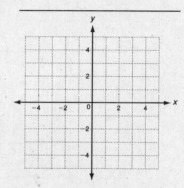

7. A school orders 25 desks for each classroom, plus 30 spare desks. The total number ordered as a function of the number of classrooms is shown in the graph.

   a. Write the equation represented by the graph.

   _____

   b. Identify the slope and *y*-intercept and describe their meanings. _____

   _____

   c. Find the total number of desks ordered if there are 24 classrooms.

   _____

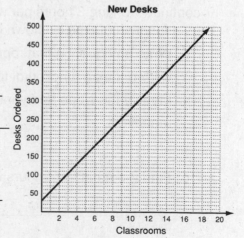

Holt McDougal Algebra 1

LESSON 4-6

Practice B

Slope-Intercept Form

Write the equation that describes each line in slope-intercept form.

1. slope = 4; y-intercept = -3

   $y =$ _____

2. slope = -2; y-intercept = 0

   $y =$ _____

3. slope = $-\dfrac{1}{3}$; y-intercept = 6

   $y =$ _____

4. slope = $\dfrac{2}{5}$, (10, 3) is on the line.

   Find the y-intercept $y = mx + b$

   ____ = (____) ____ + b

   ____ = ____ + b

   ____ = b

   Write the equation: $y =$ _____

Write each equation in slope-intercept form. Then graph the line described by the equation.

5. $y + x = 3$

6. $y + 4 = \dfrac{4}{3}x$

7. $5x - 2y = 10$

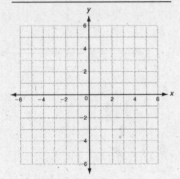

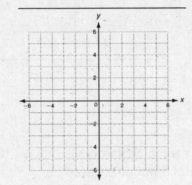

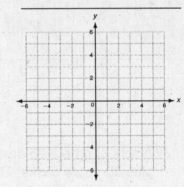

8. Daniel works as a volunteer in a homeless shelter. So far, he has worked 22 hours, and he plans to continue working 3 hours per week. His hours worked as a function of time is shown in the graph.

   a. Write an equation that represents the hours Daniel will work as a function of time. _____

   b. Identify the slope and y-intercept and describe their meanings. _____

   _____

   c. Find the number of hours worked after 16 weeks.

   _____

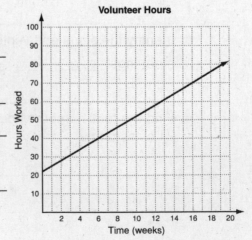

Volunteer Hours

Holt McDougal Algebra 1

LESSON 4-6

Practice C
Slope-Intercept Form

Write the equation that describes each line in slope-intercept form.

1. slope $= -\dfrac{3}{2}$; y-intercept $= 1$ 2. slope $= -3$, $(-3, 4)$ is on the line.

_____   _____

3. slope $= 0$; y-intercept $= -8$ 4. slope $= -\dfrac{4}{7}$; $(7, -8)$ is on the line.

_____   _____

5. The line that passes through $(1, 5)$ and $(4, -4)$. (*Hint:* Find the slope first.) _____

Write each equation in slope-intercept form. Then graph the line described by the equation.

6. $y - 2 = -3x$ 7. $x - y = 2$ 8. $-2y = 3x - 4$

_____   _____   _____

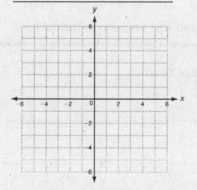 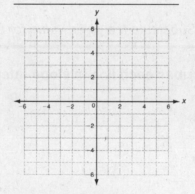 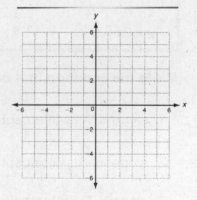

9. The Johnsons are putting new carpet in their home. Installation is $300 and the carpeting costs $4 per square foot. The total price of the job as a function of area is shown in the graph.

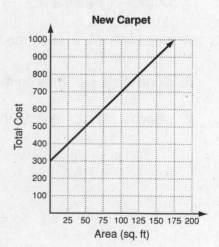

New Carpet

a. Write an equation that represents the total price as a function of area. _____

b. Identify the slope and y-intercept and describe their meanings. _____

_____

c. Find the total cost if the area is 375 square feet.

_____

Holt McDougal Algebra 1

LESSON 4-6

Review for Mastery

Slope-Intercept Form

An equation is in **slope-intercept form** if it is written as:

$$y = mx + b.$$

> *m* is the slope.
> *b* is the *y*-intercept.

A line has a slope of –4 and a *y*-intercept of 3. Write the equation in slope-intercept form.

$y = mx + b$ *Substitute the given values for m and b.*

$y = -4x + 3$

A line has a slope of 2. The ordered pair (3, 1) is on the line. Write the equation in slope-intercept form.

Step 1: Find the *y*-intercept.

$y = mx + b$

$y = 2x + b$ *Substitute the given value for m.*

$1 = 2(3) + b$ *Substitute the given values for x and y.*

$1 = 6 + b$ *Solve for b.*

$\underline{-6 \quad -6}$

$-5 = b$

Step 2: Write the equation.

$y = mx + b$

$y = 2x - 5$ *Substitute the given value for m and the value you found for b.*

Write the equation that describes each line in slope-intercept form.

1. slope $= \dfrac{1}{4}$, *y*-intercept $= 3$ _____

2. slope $= -5$, *y*-intercept $= 0$ _____

3. slope $= 7$, *y*-intercept $= -2$ _____

4. slope is 3, (4, 6) is on the line.   _____

5. slope is $\dfrac{1}{2}$, (–2, 8) is on the line.   _____

6. slope is –1, (5, –2) is on the line.   _____

      Holt McDougal Algebra 1

LESSON 4-6

Review for Mastery
Slope-Intercept Form continued

You can use the slope and *y*-intercept to graph a line.

Write $2x + 6y = 12$ in slope-intercept form. Then graph the line.

Step 1: Solve for *y*.

$2x + 6y = 12$ *Subtract 2x from both sides.*

$$\underline{-2x \qquad -2x}$$
$$6y = -2x + 12$$

$$\frac{6y}{6} = \frac{-2x + 12}{6}$$ *Divide both sides by 6.*

$$y = -\frac{1}{3}x + 2$$ *Simplify.*

Step 2: Find the slope and *y*-intercept.

slope: $m = -\frac{1}{3} = \frac{-1}{3}$

y-intercept: $b = 2$

Step 3: Graph the line.

- Plot (0, 2).
- Then count 1 **down** (because the rise is **negative**) and 3 **right** (because the run is **positive**) and plot another point.
- Draw a line connecting the points.

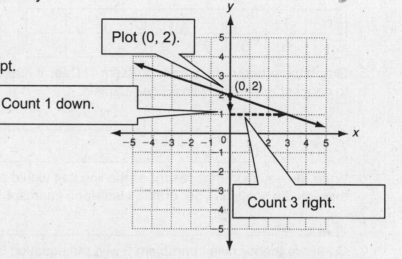

Plot (0, 2).

Count 1 down.

Count 3 right.

Write the following equations in slope-intercept form.

7. $5x + y = 30$

8. $x - y = 7$

9. $-4x + 3y = 12$

_____   _____   _____

10. Write $2x - y = 3$ in slope-intercept form.
 Then graph the line.

_____

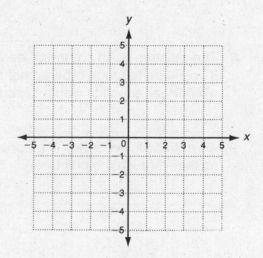

    Holt McDougal Algebra 1

Challenge
Revisiting Arithmetic Sequences

In Lesson 4-6, you learned about arithmetic sequences. In this activity, you
will see that arithmetic sequences and linear equations are closely related.

For 1–7, consider this arithmetic sequence: 3, 5, 7, 9, . . .

1. What is the first term a_1 of the sequence?   _____

2. What is the common difference d of the sequence?   _____

3. Use what you learned in Lesson 4-6 to write a
   formula for the nth term of the sequence.   _____

4. Complete this table, where x is the term number
   and y is the term.

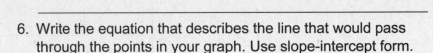

x	1	2					
y	3	5	7	9			

5. Graph the ordered pairs from problem 4. Does it make sense
   to connect the points with a line? Explain.

   _____

   _____

6. Write the equation that describes the line that would pass
   through the points in your graph. Use slope-intercept form.

   _____

7. Compare the formula in problem 3 with the equation in
   problem 6.

   a. What part of the equation relates to the common
      difference in the formula?

   _____

   b. What is the relationship between the first term in the formula and the
      y-intercept in the equation?

   _____

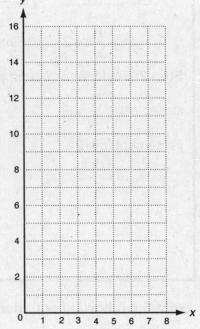

8. The nth term of an arithmetic sequence is given by the formula $a_n = 5 + (n - 1)(-3)$.
   If you were to graph ordered pairs where x is the term number and y is the term,
   what linear equation would describe the line that passes through the points?

   _____

9. An arithmetic sequence is graphed on a coordinate plane. The equation of the line that
   passes through the points is $y = 5x - 1$. What is the formula for the nth term?

   _____

Name _____ Date _____ Class _____

Problem Solving
Slope-Intercept Form

The cost of food for an honor roll dinner is $300 plus $10 per student. The cost of the food as a function of the number of students is shown in the graph. Write the correct answer.

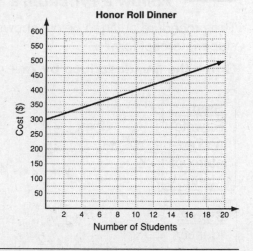

Honor Roll Dinner

1. Write an equation that represents the cost as a function of the number of students.

_____

2. Identify the slope and y-intercept and describe their meanings.

_____

_____

3. Find the cost of the food for 50 students. _____

Laura is on a two-day hike in the Smoky Mountains. She hiked 8 miles on the first day and is hiking at a rate of 3 mi/h on the second day. Her total distance as a function of time is shown in the graph. Select the best answer.

4. Which equation represents Laura's total distance as a function of time?

   A $y = 3x$ C $y = 3x + 8$

   B $y = 8x$ D $y = 8x + 3$

5. What does the slope represent?

   F Laura's total distance after one day

   G Laura's total distance after two days

   H the number of miles Laura hiked per hour on the first day

   J the number of miles Laura hikes per hour on the second day

6. What does the *y*-intercept represent?

   A Laura's total distance after one day

   B Laura's total distance after two days

   C the number of miles Laura hiked per hour on the first day

   D the number of miles Laura hikes per hour on the second day

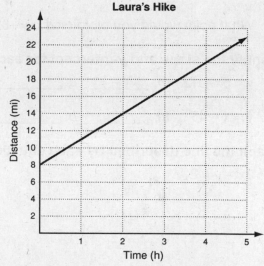

Laura's Hike

7. What will be Laura's total distance if she hikes for 6 hours on the second day?

   F 14 miles   H 26 miles

   G 18 miles   J 28 miles

Holt McDougal Algebra 1

LESSON 4-6

Reading Strategies
Follow a Procedure

The procedure outlined below shows how to graph a line using slope-intercept form.

Graph the line described by $2x + y = 4$.

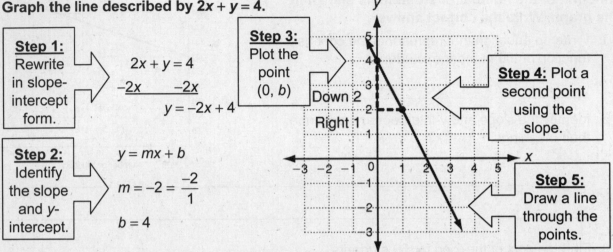

Step 1: Rewrite in slope-intercept form.

$2x + y = 4$
$\underline{-2x \qquad -2x}$
$y = -2x + 4$

Step 2: Identify the slope and y-intercept.

$y = mx + b$
$m = -2 = \dfrac{-2}{1}$
$b = 4$

Step 3: Plot the point $(0, b)$

Down 2
Right 1

Step 4: Plot a second point using the slope.

Step 5: Draw a line through the points.

Answer the following.

1. What is the benefit of always writing slope as a fraction?

_____

2. What point would you plot first if $b = -8$? _____

Identify the slope and y-intercept for each equation.

3. $y = 5x + 12$ m: _____ b: _____

4. $y = -3x$ m: _____ b: _____

5. $y = x - 4$ m: _____ b: _____

6. $3y = x + 9$ m: _____ b: _____

Graph the line described by each equation.

7. $3x + y = 2$

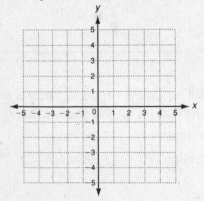

8. $x - 2y = 6$

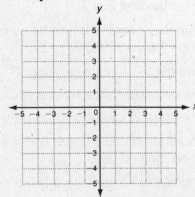

Holt McDougal Algebra 1

LESSON
4-7

Practice A
Point-Slope Form

Match each graph with the correct slope and point.

1. slope = $\frac{1}{2}$; (0, 2) _____

2. slope = $-\frac{1}{2}$; (2, 0) _____

3. slope = –2; (2, 0) _____

A
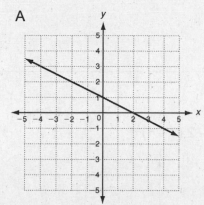

B
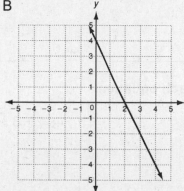

C
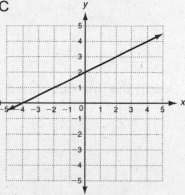

Write an equation in point-slope form for the line with the given slope that contains the given point.

4. slope = 4; (3, 8)

5. slope = $-\frac{1}{2}$; (5, –3)

_____   _____

Write the equation that describes each line in slope-intercept form.

6. slope = 5; (1, 7) is on the line

7. slope = –3; (4, 0) is on the line

_____   _____

8. (0, 2) and (2, 6) are on the line

9. (8, –2) and (4, –4) are on the line

_____   _____

Find the intercepts of the line that contains each pair of points.

10. (2, 5) and (–6, 25) _____

11. (2, 9) and (–4, –9) _____

12. The cost to have T-shirts made with the school logo is a function of the number of T-shirts ordered. The costs for 20, 50, and 100 shirts are shown. Write an equation in slope-intercept form that represents the function. Then find the cost of ordering 130 T-shirts.

_____

T-shirts	20	50	100
Cost ($)	190	430	830

Holt McDougal Algebra 1

LESSON 4-7 Practice B
Point-Slope Form

Write an equation in point-slope form for the line with the given slope that contains the given point.

1. slope = 3; (−4, 2)

2. slope = −1; (6, −1)

_____   _____

Graph the line described by each equation.

3. $y + 2 = -\dfrac{2}{3}(x - 6)$

4. $y + 3 = -2(x - 4)$

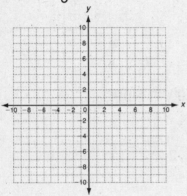   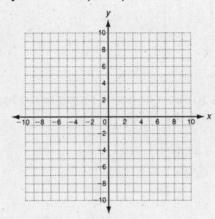

Write the equation that describes the line in slope-intercept form.

5. slope = −4; (1, −3) is on the line

6. slope = $\dfrac{1}{2}$; (−8, −5) is on the line

_____   _____

7. (2, 1) and (0, −7) are on the line

8. (−6, −6) and (2, −2) are on the line

_____   _____

Find the intercepts of the line that contains each pair of points.

9. (−1, −4) and (6, 10) _____

10. (3, 4) and (−6, 16) _____

11. The cost of internet access at a cafe is a function of time.
    The costs for 8, 25, and 40 minutes are shown. Write an equation
    in slope-intercept form that represents the function. Then find the
    cost of surfing the web at the cafe for one hour.

Time (min)	8	25	40
Cost ($)	4.36	7.25	9.80

_____

Holt McDougal Algebra 1

LESSON 4-7 Practice C
Point-Slope Form

Write an equation in point-slope form for the line with the given slope that contains the given point.

1. slope = $\frac{4}{3}$; (–5, –3)

2. slope = –3; (0, 8)

_____   _____

Graph the line described by each equation.

3. $y - 1 = -2(x - 2)$

4. $y + 3 = 2(x + 1)$

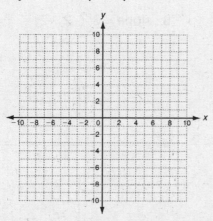

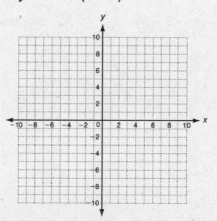

Write the equation that describes the line in slope-intercept form.

5. slope = –4; (2, –1) is on the line

6. slope = $\frac{1}{4}$; (–2, 3) is on the line

_____   _____

7. (–3, 6) and (2, 1) are on the line

8. (0, –5) and (6, –3) are on the line

_____   _____

Find the intercepts of the line that contains each pair of points.

9. (–7, 12) and (14, –6) _____

10. (2, 5) and (–6, 25) _____

11. A pool is being drained at a constant rate. The amount of water is a function of the number of minutes the pool has been draining, as shown in the table. Write an equation in slope-intercept form that represents the function. Then find the amount of water in the pool after two and a half hours.

Time (min)	12	20	50
Volume (gal)	4962	4754	3974

_____

Holt McDougal Algebra 1

LESSON 4-7

Review for Mastery
Point-Slope Form

You can graph a line if you know the slope and any point on the line.

Graph the line with slope 2 that contains the point (3, 1).

Step 1: Plot (3, 1).

Step 2: The slope is 2 or $\frac{2}{1}$; Count 2 **up** and

1 right and plot another point.

Step 3: Draw a line connecting the points.

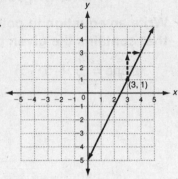

Graph the line with the given slope that contains the given point.

1. slope = $\frac{2}{3}$; (−3, −3)

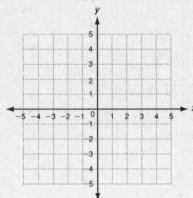

2. slope = $\frac{-1}{2}$; (−2, 4)

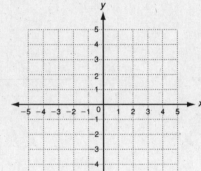

3. slope = 3; (−2, −2)

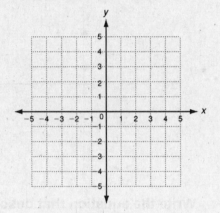

4. slope = $\frac{3}{2}$; (1, 2)

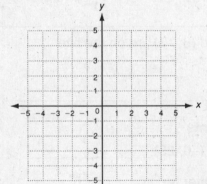

5. slope = −2; (−3, 2)

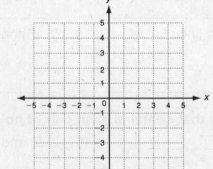

6. slope = $-\frac{2}{3}$; (2, 4)

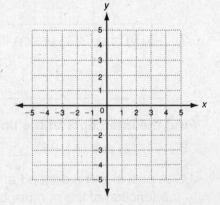

Holt McDougal Algebra 1

LESSON 4-7

Review for Mastery

Point-Slope Form continued

You can write a linear equation in slope-intercept form if you are given the slope and a point on the line, or if you are given any two points on the line.

Write an equation that describes each line in slope intercept form.

slope = 3, (4, 2) is on the line

Step 1: Write the equation in point-slope form.

$$y - 2 = 3(x - 4)$$

Step 2: Write the equation in slope-intercept form by solving for x

$$y - 2 = 3(x - 4)$$
$$y - 2 = 3x - 12$$
$$\underline{+2 \qquad\quad +2}$$
$$y = 3x - 10$$

(10, 1) and (8, 5) are on the line

Step 1: Find the slope.

$$m = \frac{y_2 - y_1}{x_2 - x_1} = \frac{5 - 1}{8 - 10} = \frac{4}{-2} = -2$$

Step 2: Substitute the slope and one point into the point-slope form. Then write in slope-intercept form.

$$y - y_1 = m(x - x_1)$$
$$y - 5 = -2(x - 8)$$
$$y - 5 = -2x + 16$$
$$\underline{+5 \qquad\quad +5}$$
$$y = -2x + 21$$

Write the equation that describes the line in slope-intercept form.

7. slope = −3; (1, 2) is on the line

8. slope = $\frac{1}{4}$; (8, 3) is on the line

_____

_____

9. slope = 4; (2, 8) is on the line

10. (1, 2) and (3, 12) are on the line

_____

_____

11. (6, 2) and (−2, −2) are on the line

12. (4, 1) and (1, 4) are on the line

_____

_____

Holt McDougal Algebra 1

LESSON 4-7

Challenge
Connect the Dots

The objective of this game is to write and graph linear equations such that each line passes through as many points as possible. Each equation must be written in slope-intercept form, but you may use point-slope form as part of your work.

Two-player version:

o Each player takes a turn writing and graphing one linear equation that passes through points on the graph. Allow time for the player to make calculations. Check each other's work for accuracy—sometimes a line may come close to a point but not actually intersect it.

o The player scores 5 points for each point on the graph that the line passes through. If the line passes through a point that was previously intersected by a line, the player does not get credit for it.

o After all points have been used, tally your scores to see who wins.

Single-player version:

o Try to write equations for the fewest number of lines that intersect all of the points.

o If other students in your class are playing as single players, compare results to see who was able to use the fewest lines. Challenge yourselves to find ways to further reduce the number of lines that you used.

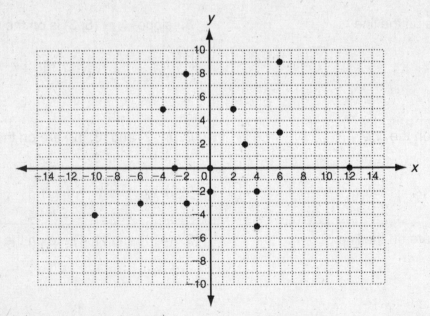

Tell how to make a game board that would result in a tie.

_____

LESSON 4-7 Problem Solving
Point-Slope Form

Write the correct answer.

1. The number of students in a school has been increasing at a constant rate. The table shows the number of students in the school for certain numbers of years since 1995.

Years Since 1995	Number of Students
0	118
5	124
10	130

Write an equation in point-slope form that represents this linear function.

_____

Write the equation in slope-intercept form.

_____

Assuming the rate of change remains constant, how many students will be in the school in 2010?

_____

2. Toni is finishing a scarf at a constant rate. The table shows the number of hours Toni has spent knitting this week and the corresponding number of rows in the scarf.

Toni's Knitting	
Hours	Rows of Knitting
2	38
4	44
6	50

Write an equation in slope-intercept form that represents this linear function.

_____

3. A photo lab manager graphed the cost of having photos developed as a function of the number of photos in the order. The graph is a line with a slope of $\frac{1}{10}$ that passes through (10, 6). Write an equation in slope-intercept form that describes the cost to have photos developed. How much does it cost to have 25 photos developed?

_____

The cost of a cell phone for one month is a linear function of the number of minutes used. The total cost for 20, 35, and 40 additional minutes are shown. Select the best answer.

4. What is the slope of the line represented in the table?

    A 0.1   C 2

    B 0.4   D 2.5

5. What would be the monthly cost if 60 additional minutes were used?

    F $64   H $84

    G $72   J $150

Cell-Phone Costs			
Number of Additional Minutes	20	35	40
Total Cost	$48	$54	$56

6. What does the *y*-intercept of the function represent?

    A total cost of the bill

    B cost per additional minute

    C number of additional minutes used

    D cost with no additional minutes used

Reading Strategies
Use a Concept Map

The point-slope form of a line can be used when writing linear equations.

Equation	**Writing Equations in Point-Slope Form**
$y - y_1 = m(x - x_1)$	A line with slope 3 which contains the point $(-6, 2)$ can be written in point-slope form as $y - 2 = 3[x - (-6)]$, or $y - 2 = 3(x + 6)$.
Changing Point-Slope Form to Slope-Intercept Form $y - 2 = 3(x + 6)$ $y - 2 = 3x + 18$ $y = 3x + 20$	**Uses** The point-slope form can be used to write a linear equation when given either... • a point and the slope • two points ...and then simplified to slope-intercept form to graph.

Point-Slope Form

Complete the following.

1. What two pieces of information do you need to write an equation in point-slope form?

   _____

2. In the concept map above, it states that you can write an equation in point-slope form if given two points on the line. What piece of information do you still need and how can you get it?

   _____

   _____

3. Write an equation in point-slope form for the line with slope 4 that contains $(3, -10)$.

   _____

4. Write an equation in slope-intercept form for the line that contains points $(2, -5)$ and $(-4, 7)$.

   _____

Holt McDougal Algebra 1

LESSON 4-8

Practice A
Line of Best Fit

1. The data in the table are graphed at the right along with two lines of fit.

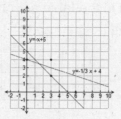

x	0	3	3	6
y	4	2	4	0

a. Find the sum of the squares of the residuals for $y = -x + 5$. _____

b. Find the sum of the squares of the residuals for $y = -\dfrac{1}{3}x + 4$. _____

c. Which line is a better fit for the data?_____

2. Use the data in the table to answer the questions that follow.

x	2	4	5	7	10
y	4.3	4.8	5.1	5.75	6.4

a. Find an equation for a line of best fit. _____

b. What is the correlation coefficient? _____

c. How well does the line represent the data? _____

d. Describe the correlation. _____

3. Use the data in the table to answer the questions that follow.

x	10	8	6	4	2
y	3	3.2	3.5	3.8	4

a. Find an equation for a line of best fit. _____

b. What is the correlation coefficient? _____

c. How well does the line represent the data? _____

d. Describe the correlation. _____

4. The table shows the average number of hours of sleep per night that four students had during the week versus their grades on a test. The equation of the line of best fit is $y \approx 4.04x + 52.70$, and $r \approx 0.97$. Discuss correlation and causation for the data set.

Hours Slept	6	6.5	7.2	8.1
Test Score	76	80	82	85

_____

_____

Holt McDougal Algebra 1

Name _____ Date _____ Class_____

Practice B

Line of Best Fit

1. The data in the table are graphed at right along with two lines of fit.

x	0	2	4	6
y	7	3	4	0

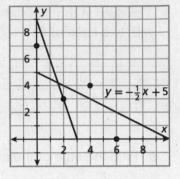

a. Find the sum of the squares of the residuals for
   $y = -3x + 9.$_____

b. Find the sum of the squares of the residuals for
   $y = -\frac{1}{2}x + 5.$_____

c. Which line is a better fit for the data?_____

2. Use the data in the table to answer the questions that follow.

x	5	6	6.5	7.5	9
y	0	−1	3	−2	4

a. Find an equation for a line of best fit. _____

b. What is the correlation coefficient? _____

c. How well does the line represent the data? _____

d. Describe the correlation. _____

3. Use the data in the table to answer the questions that follow.

x	10	8	6	4	2
y	1	1.1	1.2	1.3	1.5

a. Find an equation for a line of best fit. _____

b. What is the correlation coefficient? _____

c. How well does the line represent the data? _____

d. Describe the correlation. _____

4. The table shows the number of pickles four students ate during the week versus their grades on a test. The equation of the least-squares line is $y \approx 2.11x + 79.28$, and $r \approx 0.97$. Discuss correlation and causation for the data set.

Pickles Eaten	0	2	5	10
Test Score	77	85	92	99

_____

_____

Holt McDougal Algebra 1

LESSON 4-8

Practice C

Line of Best Fit

1. The data in the table are graphed at the right along with two lines of fit.

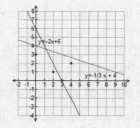

x	0	2	3	4
y	3	1	0	2

   a. Find the sum of the squares of the residuals for $y = -2x + 6$._____

   b. Find the sum of the squares of the residuals for $y = -\frac{1}{3}x + 4$._____

   c. Which line is a better fit for the data?_____

2. Use the data in the table to answer the questions that follow.

x	2.1	4.8	6.5	8.2	9.4
y	−3.08	−1.62	−5.8	0.25	0.84

   a. Find an equation for a line of best fit. _____

   b. What is the correlation coefficient? _____

   c. How well does the line represent the data? _____

   d. Describe the correlation. _____

3. The table shows the number of patients in a doctor's office and the length of time it took to see them. Use the data in the table to answer the questions that follow.

Patients	2	4	6	8	10
Time (h)	0.5	1.1	2.3	3.8	5.2

   a. Find an equation for a line of best fit. _____

   b. What is the correlation coefficient? _____

   c. How well does the line represent the data? _____

   d. Describe the correlation. _____

4. Students were surveyed about how much time they spent studying during one week and how much time they spent watching TV during the same week. The equation of the least-squares line is $y \approx -0.82x + 4.36$, and $r \approx -0.96$. Discuss correlation and causation for the data set.

Studying (h)	0	1	1.5	2	2.5	3	3.5
TV (h)	4	3.9	3.2	2.7	2.6	1.9	1.2

Holt McDougal Algebra 1

LESSON 4-8

Review for Mastery

Line of Best Fit

The data in the table are graphed along with two lines of fit. The line that is a better fit will have the lesser *sum of the square of the residuals*. A residual is the vertical distance between a data point and a line of fit.

x	1	2	3	4
y	8	5	5	2

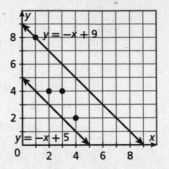

Find the sum of the squares of the residuals for $y = -x + 5$.

Step 1 Use the equation to find the y-values when $x = 1, 2, 3,$ and 4.

x	$-x + 5 = y$
1	$-1 + 5 = 4$
2	$-2 + 5 = 3$
3	$-3 + 5 = 2$
4	$-4 + 5 = 1$

Step 2 Subtract each y-value in Step 1 from the corresponding y-value in the original table to find the residuals.

$8 - 4 = 4$ $5 - 3 = 2$ $5 - 2 = 3$ $2 - 1 = 1$

Step 3 Add the squares of the residuals.

$4^2 + 2^2 + 3^2 + 1^2 = 16 + 4 + 9 + 1 = 30$

The sum of the squares of the residuals for $y = -x + 5$ is 30.

1. Find the sum of squares of the residuals for $y = -x + 9$.

   a. Use the equation to find the y-values when $x = 1, 2, 3,$ and 4.

x	1	2	3	4
y				

   b. Subtract each y-value in Step 1 from the corresponding y-value in the original table to find the residuals.

   $8 - $ _____ $= $ _____ $5 - $ _____ $= $ _____ $5 - $ _____ $= $ _____ $2 - $ _____ $= $ _____

   c. Add the squares of the residuals.

   _____^{2} + _____^{2} + _____^{2} + _____^{2} = _____ + _____ + _____ + _____ = _____

The line for which the sum of the squares of the residuals is lesser is the better fit for the data.

2. _____ is the better fit.

Holt McDougal Algebra 1

	LESSON 4-8

Review for Mastery
Line of Best Fit

Use a graphing calculator to find the line of best fit and the correlation coefficient for the data at right.

x	1	3	3.5	5
y	0	2	3	5

Step 1 Press [STAT].

Step 2 Press 1 to select **1:Edit…**.

Step 3 Enter the *x*-values into list L1.

Step 4 Enter the *y*-values into list L2.

Step 5 Press [STAT].

Step 6 Use [right arrow key] to select **CALC**.

Step 7 Press 4 to select **4:LinReg(ax+b)**.

Step 8 Press ENTER.

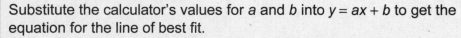

```
LinReg
  y=ax+b
  a=1.251908397
  b=-1.41221374
  r²=.9870816207
  r=.9935198139
```

Substitute the calculator's values for *a* and *b* into $y = ax + b$ to get the equation for the line of best fit.

The equation of the line of best fit is $y \approx 1.25x - 1.41$.

The correlation coefficient is *r*. When *r* is close to 1 or –1, there is a very strong correlation. The closer *r* is to 0, the weaker the correlation.

For this example, $r \approx 0.99$, so there is a strong positive correlation.

3. The table below shows the number of times four students run during the week versus how long it takes, in minutes, for each student to run one mile. Use your calculator to find the equation for the line of best fit. What is the correlation coefficient? Describe the correlation.

Number of times student runs per week	0	2	4	5
Time to run one mile (min)	14	8	7	6

$a \approx$ _____

$b \approx$ _____

The equation of the line of best fit is $y \approx$ _____ $x +$ _____.

$r \approx$ _____, so there is a _____ _____ correlation.

Holt McDougal Algebra 1

LESSON 4-8 Challenge
Line of Best Fit

Ellen holds fundraisers to help plant trees. The table below shows the earnings from the last five fundraisers.

Fundraiser	Earnings ($1000)
1	2
2	5
3	10
4	17
5	26

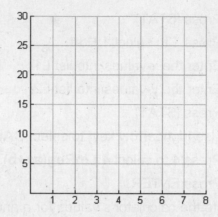

1. Plot the points on the grid at right.

2. Use a graphing calculator to find the equation of the line of best fit for the fundraiser earnings.

   $y =$ _____

3. Sketch the line of best fit on your graph.

4. What is the value of *r* for this line? _____

5. Use the QuadReg function of a graphing calculator to find a quadratic equation to represent the fundraiser earnings.

   $y =$ _____

6. Sketch this parabola on your graph.

7. What is the value of *r* for the parabola? _____

8. Explain the significance of *r* for each case. Predict how much money the next fundraiser will earn using both equations.

_____

_____

_____

_____

_____

_____

Holt McDougal Algebra 1

LESSON 4-8	# Problem Solving
	Line of Best Fit

1. The table shows the number of hours different players practice basketball each week and the number of baskets each player scored during a game.

Player	Alan	Brenda	Caleb	Shawna	Fernando	Gabriela
Hours Practiced	5	10	7	2	0	21
Baskets Scored	6	11	8	4	2	19

a. Find an equation for a line of best fit. Round decimals to the nearest tenth.

_____

b. Interpret the meaning of the slope and *y*-intercept.

_____

_____

c. Find the correlation coefficient. _____

Select the best answer.

2. Use your equation above to predict the number of baskets scored by a player who practices 40 hours a week. Round to the nearest whole number.

  A 32 baskets

  B 33 baskets

  C 34 baskets

  D 35 baskets

3. Which is the best description of the correlation?

  F strong positive

  G weak positive

  H weak negative

  J strong negative

4. Given the data, what advice can you give to a player who wants to increase the number of baskets he or she scores during a game?

  A Practice more hours per week.

  B Practice fewer hours per week.

  C Practice the same hours per week.

  D There is no way to increase baskets.

5. Do the data support causation, correlation, or chance?

  F correlation

  G causation

  H chance

  J chance and correlation

        Holt McDougal Algebra 1

LESSON 4-8

Reading Strategies
Line of Best Fit

A residual is the signed vertical distance between a data point and a line of fit. The line of best fit will have the least sum of squares of residuals.

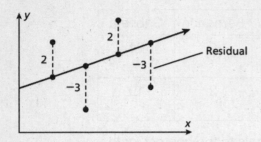

Find the line of best fit for the data set (1,1), (2, 3), (3, 2) (4, 4).

1. Enter the data into a graphing calculator.

   Use **LinReg(*ax* + *b*)** to find the equation for the line of best fit.

   _____

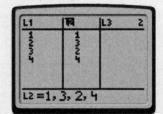

2. What is the correlation coefficient?

   r = _____

3. Use the equation of best fit to complete the table below.

x	1	2	3	4
y				

4. Find each residual. _____ _____ _____ _____

5. Find the square of each residual. _____ _____ _____

6. What is the sum of the squares? _____

Holt McDougal Algebra 1

LESSON 4-9

Practice A
Slopes of Parallel and Perpendicular Lines

Circle the equations whose lines are parallel.

1. $y = 4$; $y = \dfrac{1}{2}x + 3$; $y = \dfrac{1}{2}x$; $y = 2x$

2. $y - 5 = 6(x + 2)$; $y = -6x$; $6x + y = 4$; $y = 6$

3. Find the slope of each segment.

slope of $\overline{AB}$: _____

slope of $\overline{AD}$: _____

slope of $\overline{DC}$: _____

slope of $\overline{BC}$: _____

Explain why *ABCD* is a parallelogram.

_____

_____

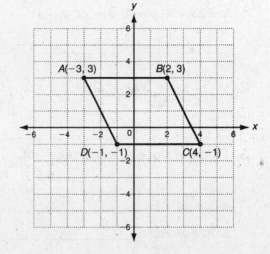

Circle the equations whose lines are perpendicular.

4. $y = x - 4$; $y = 3$; $y = -x$; $y = -3$

5. $y = 5x + 1$; $y = 3$; $y = \dfrac{1}{5}x$; $x = 5$

6. $y = \dfrac{1}{3}x - 2$; $x = 2$; $y - 4 = 3(x + 3)$; $y = -3x + 9$

7. Find the slope of each segment.

slope of $\overline{AB}$: _____

slope of $\overline{BC}$: _____

slope of $\overline{AC}$: _____

Explain why *ABC* is a right triangle.

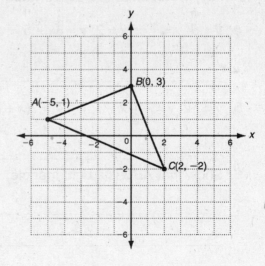

_____

_____

Holt McDougal Algebra 1

LESSON **Practice B**
4-9
Slopes of Parallel and Perpendicular Lines

Identify which lines are parallel.

1. $y = 3x + 4$; $y = 4$; $y = 3x$; $y = 3$

_____

2. $y = \frac{1}{2}x + 4$; $x = \frac{1}{2}$; $2x + y = 1$; $y = \frac{1}{2}x + 1$

_____

3. Find the slope of each segment.

slope of $\overline{AB}$: _____

slope of $\overline{AD}$: _____

slope of $\overline{DC}$: _____

slope of $\overline{BC}$: _____

Explain why $ABCD$ is a parallelogram.

_____

_____

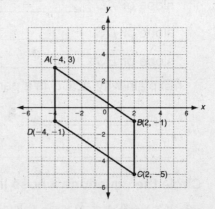

Identify which lines are perpendicular.

4. $y = 5$; $y = \frac{1}{8}x$; $x = 2$; $y = 8x - 5$

_____

5. $y = -2$; $y = -\frac{1}{2}x - 4$; $y - 4 = 2(x + 3)$; $y = -2x$

_____

6. Show that ABC is a right triangle.

_____

_____

_____

_____

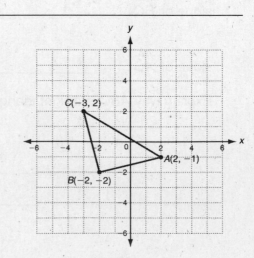

LESSON 4-9

Practice C
Slopes of Parallel and Perpendicular Lines

Identify which lines are parallel.

1. $y = \frac{1}{4}x + 2$; $y = 4$; $y = 4x$; $y = \frac{1}{4}x$

_____

2. $y - 1 = -(x + 7)$; $y = -x$; $x + y = 3$; $y = 3x$

_____

3. Show that *ABCD* is a parallelogram.

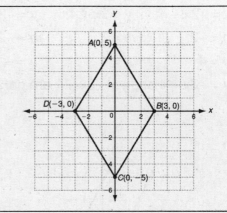

_____

_____

_____

_____

Identify which lines are perpendicular.

4. $y = 3x - 1$; $y = 3$; $x - 3y = 6$; $x = 6$

_____

5. $y = \frac{1}{2}x + 2$; $y + 1 = -2x$; $y = \frac{1}{2}$; $2x - y = 1$

_____

6. Show that *ABC* is a right triangle.

_____

_____

_____

_____

7. Line *m* contains (6, 8) and (−1, 2). Line *n* contains (−1, 5) and (5, *y*).
   What is the value of *y* if line *m* is perpendicular to line *n*? _____

LESSON 4-9

Review for Mastery

Slopes of Parallel and Perpendicular Lines

Two lines are **parallel** if they lie in the same plane and have no points in common. The lines will never intersect.

Identify which lines are parallel.

$y = -2x + 4;$ $y = 3x + 4;$ $y = -2x - 1$

If lines have the same slope, but different y-intercepts, they are parallel lines.

$y = -2x + 4;$ $y = 3x + 4;$ $y = -2x - 1$

$m = -2,$ $m = 3$ $m = -2$

$b = 4$ $b = 4$ $b = -1$

$y = -2x + 4$ and $y = -2x - 1$ are parallel.

Two lines are **perpendicular** if they intersect to form right angles.

Identify which lines are perpendicular.

If the product of the slopes of two lines is −1, the two lines are perpendicular.

$y = -3x + 1;$ $y = 3x + 2;$ $y = -\dfrac{1}{3}x + 3$

$m = -3$ $m = 3$ $m = -\dfrac{1}{3}$

Because $3\left(-\dfrac{1}{3}\right) = -1$, $y = 3x + 2$ and

$y = -\dfrac{1}{3}x + 3$ are perpendicular.

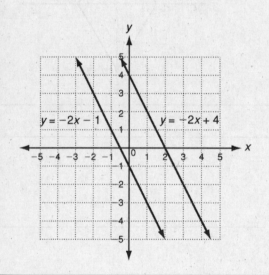

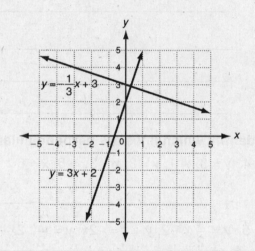

Identify which two lines are parallel. Then graph the parallel lines.

1. $y = 4x + 2;$ $y = 2x + 1;$ $y = 2x - 3$

_____

Identify which two lines are perpendicular. Then graph the perpendicular lines.

2. $y = -\dfrac{2}{3}x + 2;$ $y = \dfrac{3}{2}x + 1;$ $y = \dfrac{2}{3}x - 3$

_____

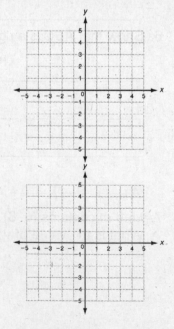

Holt McDougal Algebra 1

LESSON 4-9

Review for Mastery

Slopes of Parallel and Perpendicular Lines continued

Write an equation in slope-intercept form for the line that passes through (2, 4) and is parallel to $y = 3x + 2$.

Step 1: Find the slope of the line.

The slope is 3.

Step 2: Write the equation in point-slope form.

$$y - y_1 = m(x - x_1)$$
$$y - 4 = 3(x - 2)$$

Step 3: Write the equation in slope-intercept form.

$$y - 4 = 3(x - 2)$$
$$y - 4 = 3x - 6$$
$$\underline{+4 \qquad +4}$$
$$y = 3x - 2$$

Write an equation in slope-intercept form for the line that passes through (2, 5) and is perpendicular to $y = \frac{2}{3}x + 2$.

Step 1: Find the slope of the line and the slope for the perpendicular line.

The slope is $\frac{2}{3}$. The slope of the perpendicular line will be $-\frac{3}{2}$.

Step 2: Write the equation (with the new slope) in point-slope form.

$$y - y_1 = m(x - x_1)$$
$$y - 5 = -\frac{3}{2}(x - 2)$$

Step 3: Write the equation in slope-intercept form.

$$y - 5 = -\frac{3}{2}(x - 2)$$
$$y - 5 = -\frac{3}{2}x + 3$$
$$\underline{+5 \qquad\qquad +5}$$
$$y = -\frac{3}{2}x + 8$$

Write the slope of a line that is parallel to, and perpendicular to, the given line.

3. $y = 6x - 3$ parallel: _____   perpendicular: _____

4. $y = \frac{4}{3}x - 1$ parallel: _____   perpendicular: _____

5. Write an equation in slope-intercept form for the line that passes through (6, 5) and is parallel to $y = -x + 4$.

_____

6. Write an equation in slope-intercept form for the line that passes through (8, −1) and is perpendicular to $y = -4x - 7$.

_____

    Holt McDougal Algebra 1

LESSON
4-9
Challenge

Constructing Polygons Using Parallel and Perpendicular Lines

Two facts about parallel and perpendicular lines are summarized below.

> If two nonvertical lines are parallel, then their slopes are equal.

> If two nonvertical lines are perpendicular, then their slopes are negative reciprocals of one another.

You can use these facts if you want to construct special polygons on the coordinate plane.

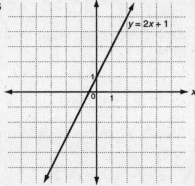

In Exercises 1–4, use the grid and the graph of $y = 2x + 1$.

1. a. Write an equation in slope-intercept form for the line parallel to the graph of $y = 2x + 1$ and having a y-intercept of 4. _____

   b. Graph your equation on the grid at right above.

2. a. Find the y-coordinate of the point on the graph of $y = 2x + 1$ for which $x = -2$. _____

   b. Find an equation for the line containing the point found in Part a and perpendicular to the graph of. $y = 2x + 1$ _____

   c. Graph your equation from Part b on the grid at right above.

3. a. Find the y-coordinate of the point on the graph of $y = 2x + 1$ for which $x = 1$. _____

   b. Find an equation for the line containing the point found in Part a and perpendicular to the graph of $y = 2x + 1$.

   _____

   c. Graph your equation from Part b on the grid at right above.

4. Identify the polygon that you formed. Explain your response.

_____

In Exercises 5 and 6, use the grid at right.

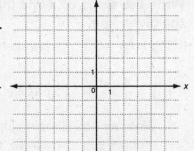

5. Suppose that you want to make a square using the graph of $x + y = 4$ to help determine one side of the square.

   Write equations in standard form to determine a square with corners at (4, 0), (0, 4), (−4, 0) and (0, −4). _____

6. On the grid at right, graph each of the equations that you wrote in Exercise 5.

Name _____ Date _____ Class_____

Problem Solving
Slopes of Parallel and Perpendicular Lines

Write the correct answer.

1. Hamid is making a stained-glass window. He needs a piece of glass that is a perfect parallelogram. Hamid lays a piece of glass that he has cut on a coordinate grid. Show that the glass is in the shape of a parallelogram.

   _____

   _____

   _____

   _____

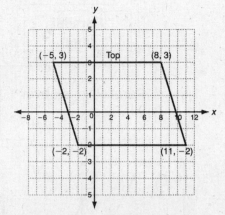

2. Norelle's garden is shown at right. Is her garden in the shape of a right triangle? Justify your answer.

   _____

   _____

   _____

   _____

Norelle's Garden

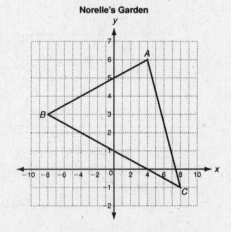

The graph shows a street map.
Use it to answer questions 3–5.

3. The district plans to add Industrial Road next year. It will run perpendicular to Smith Ave. and pass through (−14, 2). What equation will describe the location of Industrial Road?

   A $y = 14 - x$ C $y = -14$

   B $y = x - 14$ D $x = -14$

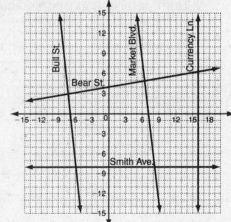

4. In two years, the business district plans to add Stock Street. It will run parallel to Market Blvd. and pass through (−1, 5). What equation will describe the location of Stock Street?

   F $y = -7x + 12$ H $y = \frac{1}{7}x + \frac{34}{7}$

   G $y = -7x - 2$ J $y = \frac{1}{7}x + \frac{36}{7}$

5. What is the slope of a street parallel to Bear Street?

   A −7   C $\frac{1}{7}$

   B $-\frac{1}{7}$ D 7

Holt McDougal Algebra 1

Name _____ Date _____ Class _____

Reading Strategies
Compare and Contrast

| **Parallel lines** | **Contrast** | **Perpendicular lines** |

| Parallel lines never intersect. | | Perpendicular lines intersect to form right angles. |

$y = -2x + 3$
$y = -2x - 2$

$y = -2x + 3$
$y = \frac{1}{2}x - 2$

| The slopes of parallel lines are the same. | | The slopes of perpendicular lines have a product of -1. |

Compare

Both parallel and perpendicular lines can be identified by their equations.

Both parallel and perpendicular lines have applications in geometry.

1. Write an equation of a line parallel to $y = 3x + 4$.

2. Write an equation of a line perpendicular to $y = 3x + 4$.

_____   _____

A(9, –4), B(–3, 0) and C(1, 4) are the vertices of a triangle.

3. Find the slope of $\overline{AB}$. _____

4. Find the slope of $\overline{BC}$. _____

5. Find the slope of $\overline{AC}$. _____

6. Is *ABC* a right triangle? Why? _____

Original content Copyright © by Holt McDougal. Additions and changes to the original content are the responsibility of the instructor.

Holt McDougal Algebra 1

LESSON 4-10

Practice A
Transforming Linear Functions

Fill in each blank with *translation*, *rotation*, or *reflection*.

1. A _____ is like a *turn*.

2. A _____ is like a *slide*.

3. A _____ is like a *flip*.

Graph *f*(x) and *g*(x). Then describe the transformation(s) from the graph of *f*(x) to the graph of *g*(x).

4. $f(x) = x$; $g(x) = x + 5$

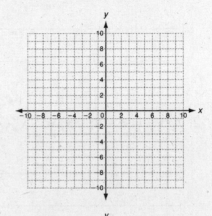

_____

_____

_____

5. $f(x) = 2x - 1$; $g(x) = 4x - 1$

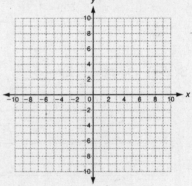

_____

_____

_____

6. $f(x) = x$; $g(x) = \dfrac{1}{2}x - 7$

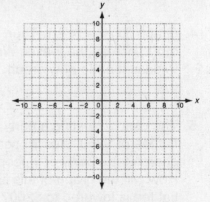

_____

_____

_____

7. The cost of making a ceramic picture frame at a paint-your-own pottery store is $12, plus $5 per hour while you paint. The total cost for the frame that you spend *x* hours painting is $f(x) = 5x + 12$.

   a. How will the graph of this function change if the cost of the frame is raised to $15?

   _____

   b. How will the graph of this function change if the hourly charge is lowered to $4?

   _____

Holt McDougal Algebra 1

LESSON
4-10

Practice B

Transforming Linear Functions

Graph *f(x)* and *g(x)*. Then describe the transformation from the graph of *f(x)* to the graph of *g(x)*.

1. $f(x) = x$; $g(x) = x + 3$

_____

_____

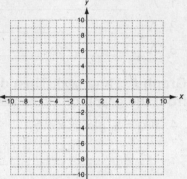

2. $f(x) = \frac{1}{3}x - 4$; $g(x) = \frac{1}{4}x - 4$

_____

_____

_____

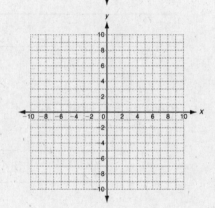

3. $f(x) = x$; $g(x) = 2x - 5$

_____

_____

_____

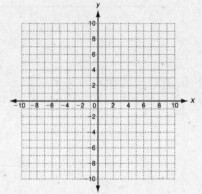

4. Graph $f(x) = -3x + 1$. Then reflect the graph of *f(x)* across the *y*-axis. Write a function *g(x)* to describe the new graph.

_____

5. The cost of hosting a party at a horse farm is a flat fee of $250, plus $5 per person. The total charge for a party of *x* people is $f(x) = 5x + 250$. How will the graph of this function change if the flat fee is lowered to $200? if the per-person rate is raised to $8?

_____

_____

_____

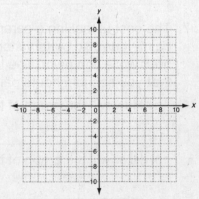

Holt McDougal Algebra 1

LESSON 4-10

Practice C
Transforming Linear Functions

Graph *f*(*x*) and *g*(*x*). Then describe the transformation from the graph of *f*(*x*) to the graph of *g*(*x*).

1. $f(x) = 2x - 4$; $g(x) = 2x + 3$

_____

_____

_____

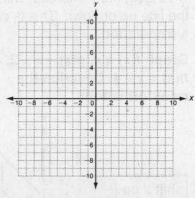

2. $f(x) = \frac{1}{2}x - 5$; $g(x) = \frac{3}{4}x - 5$

_____

_____

_____

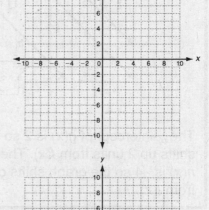

3. $f(x) = -3x + 6$; $g(x) = -x$

_____

_____

_____

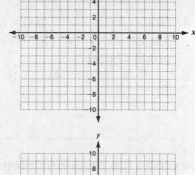

4. Graph $f(x) = 4x - 2$. Then reflect the graph of *f*(*x*) across the *y*-axis. Write a function *g*(*x*) to describe the new graph.

_____

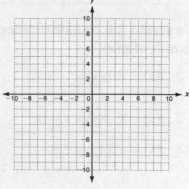

5. Joshua is planning to make a large consumer purchase. If the item costs *x* dollars in his home state of West Virginia, where the tax rate is 6%, the function $f(x) = 0.06x + x$ represents his total costs. Write a function *g*(*x*) to represent Joshua's total costs if he decides to make the purchase in his neighboring state of Virginia, where the tax rate is 5%. How will the graph of *g*(*x*) differ from *f*(*x*)?

_____

Holt McDougal Algebra 1

LESSON
4-10

Review for Mastery
Transforming Linear Functions

The function $f(x) = x$ is called the parent function for the family of linear functions.

Changing the y-intercept will shift the line up or down. This is called a **translation**.

Graph $f(x) = x$, $g(x) = x + 2$, and $h(x) = x - 4$. Describe the transformations.

Changing the slope of a line will change the steepness of the line. This is called a **rotation**.

Graph $f(x) = x$, $g(x) = 4x$, and $h(x) = \frac{1}{2}x$.

Describe the transformations.

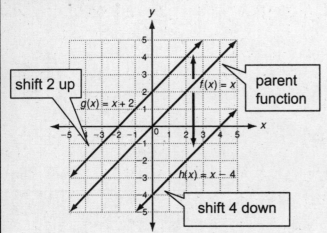

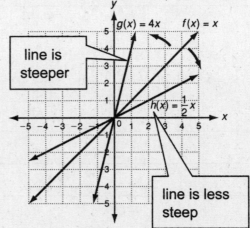

The y-intercept of $g(x)$ is 2 so the graph shifts up 2 units from $f(x)$. The y-intercept of $h(x)$ is –4 so the graph shifts down 4 units from $f(x)$.

The slope of $g(x)$ is 4 so the line is steeper than $f(x)$ which has a slope of 1. The slope of $h(x)$ is $\frac{1}{2}$ and it is less steep.

1. Graph $f(x) = x$ and $g(x) = x + 3$. Then describe the transformation from the graph of $f(x)$ to the graph of $g(x)$.

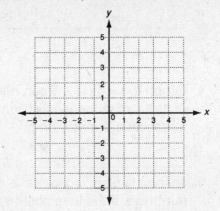

_____

Describe the transformations from the graph of $f(x)$ to the graph of $g(x)$.

2. $f(x) = x$; $g(x) = \frac{1}{3}x$ _____

3. $f(x) = x$; $g(x) = x - 5$ _____

4. $f(x) = x$; $g(x) = 6x$ _____

Holt McDougal Algebra 1

LESSON 4-10

Review for Mastery
Transforming Linear Functions continued

When the slope of a line is multiplied by −1, the graph is reflected across the *y*-axis. This is called a **reflection**.

Graph g(x) = 4x. Then reflect the graph of g(x) across the y-axis. Write a function h(x) to describe the new graph.

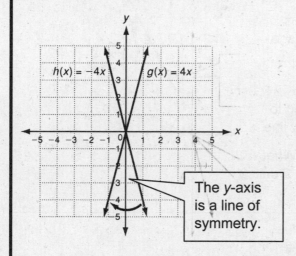

The new function is $h(x) = -4x$. The slopes of $g(x)$ and $h(x)$ are opposites.

More than one transformation can be applied to a linear function.

Graph f(x) = x and g(x) = 2x − 3. Then describe the transformations from the graph of f(x) to the graph of g(x).

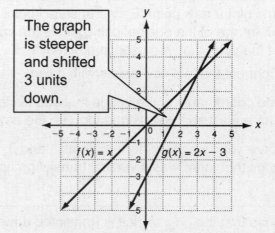

The slope of $g(x)$ is 2 so the line is steeper than $f(x)$ which has a slope of 1. The *y*-intercept of $g(x)$ is −3 so it is also translated down 3 units after it has been rotated.

Each function below is reflected across the y-axis. Write a function h(x) to describe each new graph.

5. $f(x) = 5x$

6. $f(x) = -9x$

7. $f(x) = 2x + 7$

_____ _____ _____

Describe the transformations from the graph of f(x) to the graph of g(x).

8. $f(x) = x, g(x) = 4x - 2$ _____

9. $f(x) = x, g(x) = 0.25x + 3$ _____

10. $f(x) = 2x, g(x) = x + 8$ _____

11. $f(x) = -5x, g(x) = x$ _____

Holt McDougal Algebra 1

LESSON **Challenge**
4-10 *Translations and Point-Slope Form*

For 1–5, use the two points and line graphed at right.

1. Write an equation in point-slope form for the line. Circle the point that you used as (x_1, y_1).

   _____

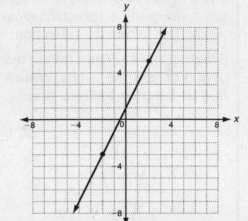

2. Translate the line up 2 units by doing the following:

   a. Translate each of the two points up 2 units and plot a new point. Each translated point is an **image** of the original point. Circle the image of the point that you used in problem 1.

   b. Connect the two new points with a line.

3. Use the coordinates of the image that you circled to write an equation in point-slope form for the new line. _____

4. Compare your equations for problems 1 and 3. What indicates that there was a vertical translation up 2 units?

   _____

5. Suppose that the *original* line is translated down 6 units. Without graphing the transformation, write an equation in point-slope form for the new line. _____

For 6–10, use the graph at right.

6. Translate the line right 5 units. (Use a process similar to problem 2.) Again, circle the image of the point that you used in problem 1.

7. Use the coordinates of the image that you circled to write an equation in point-slope form for the new line.

   _____

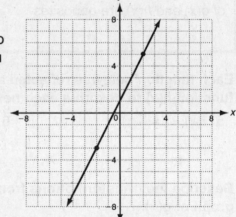

8. Compare your equations for problems 1 and 7. What indicates a horizontal translation right 5 units?

   _____

9. Suppose that the *original* line was translated left 3 units. Without graphing the transformation, write an equation in point-slope form for the new line. _____

10. The equation $y - 3 = -4(x + 2)$ is transformed into $y + 1 = -4(x - 7)$. Describe the transformations from the graph of the first line to the graph of the second.

   _____

Holt McDougal Algebra 1

LESSON 4-10

Problem Solving

Transforming Linear Functions

Write the correct answer.

1. The number of camp counselors at a day camp must include 1 counselor for every 8 campers, plus 3 camp directors. The function describing the number of counselors is $f(x) = \frac{1}{8}x + 3$ where x is the number of campers. How will the graph change if the number of camp directors is reduced to 2?

   _____

2. A city water service has a base cost of $12 per month plus $1.50 per hundred cubic feet (HCF) of water. Write a function $f(x)$ to represent the cost of water as a function of x, amount used. Then write a second function $g(x)$ to represent the cost if the rate rises to $1.60 per HCF.

   _____

   How would the graph of $g(x)$ compare to the graph of $f(x)$?

   _____

   _____

3. Owen earns a base salary plus a commission that is a percent of his total sales. His total weekly pay is described by $f(x) = 0.15x + 325$, where x is his total sales in dollars. What is the change in Owen's salary plan if his total weekly pay function changes to $g(x) = 0.20x + 325$?

   _____

   _____

An attorney charges $250 per hour. The graph represents the cost of the attorney as a function of time. Select the best answer.

4. When a traveling fee is added to the attorney's rate for cases outside the city limits, the graph is translated up 50 units. What function $h(x)$ would describe the attorney's rate with the traveling fee?

   A $h(x) = 250x - 50$

   B $h(x) = 250x + 50$

   C $h(x) = 200x$

   D $h(x) = 300x$

5. The attorney's paralegal has an hourly rate of $150. How would you transform the graph of $f(x)$ into a graph for the paralegal's rate?

   F Reflect it over the y-axis.

   G Translate it down 100 units.

   H Translate it to the left 100 units.

   J Rotate it clockwise about (0, 0).

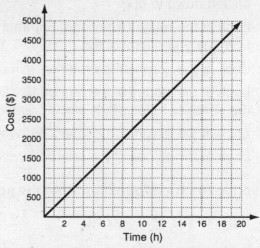

6. Which hourly rate would NOT make the attorney's graph steeper?

   A $225   C $300

   B $275   D $325

Holt McDougal Algebra 1

Reading Strategies

LESSON 4-10

Identify Relationships

The table shows three types of transformations.

Transformation	Translation	Rotation	Reflection
Description	When b in $y = mx + b$ increases (decreases), the line is translated up (down).	When $|m|$ in $y = mx + b$ increases (decreases), the line becomes more steep (less steep).	When m in $y = mx + b$ is multiplied by -1, the line is reflected across the y-axis.
Graph			
Equations	$f(x) = -3x + 2$ $g(x) = -3x - 3$	$f(x) = -3x + 2$ $g(x) = -1x + 2$	$f(x) = -3x + 2$ $g(x) = 3x + 2$

Answer the following.

1. Look at the graph of the translation. How many vertical units is $f(x)$ shifted down to $g(x)$? _____

   Look at the related functions. Subtract the y-intercept of $g(x)$ from the y-intercept of $f(x)$. _____

2. Look at the graph of the rotation. Which graph is steeper? _____

   Look at the slopes of the related functions. For which function is the absolute value of the slope greater? _____

3. Look at the graph of the reflection. Which axis is a line of symmetry? _____

   Look at the slopes of the related functions. Are they the same or opposite? _____

Describe the transformation from the graph of $f(x)$ to the graph of $g(x)$.

4. $f(x) = 4x - 3$, $g(x) = 2x - 3$ _____

5. $f(x) = -2x + 2$, $g(x) = 2x + 2$ _____

6. $f(x) = x + 2$, $g(x) = x + 8$ _____

Holt McDougal Algebra 1

Date _____

Dear Family,

Your child will study systems of linear equations and inequalities.

A **system of linear equations** is a set of two or more linear equations containing two or more variables. A **solution to the system** is a point that makes all of the equations true.

Graphically, a solution to a system of two linear equations in two variables is the point where the two lines intersect.

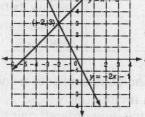

linear system:
$$\begin{cases} y = -2x - 1 \\ y = x + 5 \end{cases}$$

solution to the system:

$(-2, 3)$

check:

$y = -2x - 1$	
3	$-2(-2) - 1$
3	3 ✓

$y = x + 5$	
3	$-2 + 5$
3	3 ✓

One algebraic method of solving a system is called **substitution**.

system: $\begin{cases} 2x + y = -4 \\ x + y = -7 \end{cases}$

$2x + y = -4$
$\quad y = -2x - 4$

Step 1: Solve one equation for one variable (if necessary).

$x + y = -7$

Step 2: **Substitute** the expression into the other equation.

$x + (-2x - 4) = -7$
$\quad -x - 4 = -7$
$\quad\quad\quad x = 3$

Step 3: Solve for the value of the first variable.

$x + y = -7$
$3 + y = -7$
$\quad\quad y = -10$

Step 4: Substitute the value into one of the original equations and solve for the value of the other variable.

$(3, -10)$

Step 5: Write the values as an ordered pair.

Another algebraic method is called **elimination**.

$2x + y = -4$

Step 1: Write the system so that like terms are aligned.

$\dfrac{-(x + y = -7)}{1x + 0 = 3}$
$\quad\quad x = 3$

Step 2: Add or subtract multiples of the equations in order to **eliminate** one of the variables...
... and solve for the value of the remaining variable.

$3 + y = -7$
$\quad\quad y = -10$

Step 3: Substitute and solve for the other variable.

$(3, -10)$

Step 4: Write the values as an ordered pair.

Holt McDougal Algebra 1

Not all linear systems have exactly one solution. If the lines coincide, then there are infinitely many solutions. If the lines are parallel and never intersect, then there is no solution. Based on their solutions, systems are classified as **consistent** (at least one), **inconsistent** (none), **independent** (exactly one), or **dependent** (infinitely many).

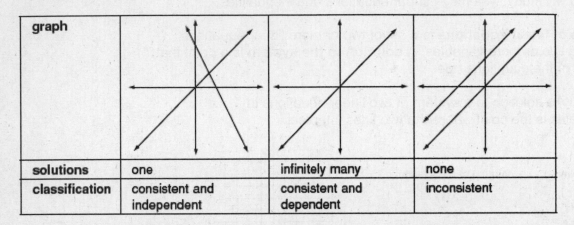

graph			
solutions	one	infinitely many	none
classification	consistent and independent	consistent and dependent	inconsistent

A **linear inequality** in two variables is similar to a linear equation, but the equal sign is replaced with an inequality ($>$, $<$, $\geq$, or $\leq$). Similarly, a **solution of a linear inequality** is any ordered pair that makes the inequality true.

Linear inequalities are graphed first with a dashed or solid boundary line. Then you shade above or below the line to show all of the points that satisfy the inequality. The graph of a linear inequality is called a **half-plane**.

Graphing a Linear Inequality Solved for y (slope-intercept form)		
Boundary	$\leq$ or $\leq$ (equal to)	Solid
	$>$ or $<$ (not equal to)	Dashed
Shading	$>$ or $\geq$ (greater than)	Above
	$<$ or $\leq$ (less than)	Below

linear inequality: $y < x + 1$

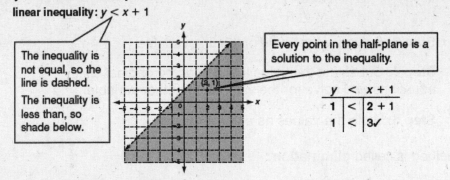

The inequality is not equal, so the line is dashed.

The inequality is less than, so shade below.

Every point in the half-plane is a solution to the inequality.

$$\begin{array}{c|c}
y & < x + 1 \\
\hline
1 & < 2 + 1 \\
1 & < 3 \checkmark
\end{array}$$

A **system of linear inequalities** is a set of two or more linear inequalities containing two or more variables. The **solution of a system of linear inequalities** consists of all the ordered pairs that satisfy all of the linear inequalities. Graphically, the solution occurs where the half-planes of the linear inequalities intersect, or the overlapping shaded regions.

Holt McDougal Algebra 1

LESSON 5-1

Practice A

Solving Systems by Graphing

Complete the steps to determine whether the ordered pair is a solution of the given system. Circle ✓ or ✗ for each equation. Then, write *is* or *is not* to complete the sentence.

1. $(2, 4)$; $\begin{cases} x - y = -2 \\ 2x + y = 6 \end{cases}$

2. $(1, -2)$; $\begin{cases} 2x + y = 0 \\ x + 4y = -7 \end{cases}$

$x - y = -2$	
$(2)-(4)$	-2
___	-2

✓ or ✗

$2x + y = 6$	
$2(2) + (\_\_)$	6
$(\_\_) + (\_\_)$	6
$(\_\_)$	6

✓ or ✗

$(2, 4)$ _____ a solution of the system.

$2x + y = 0$	
$2(1) + (-2)$	0
$(\_\_) + (-2)$	0
$(\_\_)$	0

✓ or ✗

$x + 4y = -7$	
$(1) + 4(\_\_)$	-7
$(\_\_) + (\_\_)$	-7
$(\_\_)$	-7

✓ or ✗

$(1, -2)$ _____ a solution of the system.

Solve each system by graphing. One of the lines has been graphed for you.

3. $\begin{cases} y = 3x - 5 \\ y = x - 3 \end{cases}$ Solution: _____

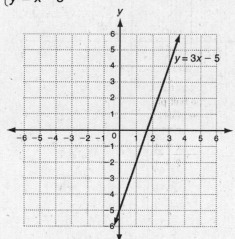

4. $\begin{cases} y = x + 7 \\ y = -2x - 2 \end{cases}$ Solution: _____

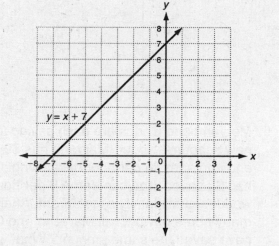

5. The Science Club needs to rent a bus for a field trip. Main Street Buses charges a $40 rental fee, plus $2 per mile. County Bus Line charges a $20 rental fee, plus $3 per mile. For what number of miles will the total charge be the same? What will that charge be?

_____

Holt McDougal Algebra 1

LESSON 5-1

Practice B

Solving Systems by Graphing

Tell whether the ordered pair is a solution of the given system.

1. (3, 1); $\begin{cases} x + 3y = 6 \\ 4x - 5y = 7 \end{cases}$ _____

2. (6, –2); $\begin{cases} 3x - 2y = 14 \\ 5x - y = 32 \end{cases}$ _____

$x + 3y = 6$	$4x - 5y = 7$		$3x - 2y = 14$	$5x - y = 32$

Solve each system by graphing. Check your answer.

3. $\begin{cases} y = x + 4 \\ y = -2x + 1 \end{cases}$ Solution : _____

4. $\begin{cases} y = x + 6 \\ y = -3x + 6 \end{cases}$ Solution : _____

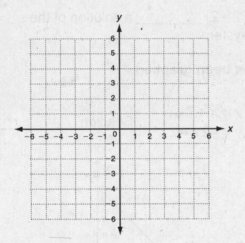

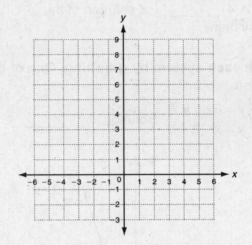

5. Maryann and Carlos are each saving for new scooters. So far, Maryann has $9 saved, and can earn $6 per hour babysitting. Carlos has $3 saved, and can earn $9 per hour working at his family's restaurant. After how many hours of work will Maryann and Carlos have saved the same amount? What will that amount be?

_____

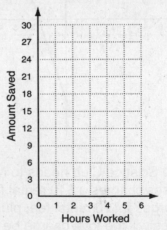

Holt McDougal Algebra 1

LESSON 5-1

Practice C

Solving Systems by Graphing

Tell whether the ordered pair is a solution of the given equation.

1. $(6, -2)$; $\begin{cases} 2x - y = 14 \\ x + 4y = -2 \end{cases}$

2. $(4, 0)$; $\begin{cases} x - 2y = 4 \\ -x + y = -8 \end{cases}$

3. $(-6, -2)$; $\begin{cases} 2x - y = -10 \\ -x + y = 4 \end{cases}$

_____   _____   _____

Solve each system by graphing.

4. $\begin{cases} y = 2x + 4 \\ y = -x + 7 \end{cases}$

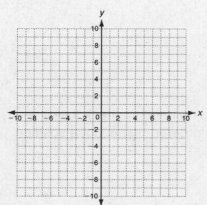

5. $\begin{cases} y = 2x - 6 \\ y = 3x - 8 \end{cases}$

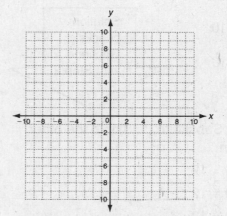

Solution: _____

Solution: _____

6. $\begin{cases} x + y = -2 \\ y = 4x - 7 \end{cases}$

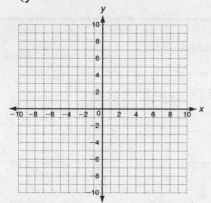

7. $\begin{cases} x = y + 2 \\ 2x = y \end{cases}$

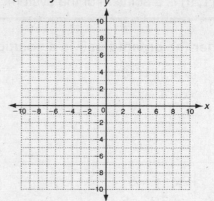

Solution: _____

Solution: _____

Use a graphing calculator to solve.

8. To sell an item in an online auction, WebAuctions charges a $5 listing fee plus 10% of the final selling price. AuctionsOnline charges a $3 listing fee plus 15% of the final selling price. For what final selling price do both companies charge the same amount? What will that amount be? _____

Holt McDougal Algebra 1

Name _____ Date _____ Class_____

Review for Mastery

Solving Systems by Graphing

You have checked to see if an ordered pair was a solution of an equation. Now you will check to see if an ordered pair is a solution of a system of equations.

Tell whether (1, 9) is a solution of
$$\begin{cases} x + y = 10 \\ 3x + y = 12 \end{cases}$$

Step 1: Substitute (1, 9) into one of the equations.

(1, 9) means that $x = 1$ and $y = 9$.

$x + y \overset{?}{=} 10$

$1 + 9 \overset{?}{=} 10$

$10 \overset{?}{=} 10 \checkmark$

Solution checks. Continue with Step 2

Step 2: Substitute (1, 9) into the other equation.

$3x + y = 12$

$3(1) + 9 \overset{?}{=} 12$

$3 + 9 \overset{?}{=} 12$

$12 \overset{?}{=} 12 \checkmark$

The ordered pair makes both equations true. So (1, 9) is a solution of the system.

Tell whether (2, –3) is a solution of
$$\begin{cases} x + y = 5 \\ 2x + 5y = -11 \end{cases}$$

Step 1: Substitute (2, –3) into one of the equations.

$x + y = 5$

$2 + -3 \overset{?}{=} 5$

$-1 \overset{?}{=} 5$ ✗

Stop! There is no need to check the other equation. The ordered pair is not a solution of the system.

Tell whether the ordered pair is a solution of the given system.

1. (0, –4); $\begin{cases} x + 2y = -8 \\ x = 4 + y \end{cases}$

2. (2, 5); $\begin{cases} x + y = 7 \\ 3x + y = 10 \end{cases}$

_____

3. (–3, 1); $\begin{cases} 2x + y = 5 \\ x + 3y = -6 \end{cases}$

4. (–3, 9); $\begin{cases} y = x + 12 \\ y = -3x \end{cases}$

_____

Holt McDougal Algebra 1

LESSON 5-1

Review for Mastery

Solving Systems by Graphing continued

Graph to check if (5, 7) is a solution of $\begin{cases} y = x + 2 \\ y = 2x + 3 \end{cases}$.

If (5, 7) is not the solution, find the solution from the graph.

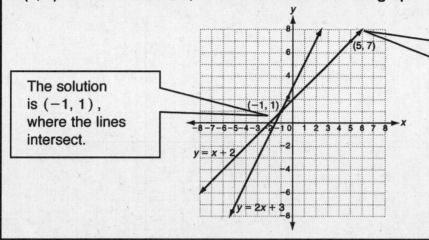

The solution is $(-1, 1)$, where the lines intersect.

(5, 7) satisfies one equation but not the other. Therefore, (5, 7) is not a solution of this system.

Find the solution of each system of equations graphed below.

5.

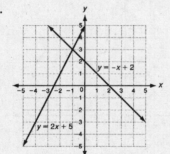

6.

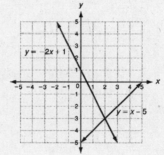

_____   _____

Solve each system by graphing.

7. $\begin{cases} y = -3 \\ y = x + 2 \end{cases}$

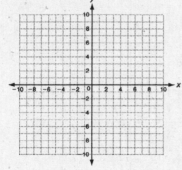

8. $\begin{cases} y = x - 6 \\ y = -x \end{cases}$

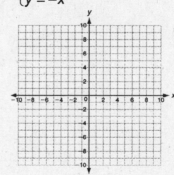

_____   _____

Name _____ Date _____ Class_____

LESSON 5-1

Challenge

Solving Systems by Graphing

Sometimes one or both equations in a system will be non-linear. The solutions to these systems will still be where the graphs intersect. This can happen in more than one place. Recall that you can graph any equation by generating and plotting ordered pairs.

Solve each system by graphing.

1. $\begin{cases} y = x^2 - 4 \\ y = x + 2 \end{cases}$

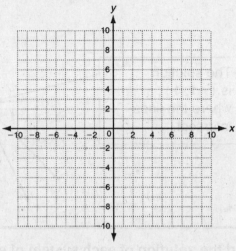

_____

2. $\begin{cases} y = -x^2 + 5 \\ y = x^2 - 5 \end{cases}$

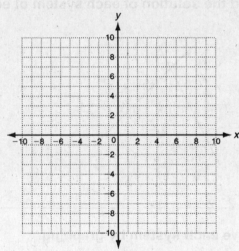

_____

3. $\begin{cases} y = |x + 1| \\ y = \dfrac{1}{2}x + 3 \end{cases}$

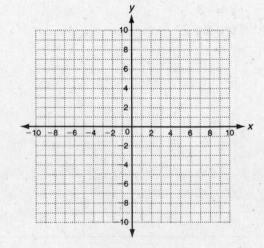

_____

_____

Original content Copyright © by Holt McDougal. Additions and changes to the original content are the responsibility of the instructor.

5-8   Holt McDougal Algebra 1

LESSON 5-1

Problem Solving

Solving Systems by Graphing

Write the correct answer.

1. Mr. Malone is putting money in two savings accounts. Account A started with $200 and Account B started with $300. Mr. Malone deposits $15 in Account A and $10 in Account B each month. In how many months will the accounts have the same balance? What will that balance be?

_____

2. Tom currently has 5 comic books in his collection and has subscribed to receive 5 new comic books each month. His uncle has 145 comic books, but sends 5 to each of his 3 nieces each month. In how many months will they have the same number of comic books? How many books will that be?

_____

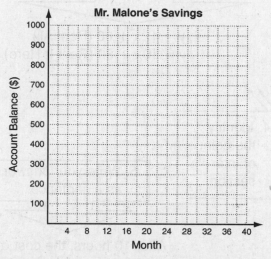

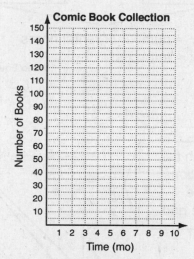

The graph below compares the heights of two trees. Use the graph to answer questions 3–6. Select the best answer.

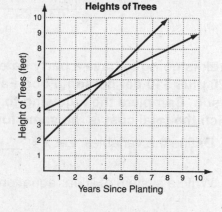

3. How many years after planting will the trees be the same height?

   A 1 years   C 4 years

   B 2 years   D 6 years

4. Which system of equations is represented by the graph?

   F $\begin{cases} y = x+2 \\ y = 0.5x+2 \end{cases}$ H $\begin{cases} y = 2x+4 \\ y = x+4 \end{cases}$

   G $\begin{cases} y = x+2 \\ y = 0.5x+4 \end{cases}$ J $\begin{cases} y = 4x-2 \\ y = 2x+2 \end{cases}$

5. How fast does the tree that started at 2 feet tall grow?

   A 0.5 ft/yr   C 1.5 ft/yr

   B 1 ft/yr   D 2 ft/yr

6. How fast does the tree that started at 4 feet tall grow?

   F 0.5 ft/yr   H 1.5 ft/yr

   G 1 ft/yr   J 2 ft/yr

LESSON 5-1

Reading Strategies
Follow a Procedure

In the example below, the steps show how to set up and solve a system of linear equations.

A teacher needs to rent video equipment. Rent All charges $60 plus $12 for each hour. Rent It Here charges $80 plus $10 per hour. After how many hours is the cost of renting video equipment the same from both companies?

1. Define variables for the unknowns.

2. Write a system of linear equations.

- Let x = number of rental hours
- Let y = total cost

$$\begin{cases} y = 12x + 60 \text{ (Rent All)} \\ y = 10x + 80 \text{ (Rent It Here)} \end{cases}$$

3. Graph the equations on the same grid.

4. Identify the point of inter- section.

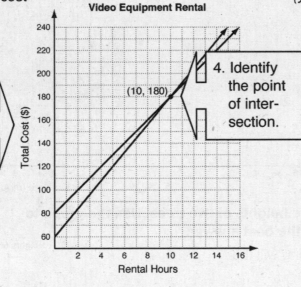

Video Equipment Rental

(10, 180)

5. Write your answer as a sentence.

After 10 hours, the cost of renting video equipment is $180 from both companies.

Derek is going to have a party catered. Good Eats charges $120 plus $10 per person. Food Fare charges $150 plus $8 per person. Complete the following to find the number of people for which the total cost is the same for both catering companies.

1. Define the variables. Let x = _____, Let y = _____

2. Write a system of linear equations. {_____
   _____

3. Graph the equations.

4. What is the point of intersection?_____

5. Write your answer. _____

_____

_____

Catering Costs

Holt McDougal Algebra 1

LESSON 5-2

Practice A

Solving Systems by Substitution

Fill in the blanks to solve each system by substitution.

1. $\begin{cases} y=3x \\ y=x+4 \end{cases}$

Substitute _____ for y in the second equation.

_____ $= x + 4$

$-$ _____ $- x$

_____ $= 4$

$\div$ _____ $\div$ _____

_____ $=$ _____

Since $x =$ _____, substitute _____ for x in one of the equations to find the value of y:

$y = 3x$

$y = 3(\underline{})$

$y =$ _____

Solution: (_____, _____)

2. $\begin{cases} 3x+y=25 \\ y=x-3 \end{cases}$

Substitute _____ for y in the first equation.

$3x + ($ _____ $) = 25$

_____ $-3 = 25$

 $+3$ $+3$

_____ $= 28$

$\div$ _____ $\div$ _____

_____ $=$ _____

Since $x =$ _____, substitute _____ for x in one of the equations to find the value of y:

$y = x - 3$

$y =$ _____ $- 3$

$y =$ _____

Solution: (_____, _____)

Solve each system by substitution. Check your answer.

3. $\begin{cases} y=4x \\ y=2x+6 \end{cases}$

_____

4. $\begin{cases} y=x-2 \\ 2x+y=4 \end{cases}$

_____

5. $\begin{cases} 2x+y=-1 \\ -x+y=-7 \end{cases}$

_____

6. A professional organizer charges a $45 consultation fee, plus $20 per hour. Her competitor charges a $30 consultation fee, plus $26 per hour.

   a. Write a system of equations to represent the situation.

   _____

   b. Solve the system by substitution. For what number of hours will the total charge be the same? _____

   c. What will that charge be? _____

Holt McDougal Algebra 1

LESSON
5-2

Practice B

Solving Systems by Substitution

Solve each system by substitution. Check your answer.

1. $\begin{cases} y=x-2 \\ y=4x+1 \end{cases}$

2. $\begin{cases} y=x-4 \\ y=-x+2 \end{cases}$

3. $\begin{cases} y=3x+1 \\ y=5x-3 \end{cases}$

_____ _____ _____

4. $\begin{cases} 2x-y=6 \\ x+y=-3 \end{cases}$

5. $\begin{cases} 2x+y=8 \\ y=x-7 \end{cases}$

6. $\begin{cases} 2x+3y=0 \\ x+2y=-1 \end{cases}$

_____ _____ _____

7. $\begin{cases} 3x-2y=7 \\ x+3y=-5 \end{cases}$

8. $\begin{cases} -2x+y=0 \\ 5x+3y=-11 \end{cases}$

9. $\begin{cases} \dfrac{1}{2}x+\dfrac{1}{3}y=5 \\ \dfrac{1}{4}x+y=10 \end{cases}$

_____ _____ _____

Write a system of equations to represent the situation. Then, solve the system by substitution.

10. The length of a rectangle is 3 more than its width. The perimeter of the rectangle is 58 cm. What are the rectangle's dimensions?

_____

11. Carla and Benicio work in a men's clothing store. They earn commission from each suit and each pair of shoes they sell. For selling 3 suits and one pair of shoes, Carla has earned $47 in commission. For selling 7 suits and 2 pairs of shoes, Benicio has earned $107 in commission. How much do the salespeople earn for the sale of a suit? for the sale of a pair of shoes?

_____

Holt McDougal Algebra 1

LESSON
5-2

Practice C

Solving Systems by Substitution

Solve each system by substitution. Check your answer.

1. $\begin{cases} y=x-6 \\ y=2x-8 \end{cases}$

2. $\begin{cases} y=x-4 \\ y=-2x+5 \end{cases}$

3. $\begin{cases} y=2x+8 \\ y=8 \end{cases}$

_____ _____ _____

4. $\begin{cases} x+y=-3 \\ x-y=-1 \end{cases}$

5. $\begin{cases} 4x+2y=-2 \\ y=6x-5 \end{cases}$

6. $\begin{cases} \dfrac{1}{2}x=y-1 \\ \dfrac{1}{3}x=y \end{cases}$

_____ _____ _____

7. $\begin{cases} 4x+y=3.4 \\ x=4y \end{cases}$

8. $\begin{cases} x=-\dfrac{1}{4}y+5 \\ 3x+2y=0 \end{cases}$

9. $\begin{cases} 3x=-y+10 \\ 2x+3y=-12 \end{cases}$

_____ _____ _____

Solve.

10. The sum of two numbers is 39. The greater number is 5 less than 3 times the smaller number. What are the two numbers?

_____

11. Adam has dimes and quarters in his pocket. There are 28 coins in all, and they are worth $4.60 altogether. How many quarters does Adam have?

_____

12. At a pet store, Rhonda paid $11.50 for 3 dog bowls and 4 bones. Kelly paid $13 for 2 dog bowls and 8 bones. How much will Andrew pay for 4 dog bowls and 2 bones?

_____

Holt McDougal Algebra 1

LESSON 5-2

Review for Mastery

Solving Systems by Substitution

You can use substitution to solve a system of equations if one of the equations is already solved for a variable.

Solve $\begin{cases} y = x + 2 \\ 3x + y = 10 \end{cases}$

Step 1: Choose the equation to use as the substitute.

> Use the first equation $y = x + 2$ because it is already solved for a variable.

Step 2: Solve by substitution.

$$\boxed{x + 2}$$

$3x + y = 10$

$3x + (x + 2) = 10$ *Substitute $x + 2$ for y.*

$4x + 2 = 10$ *Combine like terms.*

$\dfrac{ -2 \quad -2}{4x = 8}$

$\dfrac{4x}{4} = \dfrac{8}{4}$

$x = 2$

Step 3: Now substitute $x = 2$ back into one of the original equations to find the value of y.

$y = x + 2$

$y = 2 + 2$

$y = 4$

The solution is (2, 4).

Check:

Substitute (2, 4) into both equations.

$y = x + 2$ $3x + y = 10$

$4 \overset{?}{=} 2 + 2$ $3(2) + 4 \overset{?}{=} 10$

$4 \overset{?}{=} 4 \checkmark$ $6 + 4 \overset{?}{=} 10$

                              $10 \overset{?}{=} 10 \checkmark$

Solve each system by substitution. Check your answer.

1. $\begin{cases} x = y - 1 \\ x + 2y = 8 \end{cases}$

2. $\begin{cases} y = x + 2 \\ y = 2x - 5 \end{cases}$

3. $\begin{cases} y = x + 5 \\ 3x + y = -11 \end{cases}$

4. $\begin{cases} x = y + 10 \\ x = 2y + 3 \end{cases}$

                 Holt McDougal Algebra 1

LESSON 5-2 **Review for Mastery**

Solving Systems by Substitution continued

You may need to solve one of the equations for a variable before solving with substitution.

Solve $\begin{cases} y - x = 4 \\ 2x + 3y = 27. \end{cases}$

Step 1: Solve the first equation for y.

$y - x = 4$

$\underline{+x \quad +x}$

$\quad\quad y = x + 4$

Step 2: Solve by substitution.

$\boxed{x + 4}$

$2x + 3y = 27$

$2x + 3(x + 4) = 27$ *Substitute $x + 4$ for y.*

$2x + 3x + 12 = 27$ *Distribute.*

$5x + 12 = 27$ *Combine like terms.*

$\underline{-12 \quad -12}$

$\quad\quad 5x = 15$

$\quad\quad \dfrac{5x}{5} = \dfrac{15}{5}$

$\quad\quad x = 3$

Step 3: Now substitute $x = 3$ back into one of the original equations to find the value of y.

$y - x = 4$

$y - 3 = 4$

$\underline{+3 \quad +3}$

$\quad\quad y = 7$

The solution is (3, 7).

Check:

Substitute (3, 7) into both equations.

$y - x = 4 \qquad\qquad 2x + 3y = 27$

$7 - 3 \overset{?}{=} 4 \qquad\qquad 2(3) + 3(7) \overset{?}{=} 27$

$4 \overset{?}{=} 4\ \checkmark \qquad\qquad 6 + 21 \overset{?}{=} 27$

$\qquad\qquad\qquad\qquad 27 \overset{?}{=} 27\ \checkmark$

Solve each system by substitution. Check your answer.

5. $\begin{cases} x - y = -3 \\ 2x + y = 12 \end{cases}$

6. $\begin{cases} y - x = 8 \\ 5x + 2y = 9 \end{cases}$

Holt McDougal Algebra 1

LESSON 5-2 Challenge

Three Equations in Three Variables

To solve a system with two variables, you must have two equations. To solve a system in three variables, you must have three equations.

Use substitution to find the values of *x*, *y*, and *z*.

1. $\begin{cases} 2x+4y+3z=14 \\ y+3z=11 \\ z=4 \end{cases}$

2. $\begin{cases} 4x+y+3z=-9 \\ 2y-5z=23 \\ z=-3 \end{cases}$

_____   _____

3. $\begin{cases} 2x+3y+2z=18 \\ -4x+y-z=5 \\ 2z=-10 \end{cases}$

4. $\begin{cases} x+y+z=15 \\ 2x-y+3z=-5 \\ -x-y+z=-7 \end{cases}$

[Hint: Solve for *z* and get two equations to have *x* and *y* only.]

_____   _____

Holt McDougal Algebra 1

LESSON 5-2

Problem Solving

Solving Systems by Substitution

Write the correct answer.

1. Maribel has $1.25 in her pocket. The money is in quarters and dimes. There are a total of 8 coins. How many quarters and dimes does Maribel have in her pocket?

   _____

   _____

2. Fabulously Fit offers memberships for $35 per month plus a $50 enrollment fee. The Fitness Studio offers memberships for $40 per month plus a $35 enrollment fee. In how many months will the fitness clubs cost the same? What will the cost be?

   _____

   _____

3. Vong grilled 21 burgers at a block party. He grilled the same number of pounds of turkey burgers as hamburgers. Each turkey burger weighed $\frac{1}{4}$ pound and each hamburger weighed $\frac{1}{3}$ pound. How many of each did Vong grill?

   _____

   _____

4. Kate bought 3 used CDs and 1 used DVD at the bookstore. Her friend Joel bought 2 used CDs and 2 used DVDs at the same store. If Kate spent $20 and Joel spent $22, determine the cost of a used CD and a used DVD.

   _____

   _____

Use the chart below to answer questions 5–8. Select the best answer. The chart compares the quotes that the Masons received from four different flooring contractors to tear out and replace a floor.

5. Which expression shows the total cost if the work is done by Dad's Floors?

   A $8 + 150x$ C $150(8x)$

   B $150 + 8x$ D $158x$

6. How many square feet would the Masons need to have installed to make the total cost of V.I.P. Inc. the same as the total cost of Floorshop?

   F 10 sq ft   H 100 sq ft

   G 200 sq ft   J 350 sq ft

7. When the total costs of V.I.P. Inc. and Floorshop are the same, what is the total cost?

   A $1125.00   C $1950.00

   B $1900.00   D $3187.50

Contractor	Cost to tear out old floor	Cost of new floor per square foot
Smith & Son	$250	$8.00
V.I.P. Inc.	$350	$7.75
Dad's Floors	$150	$8.00
Floorshop	$300	$8.25

8. How many square feet would the Masons need to have installed to make the total cost of Smith & Son the same as the total cost of V.I.P. Inc.?

   F 80 sq ft   H 400 sq ft

   G 100 sq ft   J 1000 sq ft

LESSON 5-2

Reading Strategies
Use a Sequence Chain

Use the sequence chain below to guide you in solving systems of linear equations by the method of substitution.

Step 1: Isolate one variable in one equation.	**Step 2:** Substitute the expression for that variable into the other equation.	**Step 3:** Solve for the variable remaining in that equation.

Sequence Chain: *Solving Systems by Substitution*

Step 4: Substitute the value for that variable into either original equation and solve for the other variable.	**Step 5:** Write the found values for x and y as an ordered pair (x, y).	**Step 6:** Check your answer by substituting (x, y) into both equations.

Answer each question.

1. Perform Step 1 for $\begin{cases} x+y=5 \\ -3x+5=\dfrac{1}{2}y \end{cases}$ by solving the first equation for y.

   _____

2. To solve the system $\begin{cases} y=x+2 \\ 2x+y=6 \end{cases}$ by substitution, you can start at Step 2. Explain why.

   _____

3. Why does Step 6 specify substituting into *both* equations?

   _____

Solve each system of equations by substitution.

4. $\begin{cases} 2x=3y \\ y=x-2 \end{cases}$

5. $\begin{cases} x+y=2 \\ -x=2y-7 \end{cases}$

   _____   _____

Holt McDougal Algebra 1

LESSON 5-3

Practice A
Solving Systems by Elimination

Fill in the blanks to solve each system by elimination.

1. $\begin{cases} x + 3y = 14 \\ 2x - 3y = -8 \end{cases}$

   Add the equations:
   $x + 3y = 14$
   $+2x - 3y = 28$
   _____
   $3x + \underline{\quad} = 6$

   $\underline{\quad} = 6$

   $\div \underline{\quad} \div \underline{\quad}$

   $x = \underline{\quad}$

   Substitute ___ for x in one of the equations:
   $x + 3y = 14$
   $\underline{\quad} + 3y = 14$
   $- \underline{\quad} - \underline{\quad}$
   $3y = \underline{\quad}$
   $\div 3 \div 3$
   $y = \underline{\quad}$

   Solution: (___ , ___)

2. $\begin{cases} 2x + 2y = 4 \\ 3x + 2y = 7 \end{cases}$

   Subtract the equations:
   $2x + 2y = 4$
   $-(3x + 2y = 7)$
   _____

   or

   $2x + 2y = 4$
   $\underline{-3x -\underline{\quad} = \underline{\quad}}$
   $-x + \underline{\quad} = \underline{\quad}$
   $-x = \underline{\quad}$
   $\div \underline{\quad} \div \underline{\quad}$
   $x = \underline{\quad}$

   Substitute ___ for x in one of the equations:
   $3x + 2y = 7$
   $3(\underline{\quad}) + 2y = 7$
   $\underline{\quad} + 2y = 7$
   $\underline{- \underline{\quad}} \underline{- \underline{\quad}}$
   $2y = \underline{\quad}$
   $\div \underline{\quad} \div \underline{\quad}$
   $y = \underline{\quad}$

   Solution: (___ , ___)

3. $\begin{cases} 3x + 4y = 26 \\ x - 2y = -8 \end{cases}$

   Multiply the second equation by 2. Then, add the equations:
   $\begin{cases} 3x + 4y = 26 \\ 2(x - 2y = -8 \end{cases}$

   $3x + 4y = 26$
   $\underline{+ \underline{\quad} x - \underline{\quad} y = \underline{\quad}}$
   $\underline{\quad} x + 0 = \underline{\quad}$
   $\underline{\quad} x = \underline{\quad}$
   $\div \underline{\quad} \div \underline{\quad}$
   $x = \underline{\quad}$

   Substitute ___ for x in one of the equations:
   $x - 2y = -8$
   $\underline{\quad} - 2y = -8$
   $\underline{- \underline{\quad}} \underline{- \underline{\quad}}$
   $-2y = \underline{\quad}$
   $\div \underline{\quad} \div \underline{\quad}$
   $y = \underline{\quad}$

   Solution: (___ , ___)

Solve each system by elimination.

4. $\begin{cases} 3x - 2y = 1 \\ 2x + 2y = 14 \end{cases}$

   _____

5. $\begin{cases} x + y = 4 \\ 3x + y = 16 \end{cases}$

   _____

6. $\begin{cases} 3x + 2y = -26 \\ 2x - 6y = -10 \end{cases}$

   _____

7. The sum of two numbers is −1. When twice the first number and four times the second number are added, the sum is −10. What are the two numbers?

   _____

Holt McDougal Algebra 1

LESSON 5-3 Practice B

Solving Systems by Elimination

Follow the steps to solve each system by elimination.

1. $\begin{cases} 2x - 3y = 14 \\ 2x + y = -10 \end{cases}$

   Subtract the second equation:

   $2x - 3y = 14$
   $\underline{-(2x + y = -10)}$

   _____

   Solve the resulting equation:

   $y = $ _____

   Use your answer to find the value of x:

   $x = $ _____

   Solution: (_____, _____)

2. $\begin{cases} 3x + y = 17 \\ 4x + 2y = 20 \end{cases}$

   Multiply the first equation by –2. Then, add the equations:

   $\underline{\quad} x - \underline{\quad} y = \underline{\quad\quad}$
   $\underline{+ 4x + 2y = 20}$

   _____

   Solve the resulting equation:

   $x = $ _____

   Use your answer to find the value of y:

   $y = $ _____

   Solution: (_____, _____)

Solve each system by elimination. Check your answer.

3. $\begin{cases} x + 3y = -7 \\ -x + 2y = -8 \end{cases}$

4. $\begin{cases} 3x + y = -26 \\ 2x - y = -19 \end{cases}$

5. $\begin{cases} x + 3y = -14 \\ 2x - 4y = 32 \end{cases}$

_____   _____   _____

6. $\begin{cases} 4x - y = -5 \\ -2x + 3y = 10 \end{cases}$

7. $\begin{cases} y - 3x = 11 \\ 2y - x = 2 \end{cases}$

8. $\begin{cases} -10x + y = 0 \\ 5x + 3y = -7 \end{cases}$

_____   _____   _____

Solve.

9. Brianna's family spent $134 on 2 adult tickets and 3 youth tickets at an amusement park. Max's family spent $146 on 3 adult tickets and 2 youth tickets. What is the price of a youth ticket? _____

10. Carl bought 19 apples of 2 different varieties to make a pie. The total cost of the apples was $5.10. Granny Smith apples cost $0.25 each and Gala apples cost $0.30 each. How many of each type of apple did Carl buy? _____

_____

Holt McDougal Algebra 1

Practice C
Solving Systems by Elimination

Solve each system by elimination.

1. $\begin{cases} x + y = 2 \\ 2x - y = 7 \end{cases}$

2. $\begin{cases} 3x - 2y = -2 \\ 3x + y = 10 \end{cases}$

3. $\begin{cases} x + y = -7 \\ x - y = 5 \end{cases}$

_____   _____   _____

4. $\begin{cases} -3x - 4y = -2 \\ 6x + 4y = 3 \end{cases}$

5. $\begin{cases} 2x - 2y = 14 \\ x + 4y = -13 \end{cases}$

6. $\begin{cases} y - x = 17 \\ 2y + 3x = -11 \end{cases}$

_____   _____   _____

7. $\begin{cases} x + 6y = 1 \\ 2x - 3y = 32 \end{cases}$

8. $\begin{cases} -\dfrac{1}{2}x + y = 4 \\ \dfrac{1}{3}x - y = -3 \end{cases}$

9. $\begin{cases} 3x + y = -15 \\ 2x - 3y = 23 \end{cases}$

_____   _____   _____

10. $\begin{cases} 5x - 2y = -48 \\ 2x + 3y = -23 \end{cases}$

11. $\begin{cases} 4x - 3y = -9 \\ 5x - y = 8 \end{cases}$

12. $\begin{cases} 3x - 3y = -1 \\ 12x - 2y = 16 \end{cases}$

_____   _____   _____

13. At a bakery, Riley bought 3 bagels and 2 muffins for $7.25.
Karen bought 5 bagels and 4 muffins for $13.25. What is
the cost of each item?   _____

14. A chemist has a beaker of a 3% acid solution and a beaker of
a 7% acid solution. He needs to make 75 mL of a 4% acid solution.

a. Complete the table.

	3% solution	+	7% solution	=	4% solution
Amount of Solution (mL)	x	+	y	=	_____
Amount of Acid (mL)	_____ x	+	_____ y	=	0.04(75)

b. Use the information in the table to write a system of
linear equations.

_____

c. Solve the system of equations to find how much he
will use from each beaker.

_____

LESSON 5-3

Review for Mastery

Solving Systems by Elimination

Elimination can be used to solve a system of equations by adding terms vertically. This will cause one of the variables to be eliminated. It may be necessary to multiply one or both equations by some number to use this method.

I. Elimination may require no change to either equation.

$\begin{cases} 3x + y = 6 \\ 5x - y = 10 \end{cases}$

Adding vertically will eliminate y.

$3x + y = 6$
$\underline{5x - y = 10}$
$8x + 0 = 16$

II. Elimination may require multiplying one equation by an appropriate number.

$\begin{cases} 2x + 5y = 9 \\ x - 3y = 10 \end{cases}$

Multiply bottom equation by –2.

$2x + 5y = 9$
$-2(x - 3y) = -2(10)$

$2x + 5y = 9$
$\underline{-2x + 6y = -20}$
$0 + 11y = -11$

III. Elimination may require multiplying both equation by different numbers.

$\begin{cases} 5x + 3y = 2 \\ 4x + 2y = 10 \end{cases}$

Multiply the top by –2 and the bottom by 3.

$-2(5x + 3y = 2)$
$3(4x + 2y = 10)$

$-10x + -6y = -4$
$\underline{12x + 6y = 30}$
$2x + 0 = 26$

Solve each system by elimination.

1. $\begin{cases} 2x - y = 20 \\ 3x + 2y = -19 \end{cases}$

2. $\begin{cases} 3x + 2y = 10 \\ 3x - 2y = 14 \end{cases}$

3. $\begin{cases} x + y = 12 \\ 2x + y = 6 \end{cases}$

4. $\begin{cases} 3x - y = 2 \\ -8x + 2y = 4 \end{cases}$

LESSON 5-3 — Review for Mastery

Solving Systems by Elimination *continued*

A system of equations can be solved by graphing, substitution, or elimination.

- Use graphing if both equations are solved for y, or if you want an estimate of the solution.

- Use substitution if either equation is solved for a variable, or has a variable with a coefficient of 1 or -1.

- Use elimination if both equations have the same variable with the same or opposite coefficients.

It may be necessary to manipulate your equations to get them in any of the three forms above.

Solve $\begin{cases} y = 3 - x \\ 2x - y = 6 \end{cases}$.

> One equation is solved for a variable. Use substitution.

$\boxed{3 - x}$

$2x - y = 6$

$2x - (3 - x) = 6$

$3x - 3 = 6$

$\underline{+3 \qquad +3}$

$3x = 9$

$x = 3$

Substitute $x + 2$ for y.

Substitute $x = 3$ into one of the original equations to find the value of y.

$y = 3 - x$

$y = 3 - 3$

$y = 0$ — The solution is $(3, 0)$.

Solve $\begin{cases} -2x - y = -5 \\ 3x + y = -1 \end{cases}$.

$-2x - y = -5$

$\underline{3x + y = -1}$

$x + 0 = -6$

$x = -6$

> The equations have the same variable with opposite coefficients. Use elimination.

Substitute $x = -6$ into one of the original equations to find the value of y.

$3x + y = -1$

$3(-6) + y = -1$

$-18 + y = -1$

$\underline{+18 \qquad +18}$

$y = 17$

The solution is $(-6, 17)$.

Solve each system by any method.

5. $\begin{cases} y = x + 3 \\ -2x + y = -4 \end{cases}$

6. $\begin{cases} 4x + y = 10 \\ -2x - y = 4 \end{cases}$

7. $\begin{cases} 2x + y = 8 \\ 3x + 5y = 5 \end{cases}$

_____   _____   _____

Holt McDougal Algebra 1

Challenge

Solving Systems by Elimination

The elimination method can also be used for a system of three equations in three unknowns.

Three camp leaders purchased equipment for a camping trip.
Max bought 10 sleeping bags, 2 tents, and 1 can of bug repellant for $885.
Carlos bought 5 sleeping bags, 4 tents, and 1 can of bug repellant for $865.
Amy bought 9 sleeping bags, 6 tents, and 6 cans of bug repellant for $1410.
If they made their purchases at the same store, how much did each item cost?

1. Write the 3 equations:
$$\begin{cases} 10x + 2y + z = 885 \\ \rule{3cm}{0.4pt} \\ \rule{3cm}{0.4pt} \end{cases}$$

2. Subtract the second equation from the first. _____

3. Multiply the second equation by –6 ,
   and add the second and third equations. _____

4. The equations in steps 2 and 3 form a linear
   system in two variables. Solve this system for *x*. _____

5. Substitute the value of *x* into the first two
   equations. Write the resulting system. _____

6. Solve the system in problem 5 for *y* and *z*. _____

7. Write the cost of each item. _____

Holt McDougal Algebra 1

LESSON 5-3
Problem Solving
Solving Systems by Elimination

Write the correct answer.

1. Mr. Nguyen bought a package of 3 chicken legs and a package of 7 chicken wings. Ms. Dawes bought a package of 3 chicken legs and a package of 6 chicken wings. Mr. Nguyen bought 45 ounces of chicken. Ms. Dawes bought 42 ounces of chicken. How much did each chicken leg and each chicken wing weigh?

_____

_____

2. Jayce bought 2 bath towels and returned 3 hand towels. His sister Jayna bought 3 bath towels and 3 hand towels. Jayce's bill was $5. Jayna's bill was $45. What are the prices of a bath towel and a hand towel?

_____

3. The Lees spent $31 on movie tickets for 2 adults and 3 children. The Macias spent $26 on movie tickets for 2 adults and 2 children. What are the prices for adult and child movie tickets?

_____

_____

4. Last month Stephanie spent $57 on 4 allergy shots and 1 office visit. This month she spent $9 after 1 office visit and a refund for 2 allergy shots from her insurance company. How much does an office visit cost? an allergy shot?

_____

Use the chart below to answer questions 5–6. Select the best answer. The chart shows the price per pound for dried fruit.

Dried Fruit Price List			
Pineapple	Apple	Mango	Papaya
$7.50/lb	$7.00/lb	$8.00/lb	$7.25/lb

5. A customer bought 5 pounds of mango and papaya for $37.75. How many pounds of each fruit did the customer buy?

   A 2 lbs mango and 3 lbs papaya

   B 3 lbs mango and 2 lbs papaya

   C 1 lb mango and 4 lbs papaya

   D 4 lbs mango and 1 lb papaya

6. A store employee made two gift baskets of dried fruit, each costing $100. The first basket had 12 pounds of fruit x and 2 pounds of fruit y. The second basket had 4 pounds of fruit x and 9 pounds of fruit y. Which two fruits did the employee use in the baskets?

   F pineapple and apple

   G apple and mango

   H mango and papaya

   J papaya and pineapple

Holt McDougal Algebra 1

Name _____ Date _____ Class_____

Reading Strategies
Connecting Concepts

When solving systems of linear equations using elimination, you will sometimes need to multiply one or both equations by a factor in order to get the same coefficients for a variable. This process is very similar to getting a common denominator for fractions. Look at the example below.

$$\begin{cases} 6x - 5y = 16 \\ 4x - 3y = 12 \end{cases}$$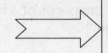

To eliminate the x–terms, you need to get the same or opposite coefficients for x in both equations.

Add: $\dfrac{5}{6} + \dfrac{1}{4} = ?$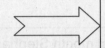

Think about finding a common denominator for 4 and 6.

4: 4, 8, ⟨12⟩ 16, 20
6: 6, ⟨12⟩ 18, 24, 30

Find the least common multiple (LCM) of 4 and 6 by listing their multiples in order. The LCM is 12.

$$\begin{cases} 2(6x - 5y = 16) \\ 3(4x - 3y = 12) \end{cases}$$

Determine what you have to multiple 4 and 6 by to get 12. Multiply each equation by the appropriate number.

$$\begin{cases} 12x - 10y = 32 \\ 12x - 9y = 36 \end{cases}$$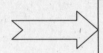

Now either add or subtract the equations. In this case, you will subtract the equations.

1. Describe how you would get common y-coefficients (instead of x-) in the example above.

_____

_____

2. Show how to get a set of common y-coefficients for the system $\begin{cases} 9x - 10y = 7 \\ 5x + 8y = 31 \end{cases}$.

_____

_____

Solve each system of equations by elimination.

3. $\begin{cases} 9x - 2y = 15 \\ 4x + 3y = -5 \end{cases}$

4. $\begin{cases} 2x - 3y = 50 \\ 7x + 8y = -10 \end{cases}$

_____   _____

Holt McDougal Algebra 1

LESSON 5-4	**Practice A**
	Solving Special systems

Solve each system of linear equations. Tell whether the system has no solution or infinitely many solutions.

1. $\begin{cases} 2x + y = 1 \\ 2x + y = -3 \end{cases}$

2. $\begin{cases} y = 5x + 2 \\ y - 5x = 2 \end{cases}$

_____

3. $\begin{cases} y - 3x + 2 = 0 \\ 2 = -y + 3x \end{cases}$

4. $\begin{cases} x + y = 4 \\ y - 4 = 1 - x \end{cases}$

_____

Give the number of solutions to each system. Then classify the system as "consistent, independent", "consistent, dependent", or "inconsistent".

5. $\begin{cases} y = 2(x + 1) \\ y - 2x = 2 \end{cases}$

6. $\begin{cases} y - 4x + 5 = 0 \\ 4x = y - 1 \end{cases}$

_____

7. Marquis opens a savings account with $60 and adds
$20 each month. His brother Jibran adds $20 each month
to the savings account that his grandmother opened with
$60. If the brothers continue to make deposits to their savings
accounts at the same rate, when will they have the same
amount of money? Explain.

_____

_____

Holt McDougal Algebra 1

LESSON 5-4 Practice B

Solving Special Systems

Solve each system of linear equations.

1. $\begin{cases} y = 2x - 3 \\ y - 2x = -3 \end{cases}$

2. $\begin{cases} 3x + y = 4 \\ -3x = y - 7 \end{cases}$

_____

3. $\begin{cases} y = -4x + 1 \\ 4x = -y - 6 \end{cases}$

4. $\begin{cases} y - x + 3 = 0 \\ x = y + 3 \end{cases}$

_____

Classify each system. Give the number of solutions.

5. $\begin{cases} y = 3(x - 1) \\ -y + 3x = 3 \end{cases}$

6. $\begin{cases} y - 2x = 5 \\ x = y - 3 \end{cases}$

_____

7. Sabina and Lou are reading the same book. Sabina reads 12 pages a day. She had read 36 pages when Lou started the book, and Lou reads at a pace of 15 pages per day. If their reading rates continue, will Sabina and Lou ever be reading the same page on the same day? Explain.

_____

_____

8. Brandon started jogging at 4 miles per hour. After he jogged 1 mile, his friend Anton started jogging along the same path at a pace of 4 miles per hour. If they continue to jog at the same rate, will Anton ever catch up with Brandon? Explain.

_____

_____

Holt McDougal Algebra 1

LESSON 5-4

Practice C

Solving Special systems

Solve each system of linear equations.

1. $\begin{cases} y + 2x + 4 = 0 \\ 2x = -y - 4 \end{cases}$

2. $\begin{cases} 5x + y = 8 \\ -5x = 8 + y \end{cases}$

3. $\begin{cases} 2x - y = 4 \\ 1 = y - 2x + 5 \end{cases}$

4. $\begin{cases} y = -x - 6 \\ y - 2x = -3x + 6 \end{cases}$

Classify each system. Give the number of solutions.

5. $\begin{cases} y + 2(x - 3) = 0 \\ 2x = -y - 3 \end{cases}$

6. $\begin{cases} y + 3x = -1 \\ x = y + 3x - 1 \end{cases}$

7. At a factory, Jin assembles 12 parts each minute. He has assembled 156 parts when Summer starts on the line, assembling at a pace of 15 parts per minute. If their assembly rates continue, will Summer ever catch up to Jin? Explain.

8. Kat is comparing monthly sales at her bookstore with those of her competitor, Gill. If the sales rates continue, will Kat's book sales ever catch up with her competitor's? Explain.

Kat's sales	112	118	124	130
Gill's sales	138	144	150	156

LESSON 5-4

Review for Mastery

Solving Special systems

When solving equations in one variable, it is possible to have one solution, no solutions, or infinitely many solutions. The same results can occur when graphing systems of equations.

Solve $\begin{cases} 4x + 2y = 2 \\ 2x + y = 4 \end{cases}$.

Multiplying the second equation by –2 will eliminate the *x*-terms.

$4x + 2y = 2$ $4x + 2y = 2$
$-2(2x + y = 4)$ $\underline{-4x - 2y = -8}$
                       $0 + 0 = -6$
                           $0 = -6$ ✗

The equation is a contradiction. **There is no solution.**

Solve $\begin{cases} y = 4 - 3x \\ 3x + y = 4 \end{cases}$.

Because the first equation is solved for a variable, use substitution.

$3x + y = 4$
$3x + (4 - 3x) = 4$ *Substitute* $4 - 3x$ *for y*
       $0 + 4 = 4$

         $4 = 4$ ✓

The equation is true for all values of *x* and *y*. **There are infinitely many solutions.**

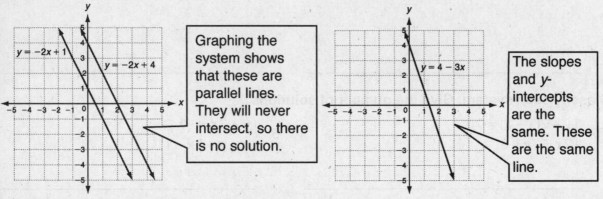

Graphing the system shows that these are parallel lines. They will never intersect, so there is no solution.

The slopes and *y*-intercepts are the same. These are the same line.

Solve each system of linear equations algebraically.

1. $\begin{cases} y = 3x \\ 2y = 6x \end{cases}$

2. $\begin{cases} y = 2x + 5 \\ y - 2x = 1 \end{cases}$

3. $\begin{cases} 3x - 2y = 9 \\ -6x + 4y = 1 \end{cases}$

_____   _____   _____

LESSON 5-4

Review for Mastery

Solving Special Systems continued

A system of linear equations can be classified in three ways.

I. Consistent and independent one solution different slopes	Example: $\begin{cases} y = x + 3 \\ y = -x + 6 \end{cases}$	
II. Consistent and dependent infinitely many solutions same slope, same y-intercepts	Example $\begin{cases} y = 3x + 4 \\ y - 3x = 4 \end{cases}$	
III. Inconsistent no solutions same slope, different y-intercepts	Example $\begin{cases} y = 2x + 5 \\ y = 2x + 2 \end{cases}$	

Classify each system below by comparing the slopes and y-intercepts. Then give the number of solutions.

4. $\begin{cases} y = -3x - 2 \\ y = -3x - 4 \end{cases}$

5. $\begin{cases} y = 2x + 5 \\ y = 5 + 2x \end{cases}$

6. $\begin{cases} y = -4x + 3 \\ y = 2x + 7 \end{cases}$

_____   _____   _____

_____   _____   _____

Classify each system and give the number of solutions. If there is one solution, provide it.

7. $\begin{cases} y = 2x + 8 \\ y - 4x = 8 \end{cases}$

8. $\begin{cases} y + 3x - 2 = 0 \\ 9x + 3y = 6 \end{cases}$

_____   _____

_____   _____

Holt McDougal Algebra 1

LESSON 5-4

Challenge

Pick a Path

The puzzle below contains 23 linear equations. You goal is to find paths through the puzzle such that each pair of equations along your path forms a special type of system.

You must begin in the **Start** square, and end in the **Finish** square. Moves can be horizontal, vertical, or diagonal between adjacent squares. Each individual path cannot cross itself, but your answers to 1 and 2 might cross.

	1	2	3	4
Start → ↘ ↓	$y = x + 2$	$3x = 3y - 6$	$3x + y = -1$	$8y = 8x + 16$
5	6	7	8	9
$y = 2x + 3$	$y = 3x - 1$	$y - x = 2$	$\frac{1}{3}x + \frac{1}{3}y = 1$	$3x = y + 1$
10	11	12	13	14
$2y = 6x + 6$	$2x - y = -3$	$2x + 2y = 4$	$2y - 4 = 2x$	$x - y = -2$
15	16	17	18	19
$\frac{1}{2}y = \frac{3}{2}x + \frac{1}{2}$	$3y = 2x + 1$	$3x - y = 4$	$\frac{1}{6}y = \frac{1}{3}x + \frac{1}{2}$	$\frac{1}{2}y = \frac{1}{2}x + 1$
20	21	22	23	↓
$10x + 15y = 5$	$-12x + 4y = 8$	$\frac{1}{2}y = \frac{1}{3}x + \frac{1}{6}$	$x = \frac{1}{3}y + 1$	↘ ↓ → **Finish**

Find a path through the puzzle such that each pair of equations forms...

1. ...a consistent and dependent system.

_____

2. ...an inconsistent system.

_____

Holt McDougal Algebra 1

LESSON 5-4

Problem Solving

Solving Special systems

Write the correct answer.

1. Tyra and Charmian are training for a bike race. Tyra has logged 256 miles so far and rides 48 miles per week. Charmian has logged 125 miles so far and rides 48 miles per week. If these rates continue, will Tyra's distance ever equal Charmian's distance? Explain.

_____

_____

2. Metroplexpress and Local Express are courier companies. Metroplexpress charges $15 to pick up a package and $0.50 per mile. Local Express charges $10 to pick up a package and $0.55 per mile. Classify this system and find its solution, if any.

_____

3. The Singhs start savings accounts for their twin boys. The accounts earn 5% annual interest. The initial deposit in each account is $200. Classify this system and find its solution, if any.

_____

_____

4. Frank earns $8 per hour. Madison earns $7.50 per hour. Frank started working after Madison had already earned $300. If these rates continue, will Frank's earnings ever equal Madison's earnings? If so, when?

_____

_____

Select the best answer.

5. A studio apartment at The Oaks costs $400 per month plus a $350 deposit. A studio apartment at Crossroads costs $400 per month plus a $300 deposit. How many solutions does this system have?

   A no solutions

   B 1 solution

   C 2 solutions

   D an infinite number of solutions

6. Jane and Gary are both landscape designers. Jane charges $75 for a consultation plus $25 per hour. Gary charges $50 for a consultation plus $30 per hour. For how many hours will Jane's charges equal Gary's charges?

   F never

   G after 2 hours

   H after 5 hours

   J always

7. A tank filled with 75 liters of water loses 0.5 liter of water per hour. A tank filled with 50 liters of water loses 0.1 liter of water per hour. How would this system be classified?

   A inconsistent

   B dependent

   C consistent and independent

   D consistent and dependent

8. Simon is 3 years older than Renata. Five years ago, Renata was half as old as Simon is now. How old are Simon and Renata now?

   F Simon is 13 and Renata is 10.

   G Simon is 15 and Renata is 10.

   H Simon is 16 and Renata is 8.

   J Simon is 16 and Renata is 13.

Holt McDougal Algebra 1

LESSON 5-4

Reading Strategies

Use a Table

The table below can help you answer questions about linear systems.

Classification	Number of Solutions	Similarities and Differences in $y = mx + b$	Description of Graphed Lines	Result of Solving with Algebra
Consistent, Independent	1	different slopes (m)	intersecting	values for x and y ex. $x = 3$, $y = -5$
Consistent, Dependent	infinitely many	same slope (m) same y-int. (b)	coincident	identity statement ex. $4 = 4$
Inconsistent	0	same slope (m) different y-int. (b)	parallel	false statement ex. $-2 = 3$

1. Mary Kate solved a system by elimination as shown below. Classify the system.

$$\begin{cases} 2x + 3y = 5 \\ 2x + 3y = 7 \end{cases} \Rightarrow \begin{array}{r} 2x + 3y = 5 \\ -(2x + 3y = 7) \\ \hline 0 = -2 \end{array}$$

_____

2. Raul solved a system of equations by substitution. He ended up with an identity statement. How many solutions does his system have?

_____

3. How many solutions does a system have if, when graphed, the lines are the same line?

_____

4. Two equations in a system have the same slope. Which classification can NOT describe the system?

_____

5. The graph of a system consists of two intersecting lines. How many solutions does the system have? _____

Classify each system, give the number of solutions, and describe its graph.

6. $\begin{cases} y = -3x \\ y = -3x + 2 \end{cases}$

7. $\begin{cases} y = -x + 4 \\ x + y = 4 \end{cases}$

8. $\begin{cases} y = 2x - 1 \\ x = y \end{cases}$

_____   _____   _____

_____   _____   _____

Holt McDougal Algebra 1

LESSON 5-5

Practice A
Solving Linear Inequalities

Use substitution to tell whether the ordered pair is a solution of the given inequality.

1. $(3, 4)$; $y > x + 2$

2. $(4, 2)$; $y \le 2x - 3$

3. $(2, -1)$; $y < -x$

_____   _____   _____

Rewrite each linear inequality in slope-intercept form. Then graph the solutions in the coordinate plane.

4. $y - x \le 3$

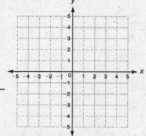

5. $6x + 2y > -2$

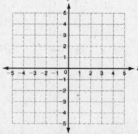

_____   _____

6. Trey is buying peach and blueberry yogurt cups. He will buy at most 8 cups of yogurt. Let x be the number of peach yogurt cups and y be the number of blueberry yogurt cups he buys.

a. Write an inequality to describe the situation.

_____

b. Graph the solutions.

c. Give two possible combinations of peach and blueberry yogurt that Trey can choose.

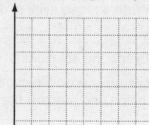

_____

_____

Write an inequality to represent each graph.

7.

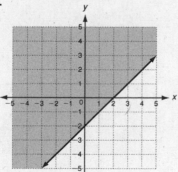

8

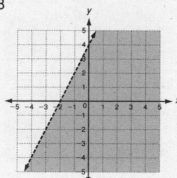

9.

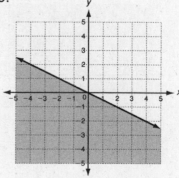

_____   _____   _____

Holt McDougal Algebra 1

Practice B
Solving Linear Inequalities

Tell whether the ordered pair is a solution of the given inequality.

1. $(1, 6)$; $y < x + 6$ 2. $(-3, -12)$; $y \geq 2x - 5$ 3. $(5, -3)$; $y \leq -x + 2$

_____   _____   _____

Graph the solutions of each linear inequality.

4. $y \leq x + 4$

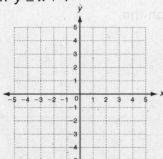

5. $2x + y > -2$

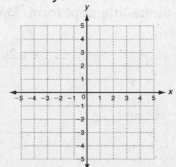

6. $x + y - 1 < 0$

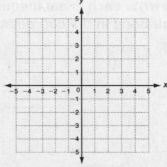

7. Clark is having a party at his house. His father has allowed him to spend at most $20 on snack food. He'd like to buy chips that cost $4 per bag, and pretzels that cost $2 per bag.

   a. Write an inequality to describe the situation.

   _____

   b. Graph the solutions.

   c. Give two possible combinations of bags of chips and pretzels that Clark can buy.

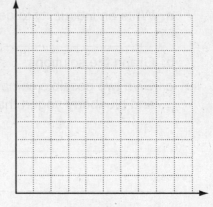

   _____

   _____

Write an inequality to represent each graph.

8.

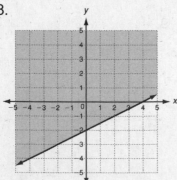

9.

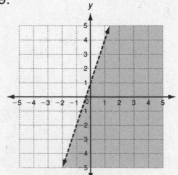

10.

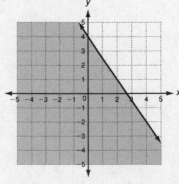

_____   _____   _____

     Holt McDougal Algebra 1

LESSON 5-5

Practice C
Solving Linear Inequalities

Tell whether the ordered pair is a solution of the given inequality.

1. $(-1, -4)$; $y \geq 2x - 1$

2. $(-6, 2)$; $y < -x - 4$

3. $(4, -8)$; $y \leq \frac{1}{2}x + 5$

_____   _____   _____

Graph the solutions of each linear inequality.

4. $y \leq x + 2$

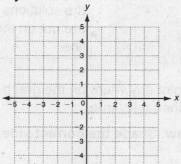

5. $-3x < y$

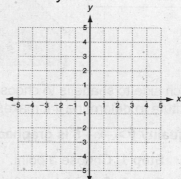

6. $2x - y - 4 > 0$

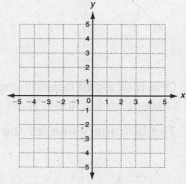

7. Adam is ordering helium balloons for his sister's birthday. He has up to $15 to spend. Decorative balloons cost $3.00 each and solid colored balloons cost $0.50 each.

   a. Write an inequality to describe the situation.

   _____

   b. Graph the solutions.

   c. Give two possible combinations of decorative and solid colored balloons Adam can order.

   _____

   _____

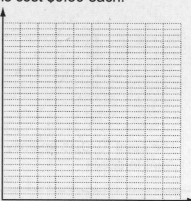

Write an inequality to represent each graph.

8.

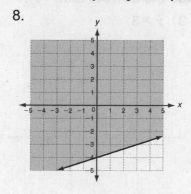

_____

9.

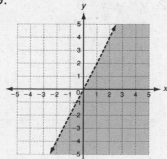

_____

10.

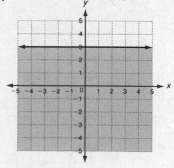

_____

        Holt McDougal Algebra 1

LESSON 5-5

Review for Mastery

Solving Linear Inequalities

When graphing an equation, the solutions are all the points on the line. When graphing an inequality, the solutions are all the points above or below the line (and may include the line).

Graph $y = x + 4$.

Graph $y < x + 4$.

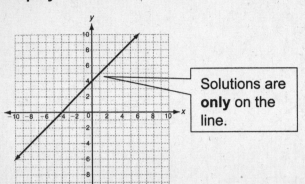

Solutions are **only** on the line.

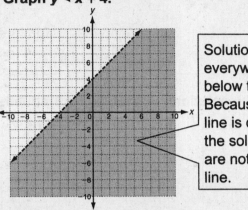

Solutions are everywhere below the line. Because the line is dashed, the solutions are not on the line.

One method of determining which side to shade is to choose a point anywhere on the graph (except on the line). Then substitute to determine if it makes the inequality true.

The boundary line for the inequality $y > -x + 5$ is graphed below. Shade the correct side.

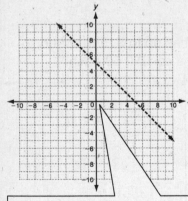

The point (0, 0) is an easy point to check.

Step 1: Choose a point.

Step 2: Substitute (0, 0) in the inequality $y > -x + 5$.

$$y > -x + 5$$
$$0 \overset{?}{>} -0 + 5$$
$$0 \overset{?}{>} 5$$

The statement is false.

Step 3: Because (0, 0), which is below the line, resulted in a false statement, it is not a solution. Shade above the line.

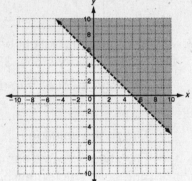

The boundary lines for each inequality are graphed below. Shade the correct side

1. $y > 5x + 7$

2. $y < -2x - 9$

3. $x > 3$

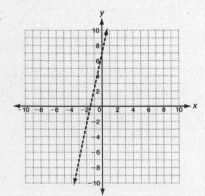

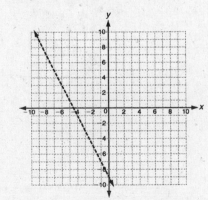

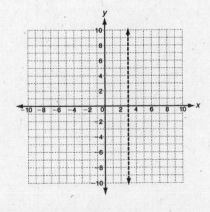

Holt McDougal Algebra 1

**LESSON
5-5**

Review for Mastery

Solving Linear Inequalities continued

To graph a linear inequality:

Step 1: Solve the inequality for y.

Step 2: Graph the boundary line. If $\leq$, or $\geq$ use a solid line. If $<$ or $>$ use a dashed line.

Step 3: Determine which side to shade.

Graph the solutions of $2x + y \leq 4$.

Step 1: Solve for y. $\qquad 2x + y \leq 4$

$$\underline{-2x \quad -2x}$$

$$y \leq -2x + 4$$

Step 2: Graph the boundary line.

Use a solid line for $\leq$.

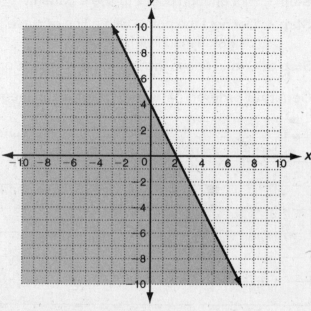

Step 3: Determine which side to shade.

Substitute (0, 0) into $2x + y \leq 4$.

$$2x + y \leq 4$$

$$2(0) + 0 \overset{?}{\leq} 4$$

$$0 \overset{?}{\leq} 4. \text{ The statement is true. Shade the side that contains the point (0, 0).}$$

Graph the solutions of each linear inequality.

4. $y - x < 3$

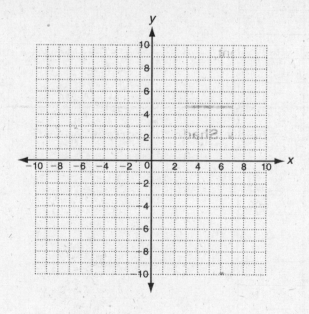

5. $x + y + 2 \geq 0$

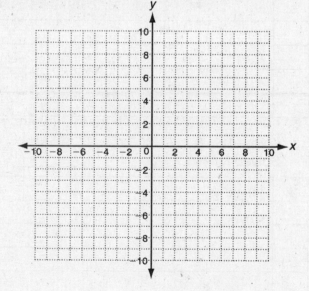

Holt McDougal Algebra 1

LESSON 5-5

Challenge

Graphing Non-Linear Inequalities

To graph non-linear inequalities, follow the steps below.

Step 1: Solve the inequality for *y*.

Step 2: Write the related equation and generate ordered pairs.

Step 3: Plot enough points to see a pattern.

Step 4: Connect the points with a line or curve. Use a solid line for ≤ or ≥.
Use a dashed line for < or >.

Step 5: Shade above the line or curve for *y* > or *y* ≥. Shade below for *y* < or *y* ≤.

Generate ordered pairs and graph each inequality.

1. $y > (x + 3)^2 - 4$

x	Think: $y = (x + 3)^2 - 4$	(x, y)

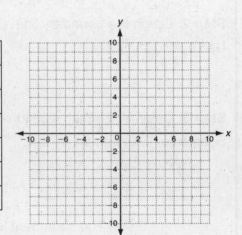

2. $|x| + y \le 5$
   Solved for *y*: _____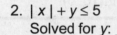

x	Think: y =	(x, y)

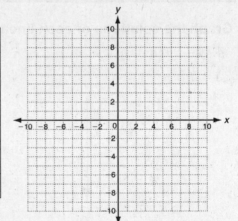

3. $2x^2 - 4y > 8$
   Solved for *y*: _____

x	Think: y =	(x, y)

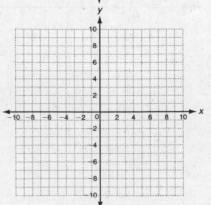

Holt McDougal Algebra 1

LESSON 5-5

Problem Solving

Solving Linear Inequalities

Write the correct answer.

1. Shania would like to give $5 gift cards and $4 teddy bears as party favors. Sixteen people have been invited to the party. Shania has $100 to spend on party favors. Write and graph an inequality to find the number of gift cards x and teddy bears y Shania could purchase.

2. Hank has 20 yards of lumber that he can use to build a raised garden. Write and graph a linear inequality that describes the possible lengths and widths of the garden. If Hank wants the dimensions to be whole numbers only, what dimensions would produce the largest area?

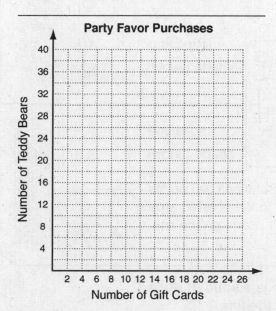

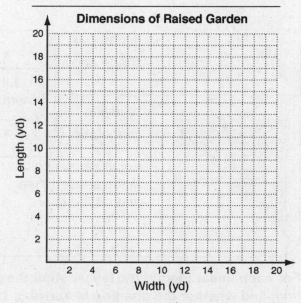

Select the best answer.

3. The royalties for the high school play are $250. Tickets to the play cost $5 for students and $8 for nonstudents. What linear inequality describes the number of student and nonstudent tickets that need to be sold so that the drama class can pay the royalties?

   A $5x + 8y \geq 250$ C $5xy + 8 < 250$

   B $5x + 8y > 250$ D $5xy + 8 \geq 250$

4. The inequality $x + y \leq 8$ describes the amounts of two juices Annette combines to make a smoothie. Which is a solution to the inequality?

   F (3, 6)   H (7, 2)

   G (6, 1)   J (0, 10)

5. A baker is making chocolate and lemon pound cakes. He can make at most 12 cakes at one time. Which inequality describes the situation?

   A $x + y > 12$ C $x + y \leq 12$

   B $x + y \geq 12$ D $x + y < 12$

6. Erasmus is the master gardener for a university. He wants to plant a mixture of purple and yellow pansies at the west entrance to the campus. From past experience, Erasmus knows that fewer than 350 pansies will fit in the planting area. Which inequality describes the situation?

   F $x + y \geq 350$ H $x + y \leq 350$

   G $x + y > 350$ J $x + y < 350$

Holt McDougal Algebra 1

LESSON 5-5

Reading Strategies
Use Graphic Aids

There are infinitely many solutions for linear inequalities. That's why the solutions are shown as a graph on a coordinate plane. There are four possible ways to draw the line and shade the correct half plane. These correspond to the four inequality symbols >, ≥, <, ≤. Use the graphic aid below as a guide.

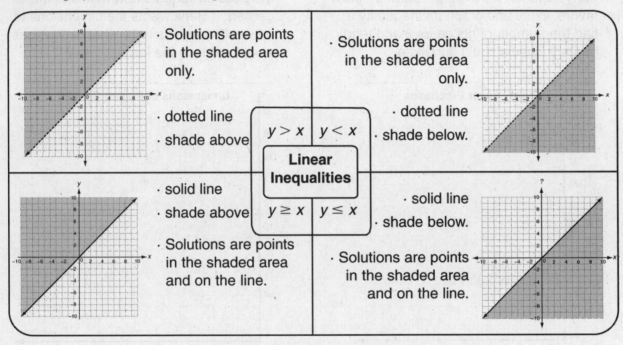

· Solutions are points in the shaded area only.

· dotted line
· shade above

· Solutions are points in the shaded area only.

· dotted line
· shade below.

$y > x$ | $y < x$

Linear Inequalities

$y \geq x$ | $y \leq x$

· solid line
· shade above

· Solutions are points in the shaded area and on the line.

· solid line
· shade below.

· Solutions are points in the shaded area and on the line.

For each linear inequality, tell whether the graph is a solid or dotted line, and whether the shading is above or below the line.

1. $y \leq x + 7$

2. $y > -5x$

3. $y \geq 3x - 2$

_____ _____ _____

_____ _____ _____

Graph each linear inequality. Name one point that is a solution, and one point that is not a solution.

4. $y \geq -\dfrac{1}{2}x + 3$

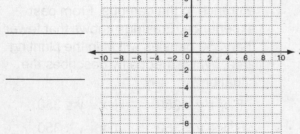

_____

_____

5. $y < x + 5$

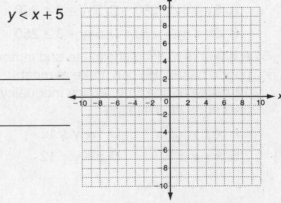

Holt McDougal Algebra 1

**LESSON
5-6**

Practice A

Solving Systems of Linear Inequalities

Tell whether the ordered pair is a solution of the given system.

1. $(4, 5);$ $\begin{cases} y \leq x + 2 \\ y \geq x - 1 \end{cases}$

2. $(1, 3);$ $\begin{cases} y > 3x \\ y < x + 2 \end{cases}$

3. $(2, 3);$ $\begin{cases} y < 5x - 3 \\ y \geq -x \end{cases}$

_____   _____   _____

Graph the system of linear inequalities. a. Give two ordered pairs that are solutions. b. Give two ordered pairs that are not solutions.

4. $\begin{cases} y \geq x + 1 \\ y \leq -2x \end{cases}$

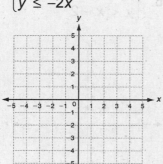

5. $\begin{cases} y < 2x + 4 \\ y > x - 1 \end{cases}$

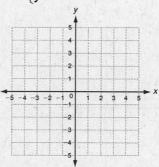

6. $\begin{cases} y > -x \\ y > -x + 3 \end{cases}$

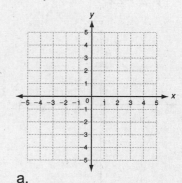

a. _____   a. _____   a. _____

b. _____   b. _____   b. _____

7. Lou is buying macaroni salad and potato salad for a picnic. Macaroni salad costs $4 per pound and potato salad costs $2 per pound. Lou would like to buy at least 6 pounds of salads and wants to spend no more than $20.

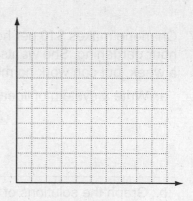

   a. Write a system of linear inequalities.
      Let x = pounds of macaroni salad
      Let y = pounds of potato salad

_____

   b. Graph the solutions of the system.

   c. Describe all the possible combinations of pounds of salads that Lou could buy.

_____

_____

   d. List two possible combinations. _____

                                  _____

Holt McDougal Algebra 1

LESSON 5-6

Practice B

Solving Systems of Linear Inequalities

Tell whether the ordered pair is a solution of the given system.

1. $(2, -2); \begin{cases} y < x - 3 \\ y > -x + 1 \end{cases}$

2. $(2, 5); \begin{cases} y > 2x \\ y \geq x + 2 \end{cases}$

3. $(1, 3); \begin{cases} y \leq x + 2 \\ y > 4x - 1 \end{cases}$

_____ _____ _____

Graph the system of linear inequalities. a. Give two ordered pairs that are solutions. b. Give two ordered pairs that are not solutions.

4. $\begin{cases} y \leq x + 4 \\ y \geq -2x \end{cases}$

5. $\begin{cases} y \leq \dfrac{1}{2}x + 1 \\ x + y < 3 \end{cases}$

6. $\begin{cases} y > x - 4 \\ y < x + 2 \end{cases}$

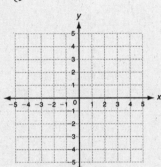 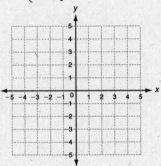 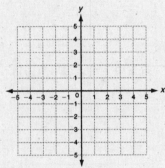

a. _____ a. _____ a. _____

b. _____ b. _____ b. _____

7. Charlene makes $10 per hour babysitting and $5 per hour gardening. She wants to make at least $80 a week, but can work no more than 12 hours a week.

   a. Write a system of linear equations.

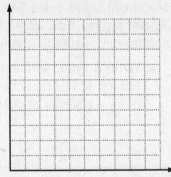

_____

   b. Graph the solutions of the system.

   c. Describe all the possible combinations of hours that Charlene could work at each job.

_____

_____

   d. List two possible combinations. _____

_____

Holt McDougal Algebra 1

LESSON 5-6

Practice C

Solving Systems of Linear Inequalities

Tell whether the ordered pair is a solution of the given system.

1. $(-2, 3); \begin{cases} y \le x + 5 \\ y > -2x - 1 \end{cases}$

   _____

2. $(-3, 3); \begin{cases} y < -x + 1 \\ y > x - 4 \end{cases}$

   _____

3. $(-1, -2); \begin{cases} y > x - 3 \\ y < 3x \end{cases}$

   _____

Graph the system of linear inequalities. a. Give two ordered pairs that are solutions. b. Give two ordered pairs that are not solutions.

4. $\begin{cases} y \le 3x + 2 \\ y \ge -x \end{cases}$

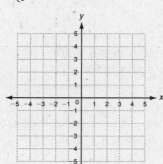

5. $\begin{cases} y > \dfrac{1}{3}x - 2 \\ x + y > -3 \end{cases}$

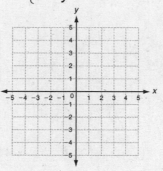

6. $\begin{cases} 3x - 2y < 8 \\ y - 1 \le \dfrac{3}{2}x \end{cases}$

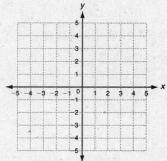

a. _____

a. _____

a. _____

b. _____

b. _____

b. _____

7. Dennis works at a frozen yogurt store in the summer. He needs to order boxes of small cups and boxes of large cups. The storage room can hold up to 10 more boxes of cups. Each box of small cups costs $100 and each box of large cups costs $150. A maximum of $1200 is budgeted for cups.

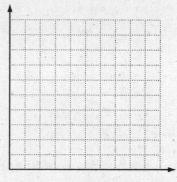

a. Write a system of linear equations.

_____

b. Graph the solutions of the system.

c. Describe all the possible combinations of boxes of cups that Dennis can order.

_____

_____

d. List two possible combinations. _____

_____

Holt McDougal Algebra 1

Review for Mastery

Solving Systems of Linear Inequalities

You can graph a system of linear inequalities by combining the graphs of the inequalities

Graph of $y \le 2x + 3$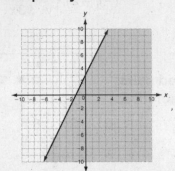

Graph of $y > -x - 6$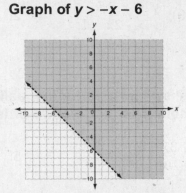

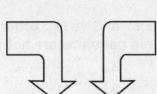

Graph of the system

$$\begin{cases} y \le 2x + 3 \\ y > -x - 6 \end{cases}$$

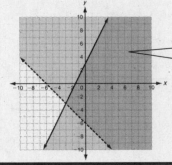

All solutions are in this double shaded area.

Two ordered pairs that are solutions: (3, 4) and (5, −2)

For each system below, give two ordered pairs that are solutions and two that are not solutions.

1.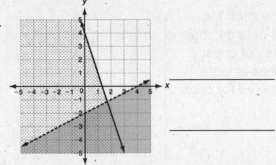

2.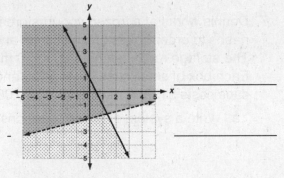

Graph each system of linear inequalities

3. $\begin{cases} y > x - 3 \\ y \ge -x + 6 \end{cases}$

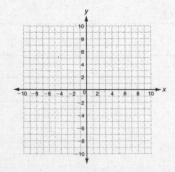

4. $\begin{cases} y < x \\ y > -2x + 1 \end{cases}$

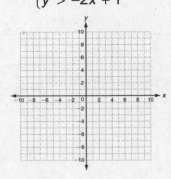

Holt McDougal Algebra 1

LESSON 5-6

Review for Mastery

Solving Systems of Linear Inequalities *continued*

A system of equations with parallel lines has no solutions.
Parallel lines in a system of inequalities might have solutions.

Graph $\begin{cases} y < x + 4 \\ y > x - 2 \end{cases}$.

Graph $\begin{cases} y \geq 2x + 4 \\ y > 2x - 1 \end{cases}$.

Graph $\begin{cases} y > -3x + 5 \\ y < -3x - 3 \end{cases}$.

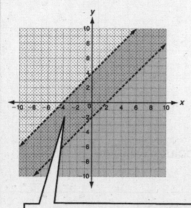

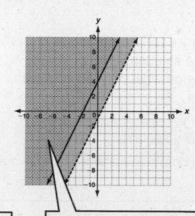

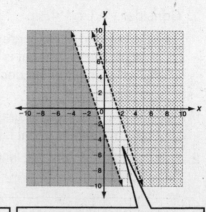

Solutions are in the double shaded area between the parallel lines.

Solutions are in the double shaded area to one side of the line.

There are no overlapping areas. There are no solutions.

Graph the solutions of each linear inequality.

5. $\begin{cases} y \leq x - 3 \\ y > x + 3 \end{cases}$

6. $\begin{cases} y > 2x - 2 \\ y \leq 2x + 3 \end{cases}$

7. $\begin{cases} y > -x - 1 \\ y > -x - 5 \end{cases}$

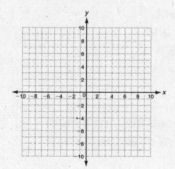

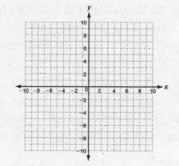

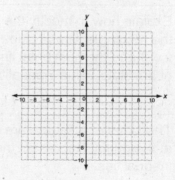

Holt McDougal Algebra 1

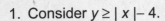

LESSON
5-6

Challenge

Solving Systems of Linear Inequalities

Recall that $|x|$ has two parts in its definition. If $x \geq 0$, then $|x| = x$. If $x < 0$, then $|x| = -x$. This definition is useful when dealing with systems of inequalities that involve absolute value.

In Exercises 1 and 2, consider $\begin{cases} y \geq |x| - 4 \\ y \leq -|x| + 4 \end{cases}$.

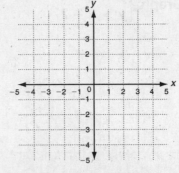

1. Consider $y \geq |x| - 4$.

   a. On the grid at right, graph $y = |x| - 4$. Shade the part of the plane that is the solution to $y \geq |x| - 4$. (Test points to help decide on what part of the plane to shade.)

   b. On the grid at right, graph $y = -|x| + 4$. Shade that part of the plane that is the solution to $y \geq -|x| + 4$.

2. Describe the region that is the common solution to the two absolute-value inequalities.

_____

You can reverse the process and represent a specified region by using a system of inequalities.

3. On the grid at right, graph the vertical lines $x = 3$ and $x = -3$. Also graph the horizontal lines $y = 5$ and $y = -5$.

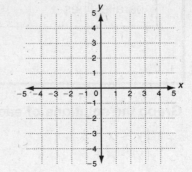

   a. Write a pair of absolute-value inequalities whose graphs are the interior of the rectangle formed.

_____

   b. Write a pair of absolute-value inequalities whose graphs are the exterior of the rectangle formed.

_____

4. Explain how to modify the solution to Exercise 3 in order to represent the rectangle whose sides are bounded by the vertical lines $x = -1$ and $x = 3$ and the horizontal lines $y = -2$ and $y = 8$. Then write the system of absolute-value inequalities.

_____

5. The sides of a square are horizontal and vertical line segments whose diagonals meet at the origin. Represent the square and its interior by using a system of absolute-value inequalities.

_____

LESSON 5-6

Problem Solving

Solving Systems of Linear Inequalities

Write the correct answer.

1. Paul earns $7 per hour at the bagel shop and $12 per hour mowing lawns. Paul needs to earn at least $120 per week, but he must work less than 30 hours per week. Write and graph the system of linear inequalities that describes this situation.

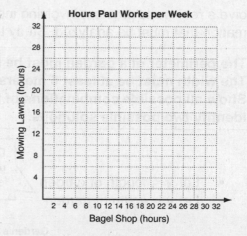

Hours Paul Works per Week

2. Zoe plans to knit a scarf. She wants the scarf to be more than 1 but less than 1.5 feet wide, and more than 6 but less than 8 feet long. Graph all possible dimensions of Zoe's scarf. List two possible combinations.

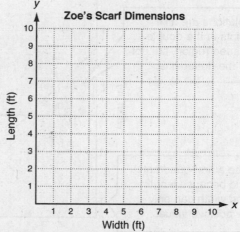

Zoe's Scarf Dimensions

The graph shows the numbers of two types of custom wood tables that can be made to fit a client's needs. Select the best answer.

3. Which system of linear inequalities represents the graph?

A $\begin{cases} x + y \le 15 \\ y \ge 12 - \dfrac{4}{3}x \end{cases}$　　C $\begin{cases} x + y \ge 15 \\ y \ge \dfrac{4}{3}x - 12 \end{cases}$

B $\begin{cases} y \le x + 15 \\ y \ge 12 - \dfrac{4}{3}x \end{cases}$　　D $\begin{cases} y \le 15 - x \\ y \le \dfrac{4}{3}x - 12 \end{cases}$

4. If 6 buffet tables are built, which can NOT be the number of dining tables built?

　F 4　　　　H 8

　G 6　　　　J 10

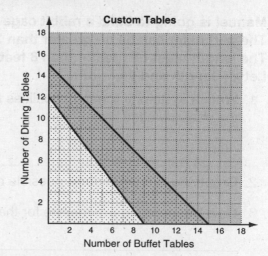

Custom Tables

Name _____ Date _____ Class _____

Reading Strategies
Analyze Information

To solve a real-world problem involving inequalities, there is a lot of information that must be analyzed. Study the example below.

> **The perimeter of a garden must be less than 20 meters.**
> **The width must be at least 6 meters.**
> **Show all possible combinations of the garden's length and width.**
> **Identify two possible solutions.**

- Let x = length of garden
- Let y = width of garden

Define variables for the unknowns: "the garden's length and width."

The perimeter must be less than 20 meters: $P = 2l + 2w$; and "less than" means $<$.

$$\begin{cases} 2x + 2y < 20 \\ y \ge 6 \end{cases}$$

Garden's Dimension

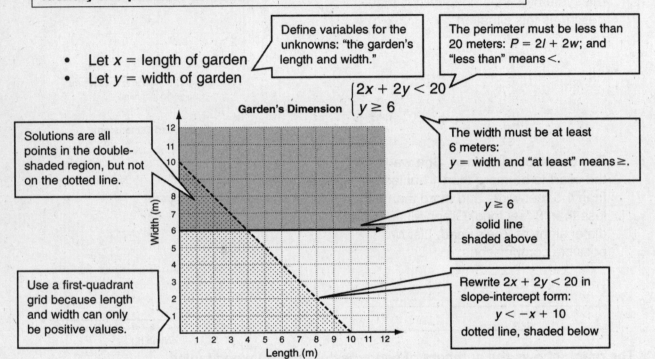

Solutions are all points in the double-shaded region, but not on the dotted line.

The width must be at least 6 meters: y = width and "at least" means $\ge$.

$y \ge 6$
solid line
shaded above

Use a first-quadrant grid because length and width can only be positive values.

Rewrite $2x + 2y < 20$ in slope-intercept form:
$y < -x + 10$
dotted line, shaded below

Possible solutions: $l = 2$ m, $w = 7$ m and $l = 1$ m, $w = 8$ m

Manuel is going to build a rabbit cage with a rectangular base.
The perimeter can be no greater than 30 feet.
The length must be greater than 8 feet.
Let x = length and y = width.

1. Write a system of linear inequalities to describe the possible cage sizes.

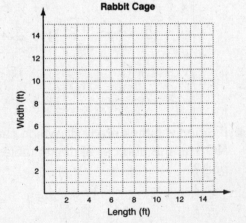

Rabbit Cage

_____

2. Graph the system to show possible dimensions.

3. Give two possible dimensions for the cage.

_____

_____

Holt McDougal Algebra 1

Answer Key For Equations

1-1 VARIABLES AND EXPRESSIONS

Practice A

1. the sum of a and 3
2. 2 times x
3. y less than 5
4. the quotient of n and 4
5. 10 increased by t
6. the product of 3 and s
7. $c + 2$
8. $5m$
9. 8
10. 4
11. 12
12. 3
13. 16
14. 8
15. a. $j - 4$
    b. 11 years old; 16 years old; 54 years old

Practice B

1. the difference of 15 and b; b less than 15
2. the quotient of x and 16; x divided by 16
3. the sum of x and 9; 9 more than x
4. the product of 2 and t; 2 times t
5. the difference of z and 7; 7 less than z
6. the product of 4 and y; 4 times y
7. $g - 6$
8. $10m$
9. 10
10. 4
11. 7
12. 3
13. 16
14. 3
15. a. $d + 20$
    b. 40 dollars; 80 dollars; 95 dollars

Practice C

1. the sum of k and 2.5; 2.5 more than k
2. the product of -5 and n; -5 times n
3. the quotient of b and 25; b divided by 25
4. the difference of 100 and x; x less than 100
5. $35g$
6. $150 \div p$
7. 14
8. 56
9. $\dfrac{1}{7}$

10. a. $25 - 2g$
    b. 23 tokens; 17 tokens; 5 tokens; 1 token
11. $n - 8$, Possible answer: Tammy is 8 years younger than Nate, who is n years old
12. $4x$, Possible answer: Bo had 4 times as many votes as Scott, who had x votes

Review for Mastery

1. $35m$
2. $h - 0.5$
3. $c \div 25$
4. $152 + b$
5. $r - 50$
6. 8
7. 10
8. 29
9. 19
10. 18
11. 12
12. 18
13. 16
14. 2
15. 9
16. 36
17. 7

Challenge

1. $70 + 0.35(m)$

Expression for Plan A	Cost of Plan A
$40 + 0.45(200)$	$130
$40 + 0.45(300)$	$175
$40 + 0.45(400)$	$220
$40 + 0.45(500)$	$265

Expression for Plan B	Cost of Plan B
$70 + 0.35(100)$	$105
$70 + 0.35(200)$	$140
$70 + 0.35(300)$	$175
$70 + 0.35(400)$	$210
$70 + 0.35(500)$	$245

2. Plan A
3. Plan B

4. Possible answer: It depends on the number of minutes used. Plan A is cheaper if you use less than 300 minutes each month. Plan B is cheaper if you use more than 300 minutes each month. If you use exactly 300 minutes each month, the plans cost the same.

Problem Solving

1. $45d$
2. $5.15 - w$
3. $216 + t$
4. $\dfrac{550}{p}$; $22, $11, $10
5. C
6. F
7. B

Reading Strategies

1. Possible answers: $10y$, $10 \cdot y$, and $10(y)$
2. Possible answers: k divided by 6, the quotient of k and 6
3. $b - 4$
4. $4 - b$
5. $20m$
6. $58 + t$

1-2 SOLVING EQUATIONS BY ADDING OR SUBTRACTING

Practice A

1. $m = 7$
2. $t = 23$
3. $p = 4$
4. $a = 8$
5. $c = 5$
6. $y = \dfrac{3}{5}$
7. $b = 0$
8. $w = 9$
9. $p = 4$
10. $x = 4$
11. $x = -2$
12. $r = 14.4$
13. $x + 18 = 86$; 68; The score on the second test was higher than the first, so the score on the first test should be less than 86.
14. $x - 4 = 29$; 33°F; The actual temperature was lower than predicted, so the predicted temperature should be greater than 29°F.
15. $x + 72 = 122$; $50; The amount of money raised in one week should be less than the two-week total of $122.

Practice B

1. $g = 22$
2. $t = 2$
3. $m = 20$
4. $x = 5.7$
5. $n = \dfrac{1}{2}$
6. $p = 1$
7. $k = 38$
8. $w = -2.3$
9. $r = -4$
10. $y = 17$
11. $b = -2$
12. $a = 0$
13. $x + 0.75 = 12.25$; $11.50; Marietta received a raise, so her previous wage should be less than $12.25.
14. $x + 4\dfrac{1}{4} = 56\dfrac{7}{8}$; $52\dfrac{5}{8}$ in.; Brad's height increased, so his previous height should be less than $56\dfrac{7}{8}$ inches.
15. $x - 2.6 = 58.4$; 61 s; Heather's race time was less than her practice time, so her practice time should be greater than 58.4 s.
16. $x + 2981.1 = 6378.1$; 3397 km; Earth is larger than Mars, so the radius of Mars should be less than 6378.1 km.

Practice C

1. $d = 21$
2. $f = -1.3$
3. $n = 1$
4. $x = 13$
5. $h = -\dfrac{1}{2}$
6. $y = -17$
7. $x + 12 = 27$; $x = 15$
8. $x - 7 = 3$; $x = 10$
9. $x - 6 = -2$; $x = 4$
10. $x + 4.7 = 8.1$; $x = 3.4$
11. $x + 2\dfrac{5}{8} = 7\dfrac{1}{4}$; $4\dfrac{5}{8}$ in.; The plant grew, so the previous height should be less than $7\dfrac{1}{4}$ inches.
12. $x - 36.8 = 475.2$; 512 MB; The new software used some of the available memory, so the amount of memory before the new software should be more than 475.2 MB.
13. $x - 0.43 = 28.3$; 28.73 s; The time was faster in 2004 than 2002, so the 2002 time should be slower than 28.3 s.

Holt McDougal Algebra 1

Review for Mastery

1.
$$x + \bigcirc = \bigcirc\bigcirc\bigcirc$$

4

2.
$$\bigcirc\bigcirc\bigcirc\bigcirc = x + \bigcirc\bigcirc$$

5

3. 8   4. 19

5. 5   6. $x + -7 = 12$; 7

7. $x + 1 = -5$; -1 8. $-4 = x + -2$; 2

9. -16 10. -6

11. -7

Challenge

1. a. Let x represent the distance traveled.
   $37,538 + x = 37,781$

   b. 243 miles

2. $s + d = e$

3. a. $e - d$
   b. $e - s$
   c. $s + d$

4. a. $d = 1697$
   b. $s = 17,152$
   c. $e = 63,777$
   d. $d = 1111$

5. $7\frac{2}{3}$ feet

6. $f = o + d$, $o = f - d$, and $d = f - o$

7. $9\frac{5}{12}$ feet

Problem Solving

1. $m - 120 = 3345$; \$3465

2. $w - 23 = 184$; 207 lbs

3. $365 + d = 687$; 322 days

4. $p + 19.9 = 53.4$; 33.5%

5. A   6. G

7. B

Reading Strategies

1. addition

2. Add 5 to the left side.

3. Add 4 to both sides.

4. $m = 13$ 5. $g = 5$

6. $k = -3$ 7. $t = -15$

8. $y = 2$ 9. $h = 11$

1-3 SOLVING EQUATIONS BY MULTIPLYING OR DIVIDING

Practice A

1. $d = 18$ 2. $n = -21$

3. $t = -15$ 4. $r = 20$

5. $b = 17.5$ 6. $v = 36$

7. $y = -5$ 8. $p = 10$

9. $m = 1$ 10. $x = 2$

11. $y = -\frac{1}{7}$ 12. $k = 12$

13. $\frac{x}{4} = 63$; 252 students

14. $5x = 1.15$; \$0.23   15. $4x = 64$; 16 mm

Practice B

1. $d = 48$ 2. $n = -10$

3. $p = 27$ 4. $t = -24$

5. $x = 10$ 6. $r = 24$

7. $y = -7$ 8. $n = 25$

9. $m = \frac{2}{3}$ 10. $v = 18$

11. $b = 11.2$ 12. $r = \frac{1}{6}$

13. $5x = 41.5$; 8.3 cm

14. $0.23x = 2.07$; 9 oz   15. $\frac{1}{3}x = 8$; \$24

Practice C

1. $e = 75$ 2. $g = 56$

3. $d = 7$ 4. $n = -9$

5. $t = 13$ 6. $r = 40$

7. $y = -9$ 8. $f = \frac{6}{7}$

9. $m = -\dfrac{2}{3}$

10. $9x = -72$; $x = -8$

11. $\dfrac{x}{-3} = -2.8$; $x = 8.4$

12. $\dfrac{2}{3}x = 14$; $x = 21$

13. $8x = 55.2$; 6.9 mm

14. $0.23x = 2.76$; 12 oz

15. $\dfrac{x}{6} = 34{,}250$; 205,500 points

Review for Mastery

1. (divided); (multiply); −14

2. (multiplied); (divide); −8

3. 10

4. −35

5. −7

6. $\dfrac{5}{2}$

7. $-\dfrac{7}{5}$

8. $\dfrac{1}{7}$

9. 12

10. −10

11. $-\dfrac{9}{10}$

Challenge

1. $x = 3$

2. $x = -5$

3. $x = 3$

4. $t = \dfrac{6}{5}$

5. $w = \dfrac{1}{2}$

6. $d = 30$

7. $ax = b$; $\dfrac{1}{a} \cdot ax = \dfrac{1}{a} \cdot b$; $1 \cdot x = \dfrac{1}{a} \cdot b$;

$x = \dfrac{b}{a}$

8. $\dfrac{ax}{a} = \dfrac{b}{a}$; $1x = \dfrac{b}{a}$; $x = \dfrac{b}{a}$

9. Using the Multiplication Property of Equality, multiply each side of the equation by the reciprocal of the coefficient of the x-term. Using the Division Property of Equality, divide each side of the equation by the coefficient of the x-term. By either method, the solution is the same.

Problem Solving

1. $32c = 480$; $15

2. $4x = 10$; 2.5 grams

3. $10.50h = 147$; 14 hours

4. $\dfrac{1}{5}w = 61.50$; $307.50

5. A

6. J

7. B

Reading Strategies

1. less

2. greater

3. greater

4. $b = 4$

5. $c = 18$

6. $k = 20$

1-4 SOLVING TWO-STEP AND MULTI-STEP EQUATIONS

Practice A

1. 2; 10; 2

2. 3; 8; 4

3. 21; 9; 3

4. $t = -2$

5. $x = 5.4$

6. $r = -23$

7. $y = 3$

8. $b = 24$

9. $m = \dfrac{1}{8}$

10. $x = 6$

11. $y = -3$

12. $d = -1$

13. −8

14. $7x + 6 + 5x = 90$

15. $x = 7$

Practice B

1. $x = -1$

2. $y = 4$

3. $p = -7$

4. $m = -1$

5. $g = 8$

6. $h = 6$

7. $y = -50$

8. $n = \dfrac{1}{3}$

9. $t = -\dfrac{1}{3}$

10. $x = 3$

11. $b = -2$

12. $q = 3$

13. −4

14. −5

15. $3x - 5 + 2x = 90$; 19

16. 20 minutes

Holt McDougal Algebra 1

Practice C

1. $r = 3$
2. $w = -14$
3. $y = -4$
4. $f = 5$
5. $p = 10$
6. $r = 7$
7. $y = 27$
8. $h = \dfrac{7}{8}$
9. $m = 3$
10. $v = -\dfrac{1}{2}$
11. $b = -7$
12. $n = -\dfrac{5}{8}$
13. -10
14. -12
15. 30
16. $0.75x - 18.50 = 24.25$, 57 cookies

Review for Mastery

1. 4
2. 60
3. $\dfrac{5}{3}$
4. 5
5. $\dfrac{5}{4}$
6. -1
7. $\dfrac{25}{2}$

Challenge

1. 4 inches
2. 8 inches
3. 1 inch
4. 9 inches
5. 15 inches
6. 7 inches
7. 3 inches
8. 7 inches
9. 6 inches
10. 11 inches
11. 15 inches
12. 4 inches
13. 5 sides
14. 12 sides
15. 7 sides
16. 18 sides

Problem Solving

1. $39.95 + 0.99d = 55.79$; 16 DVDs
2. $12.6 = 4p + 1$; 2.9 million
3. 9 years old
4. 10 weeks
5. D
6. F
7. B

Reading Strategies

1. like terms
2. subtraction
3. Subtract 3 from both sides, then multiply by 5.
4. $n = 5$
5. $d = 7$
6. $j = -2$

1-5 SOLVING EQUATIONS WITH VARIABLES ON BOTH SIDES

Practice A

1. $2a$; 3; 10; 5
2. $4r$; 9; -4
3. $-5b$; 30; $5b$; $3b$; 10
4. $c = -19$
5. all real numbers
6. no solution
7. a. 3 hours
   b. 75° F
8. a. 2 hours
   b. $12

Practice B

1. $d = -25$
2. $n = 1$
3. $p = 4$
4. $t = 12$
5. $x = \dfrac{1}{2}$
6. $r = -2$
7. $y = -18$
8. all real numbers
9. $m = -3$
10. no solution
11. $b = \dfrac{3}{2}$
12. $r = -3$
13. a. 8 years
    b. $52,000
14. a. 6 months
    b. 128 stamps

Practice C

1. $x = 2$
2. $a = 3$
3. $c = -1$
4. $y = -3$
5. $d = -\dfrac{11}{2}$
6. $t = -2$
7. $m = 9$
8. all real numbers
9. no solution
10. all real numbers
11. 6 shirts, $61
12. 5 weeks, $85

Review for Mastery

1. Possible answers: add $-3x$ to each side, add $-7x$ to each side
2. Possible answers: add $4x$ to each side, add $10x$ to each side

Holt McDougal Algebra 1

3. Possible answers: add $3x$ to each side, add $-15x$ to each side

4. -48
5. 2

6. 5
7. no solution

8. 1
9. all real numbers

10. no solution
11. all real numbers

12. -1

Challenge

1. $x = -\dfrac{7}{3}$
2. $x = -4$

3. $x = 7\dfrac{1}{2}$
4. $x = -2$

5. $2x + (-6) = 0$ or $-2x + 6 = 0$

6. $9x + 18 = 0$ or $-9x + (-18) = 0$

7. $5x + 27 = 0$ or $-5x + (-27) = 0$

8. $3x + (-21) = 0$ or $-3x + 21 = 0$

9. a. $x = -\dfrac{b}{a}$

   b. After writing the equation in the form $ax + b = 0$, substitute the values of a and b into the formula found in part a.

10. $x = 3$
11. $x = -2$

12. $x = -5\dfrac{2}{5}$
13. $x = 7$

14. a. infinitely many solutions

    b. no solution

Problem Solving

1. 28 feet
2. 7 days

3. 16 hours
4. 20 months

5. B
6. G

7. C

Reading Strategies

1. Look for an opportunity to use the Distributive Property.

2. Combine any like terms.

3. Collect the variable terms on one side of the equal sign.

4. $p = -6$
5. $x = 1$

6. $t = -2$

1-6 SOLVING FOR A VARIABLE

Practice A

1. $C = K - 273$
2. $f = \dfrac{1}{T}$

3. $y = \dfrac{x}{5}$
4. $s = r - 4t$

5. $m = \dfrac{p + 7n}{3}$
6. $j = \dfrac{6 - k}{h}$

7. $w = \dfrac{v}{9}$
8. $a = bc - 3$

9. a. $t = \dfrac{d}{r}$
10. a. $F = 2 + E - V$

   b. 3
   b. 12

Practice B

1. $r = \dfrac{C}{2\pi}$
2. $m = \dfrac{y - b}{x}$

3. $c = \dfrac{d}{4}$
4. $n = 8 + 6m$

5. $p = \dfrac{q - 5r}{2}$
6. $x = \dfrac{-10 - z}{y}$

7. $b = \dfrac{a}{c}$
8. $j = \dfrac{h - 4}{k}$

9. a. $p = \dfrac{c - 215}{5}$
10. a. $b = \dfrac{2A}{h}$

   b. 17
   b. 32 mm

Practice C

1. $w = \dfrac{P - 2l}{2}$
2. $v_f = at + v_i$

3. $f = \dfrac{g}{-3}$
4. $a = 12 - 5b$

5. $x = \dfrac{z + 7y}{3}$
6. $h = \dfrac{jk + g}{5}$

7. $r = s(t - 9)$
8. $n = \dfrac{m + 3}{p}$

9. a. $a = \dfrac{F}{m}$
10. a. $t = \dfrac{I}{Pr}$

   b. 19 m/s^2
   b. 8 years

Holt McDougal Algebra 1

Review for Mastery

1. $s = \dfrac{P}{4}$ 2. $b = 180 - a - c$

3. $K = \dfrac{VP}{T}$ 4. $w = \dfrac{3V}{lh}$

5. 12 in.

6. add $-x$ to both sides

7. multiply both sides by 2

8. add $3r$ to both sides

9. $a = \dfrac{c}{3b}$ 10. $z = 3(y - x)$

11. $m = pn - 3$

Challenge

1. $l = 375$ 2. $P = 2000$

3. $t = 5$ years

4. $r = 0.032$ or 3.2%

5. $351   6. 3 years

7. $2200   8. 0.03 or 3%

9. $247   10. 5 years

11. 0.027 or 2.7%

Problem Solving

1. $r = \dfrac{d}{t}$ 2. 9.1 m/s

3. 8.5 m/s   4. 0.4 m/s

5. B   6. F

7. D   8. J

Reading Strategies

1. Possible answer: $3x + 2y = 9$

2. The equation contains only one variable, n.

3. Yes, because it has two or more variables.

4. Divide both sides by r.

5. $t = \dfrac{b - 8}{3}$

6. a. $h = \dfrac{V}{lw}$

    b. 3 cm

1-7 SOLVING ABSOLUTE-VALUE EQUATIONS

Practice A

1. -3; 2; -2; 2

2. -7; 7; 4; 4; 4; 4; -11; 3

3. 6; -6; 6; -5; 7

4. $\{-8, 8\}$ 5. $\{-14, 14\}$

6. $\{-9, 9\}$ 7. $\{-17, 17\}$

8. $\{-11, 7\}$ 9. $\{-1, 11\}$

10. $\{-5, 5\}$ 11. $\{-7, 3\}$

12. $\{-11, 9\}$

13. $|x - 24| = 2$

14. 22 miles per gallon; 26 miles per gallon

Practice B

1. $\{-12, 12\}$

2. $\left\{-\dfrac{1}{2}, \dfrac{1}{2}\right\}$

3. $\{-10, 10\}$

4. $\{-9, 9\}$

5. $\{-8, 8\}$

6. $\{-13, 7\}$

7. $\{-1, 3\}$

8. $\{2, 8\}$

9. $\{-14, 10\}$

10. $\{-3, 3\}$

11. $\{1\}$

12. $\{3\}$

13. two   14. one

15. none   16. $|x - 68| = 3.5$

14. 64.5°; 71.5°

Practice C

1. $\left\{-\dfrac{3}{5}, \dfrac{3}{5}\right\}$ 2. $\{0\}$

3. $\{-10.5, 10.5\}$ 4. $\varnothing$

5. $\{-7, 7\}$ 6. $\{-11\}$

7. $\left\{-\dfrac{3}{2}, \dfrac{5}{2}\right\}$ 8. $\varnothing$

Holt McDougal Algebra 1

9. $\{-6.6, 8.6\}$ 10. $\{-8, 3\}$
11. $\varnothing$ 12. $\varnothing$
13. $|x - 3| = 0.005$; 2.995 m; 3.005 m
14. $|x + 5| = 1.5$; $-6.5°C$; $-3.5°C$

Review for Mastery

1. $\{-6, 10\}$ 2. $\{-15, 1\}$
3. $\{0, 10\}$ 4. $\{-3, 3\}$
5. $\{2\}$ 6. $\varnothing$
7. $\varnothing$ 8. $\{-10\}$

Challenge

1. $|(-3) - 2| = |-5| = 5; |7 - 2| = |5| = 5$

2. yes; possible answer: $|x - 2| + 1 = 6$

3. $|x - 5| = 4$

4. $|x - 2| = 6$

5. $|x - 3| = 8$

6. $|x + 5| = 4$

7. $|x| = \dfrac{1}{3}$

8. $|x - 5.5| = 0.5$

9. $|x - 2.5| = 7$

10. $|x - 1| = \dfrac{3}{2}$

Problem Solving

1. $|x - 70| = 0.02$; 69.98 cm; 70.02 cm

2. $|x - 53| = 0.021$; 52.979 m; 53.021 m

3. -1 and 11   4. 11.9 cm
5. B   6. G
7. C

Reading Strategies

1. one
2. two
3. none
4. one
5. none

6. two

1-8 RATES, RATIOS, AND PROPORTIONS

Practice A

1. 20   2. 58 ft/s
3. $1.05/lb   4. 2.5 pages/min
5. $y = 4$ 6. $x = 18$
7. $m = 2$ 8. $t = 75$
9. $b = -4$ 10. $x = 1$
11. 150 in.   12. 160 mi

Practice B

1. 15   2. $0.49/lb
3. 0.1 cars/min   4. 46.9 ft/s
5. $y = 5$ 6. $x = -0.4$
7. $m = -96$ 8. $t = \dfrac{5}{3}$
9. $b = 20$ 10. $x = 3.5$
11. 185 in.   12. 3.7 cm

Practice C

1. 18   2. 4.8 lb/book
3. $7.90/h   4. 293.3 ft/s
5. $x = -1.5$ 6. $b = -0.5$
7. $s = 0.6$ 8. $y = 2$
9. $x = 10$ 10. $y = \dfrac{3}{4}$
11. 125.5 ft   12. 3.2 in.

Review for Mastery

1. $\dfrac{3}{1}$ 2. $\dfrac{1}{100}$

3. $\dfrac{8}{1}$

4. $\dfrac{1000 \text{ m}}{1 \text{ km}}$; $\dfrac{3,391,100}{83.5}$; 40,612

5. 320 c/min   6. $x = 2.5$
7. $k = 3$ 8. $a = 10.75$
9. $y = 30$

Challenge

1. bc: $7 \cdot 15 = 105$; ad: $5 \cdot 21 = 105$

2. a. Multiply each side by $\dfrac{bd}{ac}$

   b. Cross-Product Property;
      Multiplication Property of Equality;
      Identity Property of Multiplication

3.
$$\frac{a}{b} = \frac{c}{d}$$
$$ad = bc$$
$$\left(\frac{1}{ab}\right)ad = \left(\frac{1}{ab}\right)bc$$
$$\frac{d}{b} = \frac{c}{a}$$

   Cross-Product Property;
   Multiplication Property of Equality;
   Identity Property of Multiplication

Problem Solving

1. 2.67 donuts/minute   2. $8800
3. 63,000 babies   4. 0.53 mi/min
5. C   6. G
7. D   8. F

Reading Strategies

1. $\dfrac{16\ oz}{1\ lb}$ or $\dfrac{1\ lb}{16\ oz}$

2. no; the second quality is not 1.
3. The two quantities are equal.
4. ratio; rate; ratio
5. 28 pg/hr
6. Possible answer: $\dfrac{1}{2} = \dfrac{12}{24}$

1-9 APPLICATIONS OF PROPORTIONS

Practice A

1. 4   2. 28
3. $\dfrac{5}{x} = \dfrac{4}{12}$; 15 feet
4. width = 4 cm; length = 12 cm
5. $\dfrac{1}{2}$
6. 16 cm; 32 cm;

12 cm^2; 48 cm^2

7. $\dfrac{1}{2}$

8. They are the same.   9. $\dfrac{1}{4}$

10. The ratio of the areas is the square of the ratio in problem 5.

Practice B

1. 15   2. 3.2
3. $\dfrac{5.5}{x} = \dfrac{4}{20}$; 27.5 feet
4. The ratio of the volumes is the cube of the ratio of the corresponding sides.
5. $\dfrac{1}{2}$

Practice C

1. 7.5   2. 6
3. $\dfrac{5.5}{x} = \dfrac{1.375}{11}$; 44 feet
4. 3   5. $\dfrac{1}{4}$

Review for Mastery

1. 15.6 ft
2. 6.125 cm
3. 5; 25; $(5)^3 = 125$
4. $\dfrac{2}{3}$; $\left(\dfrac{2}{3}\right)^2 = \dfrac{4}{9}$; $\dfrac{8}{27}$
5. $\dfrac{10}{7}$; $\dfrac{10}{7}$; $\dfrac{10}{7}$; $\left(\dfrac{10}{7}\right)^3 = \dfrac{1000}{343}$
6. The ratio of the areas is the square of the ratio of corresponding dimensions:
$$\left(\frac{1}{20}\right)^2 = \frac{1}{400}.$$
7. The ratio of the circumferences is equal to the ratio of corresponding dimensions: 4.

Challenge

1. $\overline{ST}$; $\overline{YZ}$
2. 1 in.; 2 in.; 3.5 in.
3. $\overline{DE}$; $\overline{XY}$ 4. 2 in.; 4 in.

Holt McDougal Algebra 1

5. $\frac{2}{4} = \frac{1}{2} = 0.5$; $\frac{3.5}{7} = \frac{1}{2} = 0.5$

6. $\frac{1}{2}$ or 0.5   7. 0.865

8. a. 0.865

   b. $\frac{1}{2}$ or 0.5

9. The sine of a 30° angle equals the cosine of a 60° angle.
   The sine of a 60° angle equals the cosine of 30° angle.

Problem Solving

1. 1:2; 1:4

2. The ratio of the volumes is the cube of the ratio of the corresponding dimensions; 8:27

3. 720 sq. ft.   4. 4

5. C   6. J

7. B   8. G

Reading Strategies

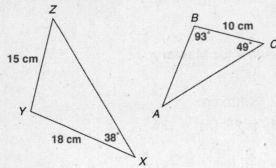

1. △ABC

2. The measure of angle B is 93 degrees.

3. Triangle XYZ is similar to triangle ABC.

5. 49°   6. 38°

7. Possible answer: $\frac{AB}{BC} = \frac{XY}{YZ}$

8. $\frac{X}{10} = \frac{18}{15}$; 12 cm

1-10 PRECISION AND ACCURACY

Practice A

1. 3215 g   2. 48 in.

3. 3.82 cm   4. 81 oz

5. 3002 mL   6. 421 cm

7. 4 qt   8. 2.9 ft

9. 25 oz   10. 19.6 lb–20.4 lb

11. 28.8 cm–31.2 cm

12. 94.8 ft–105.2 ft

13. 57.3 m–62.7 m

14. 75.2°F–84.8°F   15. 17.1 L–18.9 L

16. C, because it is to hundredths

17. C, because 16.05 is closest to 16

Practice B

1. 2782 mL   2. 72.3 in.

3. 15 oz   4. 5.24 cm

5. 47 oz   6. 5233 m

7. 48.00 m–52.00 m

8. 76.50 °F–103.50 °F

9. 14.70 L–15.30 L

10. 15.76 ft–16.24 ft

11. 8.10 in.–9.90 in.   12. 64.02 g–67.98 g

13. test tube   14. beaker

Practice C

1. 5260.0 g   2. neither

3. 420.0 mm   4. 82.1 oz

5. 4102 mL   6. 128 min

7. 65.45 m–74.55 m

8. 57.38° F–67.63° F

9. 21.38 mg–23.63 mg

10. 120 lb ± 4%   11. 300 cm ± 7.5%

12. 210 ft ± 9.1%   13. Baseball #2

Review for Mastery

1. hundredth; tenth; 73.71

2. 4.732; thousandth; hundredth; 4732 mL

3. tenth, thousandth; hundredth; 2

4. 37; 47; 37; 47

5. 3.19; 3.21; 3.19; 3.21

6. 0.05; 1.25; 1.25; 23.75; 1.25; 26.25; 23.75; 26.25

7. 0.02; 0.8; 0.8; 39.2; 0.8; 40.8; 39.2; 40.8

Challenge

1. 0.19°
2. 4.6°
3. 3000 km

Problem Solving

1. 864 in.; Rolondo's foot
2. No; it is too long
3. 1, 2, 3, 4, 5, 6, 9, 10, 11, 13
4. D
5. G
6. C
7. H

Reading Strategies

1. 7.0–9.0
2. 2.4–4.0
3. ±3
4. ±2.5
5. *B*
6. *A*

Answer Key For Inequalities

2-1 GRAPHING AND WRITING INEQUALITIES

Practice A

1. c   2. a

3. b   4. d

5.

6.

7.

8.

9. d   10. b

11. a   12. c

13. h = height; $h > 4$;

14. s = lawful speed; $s \leq 65$;

Practice B

1. all real numbers greater than or equal to 3

2. all real numbers less than 5

3. all real numbers greater than 6

4. all real numbers less than or equal to –20

5.

6.

7.

8.

9. $a > 6$ 10. $b \leq -2$

11. $c < 8.5$ 12. $d \geq 45$

13. s = hours of sleep; $s > 7$;

14. w = wage; $w \geq 0.75$;

Practice C

1. all real numbers greater than or equal to 8

2. all real numbers less than –3

3. all real numbers greater than –9

4. all real numbers less than or equal to 18

5.

6.

7.

8.

9. $a \leq 0.4$ 10. $b > 1\frac{1}{3}$

11. $c \geq 26$ 12. $d < -12$

13. y = years of experience; $y > 3$

14. s = lawful speed; $s \leq 70$

15. w = wage; $w \geq 5.15$

Review for Mastery

1.

$x = 0$	$x = 1$	$x = -3$	$x = -4$	$x = 2$	$x = 3$	$x = 1.5$
$0 \leq 10$	$5 \leq 10$	$-15 \leq 10$	$-20 \leq 10$	$10 \leq 10$	$15 \leq 10$	$7.5 \leq 10$
T	T	T	T	T	F	T

all real numbers less than or equal to 2

2.

$x = 0$	$x = 3$	$x = -4$	$x = -3$	$x = -2$	$x = -2.5$	$x = -5$
$1 < -2$	$4 < -2$	$-3 < -2$	$-2 < -2$	$-1 < -2$	$-1.5 < -2$	$-4 < -2$
F	F	T	F	F	F	T

all real numbers less than –3

3. all real numbers greater than 12

4. all real numbers less than or equal to 1

Holt McDougal Algebra 1

5.

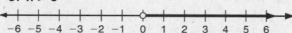

6.

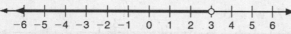

7. $x \ge -2$

8. $x < -4$

Challenge

1. $(4, \infty)$

2. $x \le -2$

3. $(-\infty, 3)$

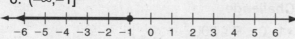

4. $x \ge -5$; $[-5, \infty)$

5. $x > 0$

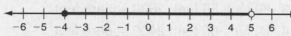

6. $(-\infty, -1]$

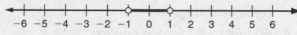

7. $[-3, 2]$

8. $0 < x \le 3$

9. $-4 \le x < 5$

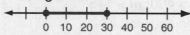

10. $(-1, 1)$

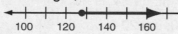

Problem Solving

1. a = age of person; $a \ge 35$

2. w = weight; $w \le 2500$

3. f = percent forested; $f \le 30$ where f is nonnegative

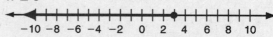

4. w = weight; $w \ge 125$

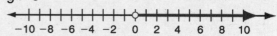

5. C

6. G

7. A

8. G

Reading Strategies

1. x is greater than or equal to 5; x is at least 5; x is no less than 5

2. empty; because the value 8 is not a solution

3.

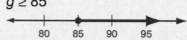

4. $t < 6.5$; t is less than 6.5

5. $g \ge 85$

2-2 SOLVING INEQUALITIES BY ADDING OR SUBTRACTING

Practice A

1. $t > 8$

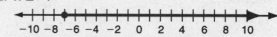

2. $x \ge -7$

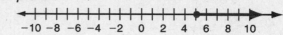

3. $p \ge 5$

4. $m > -9$

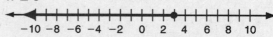

5. $w \le 3$

6. $g > 0$

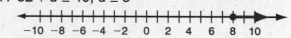

7. $32 + d \ge 40$; $d \ge 8$

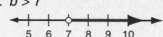

8. $11 + m \le 20$; $m \le 9$

9. $17 + h > 30$; $h > 13$

Practice B

1. $b > 7$

2. $t \ge 3$

3. $x \ge 5$

Holt McDougal Algebra 1

4. $g < -6$

5. $m \le 0$

6. $d < -4$

7. $29 + h > 40;\ h > 11$

8. $287 + m \le 512;\ m \le 225$

9. $34 + p \ge 97;\ p \ge 63$

Practice C

1. $h > 7$

2. $b \ge 5$

3. $y \ge 19$

4. $n < -6$

5. $r \le -7$

6. $t < 8$

7. $-3 + d \ge 10;\ d \ge 13$

8. $29.75 + m \le 40;\ m \le 10.25$

9. $g \ge 48 + 8;\ g \ge 56$

Review for Mastery

1. $b > 7$

2. $x < 3$

3. $x < -4$

4. $f \ge 4$

5. $c \le -5$

6. $x < 2$

7. $w > -3$

8. $n \ge 4$

Challenge

1. $0 < P \le 200$

2. No; because $2(70 + 40) = 220$ feet is greater than 200 feet

3. 80 feet; 80 feet; 1600 square feet

4. 60 feet; 60 feet; 2400 square feet

5. If the dimensions are reversed, the area remains the same.

6. 50 feet by 50 feet; a square; 2500 square feet

7. 40 feet by 40 feet

Problem Solving

1. $4 + h \le 10;\ h \le 6$

2. $m + 255 > 400;\ m > 145$

3. $q + 9 \ge 20;\ q \ge 11$

4. $40 + e \ge 60;\ e \ge 20$

5. A   **6.** J

7. C

Reading Strategies

1. Step 1

2. the direction of the inequality symbol

3. Substitute 8 for m in $14 = m + 6$.

4. Possible answer: 9

Holt McDougal Algebra 1

5. $t + 5 = -9$ $t + 5 < -9$
    $-14 + 5 = -9$; $-13 + 5 < -9$; no
      $-9 = -9$ $-8 < -9$

6. $b - 6 = 2$ $b - 6 \geq 2$
   $8 - 6 = 2$; $9 - 6 \geq 2$; yes
     $2 = 2$ $3 \geq 2$

2-3 SOLVING INEQUALITIES BY MULTIPLYING OR DIVIDING

Practice A

1. $x \geq 3$

-6 -5 -4 -3 -2 -1 0 1 2 3 4 5 6

2. $a < 5$

-6 -5 -4 -3 -2 -1 0 1 2 3 4 5 6

3. $b > 4$

-6 -5 -4 -3 -2 -1 0 1 2 3 4 5 6

4. $y \leq -2$

-6 -5 -4 -3 -2 -1 0 1 2 3 4 5 6

5. $x > -4$

-6 -5 -4 -3 -2 -1 0 1 2 3 4 5 6

6. $k < -3$

-6 -5 -4 -3 -2 -1 0 1 2 3 4 5 6

7. $n \leq 6$

-6 -5 -4 -3 -2 -1 0 1 2 3 4 5 6

8. $x \geq 0$

-6 -5 -4 -3 -2 -1 0 1 2 3 4 5 6

9. $2b \leq 15$; $b \leq 7.5$; 0, 1, 2, 3, 4, 5, 6, or 7 bags

10. $18c \leq 153$; $c \leq 8.5$; 0, 1, 2, 3, 4, 5, 6, 7, or 8 CDs

Practice B

1. $a > 8$

2 3 4 5 6 7 8 9 10 11 12 13 14

2. $y > -3$

-9 -8 -7 -6 -5 -4 -3 -2 -1 0 1 2 3

3. $n \leq -12$

-18 -17 -16 -15 -14 -13 -12 -11 -10 -9 -8 -7 -6

4. $c \leq -24$

-30 -29 -28 -27 -26 -25 -24 -23 -22 -21 -20 -19 -18

5. $y > 20$

14 15 16 17 18 19 20 21 22 23 24 25 26

6. $s \leq -1.5$

-1.5
-7 -6 -5 -4 -3 -2 -1 0 1 2 3 4 5

7. $b > 18$

12 13 14 15 16 17 18 19 20 21 22 23 24

8. $z \leq 2$

-4 -3 -2 -1 0 1 2 3 4 5 6 7 8

9. $5p \leq 16$; $p \leq 3.2$; 0, 1, 2, or 3 pieces

10. $5s \leq 128$; $s \leq 25.6$; 0 to 25 cups

11. $4b \geq 50$; $b \geq 12.50$; $12.50 each

Practice C

1. $a > 17$ 2. $b \leq -6$

3. $c \leq -1\dfrac{2}{3}$ 4. $x \geq -14.6$

5. $y \geq -7.5$ 6. $z > 5.2$

7. $n < -\dfrac{1}{8}$

8. $p > -\dfrac{12}{5}$ or $p > -2\dfrac{2}{5}$

9. $k \geq -40$ 10. $-4x \leq 24$; $x \geq -6$

-12 -11 -10 -9 -8 -7 -6 -5 -4 -3 -2 -1 0

11. $\dfrac{x}{15} \geq 3$; $x \geq 45$

39 40 41 42 43 44 45 46 47 48 49 50 51

12. $\dfrac{2}{3}x \leq -16$; $x \leq -24$

-30 -29 -28 -27 -26 -25 -24 -23 -22 -21 -20 -19 -18

13. $12d \geq 45$; $d \geq 3.75$; 4 boxes

Review for Mastery

1. $x \geq -6$

-8 -7 -6 -5 -4 -3 -2 -1 0 1 2 3 4 5 6 7 8

Holt McDougal Algebra 1

2. $g > 4$

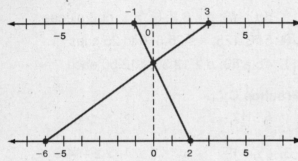

3. $v < 5$ **4.** $m > 12$

5. $q \le 2$

6. $x < -4$

7. $x \ge -5$ **8.** $d > -3$

Challenge

1. $2 > -6$

2–3.

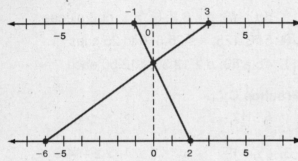

4. The segments cross each other showing that the value that was lesser (−1) now corresponds to the value that is greater (2), and vice versa.

5. The ratio of these lengths is the absolute value of −2: $\dfrac{\text{bottom}}{\text{top}} = \dfrac{2.4 \text{ cm}}{1.2 \text{ cm}} = 2$.

6. yes; the segments cross each other and the ratio of the lengths of the pieces of the dashed segment is still the absolute value of the factor: $\dfrac{\text{bottom}}{\text{top}} = \dfrac{0.9 \text{ cm}}{2.7 \text{ cm}} = \dfrac{1}{3}$.

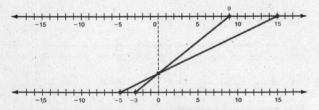

7. The segments would intersect at the midpoint of the dashed line.

Problem Solving

1. $0.50g \le 3$; $g \le 6$; 0, 1, 2, 3, 4, 5, or 6

2. $15d \le 21$; $d \le 1.40$; up to \$1.40

3. $2.5h \le 7$; $h \le 2.8$; up to 2.8 hours

4. $11q \le 50$; $q \le 4.54$; 0, 1, 2, 3, or 4

5. A **6.** G

7. A

Reading Strategies

1. No; because you are dividing by a positive number.

2. $t \le -20$; $p < -1.5$

3. Correct

4. Incorrect; $\le$ was reversed to >, instead of $\ge$.

5. Incorrect; The sign was not reversed.

2-4 SOLVING TWO-STEP AND MULTI-STEP INEQUALITIES

Practice A

1. 5; 5; 12; 6

2. 3; 3; 3; 12; > −4

3. 6; 6; 4; 5; 5; −1; 3; 3; $n > -\dfrac{1}{3}$

4. $x \ge -1$

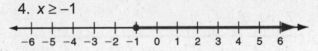

5. $z \le 2$

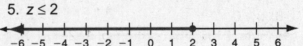

6. $a > 12$

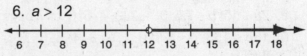

7. $x < 9$

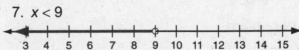

8. $\dfrac{85 + 60 + x}{3} \ge 70$; $x \ge 65$; at least 65

9. $30s + 120 \le 360$; $s \le 8$; 0, 1, 2, 3, 4, 5, 6, 7, or 8 sitcoms

Holt McDougal Algebra 1

Practice B

1. $a > 7$

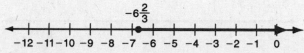

2. $x \geq 8$

3. $k < -16$

4. $z \geq -6\frac{2}{3}$

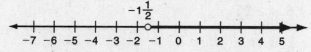

5. $n \geq 5$

6. $x > -1\frac{1}{2}$

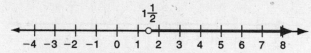

7. $c \leq 0$

8. $p > 1\frac{1}{2}$

9. $30m + 100 < 325$; $m < 7.5$; 1, 2, 3, 4, 5, 6, or 7 months

10. $x + 5 + 3x > 40$; $x > 8.75$

Practice C

1. $x \geq \frac{1}{3}$

2. $y \geq 7.8$

3. $a < \frac{1}{2}$

4. $h > 9$

5. $x \geq 3\frac{1}{2}$

6. $n < 5\frac{13}{15}$ or $n < 5.8\overline{6}$

7. $p \geq -1\frac{1}{8}$ or $p \geq -1.125$

8. $x > 5\frac{3}{5}$ or $x > 5.6$

9. $w > -3\frac{3}{5}$ or $w > -3.6$

10. $2 > 3 + \frac{1}{4}x$; $x < -4$

11. $-2(x + 3) \geq 0$; $x \leq -3$

12. $\dfrac{72 + 90 + 75 + 2f}{5} \geq 80$; $f \geq 81.5$; at least 81.5

13. $140 + 2s \leq 600$; $s \leq 230$; no more than 230 calories

Review for Mastery

1. $e \geq -2$

2. $c > 6$

3. $s \leq -3$

4. $j > 4$

5. $x > 3$

6. $b \leq -13$

7. $g < 5$

8. $k \geq 1$

Challenge

1.

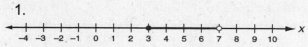

2. 3, 4, 5, 6

3. $x \geq 3$ and $x \leq 6$ where x is an integer.

4. a. $x > 55$;
   b. $x > 0$ and $x < 40$

5. No, since there is a lower limit as well as an upper limit

Holt McDougal Algebra 1

6. a. $x \geq 40$ and $x \leq 55$;
   b. $x > 0$ and $x < 40$
   or $x > 55$

7. maximum: $190,000
   minimum: $180,000
   $x \geq \$180,000$ and $x \leq \$190,000$

8. $x \geq \$75,000$ and $x \leq \$255,000$

Problem Solving

1. $\frac{p + 24}{2} > 20; p > 16$

2. $1500 + 0.15s \geq 2430; s \geq 6200$

3. $15 + 2y < 58; y < 21.5$

4. $5 + 2.5p \leq 23; p \leq 7.2; 0, 1, 2, 3, 4, 5, 6,$
   or 7 plants

5. C   6. H

7. A

Reading Strategies

1. to show the infinitely many solutions

2.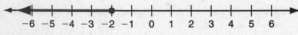

3. −1
   Possible Answer:

4. −2, −3, −4, −5, −6

5. yes; −2

2-5 SOLVING INEQUALITIES WITH VARIABLES ON BOTH SIDES

Practice A

1. $3x; -3x; 8; \geq -8$

2. $-6y; 14; 6y; 6y; 14; 14; 14; 1$

3. $15n; 18; 5n; 18; 18; 18; 5; 5; n < -4\frac{2}{5}$

4. $x \leq -2$

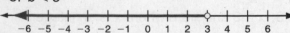

5. $b < 3$

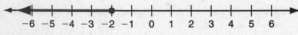

6. contradiction

7. identity

8. identity

9. $p - 0.15p + 12 < p; p > 80;$ greater than $80

10. $6x > \frac{1}{2} (4)(x + 6); x > 3$

Practice B

1. $x \leq 6$

2. $k > 3$

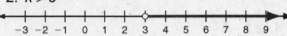

3. $b \leq 3$

4. $n > -14$

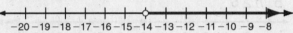

5. $s < -1$

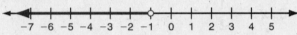

6. $x \geq 25$

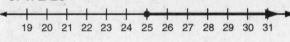

7. $z < 2$

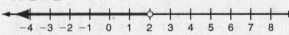

8. $p \leq \frac{2}{3}$

9. all real numbers

10. no solutions

11. no solution

12. $9.95m < 4.95 \, m + 49.95; m < 9.99;$
    for 0 to 9 months

13. $7(x + 2) > 7 + (x + 2) + 7 + (x + 2); x > 0.8$

Practice C

1. $x > \frac{1}{2}$

2. $p \geq -1\frac{3}{7}$

3. $s \geq -\frac{3}{5}$

4. all real numbers

5. $n > -12$

6. no solutions

7. $x \le 5\frac{5}{7}$

8. $z < 0$

9. no solutions

10. $b > -11$

11. $k > 1\frac{1}{3}$

12. $d < 610$

13. decreased 2000 people each year

14. $350,000 - 2000y$

15. increased 3000 people each year

16. $200,000 + 3000y$

17. $350,000 - 2000y < 200,000 + 3000y$
    $y > 30$ for years after 2010

Review for Mastery

1. add $-6y$ to both sides

2. add $-3p$ to both sides

3. add $3r$ to both sides

4. $c > -4$

5. $x < \frac{3}{2}$

6. $a > 15$

7. no solutions

8. all real numbers

9. all real numbers

10. all real numbers

11. no solutions

Challenge

1. $x = 4$; the lines intersect

2. $x < 4$; the line for y_1 is above (greater than) the line for y_2

3. $x + 3 > 2x - 1$

4. $x < 4$; same solutions as problem 2

5. Possible answer: Find the x-values for which the line for y_2 is either above (greater than) or intersects (equal to) the line for y_1. The solutions are $x \ge 4$.

6.

$y_1 = x - 3$	
x	y
-4	-7
-2	-5
0	-3
2	-1
4	1

$y_2 = -3x - 11$	
x	y
-4	1
-3	-2
-2	-5
-1	-8
0	-11

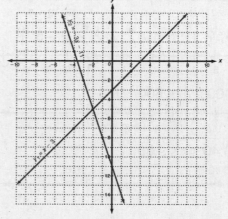

$x \le -2$

Problem Solving

1. $5r > 50 + 2r$; $r > 16$

2. $25,000 + 1000y > 19,000 + 1500y$; $y < 12$

3. $75m > 510 + 60m$; $m > 34$

4. $15 + 5s > 8s$; $s < 5$

5. B   6. F

Reading Strategies

1. Left; so he divides by a positive number.

2. $t > 8$

3. $n > 7$; left; you do not have to switch the inequality symbol.

2-6 SOLVING COMPOUND INEQUALITIES

Practice A

1.

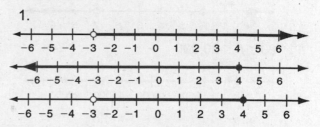

2.

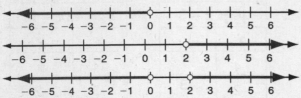

3. $x \le -1$ OR $x \ge 5$

4. $x > -4$ AND $x \le -1$

5. 5; 5; 5; 5; –3; 4

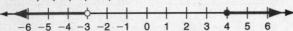

6. 1; 1; 1; 1; –10; 2; 2; 2; 2; 2; –5; 1

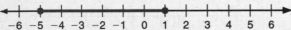

7. $400 \le m \le 600$

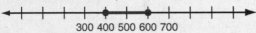

8. $6.40 \le r \le 9.80$

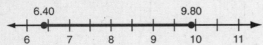

Practice B

1. $-2 < x < 4$ **2.** $x < -3$ OR $x \ge 3$

3. $x \le -15$ OR $x \ge -8$ **4.** $0 \le x < 20$

5. $-7 < x < 4$

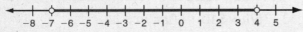

6. $3 \le n < 7$

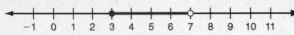

7. $-3 \le b \le 2$

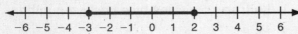

8. $x < 0$ OR $x \ge 6$

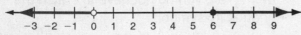

9. $k \le -4$ OR $k \ge 4$

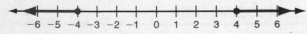

10. $s \le 2$ OR $s > 7$

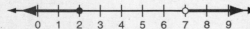

11. $20 \le h \le 20{,}000$

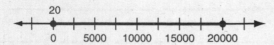

12. $140 < w \le 147$

Practice C

1. $0.5 < x < 2$

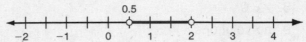

2. $a \le 1$ OR $a \ge 6$

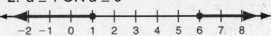

3. $y > -8$ OR $y \le 3$; all real numbers

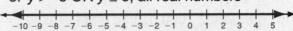

4. $-4 \le x \le -1$

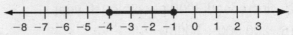

5. $k > -3$

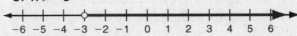

6. $z < -14$ OR $z \ge 1.8$

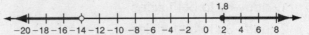

7. $-8 \le n \le 10$

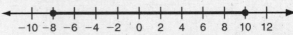

8. $p > 2$ AND $p \le -6$; no solutions

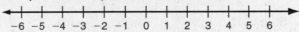

9. $0 < \ell < 4.55$ OR $\ell > 8.75$

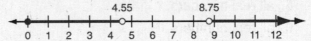

Review for Mastery

1. $-3 < x - 4$ $x - 4 \le 10$

2. $8 \le m + 4$ $m + 4 \le 15$

3.

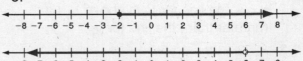

4. $-4 < k < 1$

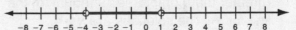

Holt McDougal Algebra 1

5. $2 < x \le 7$

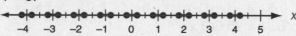

6. $x < 0$ OR $x \ge 4$ **7.** $x < -6$ OR $x > -3$

8.

9. $x \ge 3$ OR $x < -4$

10. $b \ge 7$ OR $b \le -1$

Challenge

1 – 6.

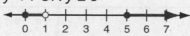
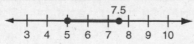

7. Answers may vary. Sample answer: closed intervals centered at each integer with each interval being $\frac{1}{2}$ unit long

8. $n \le x \le n + \frac{1}{2}$

9. $2n \le x \le 2n + 1$

10. $4n - 1 \le x \le 4n + 1$

11. a. Answers may vary. Sample answers: The center of the interval is 1, and its length is $\frac{2}{n}$.

  b. As n gets larger, the center remains at 1, but the length of the interval gets smaller.

Problem Solving

1. $68 \le t + 8 \le 77$; $60 \le t \le 69$

2. $380 \le m + 45 \le 410$; $335 \le m \le 365$

3. $y < 1$ OR $y \ge 5$

4. $10 \le 2a \le 15$; $5 \le a \le 7.5$

---

5. C   **6.** G

7. B

Reading Strategies

1. OR

2. Possible answer: 5, 6, 7

3. Possible answer: 3, 10, 11

4. AND

5. OR statement; AND statement

2-7 SOLVING ABSOLUTE-VALUE INEQUALITIES

Practice A

1. 7; 7; 2; –2; 2

2. –3; 3; 1; 1; 1; 1; –2; 4

3. $x > -4$ AND $x < 4$

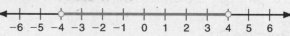

4. $x \ge -4$ AND $x \le 0$

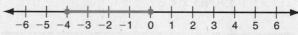

5. $x \ge -5$ AND $x \le 5$

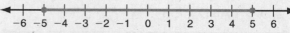

6. $x < -2$ OR $x > 2$

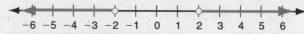

7. $x \le -2$ OR $x \ge 4$

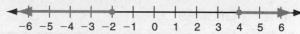

8. $x < -5$ OR $x > -1$

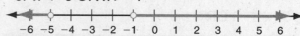

9. $\left| x - 85 \right| \le 4$; $81 \le x \le 88$

Practice B

1. $x \ge -5$ AND $x \le 5$

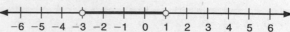

2. $x > -3$ AND $x < 1$

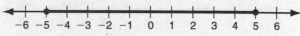

3. $x \ge 3$ AND $x \le 9$

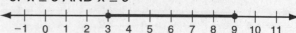

---

4. $x > -7$ AND $x < 1$

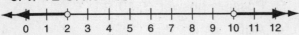

5. $x < -3$ OR $x > 3$

6. $x < 2$ OR $x > 10$

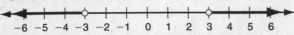

7. $x \le -9$ OR $x \ge -1$

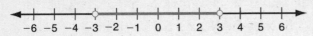

8. $x \le 0.5$ OR $x \ge 3.5$

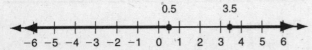

9. $\left| x - 350 \right| \le 35;\ 315 \le x \le 385$

10. $\left| x - 88 \right| \le 7.5;\ 80.5 \le x \le 95.5$

Practice C

1. $x > -3$ AND $x < 3$

2. $x > 1$ AND $x < 5$

3. $x \ge -5$ AND $x \le 1$

4. $x < 1$ OR $x > 9$

5. $x \le -3$ OR $x \ge 3$

6. $x \le -4\frac{1}{2}$ OR $x \ge 3\frac{1}{2}$

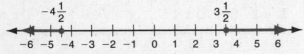

7. all real numbers

8. all real numbers

9. $\left| x - 36.5 \right| \le 1.5;\ 35 \le x \le 38$

10. $\left| x - 23.5 \right| \le 2.1;\ 21.4 \le x \le 25.6$

Review for Mastery

1. $x > -4$ AND $x < 4$

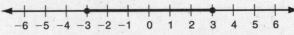

2. $x \ge -3$ AND $x \le 5$

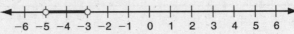

3. $x \ge -3$ AND $x \le 3$

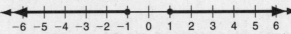

4. $x > -5$ AND $x < -3$

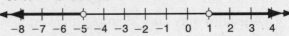

5. $x \le -1$ OR $x \ge 1$

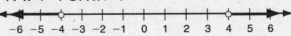

6. $x < -5$ OR $x > 1$

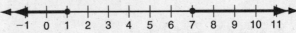

7. $x < -4$ OR $x > 4$

8. $x \le 1$ OR $x \ge 7$

Challenge

1. $3|x| < 6;\ |x| < 2;\ x > -2$ AND $x < 2$

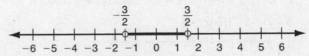

2. $9|x| \ge 27;\ |x| \ge 3;\ x \le -3$ OR $x \ge 3$

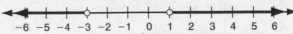

3. $x \ge -1$ AND $x \le 1$

4. $x > -\frac{3}{2}$ AND $x < \frac{3}{2}$

5. $x < -3$ OR $x > 1$

Holt McDougal Algebra 1

6. all real numbers

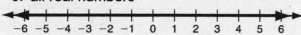

Problem Solving

1. $|x - 2| \le 0.05$; $1.95 \le x \le 2.05$

2. $|x - 134| \le 8$; $126 \le x \le 142$

3. $|x - 50| > 11$

4. $|x - 15.3| \le 0.4$

5. B   6. G

7. A

Reading Strategies

1. 5

2. 1 and 9

3.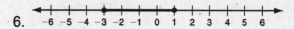

4. −1

5. −3 and 1

6.
```
◄──┼──┼──┼──●──┼──┼──●──┼──┼──┼──┼──►
  −6 −5 −4 −3 −2 −1  0  1  2  3  4  5  6
```

7.
```
◄──┼──┼──┼──○──┼──○──┼──┼──┼──┼──┼──►
  −6 −5 −4 −3 −2 −1  0  1  2  3  4  5  6
```

Holt McDougal Algebra 1

Answer Key For Functions

3-1 GRAPHING RELATIONSHIPS

Practice A

1. falling

2. staying the same

3. rising

4. Graph B

5. Graph C

6. Graph A

7.

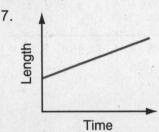

continuous

8. Possible answer: A subway train has up to 6 cars. Each car can hold 40 passengers.

Practice B

1. Graph C

2. Graph B

3. Graph A

4.

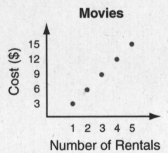

discrete

5. Possible answer: A kitten gains weight quickly after birth, then more slowly, until it reaches its maximum weight.

6. Possible answer: Each package weighs 10 pounds. The box can hold up to 60 pounds.

Practice C

1. Graph A

2. Graph C

3. Graph B

4.

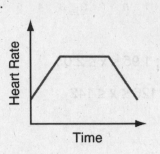

continuous

5. Possible answer: An object is thrown up in the air; drops to the ground, and bounces 3 times.

6. Possible answer: With each additional person in the group, the cost per person for a group trip drops.

Review for Mastery

1.

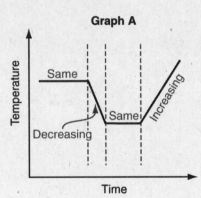

2.

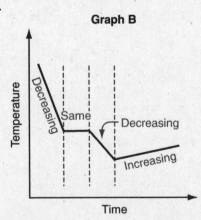

3. Graph B

4.

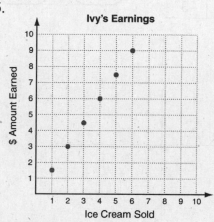

Heart Rate

continuous

5.

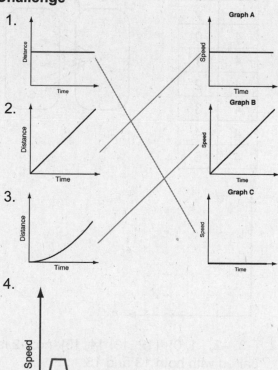

Ivy's Earnings

discrete

Challenge

1.
2.
3.
4.

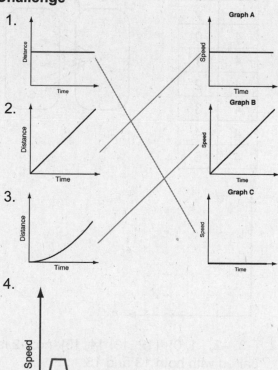

Graph A
Graph B
Graph C

1.

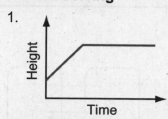

continuous

2.

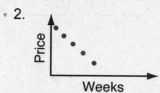

discrete

3.

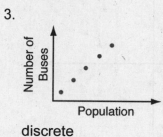

discrete

4.

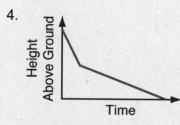

continuous

5. C   6. J

7. A   8. G

Reading Strategies

1. Possible answers: rose slowly; increased gradually

2.

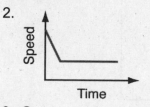

3. C   4. A

5. B

3-2 RELATIONS AND FUNCTIONS

Practice A

1.

x	y
−2	5
−1	1
3	1
−1	−2

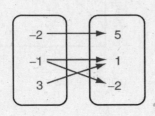

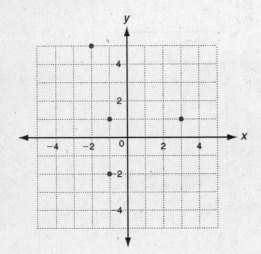

2.

x	y
5	3
4	3
3	3
2	3
1	3

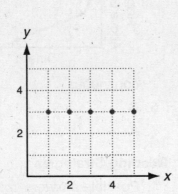

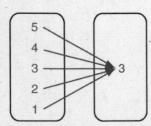

3. {0 ≤ x ≤ 4}; {0 ≤ y ≤ 4}; yes; each domain value is paired with exactly one range value.

4. {8, 9}; {−3, −4, −6, −9}; no; both domain values are paired with more than one range value.

5. {0, 1, 2}; {4, 5, 6, 7, 8}; no; two domain values are paired with two range values.

Practice B

1.

x	y
−5	3
−2	1
1	−1
4	−3

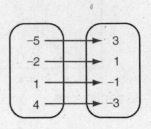

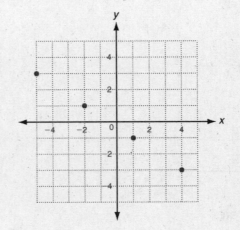

2.

x	y
4	0
4	1
4	2
4	3
4	4
4	5

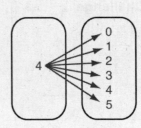

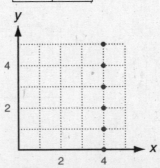

3. {−3, −2, −1, 0}; {12, 13, 14, 15}; no; −2 is paired with both 13 and 15.

4. {0 ≤ x ≤ 3}; {1 ≤ y ≤ 4}; yes; each domain value is paired with exactly one range value.

Holt McDougal Algebra 1

5. {0, 2, 4, 6, 8}; {4, 6, 8}; yes; each domain value is paired with exactly one range value.

Practice C

1.

x	y
–3	5
–2	4
–1	1
–1	–3

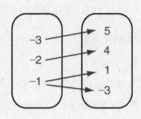

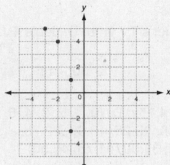

2.

x	y
–2	0
–2	1
–2	2
–2	3
–2	4
–2	5

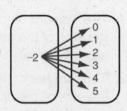

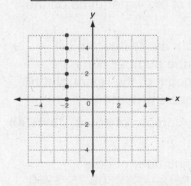

3. {1 ≤ x ≤ 5}; {1 ≤ y ≤ 4}; no; all domain values are paired with more than one range value.

4. {5, 6, 7, 8, 9}; {4}; yes; each domain value is paired with exactly one range value.

5. {1, 2, 3, 4, 5}; {1, 2, 3, 4, 5}; yes; each domain value is paired with exactly one range value.

Review for Mastery

1. D: {–2, –1, 0, 1}; R: {4, 1, 0}

2. D: {4, –2, –5}; R: {5, 6, 12}

3. D: {0, 1, 2, 3}; R: {5, 6, 7, 8}

4. D: {–3, –4, –5}; R: {10, 11, 12, 13}

5. D: $-2 \le x \le 2$; R: $1 \le y \le 4$

6. D: $-3 \le x \le 2$; R: $1 \le y \le 3$

7. No; –3 is paired with both 2 and 3.

8. Yes; each domain value is paired with exactly one range value.

9. No; several domain values are paired with more than one range value.

Challenge

1. multiples of 5: . . . , –15, –10, –5, 0, 5, 10, 15, . . .

2. multiples of k: kn

3. 0, 1, 2, 3, 4, 5, 6, 7, 8, 9

4. If P has coordinate a, Q has coordinate b, assign $\dfrac{a+b}{2}$.

5. If P has coordinate a, assign |a|.

6. If P has coordinate a and Q has coordinate b, assign |a – b|.

7. a. If the length of a side of square X is s, then P(square X) = 4s.
   b. If the length of a side of square X is s, then A(square X) = s^2.

8. a. The function rotates square A 120° counterclockwise about point O.
   b. The set of all squares.

9. a.

1, 1	1, 2	1, 3	1, 4	1, 5	1, 6
2, 1	2, 2	2, 3	2, 4	2, 5	2, 6
3, 1	3, 2	3, 3	3, 4	3, 5	3, 6
4, 1	4, 2	4, 3	4, 4	4, 5	4, 6
5, 1	5, 2	5, 3	5, 4	5, 5	5, 6
6, 1	6, 2	6, 3	6, 4	6, 5	6, 6

b. {2, 3, 4, 5, 6, 7, 8, 9, 10, 12}

Holt McDougal Algebra 1

Problem Solving

1-3. Possible answers given.

1. D: {6, 7, 8}; R: {1, 2}; no

2. D: {6, 9, 12, 15, 18}; R: {8, 10, 10.5, 11}; yes

3. D: {1, 2, 3, 4}; R: {50, 100, 150}; yes

4. D: {0, 1, 2, 3, 4, 5}; R: {2, 4.5, 7, 9.5, 12, 14.5}; yes

5. B   6. J

Reading Strategies

1.

x	1	2	3	4
y	1	2	3	4

2.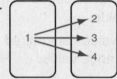

3. because the domain value 1 is paired with more than one range value.

4. no   5. no

6. yes

3-3 WRITING FUNCTIONS

Practice A

1. $y = 3x$ 2. $y = x - 3$

3. $y = -3x$

4. independent; dependent

5. dependent; independent

6. 10; 2   7. −8; 2

8. −7; 20

9. $f(b) = 10b$; D: {0, 1, 2, 3, 4, 5, 6, 7}; R: {0, 10, 20, 30, 40, 50, 60, 70}

10. $f(h) = 45 + 5h$; D: {1, 2, 3, 4}; R: {50, 55, 60, 65}

Practice B

1. $y = x + 3$ 2. $y = 2x - 1$

3. temperature; ice cream sales

4. number of people; cost of food

5. I: number of hours; D: total charge; $f(h) = 7h$

6. I: Ed's donation; D: Kay's donation; $f(d) = 2d$

7. 11; 16   8. 24; −8

9. 0; −2

10. $f(x) = 15 + 10x$; D: {0, 1, 2, 3, 4, 5, 6}; R: {15, 25, 35, 45, 55, 65, 75}

Practice C

1. $y = x^2$ 2. $y = 2x - 2$

3. population; amount of money

4. purchase price; amount of sales tax

5. I: number of students; D: money earned; $f(s) = 5 + 4.5s$

6. I: Jeb's brother's TV time; D: Jeb's TV time; $f(b) = b - 2$

7. 14; −1   8. 30; −18

9. 0; 45

10. $f(x) = 8.50 + 4.75x$; D: {0, 1, 2, 3, 4, 5, 6, 7, 8}; R: {8.50, 13.25, 18.00, 22.75, 27.50, 32.25, 37.00, 41.75, 46.50}

Review for Mastery

1. The amount of food eaten depends on the size of the animal.; pounds of food; size of animal

2. The number of firefighters depends on the size of the fire.; number of firefighters; size of the fire

3. The temperature of the water depends on the time it has been on the stove.; temperature of the water; time on the stove

4. The amount of the restaurant bill depends on the number of meals ordered.; amount of the restaurant bill; number of meals ordered

5. total charge; number of hours; $f(x) = 90x$; $180; $675

6. total charge; number of hours; $f(x) = 295 + 95(x - 1)$; $508.75; $960

Challenge

1. 104°F

2. Answers may vary. Sample answer: the 112°F may have been a "heat index" reading.

Holt McDougal Algebra 1

3. For each value of *C* there is exactly 1 value for *F*.

4. 77; 14; 64.4; 30   5. $C = \frac{5}{9}(F - 32)$

6. 15; 25; –20; $26\frac{2}{3}$

7. Yes; for each value of *F*, there is exactly one value of *C*.

8. The result is the original 35.

9. There is no temperature equivalent in both systems.

Problem Solving

1. I: number of representatives; D: number of electoral votes; $f(r) = r + 2$

2. I: number of friends; D: pieces of gum Terry has left $f(x) = 30 - 2x$

3. I: pounds of bacon; D: total price; $f(b) = 4.29b$

4. I: number of sessions; D: total cost; $f(s) = 50 + 40(s - 1)$

5. B   6. G

7. D   8. F

9. B

Reading Strategies

1. dependent; independent

2. $f(x) = 4x$

3. D: {1, 2, 3, 4, 5}

4. R: {4, 8, 12, 16, 20}

5. 12 ribbons

6. 20 ribbons

3-4 GRAPHING FUNCTIONS

Practice A

1.

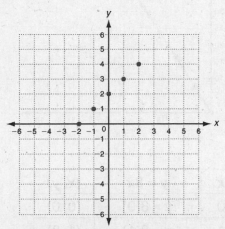

x	y = x + 2	(x, y)
–2	y = –2 + 2	(–2, 0)
–1	y = –1 + 2	(–1, 1)
0	y = 0 + 2	(0, 2)
1	y = 1 + 2	(1, 3)
2	y = 2 + 2	(2, 4)

2.

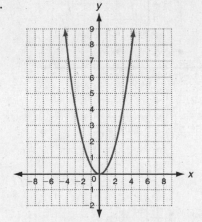

x	$y = x^2 \div 2$	(x, y)
–4	$y = (-4)^2 \div 2$	(–4, 8)
–2	$y = (-2)^2 \div 2$	(–2, 2)
0	$y = (0)^2 \div 2$	(0, 0)
2	$y = (2)^2 \div 2$	(2, 2)
4	$y = (4)^2 \div 2$	(4, 8)

3.

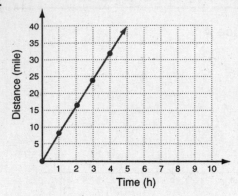

x	y = 8x	(x, y)
0	y = 8(0)	(0, 0)
1	y = 8(1)	(1, 8)
2	y = 8(2)	(2, 16)
3	y = 8(3)	(3, 24)
4	y = 8(4)	(4, 32)

about 28 miles

Practice B

1

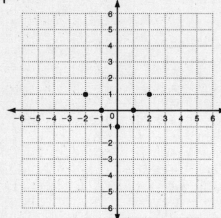

2

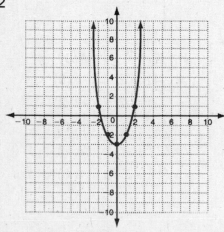

3.

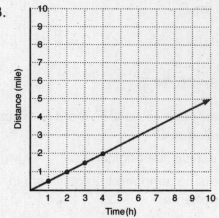

about 1.75 miles

Practice C

1.

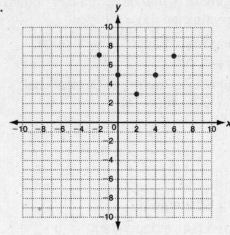

2.

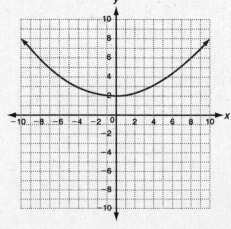

Holt McDougal Algebra 1

3.

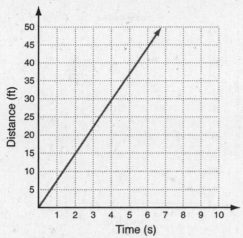

about 33 feet

x	$y = \frac{1}{2}x - 3$	(x, y)
–4	$y = \frac{1}{2}(-4) - 3 = -2 - 3 = -5$	(–4, –5)
–2	$y = \frac{1}{2}(-2) - 3 = -1 - 3 = -4$	(–2, –4)
0	$y = \frac{1}{2}(0) - 3 = 0 - 3 = -3$	(0, –3)
2	$y = \frac{1}{2}(2) - 3 = 1 - 3 = -2$	(2, –2)
4	$y = \frac{1}{2}(4) - 3 = 2 - 3 = -1$	(4, –1)

3. –3   4. 1
5. 0   6. 3
7. 1   8. 5

Review for Mastery

1.

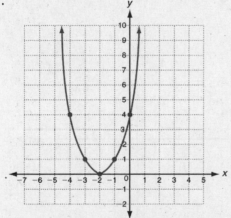

x	$y = (x + 2)^2$	(x, y)
–4	$y = (-4 + 2)^2 = (-2)^2 = \underline{4}$	(–4, 4)
–3	$y = (-3 + 2)^2 = (\underline{-1})^2 = \underline{1}$	(–3, 1)
–2	$y = (\underline{-2} + 2)^2 = (\underline{0})^2 = \underline{0}$	(–2, 0)
–1	$y = (\underline{-1} + 2)^2 = (1)^2 = \underline{1}$	(–1, 1)
0	$y = \underline{(0 + 2)^2} = (2)^2 = 4$	(0, 4)

2.

Challenge

1.

x	$g(x) = -2x$	g(x)
–1	$g(-1) = -2(-1) = 2$	2
0	$g(0) = -2(0) = 0$	0
1	$g(1) = -2(1) = -2$	–2
2	$g(2) = -2(2) = -4$	–4

g(x)	$f(x) = x^2 - 4$	f(g(x))
2	$f(2) = 2^2 - 4 = 4 - 4 = 0$	0
0	$f(0) = 0^2 - 4 = 0 - 4 = -4$	–4
–2	$f(-2) = (-2)^2 - 4 = 4 - 4 = 0$	0
–4	$f(-4) = (-4)^2 - 4 = 16 - 4 = 12$	12

Holt McDougal Algebra 1

2.

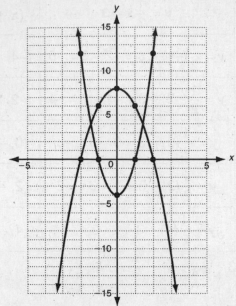

3. $y = -2x^2 + 8$

4.

x	$y = g(f(x)) = -2x^2 + 8$	$(x, g(f(x)))$
-2	$g(f(-2)) = -2(-2)^2 + 8 = -8 + 8 = 0$	(-2, 0)
-1	$g(f(-1)) = -2(-1)^2 + 8 = -2 + 8 = 6$	(-1, 6)
0	$g(f(0)) = -2(0)^2 + 8 = 0 + 8 = 8$	(0, 8)
1	$g(f(1)) = -2(1)^2 + 8 = -2 + 8 = 6$	(1, 6)
2	$g(f(2)) = -2(2)^2 + 8 = -8 + 8 = 0$	(2, 0)

5. No

Problem Solving

1.

x	$y = 8x$	(x, y)
0	0	(0, 0)
1	8	(1, 8)
2	16	(2, 16)
3	24	(3, 24)
4	32	(4, 32)

2.

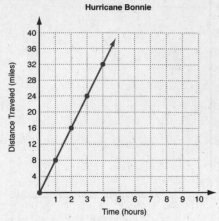

3. 28 miles

4. B   5. H

Reading Strategies

1.

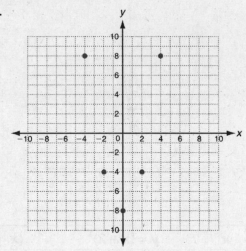

2.

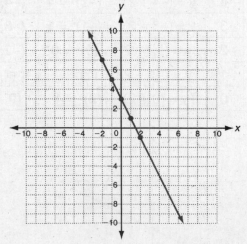

Holt McDougal Algebra 1

Practice A

1.

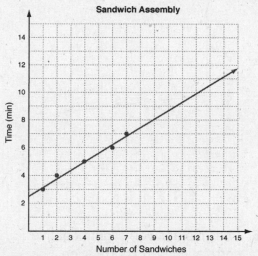

Drinks Sold

2. positive

3. negative

4. positive; as the temperature goes up, more people would go in the pool to cool off.

5. no correlation; the height of a person has nothing to do with how many phone calls they make

6. Possible answer: about 38 batteries

Practice B

1.

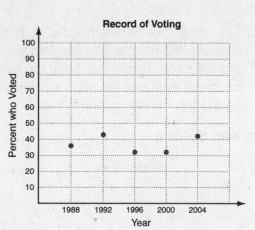

Record of Voting

2. negative   3. none

4. positive correlation; having more pets means needing more food, toys, etc.

5-6.

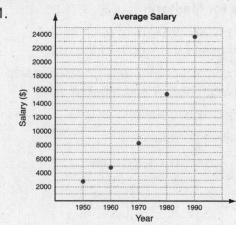

Sandwich Assembly

7. positive

8. about 10 minutes

Practice C

1.

Average Salary

2. negative correlation; as the number of vaccines goes up, the number of reported cases should go down.

3. positive correlation; as people receive more vacation days, they should be happier with their jobs because they have more leisure time

Holt McDougal Algebra 1

4-5.

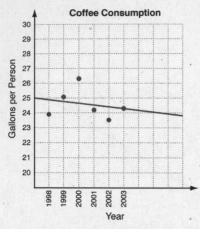

Coffee Consumption

6. Possible answer: slight negative correlation or no correlation

7. about 23.8 gallons per person

8. Possible answer: not very confident; the data fluctuates a lot from year to year.

Review for Mastery

1. Negative correlation; each knot decreases the length of the rope

2. No correlation; there is no relationship between height and algebra skill

3. negative correlation

4. positive correlation

5.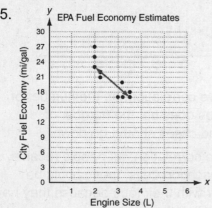

EPA Fuel Economy Estimates

6. Possible answer: 8 mi/gal
   Possible answer: 20 mi/gal
   Possible answer: 4.5 L
   Possible answer: 1.4 L

Challenge

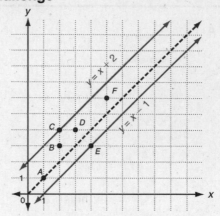

1. Yes, all the data points are either on the lines or between them.

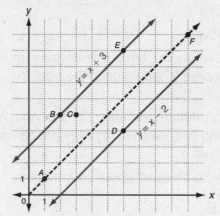

2. 3 units; 2 units

4. The closer together the parallel bounding lines are, the more tightly the data cluster around a line. The farther apart the parallel bounding lines are, the more loosely the data points cluster around a line.

Problem Solving

1.

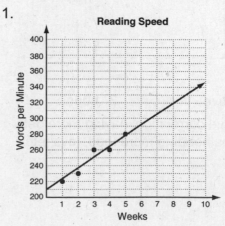

Reading Speed

2. positive correlation

3. about 320 wpm

Holt McDougal Algebra 1

4. negative correlation

5. C   6. J

7. B   8. F

Reading Strategies

1. number of children in a family; monthly cost of food; increases; positive

2. population of cities in the U.S.; average February temperature; shows no pattern; none

3. number of practice runs; finish time; decreases; negative

3-6 ARITHMETIC SEQUENCES

Practice A

1. no   2. yes

3. 3   4. –6

5. $d = -10$; –20, –30, –40

6. $d = -2$; 92, 90, 88

7. 256   8. –19

9. 30   10. 20

11. $a_{12} = 30 + 11(20)$ 12. $250

Practice B

1. arithmetic; $d = 3$; 2, 5, 8

2. arithmetic; $d = 1.5$; 6, 7.5, 9

3. not arithmetic

4. arithmetic; $d = -0.5$; –22, –22.5, 23

5. –108   6. 23

7. 97.8   8. –60.8

9. –34.5   10. 73.8

11. $213.40   12. $25.00

Practice C

1. arithmetic; $d = -0.75$; 2, 1.25, 0.5

2. arithmetic; $d = -\dfrac{1}{8}$; $\dfrac{5}{2}$, $\dfrac{19}{8}$, $\dfrac{9}{4}$

3. not arithmetic

4. arithmetic; $d = 3$; $x + 12$, $x + 15$, $x + 18$

5. –4   6. 51

7. –228   8. 14

9. 2116   10. 0

11. $339.95   12. 9

Review for Mastery

1. –2, –2, –2; yes

2. +0.3, +0.4, +0.5; no

3. –5, –8, –11

4. 15, 20, 25

5. no

6. yes; 2.5; 11.25, 13.75, 16.25

7. $a_n = 10 + (n - 1)(4)$

8. –5; 5; $a_n = -5 + (n - 1)(5)$

9. 9   10. 99

11. 190

Challenge

1. 0, 0, 0, 0, . . .

2. 0, 1, 0, 1, 0, . . .

3. 0, 1, 2, 0, 1, 2, . . .

4. 0, 1, 2, 3, 0, 1, 2, 3, . . .

5. 0, 1, 2, 3, 4, 0, 1, 2, 3, 4, . . .

6. 0, 1, 2, 3, 4, 5, 0, 1, 2, 3, 4, 5, . . .

7. a. The sequence will range from 0 to 11 and then repeat the pattern from 0 to 11. 1, 2, 3, 4, 5, 6, 7, 8, 9, 10, 11, 0, 1, 2, 3, 4, 5, 6, 7, 8, 9, 10, 11, . . .

   b. The remainder will always be a whole number ranging from 0 to 1 less than the divisor. The remainders repeat because every whole number is either a multiple of the divisor of a multiple of the divisor plus a whole number between 1 and 1 less than the divisor inclusive.

8. a. 10

   b. Every whole number divided by 10 will give a remainder that is a whole number from 0 to 9 inclusive.

9. 3:00 P.M.

Problem Solving

1. $1430   2. 1.95 ounces

3. $9400   4. $2.75

Holt McDougal Algebra 1

5. D   6. J
7. A   8. J
9. B

Reading Strategies

1. The terms do not all differ by the same number.

2. The same number is being multiplied, not added, to each term.

3. Possible answer: 1, 6, 11, 16, 21, …

4. $-\dfrac{1}{2}$; $5\dfrac{1}{2}$, 5, $4\dfrac{1}{2}$ 5. 130

6. 88

Holt McDougal Algebra 1

Answer Key For Linear Functions

4-1 IDENTIFYING LINEAR FUNCTIONS

Practice A

1. yes

2. Each domain value is paired with exactly one range value.

3. yes   4. yes

5. A constant change of +1 in x corresponds to a constant change of -2 in y.

6. $-x + y = -4$ 7. yes

8.

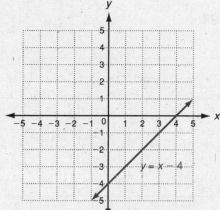

9.

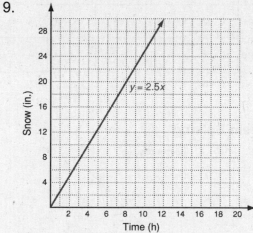

D: $x \geq 0$; R: $y \geq 0$

Practice B

1. function (not linear); each domain value is paired with exactly one range value.

2. not a function; several domain values are paired with two range values.

3. Set B; A constant change of +1 in x corresponds to a constant change of +2 in y.

4.

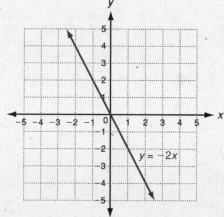

$2x + y = 0$

5.

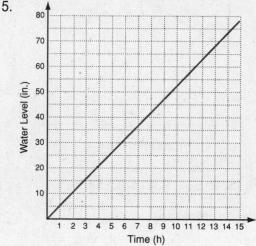

D: $0 \leq x \leq 15$; R: $0 \leq y \leq 78.75$

Practice C

1. not a function; One domain value is paired with an infinite number of range values.

2. nonlinear function; Each domain value is paired with exactly one range value.

3. Set A; A constant change of +0.1 in x corresponds to a constant change of +1.5 in y.

Holt McDougal Algebra 1

4.

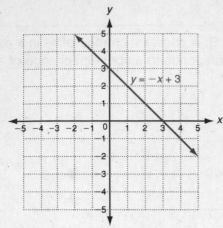

$y = -x + 3$

$x + y = 3$

10.

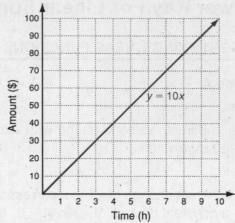

$y = 10x$

D: $x \geq 0$; R: $y \geq 0$

5.

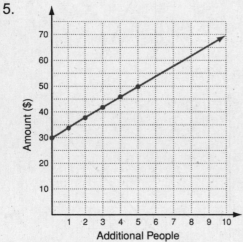

D: {0, 1, 2, 3, 4, …};
R: {$30, $34, $38, $42, $46…}

Challenge

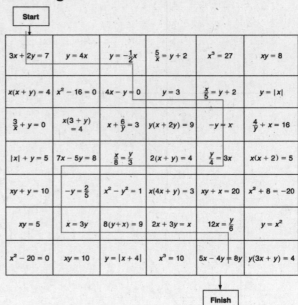

$3x + 2y = 7$	$y = 4x$	$y = -\frac{1}{2}x$	$\frac{5}{x} = y + 2$	$x^3 = 27$	$xy = 8$
$x(x + y) = 4$	$x^2 - 16 = 0$	$4x - y = 0$	$y = 3$	$\frac{x}{5} = y + 2$	$y = |x|$
$\frac{3}{x} + y = 0$	$x(3 + y) = 4$	$x + \frac{6}{y} = 3$	$y(x + 2y) = 9$	$-y = x$	$\frac{4}{y} + x = 16$
$|x| + y = 5$	$7x - 5y = 8$	$\frac{x}{8} = \frac{y}{3}$	$2(x + y) = 4$	$\frac{y}{4} = 3x$	$x(x + 2) = 5$
$xy + y = 10$	$-y = \frac{2}{5}$	$x^2 - y^2 = 1$	$x(4x + y) = 3$	$xy + x = 20$	$x^2 + 8 = -20$
$xy = 5$	$x = 3y$	$8(y + x) = 9$	$2x + 3y = x$	$12x = \frac{y}{6}$	$y = x^2$
$x^2 - 20 = 0$	$xy = 10$	$y = |x + 4|$	$x^3 = 10$	$5x - 4y = 8y$	$y(3x + y) = 4$

Start

Finish

Review for Mastery

1. no
2. yes
3. yes
4. no
5. no
6. yes
7. D: all real numbers;
   R: all real numbers
8. D: $x \geq 0$; R: $y \geq 0$
9. D: {0, 1, 2, 3, 4};
   R: {0, 0.5, 1, 1.5, 2}

Problem Solving

1.

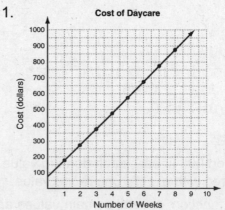

Cost of Daycare

D: {0, 1, 2, 3, …};
R: {$75, $175, $275, $375, …}

Holt McDougal Algebra 1

2.

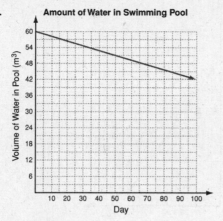

Amount of Water in Swimming Pool

D: $x \geq 0$;
R: $0 \leq y \leq 60$

3. J   4. C

5. H   6. A

Reading Strategies

1. $x + 4y = 9$

2. yes;
   Each domain value is paired with exactly
   one range value.

3. no; A constant change of +2 in x does not
   correspond to a constant change in y.

x	6	4	2	0	–2
y	–3	–1	0	2	3

4. $x + y = 4$

4-2 USING INTERCEPTS

Practice A

1. 2; 4   2. 4; –3

3. 1; –2

4.

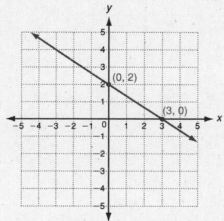

a. $x = 3$

b. 3

c. $y = 2$

d. 2

5.

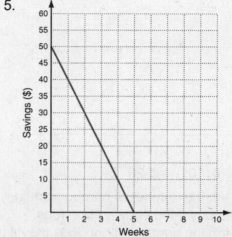

a. x-int: 5; y-int: 50

b. x-int: the amount of money after 5
   weeks. y-int: the amount of money
   before she makes any withdrawals

Practice B

1. x-int: 4; y-int: 2   2. x-int: –1; y-int: 4

3. x-int: –3; y-int: 3

4.

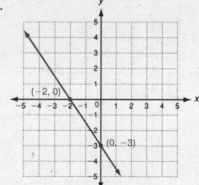

5.

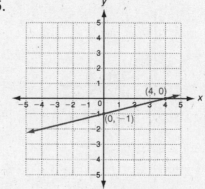

Holt McDougal Algebra 1

6.

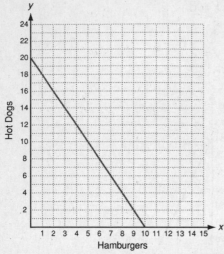

a. *x*-int: 10; *y*-int: 20

b. *x*-int: the number of hamburgers they can buy if they buy no hot dogs.
y-int: the number of hot dogs they can buy if they buy no hamburgers.

Practice C

1. *x*-int: −3.5; *y*-int: 3.5

2. *x*-int: none; *y*-int: 1

3. *x*-int: 2; *y*-int: none

4.

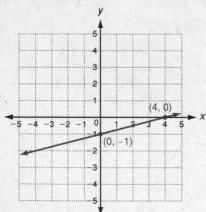

5.

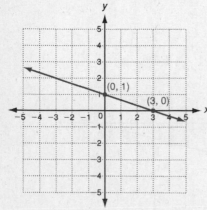

6.

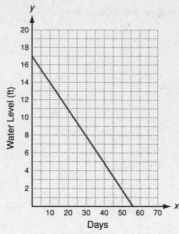

a. *x*-int: $56\frac{2}{3}$; *y*-int: 17

b. *x*-int: the number of days it will take for the river to run dry.
y-int: the water level before it falls.

Review for Mastery

1. *x*-int: 3; *y*-int: −3

2. *x*-int: −1; *y*-int: −2

3. *x*-int: −2; *y*-int: 4

4. *x*-int: 3; the time it took to complete the trip.
y-int: 120; the number of miles left to driven.

5.

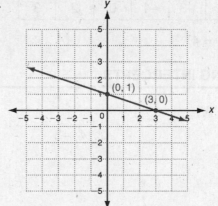

Holt McDougal Algebra 1

6.

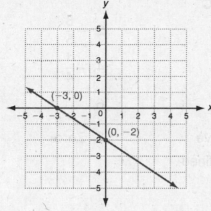

7.

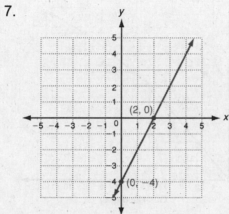

Challenge

1. ≈5.8 units   2. ≈4.5 units

3.

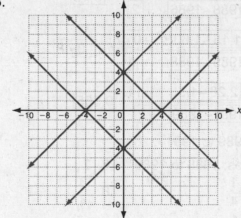

−4; 4

4; −4

4; 4

−4; −4

≈22.6 units

4.

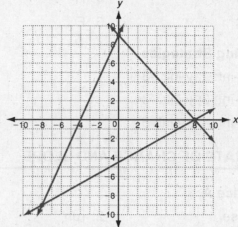

8, 9;

−4, 9;

8, −4.5;

≈50.1 units

Problem Solving

1.

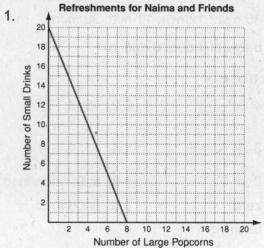

Refreshments for Naima and Friends

y-int: 20; *x*-int: 8

2.

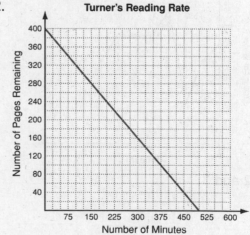

Turner's Reading Rate

y-int: 400; *x*-int: 500

Holt McDougal Algebra 1

3. B   4. H

5. C   6. F

Reading Strategies

1. x-int: 2; y-int: -3

2. x-int: 3; y-int: -3

3. x-int: -3; y-int: 5

4-3 RATE OF CHANGE AND SLOPE

Practice A

1. rise   2. run

3. rise to run   4. $\frac{1}{3}$

5. 2   6. $-\frac{3}{2}$

7. zero   8. negative

9. undefined

10. 35 mi/h; 12mi/h; 11mi/h; 39 mi/h; $\frac{1}{2}$ mi/h;

between hours 8 and 10

Practice B

1. 4; 5; $\frac{4}{5}$ 2. -6; 3; -2

3. 3; 4; $\frac{3}{4}$ 4. -1; 4; $-\frac{1}{4}$

5. 0; 4; 0   6. 6; 0; undefined

7. zero   8. undefined

9. positive

10.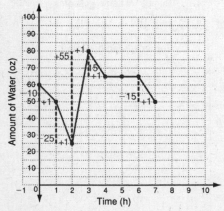

2 and 3

Practice C

1. $\frac{2}{3}$ 2. $-\frac{8}{5}$

3. $\frac{1}{9}$ 4. $-\frac{1}{4}$

5. 0   6. $-\frac{3}{5}$

7. positive   8. Zero

9. undefined

10.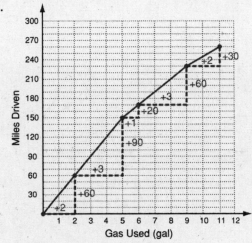

between gallons 5 and 6

Review for Mastery

1. $\frac{1.63-1.27}{1988-1986} = \frac{0.36}{2} = 0.18$

2. $\frac{1.15-1.63}{1989-1988} = \frac{-0.48}{1} = -0.48$

3. $\frac{2.26-1.5}{1991-1989} = \frac{1.11}{2} = 0.555$

4. 1989 to 1991

5. yes; 1988 to 1989   6. 2

7. $-\frac{1}{4}$ 8. $\frac{3}{4}$

9. $-\frac{1}{2}$ 10. 1

11. -5

Challenge

1. Possible answer: $\frac{2}{8}$, $\frac{3}{12}$, $\frac{4}{16}$

2.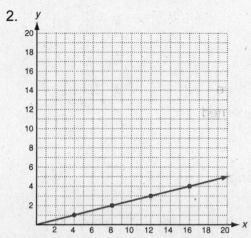
They form a straight line.

3. $\frac{1}{4}$

5.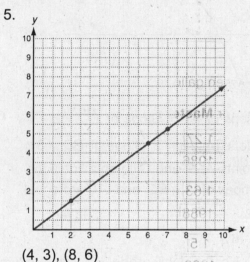
(4, 3), (8, 6)

6. $\frac{3}{4}$, $\frac{3}{4}$ 7. $\frac{3}{4}$

8. The fractions are written as $\frac{y}{x}$ and slope is defined as change in y divided by change in x.

9. yes; (−4, −3) would be written as $\frac{-3}{-4}$ which equals $\frac{3}{4}$.

Problem Solving

1. The rate of change has a constant value of 1.49.

2. 9–11: 0.75; 11–12: 2;
   12–13: 3.5; 13–15: 2;
   12–13; 9–11; 11–12 and 13–15

3. 0; she was not moving during this time.

4. D   5. G

6. C   7. G

Reading Strategies

1. temperature

2. time

3. $\frac{12}{3} = 4$; $\frac{4}{2} = 2$; $\frac{4}{4} = 1$

4. upward is vertical and the y-axis is the vertical axis.

5. people run horizontally and the x-axis is the horizontal axis.

6. $-\frac{2}{3}$

4-4 THE SLOPE FORMULA

Practice A

1. 9; 3; 6

2. $\frac{-1 - 3}{2 - (-2)}$; $\frac{-4}{4}$; −1

3. $\frac{-2 - 6}{0 - 4}$; $\frac{-8}{-4}$; 2   4. $-\frac{2}{3}$

5. −2   6. $\frac{7}{3}$

7. 2; the profit increases $2 for every box sold.

8. $\frac{3}{2}$; For each additional crust made, 1.5 cups of flour are needed.

9. a. 0;   b. 0;
      2x;   5y;
      2; 2   5; 5
      −5   −2

   c. −5; −2;
      −2; −5; $\frac{-2}{5}$

Practice B

1. $\dfrac{-3-8}{1-2}$; $\dfrac{-11}{-1}$; 11

2. $\dfrac{-2-0}{-6-(-4)}$; $\dfrac{-2}{-2}$; 1

3. $\dfrac{-7-(-2)}{4-0}$; $\dfrac{-5}{4}$

4. $\dfrac{3}{5}$

5. 1.25

6. $-\dfrac{3}{4}$

7. $\dfrac{3}{2}$; the salary increases $3 every 2 years.

8. $-\dfrac{400}{3}$; the number of people remaining decreases by 400 every 3 hours.

9. $-\dfrac{3}{4}$

10. $\dfrac{8}{3}$

Practice C

1. 4

2. $\dfrac{5}{7}$

3. $\dfrac{1}{5}$

4. 3

5. 0

6. 3

7. $\dfrac{4}{5}$

8. $\dfrac{2}{5}$

9. $-\dfrac{1}{2}$

10. $-\dfrac{50}{3}$; the number of remaining pages decreases by 50 every 3 days.

11. $\dfrac{1}{10}$; one quart of syrup can be made for every 10 gal of sap.

12. $\dfrac{7}{6}$

13. $-\dfrac{5}{2}$

14. $\dfrac{1}{4}$

15. 4

16. 2

17. 6

Review for Mastery

1. $\dfrac{3}{4}$

2. $\dfrac{1}{2}$

3. 4

4. $-\dfrac{2}{5}$

5. –2

6. 3

7. $\dfrac{1}{2}$

8. $-\dfrac{4}{3}$

9. $\dfrac{1}{4}$

Challenge

1.

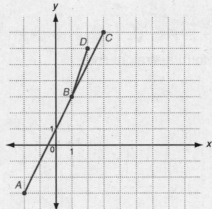

2. Slope of $\overline{AB}$ = Slope of $\overline{BC}$ = 2

4. Slope of $\overline{AB}$ = 2; Slope of $\overline{BD}$ = 3

5. Points A, B, and C lie on a line if the slopes of $\overline{AB}$, $\overline{BC}$ and $\overline{AC}$ are equal.

6. 3%

7. 300 feet

8. a. 6%

   b. No; the uphill grade is positive and the downhill grade is negative.

9. $2

Problem Solving

1. 12; the number of kits assembled per day.

2. –0.2; the number of pounds of flour used per day.

3. 20

4. B

5. J

6. A

7. G

Holt McDougal Algebra 1

Reading Strategies

1. 4

2. Possible answer: (−1, 6)

3. 2   4. (−4, 1) and (6, 5)

5. $\frac{2}{5}$ 6. 0

7. horizontal

4-5 DIRECT VARIATION

Practice A

1.	$y = 7x$	yes	yes	7
2.	$y = 4x - 10$	no	no	n/a
3.	$y = \frac{5}{2}x$	yes	yes	$\frac{5}{2}$

4.	$\frac{1}{5}; \frac{1}{5}; \frac{1}{5}$	yes	yes
5.	4; 2.5; 2	no	no

6. $\frac{1}{2}$; 8;   7. $\frac{3}{2}$; 15;

   $\frac{1}{2}$; 4 $\frac{3}{2}$; $\frac{45}{2}$

8.

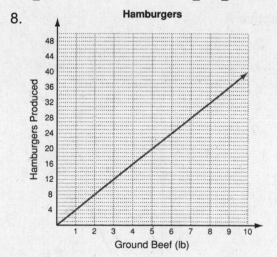

Hamburgers

$y = 4x$

Practice B

1. yes; 3   2. no

3. yes; $-\frac{2}{3}$ 4. yes; 3

5. $\frac{1}{3}; \frac{1}{3}; \frac{1}{3}$ 6. 4; 4; 4

   yes   yes

7. $\frac{3}{10}; \frac{1}{3}; \frac{9}{20}$ 8. −3; −8;

   no   −3; 24

9. $\frac{1}{10}$; 30; $\frac{1}{10}$; 3

10.

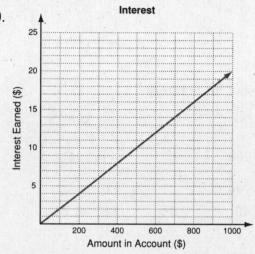

Interest

$y = 0.02x$

11. $27

Practice C

1. yes; −2   2. no

2. yes; 2   4. yes; $\frac{5}{9}$

5. no   6. no

7. yes; the ratio of y to x is −6 for each ordered pair.

8. no; the ratio of y to x is not the same for each ordered pair.

9. yes; the ratio of y to x is 1.5 for each ordered pair.

10. no; the relationship can not be expressed in the form $y = kx$.

11. 28

12. 5

13. $y = 48x$

Holt McDougal Algebra 1

14. $y = 18x$

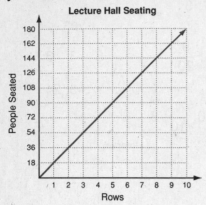

Lecture Hall Seating

Review for Mastery

1. no

2. yes; $\frac{4}{3}$

3. yes; -3

4. yes; $-\frac{1}{2}$

5. yes; 3.5

6. no

7. 40

8. -8.75

9.

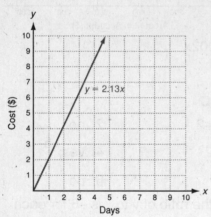

$y = 2.13x$

Challenge

1. a. $y = 5t$, 40 minutes

   b. $y = 10t$, 20 minutes

   c. $y = 15t$, $13\frac{1}{3}$ minutes

2. a. $y = 15t$

   b. $y = 25t$

   c. $y = 30t$,

3. a. $Q = 500 + 30t - 35t$

   b. emptying at 5 gallons per minute

   c. after 100 minutes, the tank will be empty

4. a. $Q = 500 + 30(t + 6) - 35t$,
   or $Q = 680 - 5t$

   b. after 136 minutes, the tank will be empty

Problem Solving

1. $y = 6.5x$

2. yes; it can be written as $y = 4x$.

3. no; it cannot be written in the form $y = kx$

4. 462 miles

5. A

6. H

7. C

8. G

Reading Strategies

1. 8

2. $\frac{1}{3}$

3. -2.5

4. $y = 12 - x$; no

5. $y = \frac{3}{2}x$; yes

6. $\frac{1}{2}, \frac{1}{2}, \frac{1}{2}$

7. yes

8. 12

4-6 SLOPE-INTERCEPT FORM

Practice A

1. $\frac{2}{3}$; 2

2. -1; 8

3. 3; -6;
   6; 6; 11;
   -2; 11

4. $y = 2x - 4$

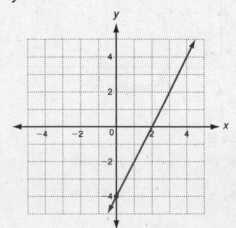

Holt McDougal Algebra 1

5. $y = -\dfrac{1}{2}x + 3$

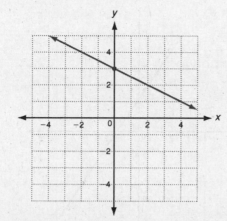

6. $y = -\dfrac{2}{3}x + 2$

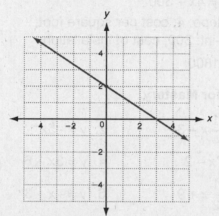

7. a. $y = 25x + 30$

b. slope: 25; number of desks per classroom; *y*-int 30; number of spare desks

c. 630

Practice B

1. $y = 4x - 3$

2. $y = -2x$

3. $y = -\dfrac{1}{3}x + 6$

4. $3 = \left(\dfrac{2}{5}\right)10 + b$

$3 = 4 + b$

$-1 = b$

$y = \dfrac{2}{5}x - 1$

5. $y = -x + 3$

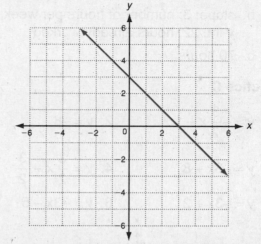

6. $y = \dfrac{4}{3}x - 4$

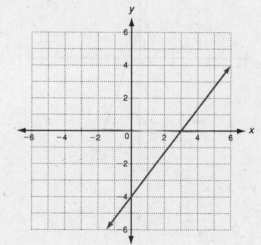

7. $y = \dfrac{5}{2}x - 5$

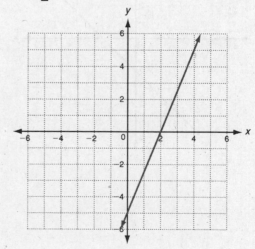

Holt McDougal Algebra 1

8. a. $y = 3x + 22$

   b. slope: 3; number of hours per week;
      y-int: 22; hours already worked

   c. 70 hours

Practice C

1. $y = -\dfrac{3}{2}x + 1$ 2. $y = -8$

3. $y = -3x + 8$ 4. $y = \dfrac{3}{2}x - \dfrac{3}{2}$

5. $y = -3x + 2$ 6. $y = -3x - 5$

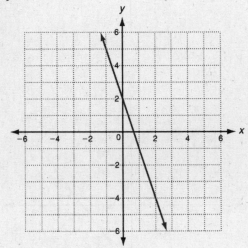

7. $y = x - 2$

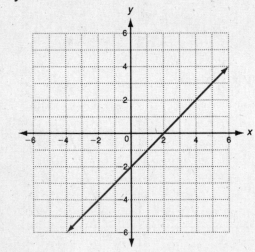

8. $y = -\dfrac{3}{2}x + 2$

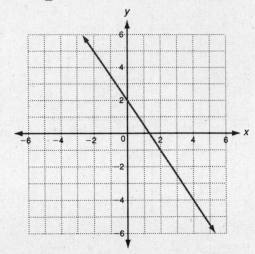

9. a. $y = 4x + 300$

   b. slope: 4; cost per square foot;
      y-int: 300; cost of installation

   c. $1800

Review for Mastery

1. $y = \dfrac{1}{4}x + 3$ 2. $y = -5x$

3. $y = 7x - 2$ 4. $y = 3x - 6$

5. $y = \dfrac{1}{2}x + 9$ 6. $y = -x + 3$

7. $y = -5x + 30$ 8. $y = x - 7$

9. $y = \dfrac{4}{3}x + 4$

10. $y = 2x - 3$

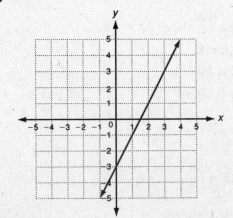

Challenge

1. $a_1 = 3$ 2. $d = 2$

3. $a_n = 3 + (n - 1)(2)$

     Holt McDougal Algebra 1

4.

x	1	2	3	4	5	6	7
y	3	5	7	9	11	13	15

5.

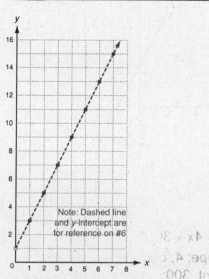

Note: Dashed line and y-intercept are for reference on #6

No, because the domain of the sequence is restricted to natural numbers: {1, 2, 3, 4, …}.

6. $y = 2x + 1$

7. a. The slope is the same as the common difference ($m = d = 2$).

   b. The y-intercept is the same as the first term less the common difference ($b = a_1 - d = 1$).

8. $y = -3x + 8$; $m = d = -3$ and $b = a_1 - d = 5 - (-3) = 8$

9. $a_n = 4 + (n - 1)(5)$; $d = m = 5$ and $a_1 = b + d = -1 + 5 = 4$

Problem Solving

1. $y = 10x + 300$

2. slope: 10, rate of the change of the cost: $10 per student; y-int: 300, the initial fee (the cost for 0 students)

3. $800

4. C   5. J

6. A   7. H

Reading Strategies

1. With a fraction, you have a "rise" and "run" for graphing.

2. (0, –8)   3. 5; 12

---

4. –3; 0   5. 1; –4

6. $\frac{1}{3}$; 3

7.

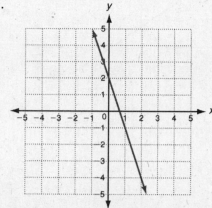

8.

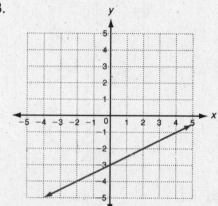

4-7 POINT-SLOPE FORM

Practice A

1. C   2. A

3. B   4. $y - 8 = 4(x - 3)$

5. $y + 3 = -\frac{1}{2}(x - 5)$ 6. $y = 5x + 2$

7. $y = -3x + 12$ 8. 2; $y = 2x + 2$

9. $\frac{1}{2}$; $y = \frac{1}{2}x - 6$ 10. x-int:4, y-int: 10

11. x-int: –1, y-int: 3

12. $y = 8x + 30$; $1070

Practice B

1. $y - 2 = 3(x + 4)$ 2. $y + 1 = -(x - 6)$

Holt McDougal Algebra 1

3.

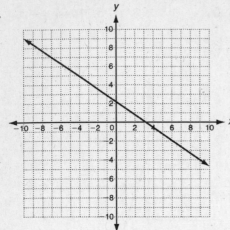

4.

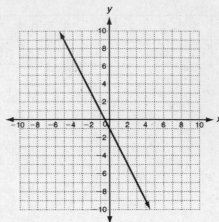

4.

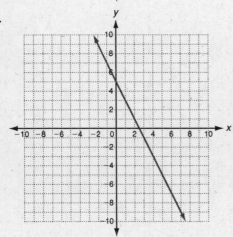

5. $y = -4x + 1$ 6. $y = \frac{1}{2}x - 1$

7. $y = 4x - 7$ 8. $y = \frac{1}{2}x - 3$

9. x-int: 1, y-int: –2   10. x-int:6, y-int: 8

11. $y = 0.17x + 3$; $13.20

Practice C

1. $y + 3 = \frac{4}{3}(x + 5)$ 2. $y - 8 = -3(x - 0)$

3.

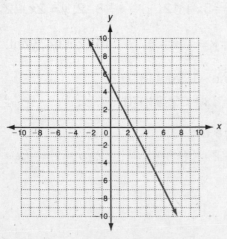

5. $y = -4x + 7$ 6. $y = \frac{1}{4}x + \frac{7}{2}$

7. $y = -x + 3$ 8. $y = \frac{1}{3}x - 5$

9. x-int: 7, y-int: 6

10. x-int: 4, y-int: 10

11. $y = -26x + 5274$; 1374 gal

Review for Mastery

1.

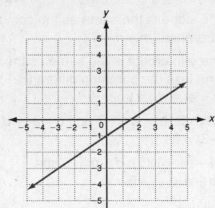

2.

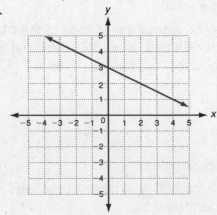

Holt McDougal Algebra 1

3.

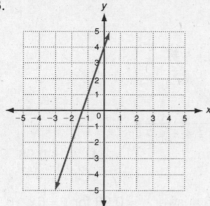

4.

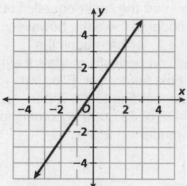

5.

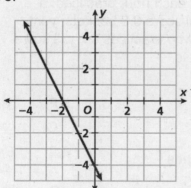

6.

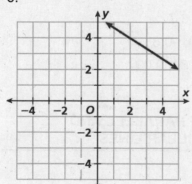

7. $y = -3x + 5$

8. $y = \frac{1}{4}x + 1$

9. $y = 4x$

10. $y = 5x - 3$

11. $y = \frac{1}{2}x - 1$

12. $y = -x + 5$

Challenge

Plot an even number of pairs of points such that the two points in each pair are collinear but neither point is collinear with any other plotted point.

Problem Solving

1. Possible answer:
   $y - 130 = 1.2(x - 10)$;
   $y = 1.2x + 118$;
   136

2. $y = 3x + 32$

3. $y = \frac{1}{10}x + 5$; \$7.50

4. B   5. F

6. D

Reading Strategies

1. the slope of the line and one point on the line

2. the slope; you can substitute the coordinates of the two given points into the slope formula.

3. $y + 10 = 4(x - 3)$ 4. $y = -2x - 1$

4-8 LINE OF BEST FIT

Practice A

1 a. 6
  b. 6
  c. neither

2 a. $y \approx 0.27x + 3.77$
  b. ≈ 0.997
  c. very well
  d. strong pos. correlation

3 a. $y = -0.13x + 4.28$
  b. ≈ -0.997
  c. very well
  d. strong neg. correlation

4. strong pos. correlation; likely cause-and-effect relationship

Holt McDougal Algebra 1

Practice B

1. a. 134

   b. 10

   c. $y = -\dfrac{1}{2}x + 5.$

2. a. $y \approx 0.78x - 4.54$

   b. 0.46

   c. moderately well

   d. weak pos. correlation

3. a. $y \approx -0.06x + 1.58$

   b. −0.99

   c. very well

   d. strong neg. correlation

4. strong pos. correlation; unlikely cause-and-effect relationship

Practice C

1. a. 26

   b. $15\dfrac{8}{9}$

   c. $y = -\dfrac{1}{3}x + 4.$

2. a. $y \approx 0.49x - 4.94$

   b. 0.53

   c. not well

   d. weak pos. correlation

3. a. $y = 0.61x - 1.05$

   b. 0.99

   c. very well

   d. strong pos. correlation

4. strong neg. correlation; likely cause-and-effect relationship

Review for Mastery

1. a. 8, 7, 6, 5

   b. 8, 0; 7, −2; 6, −1; 5, −3

   c. 0, −2, −1, −3; 0, 4, 1, 9; 14

2. $y = -x + 9$

3. −1.51; 12.90

   −1.51; 12.90

   −0.93; strong neg.

Challenge

1.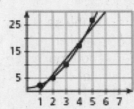

2. $6x - 6$ 4.   0.98

5. $x^2 + 1$ 7. 1

8. Possible answer: $r = 0.98$ for $y = 6x - 6$, which means there is a strong positive correlation and that the linear equation is a very good model of the data; however, $r = 1$ for $y = x^2 + 1$, which means the quadratic equation perfectly models the data. For the next fundraiser, Ellen will raise $30,000 according to the linear model $y = 6x - 6$, or $37,000 according to the quadratic model $y = x^2 + 1$.

Problem Solving

1. a. $y = 0.8x + 2.3$

   b. Slope: for each hour practiced, a player will score 0.8 baskets; y-int.: a player who practices 0 h will score 2.3 baskets.

   c. 0.998

2. C   3.   F

4. A   5.   G

Reading Strategies

1. $y = 0.8x + 0.5$

2. 0.8

3. 1.3; 2.1; 2.9; 3.7

4. 0.3; −0.9; 0.9; −0.3

5. 0.09; 0.81; 0.81; 0.09

6. 1.8

4-9 SLOPES OF PARALLEL AND PERPENDICULAR LINES

Practice A

1. $y = 4$; $y = \dfrac{1}{2}x + 3$; $y = \dfrac{1}{2}x$; $y = 2x$

Holt McDougal Algebra 1

2. $y - 5 = 6(x + 2)$; $\boxed{y = -6x}$; $\boxed{6x + y = 4}$; $y = 6$

3. 0; –2; 0; –2;
The opposite sides have the same slope which means they are parallel. ABCD is a parallelogram because both pairs of opposite sides are parallel.

4. $\boxed{y = x - 4}$; $y = 3$; $\boxed{y = -x}$; $y = -3$

5. $y = 5x + 1$; $\boxed{y = 3}$; $y = \dfrac{1}{5}x$; $\boxed{x = 5}$

6. $\boxed{y = \dfrac{1}{3}x - 2}$; $x = 2$; $y - 4 = 3(x + 3)$; $\boxed{y = -3x + 9}$

7. $\dfrac{2}{5}$; $-\dfrac{5}{2}$; $-\dfrac{3}{7}$;

$\dfrac{2}{5}\left(-\dfrac{5}{2}\right) = -1$ so $\overline{AB}$ is perpendicular to $\overline{BC}$. ABC is a right triangle because it contains a right angle.

Practice B

1. $y = 3x + 4$ and $y = 3x$; $y = 4$ and $y = 3$

2. $y = \dfrac{1}{2}x + 4$ and $y = \dfrac{1}{2}x + 1$

3. $-\dfrac{2}{3}$; undefined; $-\dfrac{2}{3}$; undefined;

The opposite sides have the same slope which means they are parallel. A quadrilateral is a parallelogram if the opposite sides are parallel.

4. $y = 5$ and $x = 2$

5. $y = -\dfrac{1}{2}x - 4$ and $y - 4 = 2(x + 4)$

6. slope of $\overline{AB} = \dfrac{1}{4}$; slope of $\overline{BC} = -4$;

$\overline{AB}$ is perpendicular to $\overline{BC}$ because $\dfrac{1}{4}(-4) = -1$. ABC is a right triangle because it contains a right angle.

Practice C

1. $y = \dfrac{1}{4}x$ and $y = \dfrac{1}{4}x + 2$

2. $y - 1 = -(x + 7)$ and $y = -x$ and $x + y = 3$

3. slope of $\overline{AB} = -\dfrac{5}{3}$; slope of $\overline{CD} = -\dfrac{5}{3}$;

slope of $\overline{BC} = \dfrac{5}{3}$; slope of $\overline{AD} = \dfrac{5}{3}$;

The opposite sides have the same slope which means they are parallel. ABCD is a parallelogram because both pairs of opposite sides are parallel.

4. $y = 3$ and $x = 6$

5. $y = \dfrac{1}{2}x + 2$ and $y + 1 = -2x$

6. slope of $\overline{AB} = \dfrac{2}{3}$; slope of $\overline{BC} = -\dfrac{3}{2}$;

$\overline{AB}$ is perpendicular to $\overline{BC}$ because $\dfrac{2}{3}\left(-\dfrac{2}{3}\right) = -1$. ABC is a right triangle because it contains a right angle.

7. –2

Review for Mastery

1. $y = 2x + 1$; $y = 2x - 3$

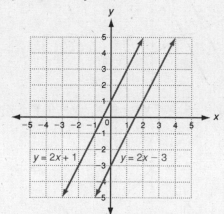

2. $y = -\dfrac{2}{3}x + 2$; $y = \dfrac{3}{2}x + 1$

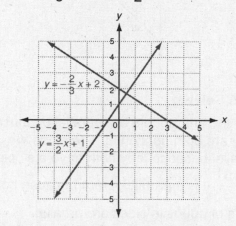

Holt McDougal Algebra 1

3. $6; -\dfrac{1}{6}$ 4. $\dfrac{4}{3}; -\dfrac{3}{4}$

5. $y = -x + 11$ 6. $y = \dfrac{1}{4}x - 3$

Challenge

1. a. $y = 2x + 4$

2. a. -3

 b. $y = -\dfrac{1}{2}x - 4$

3. a. 3

 b. $y = -\dfrac{1}{2}x + \dfrac{7}{2}$

4. It is a rectangle because it has four right angles.

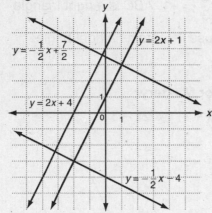

5–6. $x - y = -4; x + y = -4; x - y = 4; x + y = 4$

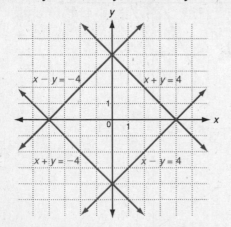

Problem Solving

1. The top and bottom are parallel because they are both horizontal. The sides are parallel because they both have a slope of $-\dfrac{5}{3}$. It is a parallelogram because both pairs of opposite sides are parallel.

2. The slope of AB is $\dfrac{1}{4}$, the slope of AC is $-\dfrac{7}{4}$, and the slope of BC is $-\dfrac{1}{4}$. None of the slopes have a product of -1 so no sides are perpendicular.

3. D   4. G

5. C

Reading Strategies

Possible answers are given for 1 and 2.

1. $y = 3x + 3$ 2. $y = -\dfrac{1}{3}x + 3$

3. $-\dfrac{1}{3}$ 4. 1

5. -1

6. yes, $\overline{BC}$ and $\overline{AC}$ are perpendicular because $1(-1) = -1$.

4-10 TRANSFORMING LINEAR FUNCTIONS

Practice A

1. rotation   2. translation

3. reflection

4.

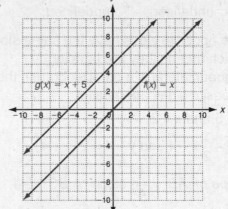

translation 5 units up

     Holt McDougal Algebra 1

5.

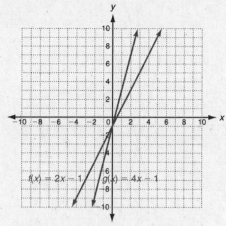

rotation (steeper) about (0, –1)

6.

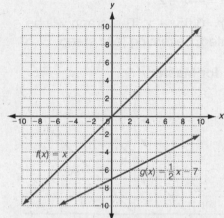

rotation (less steep) about (0, 0) and
translation 7 units down

7. a. The graph will be translated 3 units up.

   b. The graph will be rotated about (0, 12)
      and become less steep.

Practice B

1.

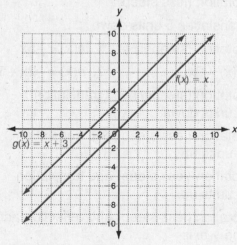

translation 3 units up

2.

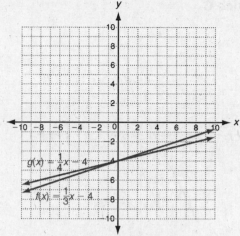

rotation (less steep) about (0, –4)

3.

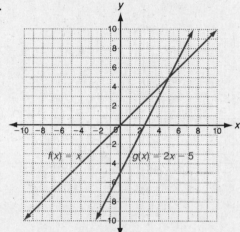

rotation (steeper) about (0, 0) and
translation 5 units down

4.

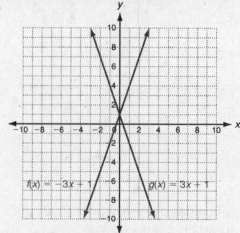

$g(x) = 3x + 1$

5. The graph will be translated 50 units
   down. The graph will be rotated about
   (0, 250) and become steeper.

Holt McDougal Algebra 1

Practice C

1.

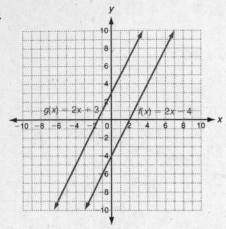

translation 7 units up

2.

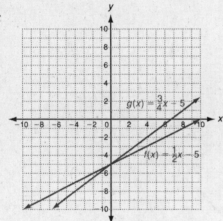

rotation (steeper) about (0, –5)

3.

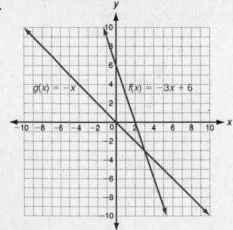

rotation (less steep) about (0, 6) and
translation 6 units down

4.

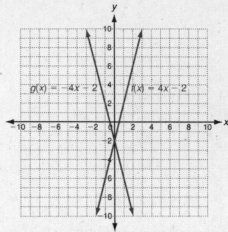

$g(x) = -4x - 2$

5. $g(x) = 0.05x + x$; The graph will be
rotated, becoming less steep.

Review for Mastery

1.

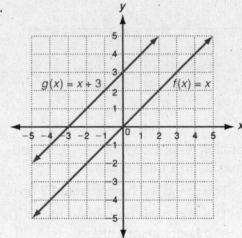

translation 3 units up

2. rotation (less steep)

3. translation 5 units down

4. rotation (steeper)   5. $h(x) = -5x$

6. $h(x) = 9x$ 7. $h(x) = -2x + 7$

8. rotation (steeper) and translation
2 units down

9. rotation (less steep) and translation
3 units up

10. rotation (less steep) and translation
8 units up.

11. rotation (less steep) and reflection across
the y-axis

Holt McDougal Algebra 1

Challenge

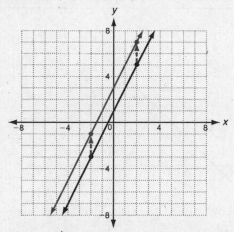

1. $y + 3 = 2(x + 2)$ OR $y - 5 = 2(x - 2)$
3. $y + 1 = 2(x + 2)$ OR $y - 7 = 2(x - 2)$
4. In the form $y - y_1 = m(x - x_1)$, the value of y_1, increased by 2 units.
5. $y + 9 = 2(x + 2)$ OR $y + 1 = 2(x - 2)$

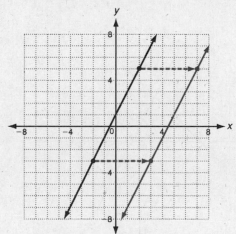

7. $y + 3 = 2(x - 3)$ OR $y - 5 = 2(x - 7)$
8. In the form $y - y_1 = m(x - x_1)$, the value of x_1, increased by 5 units.
9. $y + 3 = 2(x + 5)$ OR $y - 5 = 2(x + 1)$
10. Translated down 4 units and right 9 units.

Problem Solving

1. translation 1 unit down
2. $f(x) = 1.50x + 12$; $g(x) = 1.60x + 12$;
   it would be rotated about (0, 12), steeper.
3. His commission is raised to 20%.
4. B   5. J
6. A

Reading Strategies

1. 5; $2 - (-3) = 5$ 2. $f(x)$; $f(x)$
3. y-axis; opposite
4. rotation (less steep) about (0, –3)
5. reflection about y-axis
6. translation 6 units up

Answer Key For Systems of Equations and Inequalities

5-1 SOLVING SYSTEMS BY GRAPHING

Practice A

1.

$x - y = -2$	
$(2) - (4)$	-2
-2	-2

$2x + y = 6$	
$2(2) + (4)$	6
$(4) + (4)$	6
(8)	6

Ⓥ or ✗   ✓ or ⓧ

is not

2.

$2x + y = 0$	
$2(1) + (-2)$	0
$(2) + (-2)$	0
(0)	0

$x + 4y = -7$	
$(1) + 4(-2)$	-7
$(1) + (-8)$	-7
(-7)	-7

Ⓥor ✗   Ⓥor ✗

is

3.

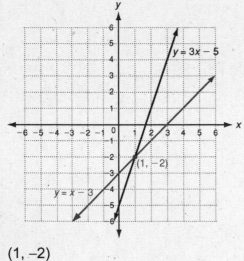

$(1, -2)$

4.

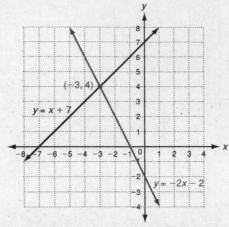

$(-3, 4)$

5. 20 miles; $80

Practice B

1. yes   2. no

3.

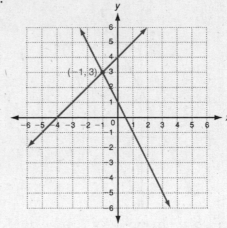

$(-1, 3)$

4.

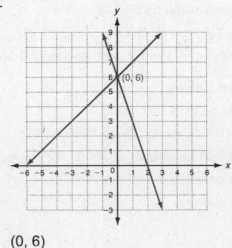

$(0, 6)$

Holt McDougal Algebra 1

5.

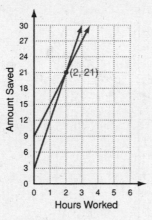

2 hours; $21

Practice C

1. yes   2. no

3. yes

4.

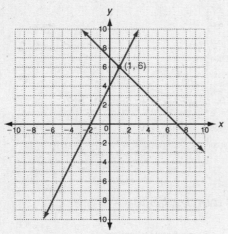

(1, 6)

5.

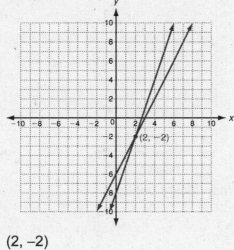

(2, −2)

6.

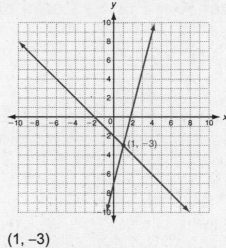

(1, −3)

7.

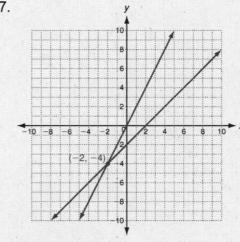

(−2, −4)

8. $40; $9

Review for Mastery

1. yes   2. no

3. no   4. yes

5. (−1, 3)   6. (2, −3)

7.

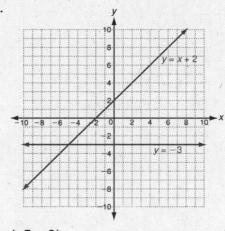

(−5, −3)

                Holt McDougal Algebra 1

8.

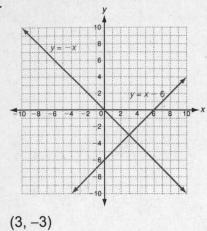

(3, –3)

Challenge

1.

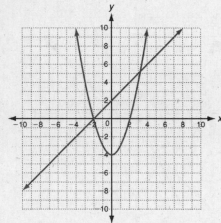

(–2, 0) and (3, 5)

2.

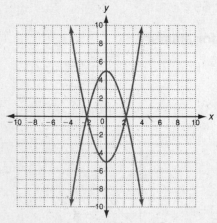

about (–2.3, 0) and about (2.3, 0)

3.

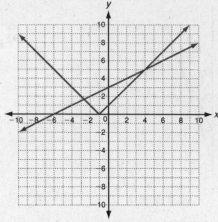

about (–2.7, 1.7) and (4, 5)

Problem Solving

1.

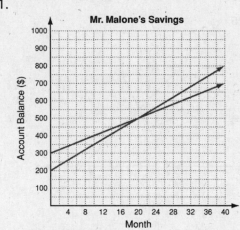

20 months, $500

2.

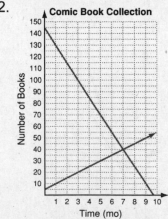

7 months, 40 books

3. C   4. G

5. B   6. F

Holt McDougal Algebra 1

Reading Strategies

1. number of people; total cost
2. $y = 10x + 120$; $y = 8x + 150$
3.

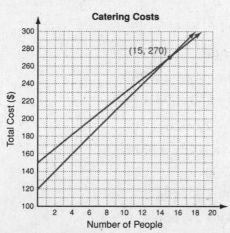

Catering Costs

(15, 270)

Total Cost ($)

Number of People

4. (15, 270)
5. For 15 people, the total cost will be $270 with both catering companies.

5-2 SOLVING SYSTEMS BY SUBSTITUTION

Practice A

1. $3x$; $3x$; x; $2x$; 2; 2; x; 2; 2; 2; 2; 6; 2; 6
2. $x - 3$; $x - 3$; $4x$; $4x$; 4; 4; x; 7; 7; 7; 7; 4; 7; 4
3. (3, 12)   4. (2, 0)
5. (2, –5)
6. a. $\begin{cases} y = 20x + 45 \\ y = 26x + 30 \end{cases}$

   b. 2.5
   c. $95

Practice B

1. (–1, –3)   2. (3, –1)
3. (2, 7)   4. (1, –4)
5. (5, –2)   6. (3, –2)
7. (1, –2)   8. (–1, –2)
9. (4, 9)
10. $\begin{cases} l = w + 3 \\ 2l = 2w + 58 \end{cases}$; 13 cm by 16 cm
11. $\begin{cases} 3s + 1p = 47 \\ 7s + 2p = 107 \end{cases}$; suit: $13; pair of shoes: $8

Practice C

1. (2, –4)   2. (3, –1)
3. (0, 8)   4. (–2, –1)
5. $\left(\dfrac{1}{2}, -2 \right)$ 6. (–6, –2)
7. (0.8, 0.2)   8. (8, –12)
9. (6, –8)   10. 11 and 28
11. 12 quarters 12. $12.00

Review for Mastery

1. (2, 3)   2. (7, 9)
3. (–4, 1)   4. (17, 7)
5. (3, 6)   6. (–1, 7)

Challenge

1. $x = 3$; $y = -1$, $z = 4$
2. $x = -1$; $y = 4$, $z = -3$
3. $x = 2$; $y = 8$, $z = -5$
4. $x = -2$; $y = 13$, $z = 4$

Problem Solving

1. 3 quarters, 5 dimes
2. 3 months; $155
3. 12 turkey burgers, 9 beef hamburgers
4. used CD $4.50, used DVD $6.50
5. B   6. H
7. A   8. H

Reading Strategies

1. $y = 5 - x$ or $y = -x + 5$
2. The first equation is already solved for y.
3. The solution of a system must satisfy both equations.
4. (6, 4)   5. (–3, 5)

Holt McDougal Algebra 1

5-3 SOLVING SYSTEMS BY ELIMINATION

Practice A

1. $0y$; $3x$; 3; 3; 2; 2; 2; 2; 2; 12; 4; 2; 4

2. $2y$; -7; $0y$; -3; -3; -1; -1; 3; 3; 3; 9; 9; 9; -2; 2; 2; -1; 3; -1

3. 2; 4; -16; 5; 10; 5; 10; 5; 5; 2; 2; 2; 2; 2; -10; -2; -2; 5; 2; 5

4. $(3, 4)$

5. $(6, -2)$

6. $(-8, -1)$

7. 3 and -4

Practice B

1. $-4y = 24$; -6; -2; -2; -6

2. -6; 2; -34; $-2x = -14$; 7; -4; 7; -4

3. $(2, -3)$

4. $(-9, 1)$

5. $(4, -6)$

6. $\left(-\dfrac{1}{2}, 3\right)$

7. $(-4, -1)$

8. $\left(-\dfrac{1}{5}, -2\right)$

9. $22

10. 7 Gala apples; 12 Granny Smith apples

Practice C

1. $(3, -1)$

2. $(2, 4)$

3. $(-1, -6)$

4. $\left(\dfrac{1}{3}, \dfrac{1}{4}\right)$

5. $(3, -4)$

6. $(-9, 8)$

7. $(13, -2)$

8. $(-6, 1)$

9. $(-2, -9)$

10. $(-10, -1)$

11. $(3, 7)$

12. $\left(\dfrac{5}{3}, 2\right)$

13. bagel: $1.25; muffin: $1.75

14. 75; 0.03; 0.07

$$\begin{cases} x + y = 75 \\ 0.03x + 0.07y = 3 \end{cases}$$

56.25 mL of the 3% solution; 18.75 mL of the 7% solution

Review for Mastery

1. $(3, -14)$

2. $(4, -1)$

3. $(-6, 18)$

4. $(-4, -14)$

5. $(7, 10)$

6. $(7, -18)$

7. $(5, -2)$

Challenge

1. $\begin{cases} 5x + 4y + z = 865 \\ 9x + 6y + 6z = 1410 \end{cases}$

2. $5x - 2y = 20$

3. $-21x - 18y = -3780$

4. $x = 60$

5. $\begin{cases} 2y + z = 285 \\ 4y + z = 565 \end{cases}$

6. $y = 140$, $z = 5$

7. sleeping bags: $60; tents: $140; bug repellant: $5

Problem Solving

1. chicken leg 8 oz., chicken wing 3 oz.

2. bath towel $10, hand towel $5

3. adult ticket $8, child ticket $5

4. office visit $25, allergy shot $8

5. A

6. G

Reading Strategies

1. Multiply the first equation by 3 and the second equation by 5 to get common coefficients of -15.

2. $\begin{cases} 4(9x - 10y = 7) \\ 5(5x + 8y = 31) \end{cases} \Rightarrow \begin{cases} 36x - 40y = 28 \\ 25x + 40y = 155 \end{cases}$

3. $(1, -3)$

4. $(10, -10)$

Holt McDougal Algebra 1

5-4 SOLVING SPECIAL SYSTEMS

Practice A

1. no solution
2. infinitely many solutions
3. infinitely many solutions
4. no solution
5. infinitely many solutions;
   consistent, dependent
6. no solution;
   inconsistent
8. They will always have the same amount of money.
   The graphs of these equations are the same line.

Practice B

1. infinitely many solutions
2. no solution
3. no solution
4. infinitely many solutions
5. consistent, dependent;
   infinitely many solutions
6. consistent, independent;
   one solution
7. Yes. The graphs of the two equations have different slopes. They will intersect.
8. No. The graphs of the two equations are parallel lines. They will never intersect.

Practice C

1. infinitely many solutions
2. no solution
3. infinitely many solutions
4. no solution
5. inconsistent;
   no solution
6. consistent, independent;
   one solution
7. Yes. The graphs of the two equations have different slopes. They will intersect.

8. No. The graphs of the two equations are parallel lines. They will never intersect.

Review for Mastery

1. infinitely many solutions
2. no solution
3. no solution
4. inconsistent;
   no solutions
5. consistent and dependent;
   infinitely many solutions
6. consistent and independent;
   one solution
7. consistent and independent;
   one solution; (0, 8)
8. consistent and dependent;
   infinitely many solutions

Challenge

1. Start –1 –2 –7 –13 –14 –19 – Finish
2. Start –6 –10 –15 –21 –17 –23 – Finish

Problem Solving

1. No; the graphs are parallel lines so there is no solution.
2. consistent and independent;
   100 mi and $65
3. consistent and dependent;
   infinitely many solutions
4. Yes;
   at 600 hours.
5. A   6. H
7. C   8. J

Reading Strategies

1. inconsistent
2. infinitely many
3. infinitely many
4. consistent, independent
5. one
6. inconsistent;
   0;
   parallel lines

Holt McDougal Algebra 1

7. consistent, dependent;

infinitely many;

coincident lines

8. consistent, independent;

1;

intersecting lines

5-5 SOLVING LINEAR INEQUALITIES

Practice A

1. no   2. yes

3. no

4.

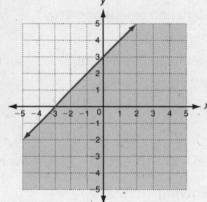

$y \leq x + 3$

5.

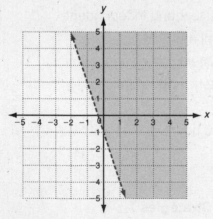

$y > -3x - 1$

6. a. $x + y \leq 8$

b.

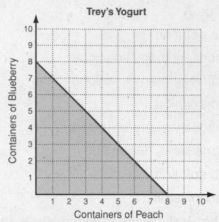

Trey's Yogurt

Containers of Blueberry

Containers of Peach

c. Possible answer: 2 peach, 6 blueberry or 4 peach, 3 blueberry

7. $y \geq x - 2$ 8. $y < 2x + 4$

9. $y \leq -\frac{1}{2}x$

Practice B

1. yes   2. no

3. yes

4.

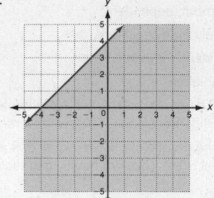

5.

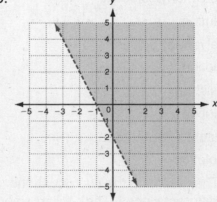

Holt McDougal Algebra 1

6.

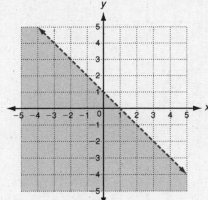

7. a. Let x = chips, y = pretzels, $4x + 2y \le 20$

b.

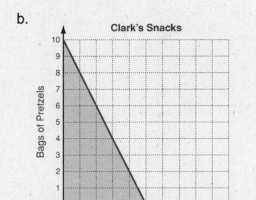

Clark's Snacks

c. Possible answer: 3 chips, 4 pretzels or 4 chips, 1 pretzel

8. $y \ge \dfrac{1}{2}x - 2$

9. $y < 3x + 1$

10. $y \le -\dfrac{3}{2}x + 4$

Practice C

1. no

2. no

3. yes

4.

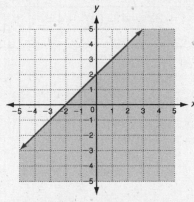

5.

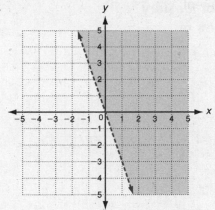

6.

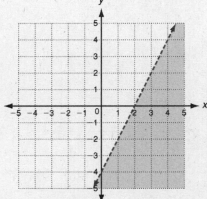

7. a. x = decorative, y – solid, $3x + 0.5y \le 15$

b.

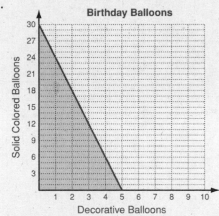

Birthday Balloons

c. Possible answer: 3 decorative, 12 solid or 2 decorative, 15 solid

8. $y \ge \dfrac{1}{3}x - 4$

9. $y < 2x$

10. $y \le 3$

Holt McDougal Algebra 1

Review for Mastery

1.

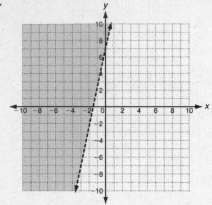

5.

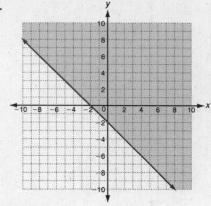

2.

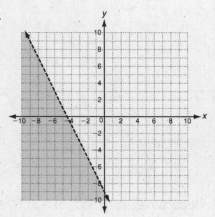

Challenge

1.

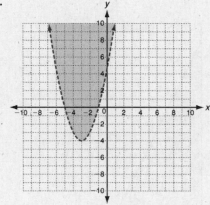

3.

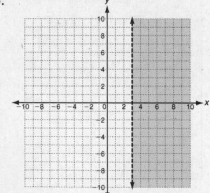

x	Think: $y = (x + 3)^2 - 4$	(x, y)
−6	$y = (-6 + 3)^2 - 4 = -(3)^2 - 4 = 9 - 4 = 5$	(−6, 5)
−5	$y = (-5 + 3)^2 - 4 = -(2)^2 - 4 = 4 - 4 = 0$	(−5, 0)
−4	$y = (-4 + 3)^2 - 4 = (-1)^2 - 4 = 1 - 4 = -3$	(−4, −3)
−3	$y = (-3 + 3)^2 - 4 = (-0)^2 - 4 = 0 - 4 = -4$	(−3, −4)
−2	$y = (-2 + 3)^2 - 4 = (1)^2 - 4 = 1 - 4 = -3$	(−2, −3)
−1	$y = (-1 + 3)^2 - 4 = (2)^2 - 4 = 4 - 4 = 0$	(−1, 0)

4.

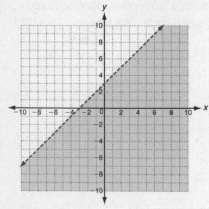

Holt McDougal Algebra 1

2. $y \leq -|x| + 5$

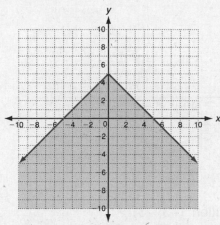

x	Think: $y = -|x| + 5$	(x, y)
–3	$y = -|-3| + 5 = -(3) + 5 =$ $-3 + 5 = 2$	(–3, 2)
–2	$y = -|-2| + 5 = -(2) + 5 =$ $-2 + 5 = 3$	(–2, 3)
–1	$y = -|-1| + 5 = -(1) + 5 =$ $-1 + 5 = 4$	(–1, 4)
0	$y = -|0| + 5 = 0 + 5 = 5$	(0, 5)
1	$y = -|1| + 5 = -1 + 5 = 4$	(1, 4)
2	$y = -|2| + 5 = -2 + 5 = 3$	(2, 3)

3. $y < \dfrac{1}{2}x^2 - 2$

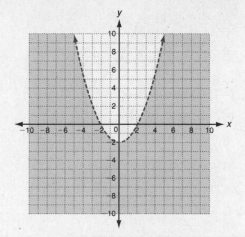

x	Think: $y = \dfrac{1}{2}x^2 - 2$	(x, y)
–4	$y = \dfrac{1}{2}(-4)^2 - 2 = \dfrac{1}{2}(16) - 2 =$ $8 - 2 = 6$	(–4, 6)
–2	$y = \dfrac{1}{2}(-2)^2 - 2 = \dfrac{1}{2}(4) - 2 -$ $2 - 2 = 0$	(–2, 0)
0	$y = \dfrac{1}{2}(0)^2 - 2 = \dfrac{1}{2}(0) - 2 =$ $0 - 2 = -2$	(0, –2)
1	$y = \dfrac{1}{2}(1)^2 - 2 = \dfrac{1}{2}(1) - 2 =$ $\dfrac{1}{2} - 2 = -1\dfrac{1}{2}$	$\left(1, -1\dfrac{1}{2}\right)$
2	$y = \dfrac{1}{2}(2)^2 - 2 = \dfrac{1}{2}(4) - 2 =$ $2 - 2 = 0$	(2, 0)
4	$y = \dfrac{1}{2}(4)^2 - 2 = \dfrac{1}{2}(16) - 2 =$ $8 - 2 = 6$	(4, 6)

Problem Solving

1.

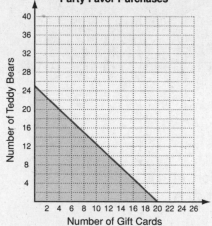

Party Favor Purchases

$5x + 4y \leq 100$

Holt McDougal Algebra 1

2.

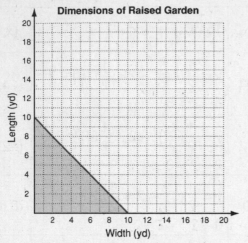

Dimensions of Raised Garden

$2x + 2y \leq 20$; 5 yd by 5 yd

3. A   4. G

5. C   6. J

Reading Strategies

1. solid;   2. dotted;
   below   above

3. solid;
   above

4.

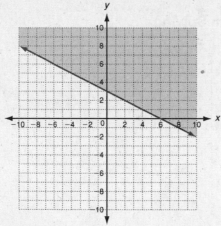

solution; (4, 1)
not: (−2, 2)

5.

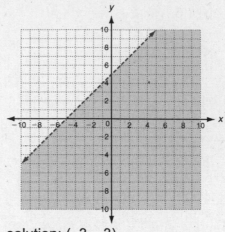

solution: (−3, −3)

not: (2, 7)

5-6 SOLVING SYSTEMS OF LINEAR INEQUALITIES

Practice A

1. yes   2. no

3. yes

4.

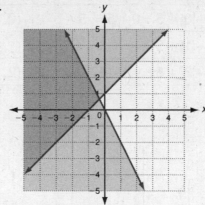

a. (−1, 0) and (−3, 2)

b. (0, −3) and (4, 0)

5.

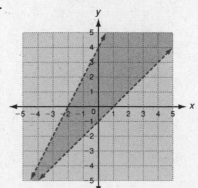

a. (0, 0) and (1, 2)

b. (1, 0) and (−4, 3)

Holt McDougal Algebra 1

6.

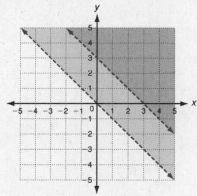

a. (3, 3) and (4, 4)

b. (0, 0) and (0, 3)

7. a.

$$\begin{cases} x + y \geq 6 \\ 4x + 2y \leq 20 \end{cases}$$

b.

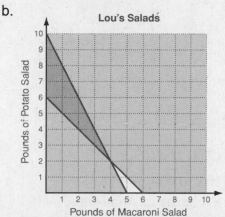

Lou's Salads

Pounds of Potato Salad (vertical axis)

Pounds of Macaroni Salad (horizontal axis)

c. Any combination represented by the ordered pairs in the solution region.

d. 2 lbs mac. salad, 5 lbs potato salad;
   3 lbs mac. salad, 4 lbs potato salad

Practice B

1. no   2. yes

3. no

4.

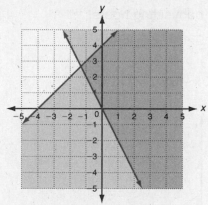

a. (0, 3) and (3, −2)

b. (−2, 0) and (−4, 3)

5.

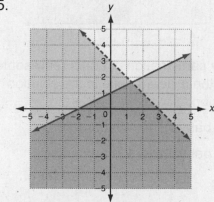

a. (0, 0) and (−2, 0)

b. (3, 0) and (2, 3)

6.

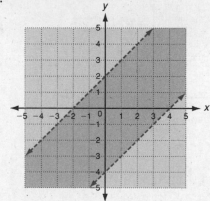

a. (0, 0) and (−2, −2)

b. (−3, 3) and (4, 0)

Holt McDougal Algebra 1

7. a. x = babysitting hours,

   y = gardening hours,

   $\begin{cases} x + y \leq 12 \\ 10x + 5y \geq 80 \end{cases}$

   b.

   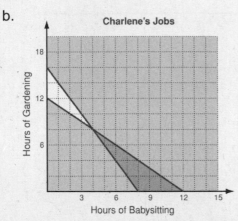

   Charlene's Jobs

   c. Any combination of hours represented by the ordered pairs in the solution region.

   d. 6 h babysitting, 4 h gardening;

   8 h babysitting, 2 h gardening

Practice C

1. no   2. yes

3. no

4.

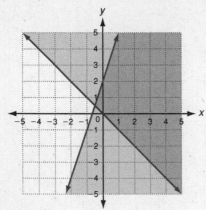

a. (0, 2) and (3, 0)

b. (0, –3) and (–4, 0)

5.

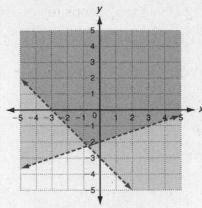

a. (–2, 0) and (0, 3)

b. (–4, –2) and (0, –4)

6.

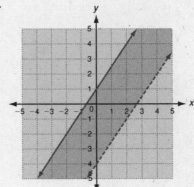

a. (0, 1) and (0, 0)

b. (4, –4) and (0, –4)

7. a. x = boxes of small cups,

   y = boxes of large cups,

   $\begin{cases} x + y \leq 10 \\ 100x + 150y \leq 1200 \end{cases}$

   b.

   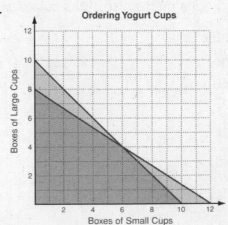

   Ordering Yogurt Cups

Holt McDougal Algebra 1

c. Any combination of cups represented by the whole number ordered pairs in the solution region.

d. 6 small, 4 large; 3 small, 5 large

Review for Mastery

1.

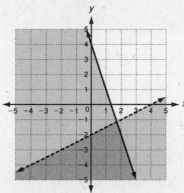

Possible Answers: Sol: (1, –3), (–2, –4)

not sol: (3, –3), (–3, 2)

2.

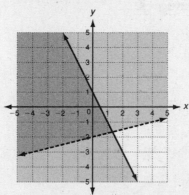

Possible Answers: Sol: (–4, 3), (–3, 1)

not sol: (3, –3), (2, 2)

3.

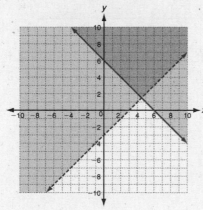

4.

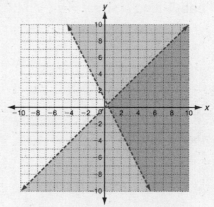

5.

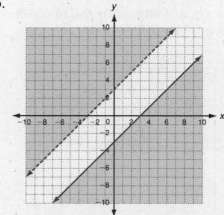

6.

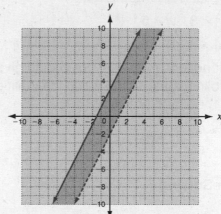

7.

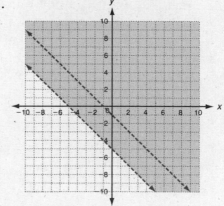

Holt McDougal Algebra 1

Challenge

1.

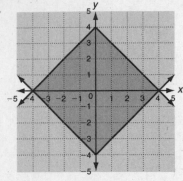

2. The solution is the interior and boundary of the square formed by the absolute value inequalities.

3.

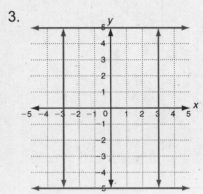

a. $|x| < 3$, $|y| < 5$

b. $|x| > 3$, $|y| > 5$

4. Explanations may vary but should give the following absolute value inequalities: $|x - 1| \le 2$ and $|y - 3| \le 5$

5. $\begin{cases} |x| \le a \\ |y| \le a \end{cases}$, where $a > 0$

Problem Solving

1.

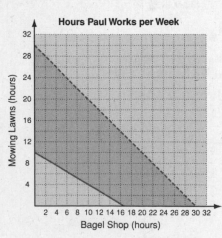

Hours Paul Works per Week

$$\begin{cases} 7x + 12y \ge 120 \\ x + y < 30 \end{cases}$$

2.

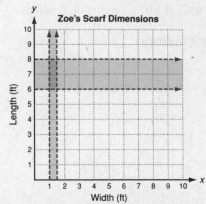

width of 1.25 ft, length of 7 ft;

width of 1.4 ft, length of 7.5 ft

3. A   4. J

Reading Strategies

1. $\begin{cases} 2x + 2y \le 30 \\ x > 8 \end{cases}$

2.

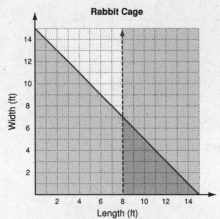

Rabbit Cage

3. $l = 10$ ft, $w = 5$ ft and $l = 11$ ft, $w = 4$ ft

Holt McDougal Algebra 1